AGILE Almanac

BOOK 1: SINGLE-TEAM PROJECTS & EXAM PREP

BOOK 1: SINGLE-TEAM PROJECTS & EXAM PREP

JOHN G. STENBECK, PMP, PMI-ACP, CSM, CSP

First Edition

Spokane, WA

Agile Almanac
Book 1: Single-Team Projects and Exam Prep

John G. Stenbeck, PMP, PMI-ACP, CSM, CSP

Published by:
GR8PM, Inc.
1818 W. Francis Ave. #228, Spokane, WA 99205 USA
(619) 890-5807
custserv@gr8pm.com; http://www.gr8pm.com/

ISBN Edition: 978-0-9846693-5-6

This book includes material based on the Project Management Institute, *A Guide to the Project Management Body of Knowledge, (PMBOK® Guide) – Fifth Edition, Project Management Institute, Inc. 2012.*

The book also contains many references to other registered terms such as PMP®, PgMP®, CAPM®, PMI-SP®, PMI-RMP®, or PMI-ACP®, which are registered marks of the Project Management Institute, Inc.

Dedication

It seems silly to me, and you may think so too, but I hope that these few brief words convey my true thankfulness for JT, Lindsey and baby Grayson, and Michael and Olivia, who inspire me, Jamie, the daughter-of-my-heart, who I admire and cherish deeply, and my Cursillo brothers who have never ceased in cheering me on. Please keep praying for me and know that I love you all!

About the Editor

Lauren Seybert Mix, President, LM Editing Co., has a unique background that makes her a gifted editor of technically sophisticated books. In addition to a Masters Degree in English, she has experience as a technical project manager in the Oil and Gas Industry as well as years of consultant engineering in the Power industry. She has also been an active member of PMI for 5 years and plans to get her PMP and PMI-ACP certifications.

She works on selected projects where she feels her background can provide more than just spelling and grammar checks. The manuscripts she edits involve collaborations where her value as a neutral and independent expert adds to the competence of the author, assisting in the struggle to find the clearest, most accessible way to create maximum knowledge transfer for the reader.

This is her fourth project with John Stenbeck who has repeatedly praised her acumen and insights, recommending many additional authors for Lauren's consideration.

Lauren Seybert Mix, President
LM Editing Co.
750 East Marshall St. #414, West Chester, PA 19380
(615) 815-7021
LMix7712@gmail.com

About the Graphic Designer

Over the last 25 years, Tamara Parsons, owner of KenType, has taken the natural gift of "an eye for graphics" and developed it into an unparalleled level of expertise in graphic design and print production.

Starting as a typographer in the printing industry, she applied passion and discipline to achieve mastery of the critical disciplines of type setting, layout and the entire printing process. Again and again she impressed clients with unexpected insights in the production of logos, branding and identity packages, advertisements, and brochures. Time after time Tamara delivered high-impact customer value with "clean and clear" messages powerfully delivered.

As the KenType client list grew Tamara remained restless, driven to achieve constantly more for her clients. The result has been extensions of service lines as clients requested help with newsletters, books and more. And all of that effort on behalf of her clients has been rewarded by consistent, organic growth based on client referrals.

It was one of those referrals that brought Tamara and John Stenbeck together for his first book. Finding that they were both driven by a desire to constantly deliver amazing world-class results, an alliance rooted in mutual respect and trust was formed. With this fourth book Tamara's unique skills both in graphic design and as an organized multitasking maven have made it possible for that alliance to deliver critically acclaimed results.

John has been quick to refer Tamara to his clients, saying her work burnishes his reputation! In fact, it was his idea – insistence really! – that this tribute be included in the Agile Almanac. He invites you to contact KenType and experience how much better your results could be!

Tamara Parsons, Owner
Kensington Type & Graphics
(619) 281-1520 | www.kentype.com
tami@kentype.com

Advance Praise

In an attempt to make this Almanac as useful as possible we sought advice from professionally qualified reviewers, many of whom are giants in the industry. Here is what they had to say:

> *I love this book! Whether you are preparing for an agile certification, seeking a pragmatic understanding of the more popular agile frameworks, looking for agile relationships with traditional methodology or simply seeking the best business outcome for your projects, Agile Almanac: Book 1 is a down-to-earth, pragmatic and fundamental view of agile. It comprehensively presents the more popular frameworks of agile, offers comparisons to the traditional methodology, and debunks myths and promotes truths that otherwise can be elusive. As a quick-reference field guide it does not disappoint. John Stenbeck is one of the best in this business who demonstrates the courage to lead and the skill to dissect and disseminate the information we need.*

Neal Whitten, PMP
The Neal Whitten Group, Inc.

> *After 48 years in the profession you can't imagine how many project management "flavor of the day" concepts and techniques I have seen come and go. But, it appears that Agile is the real deal. PM practitioners should embrace the concepts and realize the value add to be achieved through the use of Agile. As one of the "old timers" I recognized the importance of bringing my knowledge base current. This masterfully written book should be the bible for those using or thinking about using Agile on their projects. As a result of the articulate writing, the use of real world examples, and inclusion of easy to understand analogies I was able to quickly comprehend the concepts and recognize the myriad applications in my personal PM world. What a timely gift! Without question the quality and content of this book surpasses anything else available. If you can only read one Agile book – This is the ONE!!*

Lee R. Lambert, PMP, PMI Fellow
CEO at Lambert Consulting

John has packed this book full of enlightened insights that add an invaluable level of clarity to the often-distorted world of Agile. His crisp logical explanations take the reader beyond the "what and how" to address the underlying why; essential understanding for project managers aspiring to truly be great.

Michael O'Brochta PMI-ACP, PMP
Former Director of CIA's Professional Project Management Certification
President, Zozer Inc.

The Agile Almanac is an indispensable desktop reference for any organization seeking to either adopt Agile principles or extend their practice. Stenbeck's clear, friendly, and down-to-earth tone keeps the text lively and informative. If you're serious about Agile, beginner to advanced, this book is a necessity.

Peter Hodsdon, PMP, PMI-ACP
CEO, Modern Analytics Corporation

At last, a reference guide that simply gives you the facts regarding everything agile (scrum, xp, lean, etc). Here you get all the practices, roles and values so project management leadership can integrate them into their work as appropriate. The agile mindset of "do what is needed, "do it right the first time, adapt as you learn, and keep your focus on the customer" comes through in the way the author presents the complex world of agile. It is refreshing to read agile concepts and processes without a bias and fanatical viewpoint, and in a way that makes it real and easy for the project professional to incorporate desired practices into their projects, programs and organizations!

Diane Brady, CSM, PMP, PMI-ACP
Past President, PMI Portland Chapter

This Agile Almanac is a much-needed "Body of Knowledge" for the PMI-ACP exam as well as an excellent addition to the bookshelf of project management and agile practitioners. It serves as an in-depth, yet concise solution to meet the need for a body-of-knowledge in support of PMI's Agile Certified Practitioner (ACP) program. True to its name, the "Agile Almanac" is an excellent reference guide, cross-sectional collection, and historical summary of facts, data, and information about agile methods, concepts, and project management to prepare individuals to sit for the PMI-ACP exam. Its author, John Stenbeck, is a noted subject matter expert concerning project management, where he's served as PMI-San Diego's president, founder of a successful training firm, and author of numerous books. The first volume provides concise, yet complete descriptions of major agile team-level methods such as Scrum, Extreme Programming, Lean Development, and Kanban. As an added bonus, the almanac also covers hybrid methods and agile earned value management concepts. Each chapter includes extensive exercises and other tools to reinforce its key concepts and prepare the reader to sit for the PMI-ACM exam. John Stenbeck's "Agile Almanac" is a great value, combining depth, precision, and clarity for today's extremely busy professionals.

Dr. David F. Rico, PMP, CSEP, ACP, CSM, SAFe
Boeing Cyber Solutions
George Washington University, School of Engineering and Applied Science

---

The Agile Almanac is a useful resource on the values, principles and practices of Agile and Lean product development. Practitioners, coaches, managers, executives and coaches will find this an excellent desk reference as they work toward change within their organizations. I expect the Agile Almanac to enjoy pride of place on my own bookshelf in the future.

Tamara Sulaiman Runyon, PMP
Certified Scrum Trainer and Agile Coach
Managing Consultant, Advanced Project Management, Inc

Each approach, whether it be traditional project management or a flavor of Agile has its own culture. This book has been setup in such a way that it tends to bridge those cultures, explaining their differences and benefits so that you can gain the skills and knowledge yourself without the need to spend years learning each culture and its particular benefits. In my role, I teach Agile coaches and leaders the differences and benefits of many different methods, John's genius is that, without focusing too much on a single culture, he pulls a lot of those together for you to learn in one place; this book.

Robert Annis, CSM, CSP, ICP-TST, ICP-ACC, ICP-ATF
Agile Coach and Trainer

The "Agile Almanac" is clearly aligned with the word "demystify." John has successfully bridged the gaps that exist between the various factions and interpretations of Agile project management. This work is a must have for the practicing professional and for those entering the profession. The key ingredient here is the focus on the practitioner and the methods and techniques that work most effectively to achieve project success and client satisfaction. There is no doubt that "Agile" thinking has become a necessity in today's project management environment, regardless of industry, and John has provided a clear and well defined resource that will enhance the knowledge and value of every project manager!

Frank P. Saladis PMP, PMI Fellow
President, PMI New York City Chapter

Agile is not just scrum. It encompasses multiple ideas. John provides foundational insights about the agile mindset, and in a way that is straightforward and easy to understand. Without question, any reader will be able to immediately apply new ideas to improve buy-in, effectiveness, and overall success.

Tim Arthur, PMP, PMI-ACP, CSM
Distinguished R&D Program Manager, SAS Institute, Inc.

Stenbeck demystifies the attitudes that Agile can be used to shore up excuses for skipping documentation or planning and invigorates the notion that solid project management skills have been around for long before labels or formal theories were created. This is a definitive handbook that is hard to put down and navigates the reader through the numerous myths and techniques of Agile. Stenbeck brings his expertise to the page by incorporating different techniques to improve learning retention and mastery of Agile. The book is rich with stories and clear examples that give relevance and practical benefit to Agile. I'm a better Project Manager for reading it, and it's my number one book to share!

Laura Davidson, PMP, PMI-RMP, SSGB
President, PMI Atlanta Chapter

Book 1 of the Agile Almanac is an illustrative discussion of predictive and adaptive project management frameworks at the single team level – the "micro-dynamic environment". The Almanac recognizes the common denominators of various practices and equips practitioners for both CSP and PMI-ACP certifications. The integration of multiple frameworks yields a combined strategy that delivers significant business value – and has readily become a de facto standard in project management. John's book does an excellent job at interpreting the hybrid approach.

Luke Panezich
VP of Education, PMI-Puget Sound Chapter
Software Applications Project Manager, Liberty Mutual Insurance
Instructor, University of Washington, Professional & Continuing Education

---

I love this book and think it will close the gap between the two disparate camps of project management. John has put into words the best of both worlds creating the potential for a wildly successful blend.

Laurie Haberthier
President, PMI – Mile Hi Chapter

Every strategist knows that winning organizations are fast, flexible, and value creating. Agile principles provide the platform for achieving those benefits. This book provides a great introduction of the key principles of successful agile programs and projects: sensitivity to context, effective design, value, speed, and flexibility. The Agile Almanac is a fantastic addition to your bookshelf.

Greg Githens, PMP
Strategic thinking thought leader and author
Vice President, Strategic Initiatives and Innovation
Catalyst Management Consulting LLC

The Agile Almanac is an energizing mashup of the diverse collection of Agile frameworks and processes gleaned from John's expertise and other published subject matter experts.

John has demonstrated, once again, his knack of bridging Traditional and Agile Project Management processes by emphasizing and clarifying unique terms and practices. After reading the Agile Almanac, one can envision transitioning from the Traditional approach and the adoption of Agile methods and techniques.

The Agile Almanac provides a unique perspective that will serve as a valuable study aid and an excellent practitioner handbook.

Diane McCann, PhD, PMP
IT Integration Manager, Brenntag North America, Inc.
Adjunct Professor, DeSales University and DeVry University

The Agile Almanac brings clarity, in an easy to read format, to the landscape of the Agile environment. It takes the confusion out of the relationship between traditional and agile project management and gives a clear picture of how each complement the other. It's a great tool to help anyone understand the best practices of both methodologies, and how you use them together to make your project a success. This is a must read for anyone who leads projects!

Michele Terbrock, PMP
Global Marketing Communications Manager
(for a Life Science Company)

Table of Contents

FOREWORD

James H. Johnson | *Chairman and Dreamer-in-Chief, The Standish Group*

The female Dolania Americana Mayfly has a life span of five minutes. In these five minutes the Dolania Americana Mayfly is born, finds a mate, reproduces a million offspring, and dies. In a recent conversation with a large software provider we learned of a major software enhancement that was accomplished in 24 hours with a team of two very talented people. In looking at the features, functions, and capabilities, we determined through profiling the project within our CHAOS Database that by using traditional methods the project would have taken 24 months with a much bigger team. While five-minute software projects may not be in your future, please consider that the male Dolania Americana Mayfly's lifecycle is 24 hours and during that time he will father a billion new Mayflies.

The Standish Group research shows that over the last few years the life cycle of software projects has been getting shorter and shorter. Certainly the outlook is dim for software projects that are grand, long, and costly. This is good news since such projects have a poor track record in returning value. Users and stakeholders' attention spans are not only following the trend of smaller and quicker software projects, but also leading the way. The pressure for faster and faster results is changing the way many, if not most, organizations develop software products. These changes are also changing the way software projects are managed as well as the role of the project manager.

The agile process methods, such as Scrum, have advanced to the mainstream and have replaced the traditional methods, such as waterfall, for all but the most regressive organizations. The Project Management Institute (PMI), feeling its franchise slipping away, responded with Agile Certified Practitioner (PMI-ACP) certification in addition to their Project Management Professional (PMP) certification. The PMI-ACP has a very practical application. Many organizations are not ready to throw out all their project management expertise and procedures. Some of these organizations are adapting the agile and traditional methods into a hybrid method. These organizations need qualified project managers with agile expertise and education.

As of this writing, there are thousands of jobs for Scrum masters and Scrum product owners. Many of the functions of the traditional project manager are incorporated into the agile process. For example, the Scrum product owner performs about 50% of the tasks of the traditional project manager, while the Scrum master does the other half. Interested traditional project managers will need a transition method to shift to Scrum.

PMI-ACP will aid in both the hybrid integration and transition approach. The Agile Almanac provides the basic agile education for both approaches. One of the most important features of the Agile Almanac is the translation of the traditional project management language to the agile ontology.

FOREWORD

Andy Crowe | *CEO, Velociteach*

I had my first introduction to Bruce Lee on television as a young man. Like many others, I found his movements to be mesmerizing and beyond anything I had seen before. One of the most amazing things about his Jeet Kune Do fighting style was the way it was constantly changing. Lee even referred to it as "the style which has no style." It was highly adaptive in the moment, flowing, as he described, "like water" to match the demands of the situation. He borrowed liberally from fencing, boxing, and nature and incorporated all of that into his martial arts practice.

A few decades later, the project management world embarked on a similar journey and began to experiment with highly adaptive "Agile" methodologies that also looked different than anything most people had seen before. In the Agile world, only a few basic principles were sacred. The rest was adaptive and stayed in fluid evaluation and change. Constant reinvention became standard procedure in order to increase value and efficiency.

At first, many viewed Agile approaches with suspicion, feeling that these were just a reaction against the traditional approach. However, over time people came to see that there was serious value in these adaptive value-centric methodologies. As the results rolled in, skeptics were converted into believers.

John Stenbeck has delivered this book at the perfect time in Agile's evolution. His outstanding almanac is a treasure chest of resources and techniques that goes into depth on the big five Agile methodologies: Scrum, eXtreme Programming, Lean Software Development, Kanban, and Hybrid Project Management.

Readers who are new to Agile will find a wealth of information to dig into and revisit time and again. Agile embraces experimenting, so don't be shy about trying new and unfamiliar techniques for your project. Just as there is no way to learn to paint without actually painting, the only way to become truly proficient in Agile is to try things. Experiment. Evaluate. Adapt. Improve. Repeat.

For those of us who came out of a more traditional waterfall approach, Stenbeck has given us a bridge to a more adaptive, customer-centric approach. Agile's relentless focus on transparency and delivering value will benefit the organization, the customer, and the team. Readers will appreciate the fact that John is firmly grounded in the traditional approach, and he leverages this to help explain the necessary shifts in thinking and practice.

This book is a wonderful addition to the Agile world that every project manager should have on his or her desk. Think of it as a guide and not a rulebook. After all, you never know what you will find. As Bruce Lee said "Take things as they are. Punch when you have to punch. Kick when you have to kick." Whatever project circumstances you encounter, you will have a great resource on your side.

Yours in Agility,
Andy Crowe, PMP, PgMP, PMI-ACP and Author
(with book sales over 250,000 copies)

FOREWORD

Robert K. Wysocki, PhD. | *Author, Effective Project Management: Traditional, Agile, Extreme, 7th Edition*

The step from the traditional project management world into the agile complex project management world can be a traumatic experience for many project managers and fly in the face of the conventional business practices used by their managers and sponsors. For sponsors it is a step into the unknown where an acceptable solution is no longer guaranteed as it was in the traditional world. For senior managers and other decision makers the business world is no longer the same place. Gone is the comfort of a well-documented requirements document and the security of knowing how to deliver those requirements. Well-defined execution processes are the only variables separating the sponsors from a successful business result. In their place is a goal statement that could be more of a dream statement than a reality to be achieved.

The project management professional has been drawn into the world of complex projects. It was not an option. The demand for successfully managing complexity and uncertainty has been the driver of a growing portfolio of approaches to managing such projects. Furthermore, the journey to reach that goal may only be partially known. John Stenbeck has provided a guide for those project management professionals facing the transition into complexity and uncertainty.

This is the first of a 3-volume work that describes the complete journey. Volume 1 discusses the smaller self-contained agile projects (small teams, co-located). These are really introductory of the richness of the complex project landscape. In the scheme of things Volume 1 is the starter kit. Volume 2 relaxes many of those restrictions and discusses variants such as larger projects and programs and teams with virtual, distributed and remote facets. The variants are so numerous that choosing a project management approach should be seen as equivalent to creating a recipe for management based on the characteristics of the project and the internal environment and external market conditions in which it will be executed. These are cutting edge applications and will stretch the familiar models beyond their original intent. Finally, the third level is scaling to the enterprise. Complex project management is an enterprise-wide phenomenon with strategic implications but little has been done to explore that domain.

The agile movement is less than 20 years old and due mostly to the Scrum aficionados led by Ken Schwaber has dominated the agile project management space. Upon closer study and introspection I have discovered that the complex project management space goes beyond Scrum as it looks for best-fit approaches. In fact, the characteristics of the complex project and its internal constraints and external market situations require a far more complex management approach than is afforded by the Scrum Methodology. Scrum was a watershed contribution but it is not the be all and end all answer to complex project management. We all agree that projects are unique but in that uniqueness its best-fit management approach will also be unique. Cooks can manage traditional projects using pre-defined recipes but chefs, who must create the recipes to effectively management complex projects, are required.

We are at the doorstep of a major evolution in project management as it matures into the complex project landscape. One of the dimensions that will define the success of that evolution is the professional certification of those who would become the chefs of our emerging profession. John Stenbeck understands this and has shared his insight in his most recent book. Through my own client experiences as an effective complex project management consultant I have come to the validated conclusion that to be successful in complex project management means that the project manager must be a creative professional with a solid portfolio of tools, templates and processes from which to craft unique management solutions to unique complex projects. The complex project landscape is filled with critical and unsolved problems and business opportunities. Risk is high and success is not assured. The best effort may not be good enough but that is the hand we have been dealt.

We must be careful as we proceed with any certification programs. Knowledge does not equate to competency and it is competency that is required of the chefs. Perhaps knowledge is sufficient for the cooks but not for the chefs. So any valid certification program must include a significant competency validation.

Robert K. Wysocki, PhD.
President, EII Publications, LLC
Author of 25 books on project management including:

Effective Project Management: Traditional, Agile, Extreme, 7th Edition *(John Wiley & Sons, 2014)*

Effective Complex Project Management: An Adaptive Agile Framework for Delivering Business Value *(J. Ross Publishing, 2014)*

FOREWORD

Marcus Hammarberg and Joakim Sunden

Authors, Kanban In Action

This might be a certification book, but I was happy to see that the content goes way beyond that. Writing a book on "passing the exam" could very well limit the scope to just what you "need to know", but Mr Stenbeck has gone beyond that.

Already in the first three chapters a foundation for the principles, thoughts and ideas behind is presented. This is paramount I think, because the practices that a certain method is built with is just applications of those principles. Without firmly understanding the principles it's very easy to get lost in the details of the practices of a certain method. Mr Stenbeck has put in a lot of work to make sure that we understand that, BEFORE some of the agile methods around.

I enjoyed reading the summaries of Scrum and eXtreme programming (that contains many of the practices that agile teams are using, regardless of method). These two truly standout as most common applications of the agile principles.

As the author points out Lean Software Development and Kanban are less prescriptive methods and instead take a much more evolutionary approach; staring with where you are today. This makes, in my mind, those methods more powerful but also harder to grasp and describe. I think Mr Stenbeck is doing a great job giving an overview of the principles and how they might be applied. For each of the methods described there's also a recommended reading list with suggestions on how go dive deeper.

Especially around kanban I appreciate the detailed description on how one could go about to "map out the workflow". Making your work visual is often the biggest aha-moment for many teams and it's very good place to start.

There's of course a space (and focus) constraint in any book, and anyone could want "more" about their favourite method, but I'm missing a little more discussion about the Work in Progress/Process limits being improvement tools. With a WIP limit too high many improvement opportunities goes unnoticed. If the WIP limit is too low our system is very sensitive for any irregularity or problem.

The final "method" described is called "Hybrid Project Management" - likely the most common method implemented "in the wild". And that is how it should be, as pointed out early in the chapter 8, but the author. There's a reality and, especially in big organisations, the agile practices are applied within that reality.

For me personally, what stands out for those that "succeed" with agile or not is if they are willing to let the agile principles guide and change their current ways.

To me the most fundamental practice of agile is continuous improvement. Meaning that the practices we do today is just best-so-far. We will adapt, experiment and find new ones. This might be very local within the team ("let's try continuous integration next sprint", "we should do standups in the afternoon"), or it might be bigger organisational wide adjustments ("what do we need to change in our infrastructure to deploy daily", "that team should really be closer to us, maybe even take part in our daily standup")

Agile is not about following practices. It's about improving on the (so called "best") practices of today and make them better for you in your context.

Deliver business value in small increments often to increase the number of decision opportunities aka being agile. We do this by continuously improving our processes, practices and ways to move faster.

I enjoyed this book and think that especially with the thorough package of repetition and question material in the end of each chapter this will be an awesome guide for anyone wanting to pass the PMI-ACP & CSP exam.

Thank you John!

Good luck with your exams, readers!

FOREWORD

Alfonso Bucero | *PMI Fellow, CEO, BUCERO PM Consulting*

Agility to me is flexibility to be adapted to the new environment, it is a positive attitude to keep on a smile while you are working hard. It is a way of dancing according to the music the orchestra is playing at every moment in different places. Are you, the reader, agile?

I always try to be agile in my personal and professional life. My preferred sentence is "Today is a Good Day". When I agreed to write this preface, my preferred sentence came to my mind again. When I started in the project management field thirty years ago I practiced some kind of agility managing my projects. I tried to be agile in the way of minimizing bureaucracy, and keeping my team awake and productive. It was some kind of intuition as a young and inexperienced project manager. But the "Agile future" was immense.

Between 2001 and now the "Agile concept" and all the methodologies around it became formalized, and of course very popular. I also found some skeptical practitioners who refused to read anything about Agile arguing it only consisted on applying common sense. However people who do not know it are like people who are blind. I mean if you do not spend some time understanding the concepts, reading several books and trying to use it, you should not express your professional opinion because you lack information to do it. I have read a couple of books on "Agile project management" I liked but I never found real practices in those books, only theory.

However, the author of this book, John Stenbeck, used a good mix of theory, practices and exercises that created a great combination for the reader who is looking for fast results using Agile methodologies. This book is divided in parts and none of them is difficult to read. Part 1 includes the introduction, the structure and the principles of Agile. Part 2 explains the concepts and differences among Lean, Extreme Programming and Kanban. Part 3 is focused on "Agile tools".

This is a book that needs to be read by any project practitioner because it is about best practices, it is about real stories. In my opinion it is what makes a book more attractive. John made a difference with this book. The author has collected a great set of project management practices applying Agile. Nobody tried before but John achieved it. Thank you John, because this book has plenty of analogies that help the reader to understand the Agile concepts and its application. All the graphics included in this book will help you to understand the theory, and a lot of stories will be found that illustrate the concepts explained.

There is an important key point to note. The tests at the end of every chapter oblige you to review the concepts before moving forward through the material. For those people who want to be prepared for the Agile Certification Exam, this is your book. Read it, review it, answer the questions in there, and you will pass the exam easily. I envy John because his writing style, his clarity and efficiency illuminate every piece of the book. Learn from him!

Once more time, thank you John, because you have contributed to the expansion of the project management practice worldwide and we, as readers, appreciate it. Readers, enjoy this book, read each chapter, review it and take the exercises and questions and you will learn. Never stop, continue developing your skills as a project manager.

Today is a Good Day to start!

Alfonso Bucero, MSc, PMP, PMI-RMP, PfMP, Certified Speaker, PMI Fellow

PART ONE
INTRODUCTION

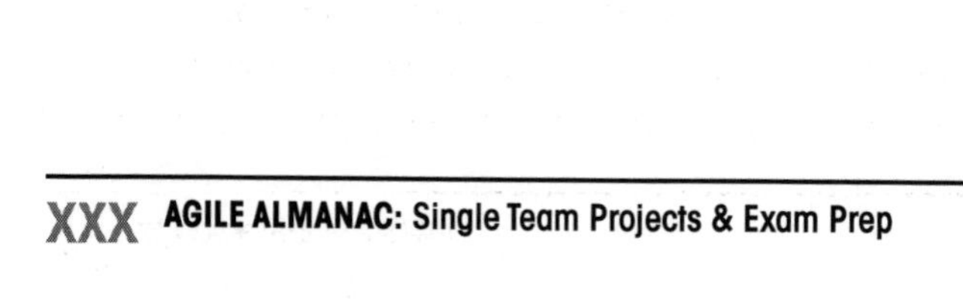

Why This *Almanac* Is Needed

Understanding This Almanac

The world of Agile Project Management has been coalescing for many years at the intersection of Lean Principles and the Project Management Institute's *A Guide to the Project Management Body of Knowledge, (PMBOK® Guide)* starting back with the *PMBOK® Guide 2000 Edition*, and continuing into the current Fifth Edition, Project Management Institute, Inc. 2012.

In February 2001, the world of Agile Project Management got a jolt of electricity infused into its development with the publication of the Agile Manifesto and the formation of the Scrum Alliance a short time later.

In the time since, multiple schools of thought developed, each with their own "evangelists" and "disciples", and Agile Project Management has come of age. However, no one has undertaken the necessary effort to collect and codify the various insights, options and best practices available for organizations, professional project managers, and product and solutions developers to use to improve project outcomes.

Perhaps that is so because no one has wanted to enter the battlefield that seems to have developed between the various camps of evangelists and adherents.

It seems that, despite their common interest in improving the world of work and project performance, a shared distrust that expresses itself as mutually exclusive worldviews has become entrenched.

The goal of this almanac is to serve the entire community by only presenting the best practices that are most used, numerically, and most proven, statistically. It will not advocate for any single school of thought. Instead, it will present thought leadership wherever it can be found.

Simply put, this almanac brings a unique perspective to the divergent, often conflicting and accusatory viewpoints expressed by the "evangelists" on all sides of the Agile versus Traditional battlefield.

Our experience delivering projects in an immense number of industries and institutions has convinced us that Agile Project Management has many patterns present in Traditional Project Management. Agile is not a "revolution" as many seem to assume because of the prominence given to the *Agile Manifesto.* Although the Manifesto may have launched a host of experimentation with product development techniques, it is not a revolution in the truest sense. It is an innovation – an extension of Lean Principles into Project Management practices.

Before you doubt that assertion, consider that the Project Management Institute's *A Guide to the Project Management Body of Knowledge, (PMBOK® Guide) 2000 Edition,* included Rolling Wave Planning, Progressive Elaboration, and Decomposition as recommended practices. All three are core Agile practices drawn from Lean Principles and Product Development best practices.

We have dealt with thousands of students, many of who are experienced Project Managers. Their most common reaction to Agile is surprise at discovering that they were already instinctually using Agile practices and that those practices were largely responsible for their projects' successful outcomes. Of course we also deal with many students who are technical professionals and new to Project Management. Their reaction is more often, "These are very good ideas that make sense to me, but I have never heard of them before!" So the difference isn't Agile. The difference is the person's experience. Most experienced Project Managers recognize pattern similarities between some Traditional and Agile practices, and also note a difference in vocabulary. Many professionals with less Project Management experience respond as if Agile is an innovation, just as they do with Traditional practices they haven't seen before.

Either way, this book is going to increase your expertise in Project Management and move you from playing checkers to playing chess when designing and executing your projects!

At GR8PM (pronounced, "Great PM") we view Traditional, Agile, and Hybrid Project Management approaches as complementary. In fact, we consider each approach a mandatory tool for professional Project Managers (PMs) to know! Selecting and using the right approach is a significant first step to delivering a successful project. We also know all successful PMs are pragmatists and once they have good command of the various Frameworks and tools, they will make the right choice in applying the best ones to their project and its success.

GR8PM understands employers and client organizations want the assurance of well-trained professionals serving their organizations. Therefore, we created this world-class book to assist in preparation for PMI's Agile Certified Practitioner (PMI-ACP®) exam. (The Certified Scrum Master exam is so simple that exam preparation is not needed, and completing it is usually done at the end of the training class.)

In addition to doing an in-depth analysis of the books[1] chosen by PMI as the basis of the PMI-ACP® test, we used our own expertise to create a useful, accessible digest of each of the Agile Frameworks and tools. That means this book will help you pass the exam and, even more importantly, succeed in using Agile methods as a professional Project Manager!

How do these books help Practitioners and Organizations?

These books allow Practitioners and Organizations to select precisely the content they need and zero in on applying it in the ways best suited to the context of their environments. We often remind students that the organization doesn't care whether they use Traditional methods, Agile techniques or Aunt Suzy's recipe. The organization only cares about results! In fact, they demand results as the validation that the project leader, regardless of their title, is a professional.

Everywhere we go to present, teach, coach and mentor, the audiences and teams we work with all acknowledge that there is not one right way to do every project. They also agree that for a specific team, on a specific project, given the available resources and constraints, there is one best way – the way with the highest probability of success – to execute that project. This means that for any project leader to be a real professional, they must have as many tools and techniques as the Team may need from both the Traditional and Agile domains. They must also be able to effectively share and apply them in ways that empower the Team's performance and growth.

The many tools and techniques used in the Traditional domain are well documented in the *PMBOK® Guide (Fifth Edition, Project Management Institute, Inc. 2012)*. However, the many tools and techniques used in the Agile domain are not comprehensively documented elsewhere, creating the need for this almanac.

At the highest level, the Agile domain can be divided into three sub-domains, Single-team Projects and Exam Prep, Programs with Multi- and Virtual-team Environments, and Portfolio Management and Enterprise Scaling. Each sub-domain is covered in its own book.

Book 1: Single-team Projects & Exam Prep

- Agile Project Management, Lean Principles & the "Big 5"
- Scrum
- eXtreme Programming (XP)
- Lean Software Development (LSD)
- Kanban Basic Practices
- Hybrid Project Management

Book One is focused on the needs of individual practitioners, whether they have a lot of experience or are new to Agile Project Management, and provides detailed insight and analysis on when and how to use the "Big 5" Frameworks. It also includes solid preparation for PMI's Agile Certified Practitioner (PMI-ACP®) exam. (The exam prep content Appendices are included in an electronic PDF format. Doing so allows them to be updated as changes occur so the reader has the latest information available. Also, because the core Agile content presented in this Almanac is mature and stable, the Desk Reference has a long-term shelf-life and won't need to be replaced frequently, saving the reader a future expense.)

Book 2: Programs with Multi- and Virtual-Team Environments

- Agile with Multi- and Virtual-Teams
- Program Integration and Scheduling
- Kanban Advanced Practices

Book Two is focused on the needs of practitioners and organizations dealing with the challenges of large programs being executed in an environment that includes the use of multiple teams and/or virtual, remote, and distributed teams. It includes many tools and techniques that optimize results when Traditional and Agile methods are being used in a customized Hybrid approach designed specifically for the organization. It provides insight and help for large teams within organizations that are a public agency, department or command competing for tax dollars in budget battles, or a commercial entity battling for consumer dollars.

Book 3: Portfolios and Enterprise Scaling

- Agile Portfolio Management
- Agile Maturity Matrix Instrument (AMMI Assessment)
- Scaling Agile to the Enterprise

Book Three is focused on the needs of organizational leaders and senior practitioners supporting Project Management Offices (PMOs), portfolios, and strategic decision-making. It includes assessment instruments, analysis tools and planning techniques that optimize total throughput within overall resource limits. It provides insight and helps increase the top and bottom line and employee engagement.

Important Structural Highlights and Conventions

This book serves the needs of various readers. First, it prepares those studying for the PMI-ACP® exam with in-depth coverage of the team-level micro-dynamic processes they must know. Second, it provides Project Management practitioners a quick reference Field Guide for clear direction about how to choose and implement the correct practices for specific teams on particular projects within the context of organizational constraints.

This book concentrates on the needs of individual practitioners, whether they have a lot of experience or are new to Agile Project Management. Its goal is to provide enough detailed insight about using the "Big 5" that practitioners can set up their teams, projects and careers for success. It also includes specific, detailed information to ensure they can pass the PMI's Agile Certified Practitioner (PMI-ACP®). (Again, the Certified Scrum Master exam uses a simple, open-book exam at the end of he class. The Certified Scrum Professional does not require an exam.)

In order to support the exam preparation needs of many readers, Chapters 2 through 8 include a Chapter Close-Out section with a Chapter Test, Fill-in-the-Blank questions, and a Terminology Matching Challenge. These various study aids should be used at the reader's discretion based on their preferred learning style in order to enhance and support understanding and retention of the content, which is designed to reinforce your command of that chapter's specific material. The answers to the Chapter Test, Fill-in-the-Blank questions, and Terminology Matching Challenge are included so you can reinforce your retention of the right answers.

Part Two – The "Big 5" Deep Dive

Based on GR8PM's experience and feedback from thousands of students, Part Two will provide an intense, thorough investigation and explanation of the "Big 5" Agile Frameworks – Scrum, eXtreme Programming (XP), Lean Software Development (LSD), Kanban, and Hybrid Project Management. It will cover their school of thought and associated approaches to delivering outcomes. Because hiring organizations have a high allegiance to project **results** not **theories,** the content is organized to support the needs of professional Project Managers wanting to advance their careers. Wherever possible we have defined the best practices currently used as well as common customizations employed to optimize outcomes.

Each chapter in Part Two is also summarized in the Quick Notes section of the Appendices. Quick Notes can be thought of like the "Cliff Notes" used by many college students. They present bulleted coverage of the most important principles and practices of the "Big 5" Agile Frameworks. Quick Notes are ideal for a final "in the parking lot" refresher before entering the testing center to sit for the PMI-ACP® exam.

Chapter Endnotes and Recommended Reading

The extensive endnotes throughout this book provide useful source information so that you can use this book as both a ***Desk Reference*** and ***Field Guide***. Although the endnotes may only be marginally helpful for exam preparation, they will be invaluable long after the pain of the exam has faded! That is when your boss and coworkers will expect you to be an expert in all things Agile, and you will refer to the sources identified in the endnotes time and time again.

As an additional source of value, each chapter includes a Recommended Reading list that can be used to increase your expertise with further in-depth study of pertinent topics. All of the recommending reading citations are well recognized and respected resources that have been thoroughly reviewed by GR8PM.

Flashcards

Throughout the book, you will find the light bulb icon (shown on the left) to call your attention to important facts included in the GR8PM Flashcard deck. This also makes it easy for you to identify good choices for creating your own flashcards if you are not using the ones from GR8PM.com. Adult Learning Theory has shown that learning through various channels increases retention and mastery. Many students use flashcards for that purpose. Use them if they appeal to your learning style; skip them if they don't!

Appendices

The Appendices provide exam prep content and are included in a PDF format. They are updated as changes are made by PMI or the Scrum Alliance so readers get the latest information available.

Appendix 1: Exam Certification Choices

There are two primary Agile certification choices with over 90% market-share combined. The Scrum Alliance offers the the Certified ScrumMaster® (CSM) and Certified Scrum Professional (CSP). PMI offers the Agile Certified Professional (PMI-ACP®). The dozens of other certifications offered by virtually unrecognized groups aren't worth pursuing so they are not covered.

Appendix 1 covers the prerequisites required for each certification as well as the process for applying, passing the exam, and receiving and maintaining them.

Appendix 2: Exam Prep "Pre-Game" Quick Notes

The Quick Notes are an excellent "parking lot" review on the day of the exam. They contain summarized content pulled together and condensed for use as a final, quick, and easily accessible exam prep ritual. Quick Notes are not a substitute for proper exam preparation, but are a great "pre-game warm-up" on exam day.

Summarizing Agile Certification Choices

Three years ago when *"PMI-ACP® and Certified Scrum Professional Exam Prep and Desk Reference"* was published, GR8PM thought it would do well but never imagined it would achieve over $1 million in sales in 26 months. However, two things were obvious from very early on. First, the PMI-ACP®

was going to be very popular. Second, PMI would recognize that trend and invest in improving the PMI-ACP® certification. Our prediction was validated in the Fall of 2014 when PMI conducted an Agile Role Delineation Study and revised the PMI-ACP® exam in 2015.

To begin, know that there are three primary certification choices of interest to 98% of technical professionals and Project Managers. Two are from the Scrum Alliance and one is from PMI.

The Scrum Alliance offers the Certified Scrum Master (CSM) and Certified Scrum Professional (CSP). If you are in a job transition, or expect to be at the time of this writing (August 2015), you should consider adding the CSM to your resume. Likewise, if you are in software development and never intend to work outside the software industry, then the CSM is fine and should be added to your resume. The CSP is entirely optional because it carries very little "brand recognition" and therefore adds very little career value.

The Project Management Institute, PMI, offers the Agile Certified Professional (PMI-ACP®) certification and it has become the fastest growing certification in PMI history. For any serious technical professional or Project Manager, adding this to their resume is not a question of "if" but only a question of "when". As we have explained to audiences across the country, PMI's brand recognition and implied credibility among Fortune 2000 companies and most public entities is dramatically higher than any of its competitors, including the Scrum Alliance.

That is so, in part, because of the objective rigor that is required to obtain any of the various PMI certifications. As we began predicting three years ago, PMI has taken the next step to improve the PMI-ACP® by conducting a Role Delineation Study in the Fall of 2014 and re-piloting a new, more stringent exam starting in July 2015.

That means that the career paths of serious technical professionals and Project Managers are on a direct collision course with the rising expectations of hiring managers that will intersect at a point where the PMI-ACP® is a threshold requirement. As it is now with the PMP® being a threshold requirement for any valuable Project Manager job or promotion, so it will be with the PMI-ACP® in the very near future. This fact is driven by an organizational need for Agile leaders who can foster and manage the innovation that defines success or failure on the battlefield for consumer dollars or taxpayer funding.

And since it is only a question of "when", most intelligent professionals are interpreting the recent investment by PMI to improve the certification and make the examination more challenging as a trigger to do it sooner and save themselves from additional future grief.

Along that same line, one additional GR8PM prediction is worth noting. We believe that the improvements being done to the PMI-ACP® now by PMI are a precursor to the final step of fully integrating Agile best practices into the *PMBOK® Guide.* Core Agile content already exists in the *PMBOK® Guide (Fifth Edition, Project Management Institute, Inc. 2012)* and we believe that the next edition of the *PMBOK® Guide* will make that content even more clear and robust. Once that is done, we believe, the PMI-ACP® exam will be based on content in the *PMBOK® Guide* and the need for a separate external list of books will be gone.

As organizations pursue competitive advantage by leveraging Agile to deliver innovation, it will translate into hiring demands that will be a significant boon to PMI as it advocates for training in multiple Agile Frameworks. Conversely, significant challenges will likely emerge for the Scrum Alliance as it advocates for training in a single Framework. That is because organizations want the right answer, customized to their needs, resources, and constraints. They consider getting the right answer more important than dogmatic allegiance to any particular Framework.

Therefore, acquiring the PMI-ACP® certification will likely provide many career opportunities. Being a PMI-ACP® could give you the chance to lead dream teams on projects of a lifetime. Additionally, if you feel like your job or your future is at risk, having the PMI-ACP® could keep you from getting passed over instead of promoted, at the next opportunity.

All that's left now is for you to decide when the time is right for you to add it to your resume.

Agile, PMP®s and 1500 Agile Hours

Before going any further, there is a common myth among PMP®s that needs to be pointed out. One of the biggest myths is PMP®s thinking that they don't already use Agile practices. They think that they don't have the 1,500 hours of Agile experience required to sit for the PMI-ACP® exam. What seems to get missed is that even though the Agile vocabulary is different from the *PMBOK® Guide,* an important number of the core principles are exactly the same.

If you take the time to remember back to that first time you opened the *PMBOK® Guide* and started reading it, was your reaction, "Wow this is exactly how we talk at work?" Of course it wasn't and that thought is ridiculous. Nobody talks that way until after they become a PMP®. So it shouldn't surprise you that the Agile vocabulary is unfamiliar when you first start investigating it.

The beauty of the *PMBOK® Guide* is that it has given us a common language. Therefore, a PM at Pfizer, another PM working at Nike® and a third PM at Ford, can still have a fruitful conversation about tricks and tips because they have a core vocabulary that transcends varying industries.

One example of a core Agile concept can be seen in the graphical Work Breakdown Structure (WBS) that is studied as part of most PMP® exam prep classes. The levels of the WBS are defined from the top down as Objectives, Phases, Work Packages, Activities and Tasks. Similarly, Agile calls the same logical device a Feature Structure, or a Feature Breakdown Structure (FBS), and though it has a different naming convention, it serves the same function. The levels of the FBS are most commonly defined from the top down as Product, Theme, Epic, Story and Task.

Recognize that what they share in common is that at the highest level they have broad details and at the lowest level they have lots of fine granularity. Also, they are both arbitrary, logical devices for bucketing and managing information. Without this logical device, if you try to carry all that information about all your projects around in your head at the task level, your head would explode.

So, if you put the names the *PMBOK® Guide* uses next to the names Agile uses for the various levels, what you find is that the definitions are virtually the same. Thus, every time you've worked on a WBS, you were doing Progressive Elaboration and Decomposition, which are two core Agile practices.

So our experience talking to PMP®s suggests that every PMP® has the 1,500 hours of required experience, but many do not know it! In a recent poll[2] done by the PMI –Washington DC Chapter, when asked, "If you are a PMP® do you think you have the 1,500 hours of Agile experience needed to sit for the PMI-ACP® exam?" just over 65% said "No" and an additional 18% said "Don't Know". That means 83% of PMP®s didn't know they were already using Agile practices! Interestingly, when asked, "Do you agree that some of Agile's best practices are simply more effective ways to implement practices from the

PMBOK® Guide?" slightly over 49% said "Yes" and almost 46% said "Don't Know", which seems to imply that PMP®s instinctively know that Agile enhances project execution without realizing they are using Agile best practices.

When you decide to pursue the PMI-ACP® certification, this book helps because it is more than just an exam preparation book. It is also a Desk Reference and Field Guide. It serves as a handy source of "how to" knowledge and best practices as you lead your teams after receiving your PMI-ACP® certification. Stepping up like that could help you unlock a leadership role in moving your organization to the next level of agility and competitive advantage!

About the Author

John G. Stenbeck, PMP, PMI-ACP, CSM, CSP, is the Founder of GR8PM, Inc., with a combined background in Accounting, Operations, I.T. and Project Management. He has the ability to manage large, complex projects to success where others have failed. John has extensive experience implementing enterprise resource planning (E.R.P.) systems at firms in the aerospace, shipbuilding, and construction industries.

John is also a respected author, sought-after Keynote speaker and trainer. He has authored three highly acclaimed books in addition to seven internationally delivered training courses for project management practitioners.

He delivers over 50 events a year. John presents programs that engage hard-to-impress technical and engineering professionals with unique Keynote-Workshops that return audiences to work... *ENABLED TO BE POWERFULLY PRODUCTIVE!*

At the 2008 PMI – Global Congress, John set the all-time attendance record for Area of Focus presentations when the first audience of ***640*** made it a ***sell-out!*** *The Five Time-tested Keys of Estimating that Successful Project Managers Can't Live Without!* continues to be popular at PMI meetings and industry events. Interestingly, at the 2010 Global Congress, John set the second highest-ever record – ***over 400*** – with *Agile Project Management Mastery in 60 Minutes…Guaranteed!*

John is available to speak to your company or group on a variety of topics, including:

- Transform Your Career Network from Unreliable to Championship!!
- Unlock Your Project Leadership Potential…NOW!
- Five Keys to Estimating Every PM Needs!
- Three Vital Steps to Mastering Risk Management
- Agile PM Mastery in 60 minutes... Guaranteed!
- Conquering Project Cost Management with a Simple, Proven System
- Successful Project Scheduling… In a Nutshell
- Why Agile is Mainstream!
- Rolling Out Enterprise Agile Practices (Advanced Topic)

Over the past fifteen years, he has coached, trained and managed projects for a host of organizations including Booz Allen Hamilton, Inc. – Defense Information Technologies Group, McLean, VA; County of Orange, Orange, CA; Guinness Bass Import Company, Greenwich, CT; Hewlett-Packard Company, Palo Alto, CA; Lucent Technologies, Allentown, PA; Nike Corp., Beaverton, OR; Oracle Corp., Redwood Shores, CA; Qualcomm, Inc., San Diego, CA; U.S. Army – Space and Terrestrial Communications Directorate, Fort Monmouth, NJ; U.S.D.A. – National Finance Center, New Orleans, LA; Visa – Smart Cards, Foster City, CA.

John was an Adjunct Instructor for the University of California – San Diego's School of Extended Studies, teaching Project Management in the Systems Engineering Certificate program prior to relocating to Spokane, Washington. As a trainer, he has taught numerous public and corporate on-site programs to over 9,500 students.

John holds the Project Management Professional (PMP®) credential and the Agile Certified Practitioner (PMI-ACP®) certification from the Project Management Institute (PMI). He is also certified by the Scrum Alliance as a Certified ScrumMaster® (CSM) and a Certified Scrum Professional (CSP). Additionally, he has an ITIL v.3 Foundations certification.

John is a Past President of the PMI – San Diego Chapter where he served as the Vice-President of Professional Development before becoming the President. Currently he serves as the Vice-President of Programs for the PMI – Inland Northwest Chapter serving eastern Washington. He is also involved in a number of professional user groups outside of the project management field.

Beyond professional and career pursuits John is a passionate supporter of youth soccer where he has been a coach and referee for many years. He was a

California licensed Soccer Coach and certified by two different officiating bodies as a Referee.

Personally, John has been active in men's ministry as part of the Cursillo Community of San Diego, prison ministry as part of Kairos International, and supports the youth ministry efforts of Steubenville Conferences.

His hobbies include cooking, swimming, hunting and enjoying an outdoor lifestyle with his two sons, daughter-in-law, grandson and many friends.

Chapter End Notes

[1]The list can be found at PMI.org.

[2]Poll was conducted as part of a webinar on May 28, 2015 and had a sample size of 205.

Agile From a PMP®'s Perspective

Chapter Highlights

In this chapter we describe how Lean principles evolved into Agile Project Management practices. We will highlight important Agile principles that impact every organization - commercial, industrial, governmental and institutional - and need to be understood in order to assess the value of agility in their environment.

Two Quick, Familiar Analogies

Years of teaching experience have shown that sharing quick, familiar examples helps students create useful mental maps as they study Agile Project Management in greater depth. Let's use building a jigsaw puzzle and also a shopping center as examples of Agile thinking being applied in situations familiar to you.

Assembling a Jigsaw Puzzle

Imagine for a moment that you and three friends decide to assemble a jigsaw puzzle. In many ways, Project Management often feels like this. The first step is to define the project objective. In this case, the objective is to assemble a 1,000-piece puzzle of a Space Shuttle Launch. You clarify the understanding of the objective by propping up the lid from the puzzle box so everyone can see a clear picture of the desired final result. In Traditional Project Management this activity would be called creating the Project Charter, while the same activities in Agile would be considered defining the Product Vision. By the way, a side objective that often goes unspoken is to finish successfully and remain

Figure 2.1 | *Jigsaw Puzzle*

friends afterwards! Next, your group agrees on the tactic it will use to complete the work. The most common tactic is to assemble the outer edge, or frame, of the puzzle as single team then work independently creating sub-assemblies of pieces that make up distinct sections of the puzzle. For example, the external fuel tank, the adjacent tower, and the steam clouds. While you are doing the work, you pause frequently and synchronize with your teammates by sharing data on what you have done and what you are trying to do. It might sound something like, "I've connected all the white steam cloud pieces. Now I'm looking for the dark pieces of the fuel tank." In Agile Project Management this activity would be called a Stand-up Meeting while the same activities in a Traditional setting would be called a Status Meeting. As the work proceeds, in order to help the team complete the project, the "expert" in white clouds and dark landscaping might begin helping the "expert" working on the external fuel tank or the "expert" working on the water tower. This concept of teamwork highlights the value of having a cross-functional team where each Subject Matter Expert (SME) is also willing to extend beyond their core skills and learn other skills in order to help the team accomplish the shared mission.

Building a Shopping Center

Expanding on the jigsaw analogy, imagine for a moment that you and three friends are investors who decide to build a shopping center on a piece of land you recently acquired.

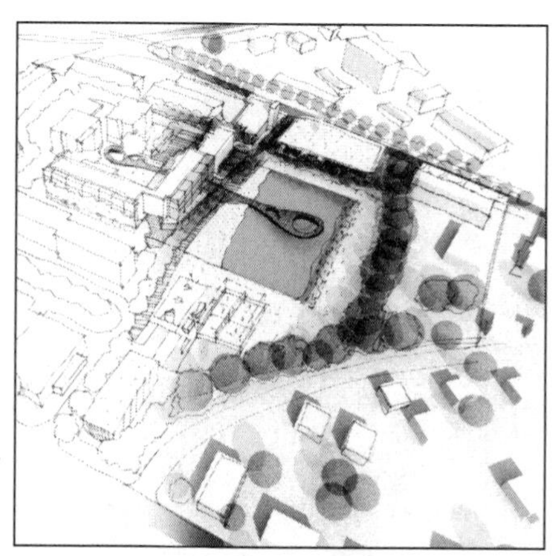
Figure 2.2 | *Plot Plan*

The first step you take is to hire an architect to help define a Project Objective, maximizing the value of your investment. The architect would then initiate a repetitive, cyclical process to help you make choices and define the

Final Objective with a set of blueprints. In Agile Project Management, each timebox in the cycle would be called an Iteration or Sprint and the expected result would be called a Potentially Shippable Product.

Iterations are single cycles of development with a fixed-length that is not varied during the Release. Commonly the length is fixed at one to four weeks. It is the basic operational process used in Agile to deliver desired results in small increments. The standard Iteration typically delivers new development work that has been subjected to full quality assurance and user acceptance testing. It begins with the Iteration Planning meeting and concludes with a Review meeting for interested stakeholders and a Retrospective meeting for the Team. In Scrum it is called a *Sprint.*

For example, Iteration 1 would likely deliver the Plot Plan, as seen in Figure 2.2, as the Potentially Shippable Product. Following your discussions with the architect, either the Plot Plan would be accepted or additional revisions would occur in the next Iteration. You would review the result, again deciding to accept it or request more revisions. Assuming for the moment that you accepted the Plot Plan at the end of the second Iteration, then Iteration 3 might deliver the Elevation Drawing, as seen in Figure 2.3.

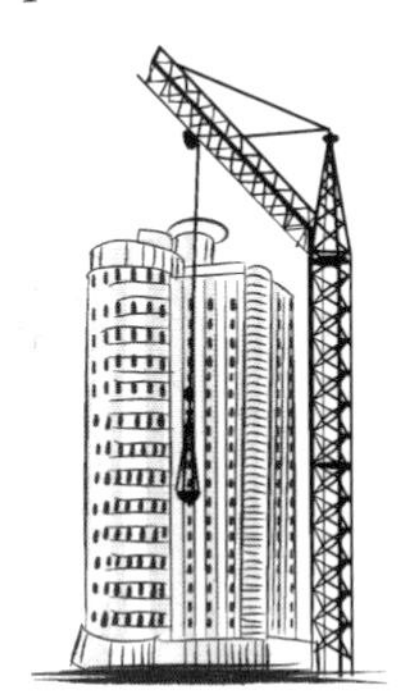

Figure 2.3
Elevation Drawing

Again, following discussions with the architect, either the Elevation Drawing would be accepted or revisions would occur during additional Iterations until you accepted the result. If, for example, you accepted the Elevation Drawing at the end of the sixth Iteration, Iteration 7 could possibly deliver a Computer Generated Walkthrough, as pictured in Figure 2.4.

Figure 2.4 | *Computer Generated Walkthrough*

By now you can see how the process works. The team does the work to deliver a result. You discuss the result with the team of SMEs, in this case the architectural firm, then you make a decision to accept or revise the Potentially Shippable Product from that Iteration.

Your decision to accept or reject the Potentially Shippable Product is either a formal or informal Test-Driven Development (TDD) process depending on the experience and maturity of your group of investors and the architectural firm. Eventually, the process will embrace a formal TDD process when another critical stakeholder – the Building Department – gets involved. Until the details in the blueprints, schedules and specifications meet the minimum standards defined by the Building Department, they will not issue the building permits and your project cannot begin the construction phase.

This same process in Traditional Project Management would be called Rolling Wave Planning and the activities would be Progressive Elaboration and Decomposition. The timeboxes might be weeks or months and the decision points would be called Milestones, Phase Gates, or Go – No Go Meetings.

The goal of the process is to reduce waste regardless of whether you use the Agile or Traditional lexicon to describe it! Waste reduction is one of the core Lean principles that drive both Agile and Traditional Project Management best practices.

There are other best practices also implied and imbedded in these analogies.

For example, your jigsaw team and the architectural team are both cross-functional. Their strength comes from the different skill sets contributed by each SME. Consequently, it is implied that the team has all the skills necessary to complete the project. Neither Agile nor Traditional Project Management are a magic potion or wand! If a team does not have the required skills, it cannot successfully complete the project.

Another example is using various meetings and techniques to solicit feedback as part of the Stakeholder Management best practice. Consider for a moment the pancake stacks in Figure 2.5 and ask, "Which one do most stakeholders want and expect if all the information they are given is what they see in Figure 2.5?" Then ask yourself, "What happens to stakeholders' expectations when they are shown the information in Figure 2.6?" Far too often Project Managers complain about irrational stakeholder behavior without identifying the underlying cause and accepting responsibility for doing their part to change the situation. Stakeholders are human and humans are irrational when they make a decision without the information needed to understand the real context of the decision.

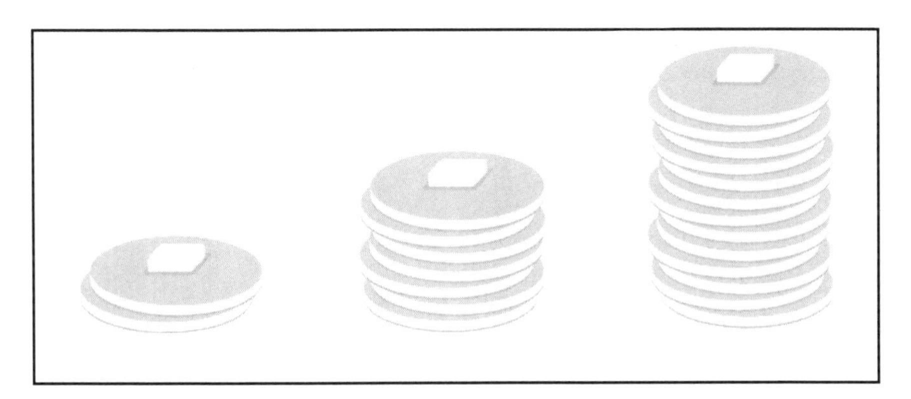

Figure 2.5 | *Stakeholder Management*

Cost and schedule are two of the key drivers in making scope decisions. A stack of pancakes I definitely wanted when I understood the cost and schedule to be $100 and 1 day becomes a stack of pancakes I absolutely don't want when I learn the cost and schedule are $10,000 and 6 months. Without complete, clear information the stakeholder could make the wrong decision and appear irrational, but it would be the Project Manager's fault. The core purpose of both Traditional Rolling Wave plans and Agile Iterative and Incremental development is to provide adequate, accurate and timely information so stakeholders can properly understand the context of their decisions.

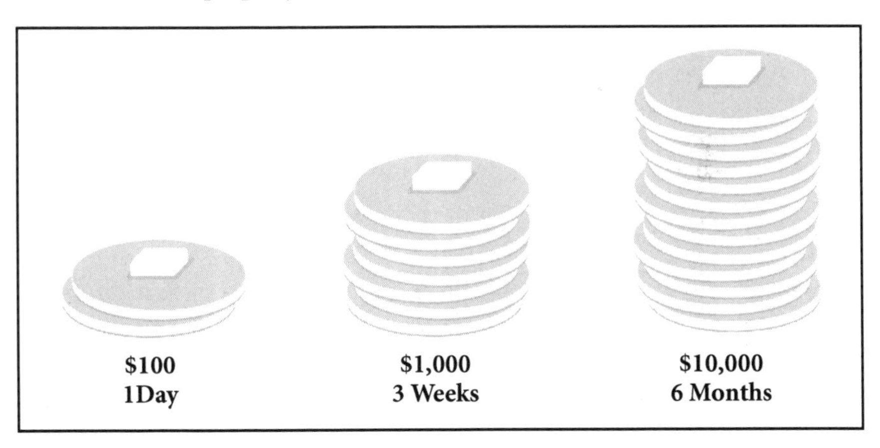

Figure 2.6 | *Stakeholder Management*

What Makes Planning Agile

Given the simple analogies just described, one of the first follow-up questions that should be asked is, "What makes project management Agile? What makes planning Agile? What is the difference between Agile and Traditional?"

Interestingly enough, Helmuth Graf von Moltke, a German Field Marshal[3] in the early 1800s summed it up when he said, "No plan survives contact with the enemy!" He was thinking of the high complexity and high uncertainty that exists and is unavoidable, by definition, on battlefields. That description also happens to be a pretty good fit for what most projects are like. Projects are challenges with high complexity, high uncertainty, and even battlefield-like atmospheres at various times.

No plan survives contact with the enemy. Is there anybody who has ever been on a project of any significance that actually went according to the original plan? Has such a project ever even been heard of? His observation is really interesting because it focuses on the core assumption of Agile that project management must be responsive to the situational reality.

So what makes project management Agile? What makes planning Agile? There are really two key characteristics. First, Agile balances resource consumption against the absolute certainty that the plan is going to change. We know the plan is going to change so spending a huge amount of time doing a super detailed plan at the very beginning – knowing that it is going to change – violates the Lean practice of always reducing avoidable waste! Instead, Agile uses an iterative and integrated cycle of development and planning that applies the best practices of Rolling Wave Planning and Progressive Elaboration in a robust and meaningful way. The second trait that makes planning and project management Agile is embracing change that is driven by two factors – the acquisition of new knowledge or the circumvention a problem in the original plan.

When either of those factors is present, we change in order to leverage the opportunity presented by the new knowledge or to avoid the mistake inherent in the original plan.

Understanding Lean's Evolution Into Agile

According to Winston Churchill, "To improve is to change; to be perfect is to change often!"

Given the wisdom in Churchill's comment, the movement to adopt and adapt Lean principles into the project management profession is not surprising. An often overlooked reality of today's workplace, now and forever into the future, is that the constantly increasing rate of technological capabilities is driving almost unimaginable levels of complexity, and therefore uncertainty, into project management. A related and unavoidable truth for organizations, whether they are competing in budget battles for tax dollars or competing in the marketplace for consumer dollars, is that every constituent and customer has had their expectations conditioned by the Internet and companies like Amazon, Facebook and Google. Good enough is no longer good enough. Speed, complexity and uncertainty are constants in the new baseline of every project!

In such a challenging environment, experience has shown the best practices available for achieving success come from the principles of Lean Manufacturing, as originally developed in the Toyota Production System with the insight and guidance of W. Edward Demings[4] and extended by Eli Goldratt[5] in his seminal work on the *Theory of Constraints* and the *Critical Chain.*

Because a great many projects today have levels of complexity and uncertainty similar to when John F. Kennedy launched the Apollo Space Program, taking a moment to reflect back can provide interesting insights into understanding how Lean was the outgrowth of iterative and adaptive development practices, and also how Lean is being adapted and adopted into the project management profession.

Agile and Apollo

If you are old enough to remember, you can still hear John F. Kennedy's clipped New England accent as he said, "We will go to the moon and return a man safely by the end of the decade!" But to really understand the power of his statement, you have to put yourself in the context of that timeframe. To fully understand how boldly he embraced a challenge with epic levels of complexity and uncertainty, you have to recall the situational context.

At the time that he made that bold proclamation, as a nation we had never put anything in orbit and engineers were using slide rules to do calculations because computers with adequate computational power did not exist. It would have been a huge claim to say that we are going to put an object into orbit and return it safely. But to say that we were going to put a man on the moon and return him safely was an outlandish claim. And part of the power that is held was that it was crystal clear; to the moon and back, safely, by the end of the decade!

There could be no fudging. It would be exactly clear whether you reached the moon, returned safely, and when! The Project Charter provided an unmistakable set of Acceptance Criteria that could be decomposed into a completely measurable series of Iterations where Test-Driven Development could harness talent and energy to create Incremental Progress at a Sustainable Pace.

He then took the next important step that is sometimes missing from projects in a lot of organizations. He recruited the right team to take on this unbelievably challenging project. And that team decided to move forward using an iterative development methodology.

Stop for a moment, again, and recognize that the Apollo team chose iterative development before Agile's Manifesto had been written, before the Project Management Institute existed, and before the Toyota Production System, the source of Lean principles, existed. They took on this project in the absence of so many of the core best practices available today and still succeeded.

So even though iterative development techniques were being employed before Lean principles were developed, and even though Lean principles were developed before the Agile movement began, the introduction of Agile to many PMP®s has still been an experience of surprise and confusion. Unfortunately, Agile has been presented by some of its early adherents as something completely new, completely foreign to project management, and completely opposed to the PMP®'s worldview. This has resulted in unnecessarily limiting Agile adoption simply because it was misrepresented by those early adherents who were misinformed about the true pedigree of Agile.

Agile and the PMBOK® Guide

For many PMP®s with a background in Traditional Project Management, the whole idea of Agile Project Management seems to have appeared out of nowhere. Additionally, it is hard for many of them to discern whether it is simply a passing fad or a source of genuine value to the project management profession. So before we begin a deep dive of the details of Agile and focus on how it works, it is useful to step back and get an overall perspective by examining the relationship between Traditional, often called Waterfall, as embodied in the *PMBOK® Guide* and Agile Project Management.

A valuable place to begin is with some common myths about Agile and its relationship to Traditional Project Management.

> **MYTH #1** – Agile is completely separate from and outside the *PMBOK® Guide.*
>
> **FACT #1** – *The PMBOK® Guide 2000 Edition* included Rolling Wave Planning, Progressive Elaboration, and Decomposition and was published a full year before the Agile Manifesto was written. All three are core Agile practices and the simple fact is that it is impossible to be a successful Project Manager and not be using those three practices.

MYTH #2 – Agile is a revolution.

FACT #2 – Suggesting Agile is a revolution is an exaggeration, at best, and a self-aggrandizing deception, at worst. At its most basic core, Agile is simply the application of proven Lean principles to the profession of project management. Because Agile draws on the proven heritage of Lean, it offers improved planning and team management practices in environments where high uncertainty and high complexity exist. The idea that the child, Agile, sprang into existence from nothing is ludicrous and insults the very fine parentage of Lean.

MYTH #3 – Agile is easily scalable to large programs and enterprise portfolios using the practices taught and utilized in Scrum, eXtreme Programming, Lean Software Development, and many other frameworks.

FACT #3 – Every Agile framework is missing two key components required for scalability. Every Agile framework is missing both budgeting and sophisticated scheduling tools. The good news is that Agile can overcome this limitation by integrating with practices from the *PMBOK® Guide* and PMI's other Practice Standards.

MYTH #4 – Agile can meet its stated goal of "changing the world of work" with the practices used by many Agilists that maintain an exclusive focus on the Customer and Team while ignoring the needs of the Organization.

FACT #4 – Any approach that fails to meet the budgeting and scheduling needs of the Organization is self-limiting because without the resources of the Organization, the Teams cannot exist to develop the products and services desired by the Customer. Without meeting the needs of the Customer, the goal of "changing the world of work" will never be achieved. Therefore, integrating the needs of the Organization is fundamental to "changing the world of work."

Beyond these very common myths, many Agilists seem to ignore the evidence that Lean-aligned organizations in every industry have planning guidelines and processes that enable and sustain the focus and productivity of teams, including Agile teams. In order for a Team to serve a Customer, it is necessary for an Organization to provide resources. Therefore, the Organizational-customer has the right to expect a reliable estimating and planning environment. The Lean-aligned, proven techniques from the *PMBOK® Guide* can be integrated in mutually beneficial ways with Agile best practices to support and enable Teams while creating a healthy and dynamic world of work in the process.

In order to understand the numerous ways in which Agile and the *PMBOK® Guide* can be complementary, a clear lexicon must be developed and used. As we like to say at GR8PM, "Power comes from using precise language ... precisely!"

We talked about Methodologies as the highest-level structure or philosophical foundation. At the highest level in project management you have two primary Methodologies, referred to as Traditional or Waterfall, on the one side and Agile or Lean on the other side. Traditional typically refers to approaches based on *A Guide to the Project Management Body of Knowledge, (PMBOK® Guide – Fifth Edition, Project Management Institute, Inc. 2012).* Agile or Lean approaches are based on iterative product development, the Toyota Production System, and the Agile Manifesto.

It is worth noting that, technically speaking, the *PMBOK® Guide* covers the entire body of knowledge about project management, which implies that Agile or Lean practices are a subset of that overall body of knowledge.

Methodologies contain Frameworks, sometimes referred to as Extensions. For example, the *PMBOK® Guide* has extensions for the Automotive, Construction and Software industries that contain best practices beyond the core of the *PMBOK® Guide.* In the Agile lexicon, instead of extensions, they refer to Frameworks and there are a variety of them. Scrum is by far the best-known and best recognized, but the list also includes eXtreme Programming (XP), Lean Software Development (LSD), Kanban and Hybrid Project Management approaches.

It is also worth noting that when you reach for a box of facial tissues, you are likely to call it a box of Kleenex regardless of the actual brand. That is because Kleenex is the best-known brand in facial tissue. Similarly, many people use Scrum and Agile interchangeably. But to be accurate, Scrum is a particular set of practices within the Agile Methodologies.

So, to use an analogy, when you choose a Framework, it is the "house" or "container" that holds the various processes, practices and protocols defining how to initiate, manage, organize, fund and report about the project being done. Therefore, different Frameworks may have similar and different processes, practices, and protocols tailored to their specific industry or environment.

Core Purpose of Project Management ... and Agile

The core purpose of project management is to aid and support stakeholder decision-making! That's it. Period. And that core purpose is the same whether Traditional or Agile Project Management methods are being used.

As mentioned earlier, many Project Managers complain about irrational stakeholders. In fact, some Project Managers insist there isn't any other kind! But the sad, self- incriminating truth is that a lot of times stakeholders are irrational precisely because the Project Manager made them that way. When the Project Manager doesn't continually teach, and reinforce, and re-impress upon stakeholders that their job is to support the stakeholder's decision making, the Project Manager becomes the decision maker. And that is a big mistake!

Stakeholders cannot make intelligent decisions if the Project Manager doesn't give them adequate, accurate, and timely information. The Project Manager's job is to be the expert source of that information and provide it with a proper frame around it. The Project Manager must be able to structure the information so the stakeholder can make a rational decision.

John Maynard Keynes, a well-known economist, said, "It is better to be roughly right than precisely wrong!" If 80% of projects are on time and on budget, deliver what they're supposed to, and do so 80% of the time, then the organization should not change! Projects are already executing at a very, very high standard. Likewise, if 80% of projects are nightmares, have members of the team quitting, have everybody else on blood pressure medicine, and deliver unhappy customers, the organizational approach is precisely wrong and **must** change!

The most common point of confusion is when senior decision makers think the organization is in situation number one, with 80% of everything going well, but the actual reality is situation number two, with 80% of everything in chaos. If senior management is living with a rose garden perception, the first critical step is to establish contact with reality. Doing so is beyond that immediate scope of any project management approach, including Agile, but it can be done. A good starting point can be a discussion of the biennial Chaos Studies (from the Standish Group) showing the reality that one third of projects actually succeed, one third are challenged, and one third outright fail. But, again, that is beyond the scope of this book as well.

The science suggests that the highest probability is that no more than 40% of projects in your organization are successful even if your project management practices are exceptionally good! Another 40% of your projects are challenged. This means that implementing Agile practices can help achieve the essential purpose of aiding and supporting better decision-making throughout the organization.

That makes it very important that your organization understand that Agile and the *PMBOK® Guide* are intertwined and that many Agile practices are important to the organization because they are a more robust way to apply core *PMBOK® Guide* principles. That central truth makes it is important to be able to express the Agile "value proposition" concisely.

Agile Value Proposition ... in a Nutshell!

As strange as it sounds, companies and organizations don't actually want agility – or at least not agility for agility's sake. They want innovation! Organizations of all types have come to recognize that the economic drivers of success have moved from information to innovation.

Although the rate of information technology innovation has cooled down over the last decade from majestic to simply exceptional, innovation in bioengineering, nanoscale science, combinatorial chemistry and big data analytics have filled any vacuum and accelerated competition along the innovation curve. Technology has fundamentally altered the innovation process so that it permanently advances on a non-linear growth curve. That vertical shift, driven by technology, has altered the process of research, experimentation and change thereby reducing the cost of discovery by rough orders of magnitude. The cost of iterating through uncertainty, and the speed at which those iterations can be done, mean that the process of finding the best possible solution has been improved so dramatically it has altered many of the fundamental rules of business and government.

That technology-driven process change means the cost of exploration and experimentation has been so drastically reduced that discovering solutions both more effective and less costly is now possible. This new dynamic can be seen in the advances driven by Lean manufacturing and Agile development in industries as varied as integrated circuits, pharmaceuticals, software, and automotive, commercial and rail transportation vehicles.

However, leveraging this technology-driven process change has proven tricky. Nowhere has it been trickier than in project management. Moving from Traditional prescriptive processes with detailed specifications, to discovery processes with experimental and exploratory methods, means organizations and people have been compelled to change. Project Managers must now facilitate the discovery process rather than design detailed, prescriptive plans. Additionally, organizations need new metrics for guiding and measuring the discovery process in order to activate lower cost and higher value performance for their customers and constituents. Therefore, it should not come as a surprise that this transformation sometimes proves difficult.

Difficult or not, it is necessary because the playing field where human communities compete, from companies to agencies, commands, and departments, requires innovation and agility to create or maintain any competitive advantage.

Sustainable advantage comes from systematic innovation. Whether enterprises, agencies, or communities thrive, survive, or fail is directly correlated to their ability to be agile and innovative. (And the same can be said for your career and future!) That core driver is behind the ever-increasing demand for Agile Project Managers. That is also the *Agile value proposition... in a nutshell!*

Stated another way, projects allow organizations to operationalize their innovative strategic vision. Executing those projects using the correct project management framework ensures those projects maximize the positive impact of the assets and people deployed to deliver them. To accomplish this, professional Project Managers are increasingly being tasked by their organizations to synthesize the best practices of Traditional and Agile frameworks into an approach that is tailored to the environmental demands they face.

Without a solid base of Agile project management knowledge it is impossible for a project manager to fulfill that responsibility effectively. Evidence strongly suggests that the future of project management is running ***Hybrid*** projects (see Figure 2.7).

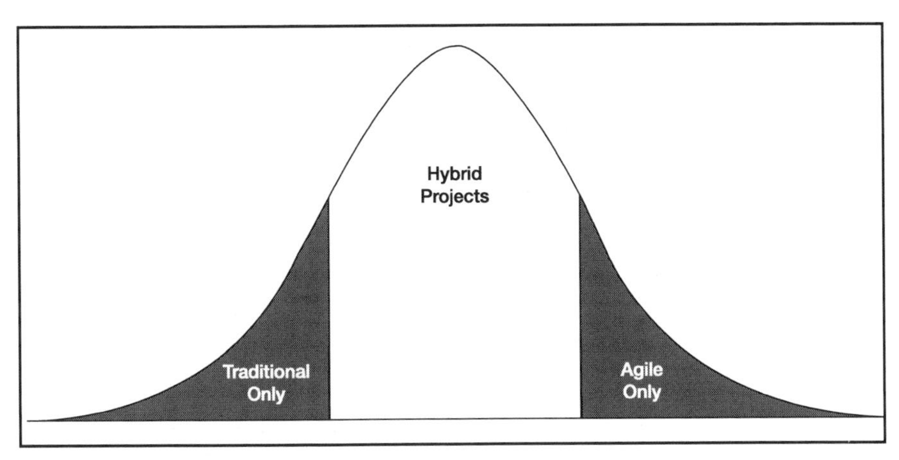

Figure 2.7 | *Total Projects by Framework*

Hybrid projects are projects managed with a combination of Traditional and Agile practices or with a combination of practices from multiple Agile frameworks.

Today's professional Project Manager cannot be effective without the ability to run Hybrid projects. Basically, the Agile Project Management value proposition is the ability to manage Hybrid projects because you have an understanding of both Traditional and Agile frameworks!

Is Agile Really Needed?

For many practitioners from a Traditional Project Management background, the whole idea of Agile Project Management seems to have appeared out of nowhere. Even though there is a core of Agile principles in the concepts of Rolling Wave Planning, Progressive Elaboration, and Decomposition, for many Project Managers it seems hard to discern whether it is simply a passing fad or a source of genuine value to our profession.

Project management, after all, is not a profession that quickly embraces change. The last major tool recognized in the Project Management Institute's "*A Guide to the Project Management Body of Knowledge (PMBOK® Guide) ¬– Second Edition* was the Critical Chain[6] in 1997.

With today's non-linear increasing rate of technology-driven process change, survival requires organizational agility. Broadly speaking, organizational agility can be described as having the capacity to quickly respond to strategic opportunities because internal structures enable shorter decision cycles through frequent market and product development reviews. Organizational agility means having an integrated view of the customers' needs and responding to those needs with desirable solutions. To accomplish that objective, cross-functional project teams must have the power to act fast while maintaining appropriate change and risk management processes.

Interestingly, the Apple iPad provides a classic case study in Agile Project Management. In Lean and Agile terminology, it was a full function device that included the minimum marketable feature set, yet it was not a full feature tablet PC. Because it was focused on what the customer wanted, it sold 3 million devices in 80 days and almost 15 million devices in its first 8 months, taking 75% market share of tablet PCs by the end of that year (2010). That meant that it sold more units than all other tablet PCs combined.

The success of the iPad speaks eloquently to the success that agility enables. It also challenges organizational leaders who may feel an expectation to produce achievements equivalent to those of Steve Jobs[7].

PMI even seems to have acknowledged the increased demands and complexity of the project management universe. They moved beyond the long-cherished Iron Triangle – time, cost, scope – that was a part of the first three editions of the *PMBOK® Guide.* With the release of the *PMBOK® Guide,* Fourth Edition, PMI took the traditional view of time, cost, scope, and added quality, risk, and customer satisfaction. The triangle became a hexagon in order to express the increased complexity that Project Managers now face in the everyday world. Soon, Project Managers around the world will be speaking about the *"Hell-of-a-Hexagon"* that replaced the "Iron Triangle." (See Figure 2.8)

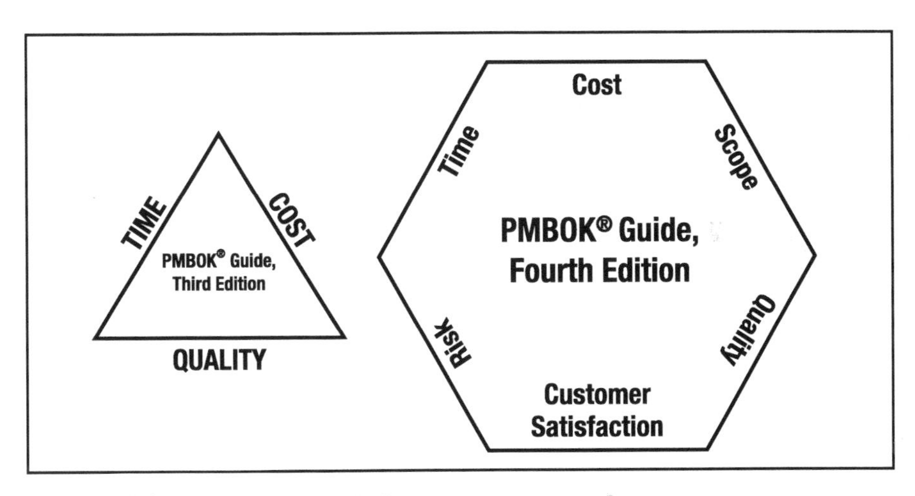

Figure 2.8 | *Iron Triangle vs. Hell-of-a-Hexagon*

In 2012, PMI released a *Pulse of the Profession In-depth Report, Organizational Agility 2012* that said in part, "Slow economic growth and shifting global market priorities have created a complex, risk-laden business environment – one that rewards innovation yet also threatens to derail projects." The annual global study of more than 1,000 project, program and portfolio managers continued, "Such a turbulent environment demands organizational agility. To forge that agility, successful organizations are aggressively reshaping their culture and business practices on a three-pronged front:

- Rigorous change management to better adapt to shifting market conditions
- More collaborative and robust risk management
- Increased use of standardized project, program and portfolio practices

The report reveals a clear payoff saying, "Highly agile organizations are twice as likely to see increased success with their new initiatives as their counterparts with low agility."

Beyond PMI, there is an abundance of additional evidence pointing to the added complexity faced by Project Managers. Consider the high project failure rates documented over the last couple of decades by the Standish Group in the aptly named CHAOS Reports[8]. Also consider the Standish report proved only 20% of the features being delivered to users are in the "Always" or "Often Used" categories, while 16% are "Sometimes Used," and a full 64% fall into the "Rarely" and "Never Used" categories.

In *Built to Last*[9], the authors wanted to answer the question, "What makes truly exceptional companies different?" One core discovery was that exceptional companies had an unchanging foundation complemented by strategies and practices that change in response to marketplace realities.

In today's challenging economic times, organizational agility is definitely necessary and best executed on a firm foundation.

Recommended Reading

Effective Project Management: Traditional, Agile, Extreme, by Robert K. Wysocki (Wiley; December 2013)

Chapter Close-Out

This section of the book is of particular interest to practitioners who are preparing to take the PMI-ACP® exam. Use the quiz and other exercises and challenges to improve your retention and recall of the material covered in this chapter.

Practice Test

1. When the Team clarifies the project objective and the desired final result, in Traditional Project Management it is called creating the ________________ while the same activities in Agile are called defining the ____________________.

   A. Project Requirements and Product Specifications
   B. Project Specifications and Product Requirements
   C. Project Charter and Product Vision
   D. Project Vision and Product Charter

2. When the Team initiates a repetitive cyclical process to make choices and define the final objective of the project in Agile Project Management, the timeboxes in the cycle are called a (n) ____.

   A. Iteration or Sprint
   B. Milestone
   C. Phase or Stage
   D. Release

3. When the Team completes the work of a specific timebox, the result is called a (n) ___________________________.

   A. Minimal Marketable Feature
   B. Blueprint or Design
   C. Customer Shippable Product
   D. Potentially Shippable Product

4. There are two key characteristics that make planning Agile. One of those factors is:

   A. Spending time carefully planning in order to manage inevitable changes.
   B. Balancing resource consumption against the certainty that the plan is going to change.
   C. Using Lean practices to reduce unavoidable waste.
   D. Applying Rolling Wave Progressive Elaboration in a robust and meaningful way.

5. An often-overlooked reality of today's competitive marketplace is:

   A. An almost unimaginable uncertainty in project management due to budget cuts.
   B. The unavoidable truth that organizations competing for tax dollars or consumer dollars must face each other.
   C. That some constituents and customers have had their expectations conditioned by the Internet, Amazon, Facebook and Google.
   D. The constantly increasing rate of technological capabilities is driving almost unimaginable levels of complexity into every project.

6. Iterative development techniques were being employed ______________________ Lean principles were developed.

   A. While Agile and
   B. Before
   C. After
   D. While best practices from the *PMBOK® Guide* and

7. The highest-level structure or philosophical foundation of a project management lexicon is called a ________________________.

   A. Methodology
   B. Frameworks
   C. Best Practice
   D. Process or Protocol

8. The core purpose of project management is to ________________ ________________________.

   A. Provide accurate estimates.
   B. Develop accurate plans and reports.
   C. Aid and support stakeholder decision-making.
   D. Create a competitive advantage by efficient delivery of customer solutions.

9. Technology-driven process change means that exploration and experimentation has been altered so that ________________ ________________________.

   A. Discovering solutions is both more effective and less costly.
   B. Discovering solutions is more effective and somewhat more costly.
   C. Discovering solutions is both more efficient and less costly.
   D. Discovering solutions is more efficient and somewhat more costly.

10. The Agile value proposition says that sustainable advantage comes from ________________________.

   A. Disruptive innovation.
   B. Discovering effective solutions quickly.
   C. Systematic innovation.
   D. Developing solutions that are cost effective.

Fill-in-the-Blank Challenge

1. In Traditional approaches, activities to clarify the project objective would be called creating the ______________________________ while the same activities in Agile would be called defining the Product Vision.

2. In Agile Project Management the Team uses a Stand-up Meeting to stay synchronized while the same activities in Traditional would be called a ____________________.

3. In Agile Project Management each Iteration or Sprint delivers an expected result be called a ____________________________.

4. The decision to accept or reject the Iteration's result is either a formal or informal ____________________________ process depending on the situational requirements.

5. In addition to balancing resource consumption against the certainty that the plan will change, the second trait that makes planning and project management Agile is embracing change ______________ ____.

6. Iterative development techniques were being employed ________ ____________________ were developed or the Agile movement began.

7. The core purpose of project management is to ______________ ____!

8. In a nutshell, the Agile value proposition says sustainable advantage comes from ____________________________________.

9. Projects being managed with a combination of Traditional and Agile practices or with a combination of practices from multiple Agile frameworks are called _______________.

10. The PMI report, "Pulse of the Profession In-depth Report, Organizational Agility 2012" revealed that "Highly agile organizations are ___________________________ increased success with their new initiatives as their counterparts with low agility."

Terminology Matching Exercise

In the blank column to the left of the Term, fill in the letter that identifies the correct Definition or Description.

	TERM		DEFINITION / DESCRIPTION
	1. Iron Triangle	A	Person who said, "To improve is to change; to be perfect is to change often!"
	2. Hybrid Projects	B	Person who said, "It is better to be roughly right than precisely wrong!"
	3. John Maynard Keynes	C	The "container" that holds the various processes, practices and protocols that define how to initiate, manage, organize, fund and report about the project.
	4. Methodology	D	Projects managed using both Traditional and Agile practices or practices from multiple Agile frameworks
	5. Framework	E	Potentially Shippable Product
	6. Winston Churchill	F	Person who said, "No plan survives contact with the enemy!"
	7. Helmuth Graf von Moltke	G	A core Lean principles that drives both Agile and Traditional Project Management best practices
	8. Expected result	H	A philosophical foundation to contain Frameworks, sometimes referred to as Extensions
	9. Waste reduction	I	Iteration or Sprint
	10. Agile timebox	J	The constraints of time, cost, and scope

Answers - Practice Test

1. **C.** When the Team clarifies the project objective and the desired final result, in Traditional Project Management it is called creating the Project Charter while the same activities in Agile are called defining the Product Vision.

2. **A.** When the Team initiates a repetitive cyclical process to make choices and define the final objective of the project in Agile Project Management the timeboxes in the cycle are called an Iteration or Sprint.

3. **D.** When the Team completes the work of a specific timebox the result is called a Potentially Shippable Product.

4. **B.** There are two key characteristics that make planning Agile. One of those factors is balancing resource consumption against the certainty that the plan is going to change.

5. **D.** An often-overlooked reality of today's competitive marketplace is the constantly increasing rate of technological capabilities is driving almost unimaginable levels of complexity into every project.

6. **B.** Iterative development techniques were being employed before Lean principles were developed.

7. **A.** The highest-level structure or philosophical foundation of a project management lexicon is called a Methodology.

8. **C.** The core purpose of project management is to aid and support stakeholder decision-making.

9. **A.** Technology-driven process change means that exploration and experimentation has been altered so that discovering solutions is both more effective and less costly.

10. **C.** The Agile value proposition says that sustainable advantage comes from systematic innovation.

Answers - Fill-in-the-Blank Challenge

1. In Traditional approaches, activities to clarify the project objective would be called creating the **PROJECT CHARTER** while the same activities in Agile would be called defining the Product Vision.

2. In Agile Project Management the Team uses a Stand-up Meeting to stay synchronized while the same activities in Traditional would be called a **STATUS MEETING.**

3. In Agile Project Management each Iteration or Sprint delivers an expected result be called a **POTENTIALLY SHIPPABLE PRODUCT.**

4. The decision to accept or reject the Iteration's result is either a formal or informal **TEST-DRIVEN DEVELOPMENT (TDD)** process depending on the situational requirements.

5. In addition to balancing resource consumption against the certainty that the plan will change, the second trait that makes planning and project management Agile is embracing change **DRIVEN BY NEW KNOWLEDGE OR TO AVOID A PROBLEM.**

6. Iterative development techniques were being employed **BEFORE LEAN PRINCIPLES** were developed or the Agile movement began.

7. The core purpose of project management is to **AID AND SUPPORT STAKEHOLDER DECISION-MAKING!**

8. In a nutshell, the Agile value proposition says sustainable advantage comes from **SYSTEMATIC INNOVATION.**

9. Projects being managed with a combination of Traditional and Agile practices or with a combination of practices from multiple Agile frameworks are called **HYBRID.**

10. The PMI® report, "Pulse of the Profession In-depth Report, Organizational Agility 2012" revealed that "Highly agile organizations are **TWICE AS LIKELY TO SEE** increased success with their new initiatives as their counterparts with low agility."

Answers - Terminology Matching

1:J, 2:D, 3:B, 4:H, 5:C, 6:A, 7:F, 8:E, 9:G, 10:I

Chapter End Notes

[3]German Field Marshal Helmuth Graf von Moltke (1800 – 1891) was chief of staff for the Prussian Army and is revered as one of the great military strategists of the latter 19th century.

[4]William Edwards Deming (October 14, 1900 – December 20, 1993) is perhaps best known for his work in Japan. He taught how to improve product quality through the application of statistical methods. Deming made a significant contribution to Japan's later reputation for innovative high-quality products. Despite being a hero in Japan, he was only beginning to be recognized in the U.S. at the time of his death.

[5]Goldratt, E. M., *Critical Chain.* Great Barrington, MA: The North River Press (1997) and *Theory of Constraints.* Great Barrington, MA: The North River Press (1999).

[6]Goldratt, E. M. (1997). *Critical Chain.* Great Barrington, MA: The North River Press.

[7]Steven Paul "Steve" Jobs (February 24, 1955 – October 5, 2011) was a visionary widely recognized as a charismatic pioneer of the personal computer revolution. He was co-founder, chairman, and chief executive officer of Apple Inc.

[8]See for example *CHAOS 2009 Report Summary*, Boston, MA, April 23, 2009, The Standish Group International, Inc. (www.standishgroup.com)

[9]*Built to Last: Successful Habits of Visionary Companies* by Jim Collins and Jerry I. Porras, HarperBusiness, November 2, 2004

Agile Project Management and Lean Principles

In the previous chapter, two quick, familiar examples were used to describe Agile Project Management. In this chapter, a more complete discussion of the Agile Lexicon, the *Agile Manifesto,* and the *Principles behind the Agile Manifesto* (commonly called "The 12 Principles") will be covered.

It will include an overview of Agile's Micro-Dynamic Workflow and the Micro-Dynamic Work Practices that are used, in common, by many of the Agile Frameworks. Those work practices include such things as Minimal Marketable Features (MMFs), Value-Driven Deliverables, Test Driven Development (TDD), Operational Ceremonies, Actionable Reports, Osmotic Communication and Agile Leadership.

Agile Lexicon - Methodologies, Frameworks and Processes

A key point to be aware of is that the lexicon used in this book is the most common taxonomy of ***methodologies, frameworks,*** and ***processes.*** However, it is important to note that unlike Traditional Project Management that has the authoritative PMBOK® Guide, there are no similar governing standards in the Agile sphere at this time. It is not unreasonable to expect that standards for Agile will become part of the *PMBOK® Guide* over time. The *PMBOK® Guide Fifth Edition* already includes some Agile content and it is likely the *PMBOK® Guide Sixth Edition* will contain significantly more.

Frameworks are context-specific foundations created to support particular industry settings, such as aerospace or automotive, or particular categories of activities, such as software or product development. Frameworks have a set of Processes that are used to execute work in a defined way.

Methodologies provide the philosophical foundation for organizing Frameworks. In project management, the two dominant choices are Traditional, as embodied in the *PMBOK® Guide,* and Agile. Methodologies contain and define various Frameworks as context-specific logical foundations.

Processes are practical "how to" protocols used to direct things like sponsoring, organizing, funding, and controlling solution development projects. The Processes guide work to follow or align with context-specific best practices.

The best-known Agile Framework is Scrum. Each of the Agile Frameworks, including Scrum, started in a specific context, such as software development. Each of the Frameworks strives to apply Lean principles to produce processes that are appropriate to a context-specific environment.

Agile Manifesto and The 12 Principles

One of the seminal events in the rise of Agile Project Management occurred in February 2001, at the Snowbird resort in Utah. Seventeen luminaries in the field of software development met to discuss the need for alternatives to the project management processes that were producing failure-prone results. Perhaps no one was more surprised than the participants themselves when they achieved a meeting of the minds and all agreed to sign the *Manifesto for Agile Software Development,* now commonly referred to as the Agile Manifesto.

The group named itself The *Agile Alliance* and published the Manifesto for Agile Software Development. It outlined fundamental beliefs that reinforce Agile software development, a precursor to Agile Project Management.

Manifesto for Agile Software Development[10]

> We are uncovering better ways of developing software by doing it and helping others do it. Through this work we have come to value:

Individuals and interactions over processes and tools
Working software over comprehensive documentation
Customer collaboration over contract negotiation
Responding to change over following a plan

That is, while there is value in the items on the right, we value the items on the left more.

Notice that the central word in the Agile Manifesto is "over." The Manifesto does not support the common, erroneous interpretations suggesting that it supports individuals and interactions "instead of" or "rejecting" processes and tools. Great damage has been done to the potential of the Agile movement by imposters claiming their focus is working software "not" comprehensive documentation, or customer collaboration "without needing" contract negotiation, or responding to change "without" following a plan. Proponents of such approaches are simply not Agile in spirit or in fact!

Understanding the Agile Manifesto

The Agile Manifesto is so widely published and well known that almost anyone with an interest in Agile has seen it, read it or heard about it at least at some level. Everybody seems to want to talk about it and some people try to use it as an excuse for bad behavior. Those folks say things like, "I'm doing Agile so I don't do planning," "I'm doing Agile so I don't do reporting" or "I'm doing Agile so I don't do documentation." That is not Agile. That is Agile as an excuse for bad behavior.

This violates the core of the Manifesto. In fact, to understand the heart of Agile, you need to notice it says, "We value these things on the left…", and there are four values listed. Then it says, "Over these things on the right" and lists four other values. That construction makes the word "over" very important. It doesn't say "in rejection of" or "in refusal of" the values on the right. It says "over" right there in the middle. What "over" implies, on some level, is the things on the left help us better understand and apply the things on the right.

It says, "We value individuals and interactions over processes and tools" and experience shows that the correct processes and tools cannot be selected and applied, especially when dealing with work that has high complexity and high uncertainty, unless you know who the individuals are and what interactions they need to have. Knowing who the team and customers are guides the process of selecting the correct processes and tools.

To be successful it is imperative to ask discovery questions like, "Who are my stakeholders and what feedback do they need? Who is my core customer or my voice of the customer and what information do they need to have? Who is on the team and what is the work composed of?"

The second 'P' in PMP stands for professional and our organizations expect us to be professional enough to ask discovery questions to guide the team to the best choices for executing this project.

The next statement says, "Working software over comprehensive documentation." It says software because the seventeen folks who were in Snowbird and signed the Manifesto all happen to be from the software industry. Today it could easily say, "Working solutions" because it is being used in so many different environments.

If you think that Agile is software only, you are talking about Agile a decade ago. Today, Agile is in all kinds of industries. Agile helps us create competitive advantage and that is what organizations really care about.

You can go right down the Manifesto. Customer collaboration over contract negotiation doesn't mean not to use contracts. That would be silly. It's the real world after all. Lean would say that contracts are an unavoidable waste and to minimize unavoidable waste. The Manifesto implies the desire to minimize waste by using the contract to develop a collaborative relationship with the customer wherever possible.

Finally it says, "Responding to change over following a plan." It doesn't say or even imply *not* to have a plan. It acknowledges that the plan is going to encounter the enemy. And by the way, the enemy is not your co-workers or your customers. The enemy is the complexity and the uncertainty. Encountering the enemy means discovery and learning by the Customer and Team can be leveraged and the plan will be adjusted to cope with those potentially good things as well as challenges.

One last thought about Agile and the Manifesto worth noting is that despite the reverential awe of some of the Agile faithful, Agile is not a magic wand. If a senior manager is insistent on creating chaos, Agile won't fix him. Agile may offer tools that are better able to manage the environment in spite of him, but it is not going to eliminate him. There are situational variables that Agile can't do anything about. Agile can help put a frame around it perhaps, create better value in spite of it perhaps, but it is not a magic wand.

Principles Behind the Agile Manifesto

The Agile Alliance also published the ***Principles behind the Agile Manifesto,*** which stated the following.

> "*We follow these principles:*
>
> Our highest priority is to satisfy the customer through early and continuous delivery of valuable software.
>
> Welcome changing requirements, even late in development. Agile processes harness change for the customer's competitive advantage.
>
> Deliver working software frequently, from a couple of weeks to a couple of months, with a preference to the shorter timescale.
>
> Business people and developers must work together daily throughout the project.
>
> Build projects around motivated individuals. Give them the environment and support they need, and trust them to get the job done.
>
> The most efficient and effective method of conveying information to and within a development team is face-to-face conversation.
>
> Working software is the primary measure of progress.
>
> Agile processes promote sustainable development. The sponsors, developers, and users should be able to maintain a constant pace indefinitely.
>
> Continuous attention to technical excellence and good design enhances Agility.
>
> Simplicity – the art of maximizing the amount of work not done – is essential.
>
> The best architectures, requirements, and designs emerge from self-organizing teams.
>
> At regular intervals, the team reflects on how to become more effective, then tunes and adjusts its behavior accordingly."

These principles address various aspects of the fact that good communication does not occur automatically and must be deliberately cultivated. Something about being human makes communicating unavoidably complex.

That fact has been observed hundreds of times during a simple exercise, called the "Stare and Share," conducted at numerous training seminars. The exercise has three steps. In Step 1, all participants are asked to stand, choose a partner, and face that partner. They are then given 20 seconds (which always seems like a lifetime to the participants) to "visually study their partner." In Step 2, they are instructed to stand with their backs turned so they cannot see each other, and change three things about their appearance. In Step 3, they are asked to turn so they can each see their partner once again, then identify the three changes their partner made. At no time are the participants told not to collaborate, and they are even referred to as "partners" repeatedly throughout the instructions. Nevertheless, there are normally less than one-third of the participants who identify all three changes, and less than five percent who ask for, or reveal, the changes to one another.

This human trait impacts many project teams. Critical information – information vital to success – will not be shared automatically, unless the people assigned to the project unite as a team. Commitment to one another's success does not begin until a team is born! Catalyzing as a team, therefore, is critical to success and only happens when communication is properly facilitated.

So the **quantitative** goal of having collocated, cross-functional, trusted teams is to reduce project risk by reducing the **unknown** about the project. The situation before a team catalyzes can be seen in Figure 3.1. The illustration shows that as long as the project is worked on by a group of people who have not become a Team, the relationship between what is known and unknown remains static. That produces a significant "blind spot," where things that are not known by the PM overlap with things that are not known by the team (i.e., the bottom right quadrant).

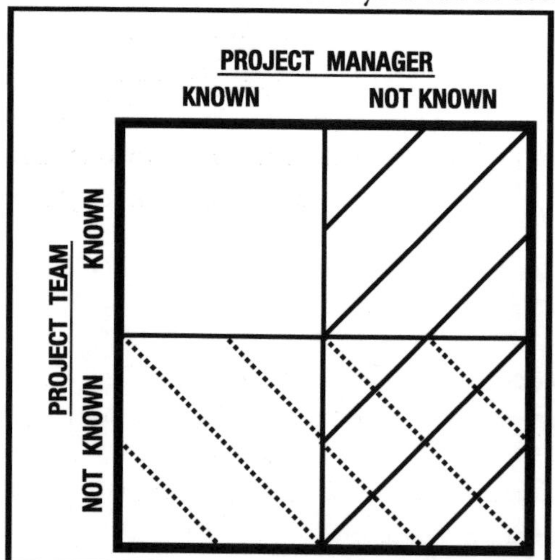

Figure 3.1 | *Risk Before Team Formation*

The situation *after* a team catalyzes can be seen in the

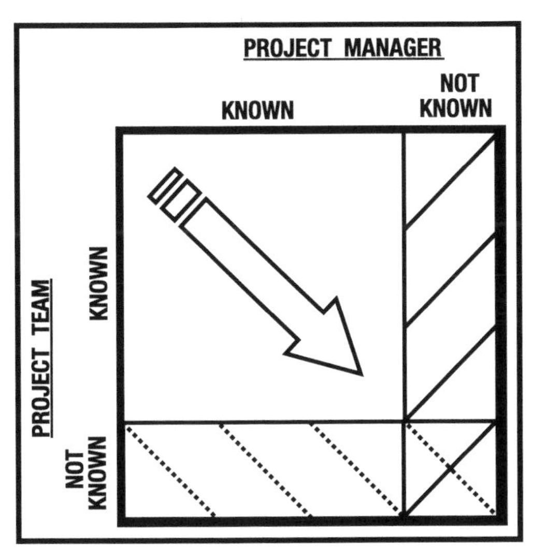

Figure 3.2| *Risk After Team Formation*

next illustration, Figure 3.2. When a team environment exists, everyone is committed to being responsible for the project's success or failure. That is because relationships formed when the Team made the hard commitment to the Iteration goal (a process that will be explained later). Those relationships engage everyone to remain vigilant, watching for areas of risk "owned" by other Team members – as naturally as soldiers covering each other's back in combat. Most importantly, the automatic disclosure of observations, insights, and information occurs.

This reduces the resulting blind spot, increasing the general level of knowledge about the project. The way this happens can almost be described as triangulation. As members of the team share what they know or have learned, other members can integrate that with their knowledge base then share observations and insights. In the process, risks that had been unrecognized, and therefore unknown, are identified by triangulating their position. This occurs much like the navigation of early mariners using a sextant and the stars. Two data points are used to help identify a third. Precisely because trusted, cross-functional teams supply a mix of skills, risk and errors are reduced. So risk is diminished and the opportunity for success is enhanced. In the Agile ethos, empowering teams is central to realizing the goal of a successful project

Agile Micro-Dynamic Workflow

As noted earlier, the Agile domain can be divided into three levels. They are Single-team Projects, Programs with Multi- and Virtual-team Environments, and finally, Portfolios and Enterprise Scaling. This book is focused on the needs of individual practitioners working on Single-team Projects and that is defined as the micro-dynamic environment. It provides detailed insight and analysis on when and how to use the "Big 5" approaches. It does not extend into the macro-dynamic of Programs, Portfolios and Enterprises.

Micro-Dynamic Team-level Workflow

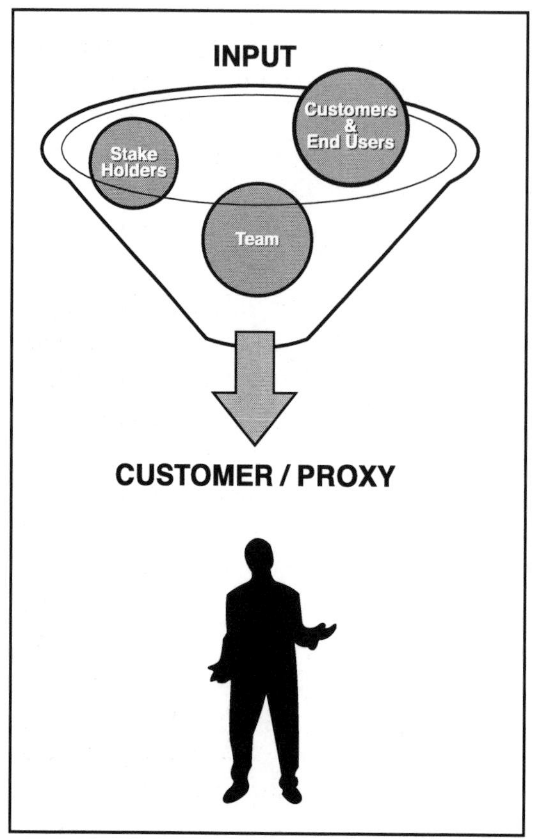

Figure 3.3| *Customer-Proxy*

Agile, at the team or micro-dynamic level, starts with the concept that all the information about the project is directed to the Customer-Proxy (Figure 3.3), sometimes called the "Voice of the Customer" or the Product Owner. The Customer-Proxy is responsible for knowing what the customer wants and deciding on the Product Roadmap that defines what is most important and will be developed first. Thus, all information related to the project is directed to them and they use it to organize the Product Backlog. The concept of a Product Backlog in Agile is similar to the concept of requirements or specifications in Traditional Project Management.

It is worth noting that the funnel above the Customer-Proxy's head that is commonly used to illustrate this concept implies that there is some organizational structure in place to direct that information to the Customer-Proxy. Many Agile evangelists present Agile as if it exists in a world where the organization doesn't provide structure and rules, yet that's just not the real world. The funnel illustration directly disputes the belief that Agile and organizational structure are incompatible.

The Customer-Proxy takes this information and creates the Product Backlog (Figure 3.4). It includes information about the features, functions, and capabilities that need to be developed in order to successfully deliver the final outcome. Notice that the image of the backlog looks like a stack of index cards. The intent is that one requirement, function or capability is on each card so that the Customer-Proxy can prioritize them. The Customer-Proxy

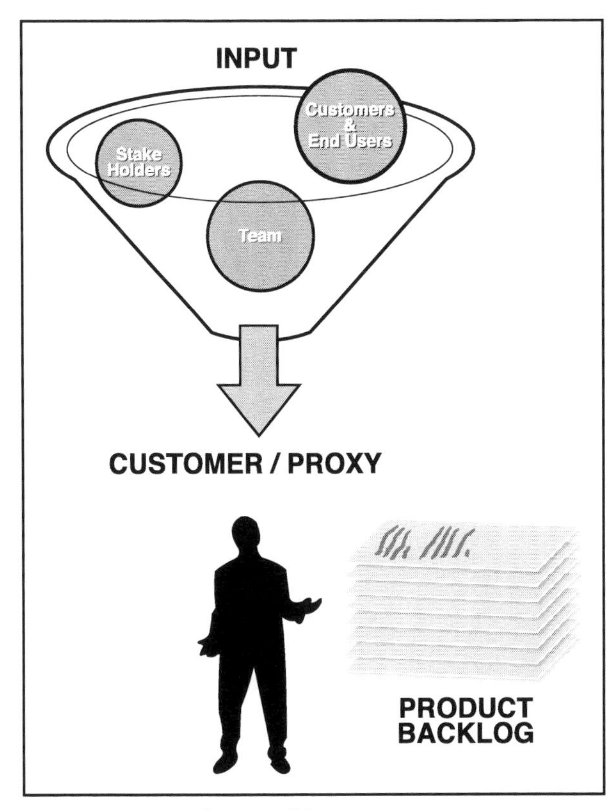

Figure 3.4| *Product Backlog*

does so by sorting the most important ones to the top of the stack and pushing the less important ones to the bottom of the stack. The idea is that the Customer-Proxy will continuously groom the Backlog. This sorting process is an important step that precedes the planning session occurring at the beginning of each Iteration or Sprint. That planning session is the next step in the process. It determines what the Team can and will be responsible for building as the next step towards the final solution.

The Customer-Proxy submits what is most important for the customer to see as the next piece of the puzzle to develop. The approach is a negotiation where the Customer-Proxy and Team define an outcome that is both valuable and doable. When they reach agreement it is called the goal of the Iteration or Sprint. The goal is documented with Stories in the Iteration or Sprint Backlog (Figure 3.5). It can be visualized as if the Customer-Proxy takes the top of the Product Backlog stack, the most important stories for the customer to see, and brings it to the Team and says, "This is what I think you can build as the next subassembly of the puzzle, as the next piece of the solution, during this next timebox." The Team then asks clarifying questions like, "Does it include wireframes or final forms? What about load testing? Does it need a security audit?" If you're developing software, you know one of the questions that always come up is, "Does it include documentation?" Because programmers love creating documentation, right?

The clarifying questions make sure the Team gets a clear idea of what the Customer-Proxy wants them to build. Sometimes the Customer-Proxy says,

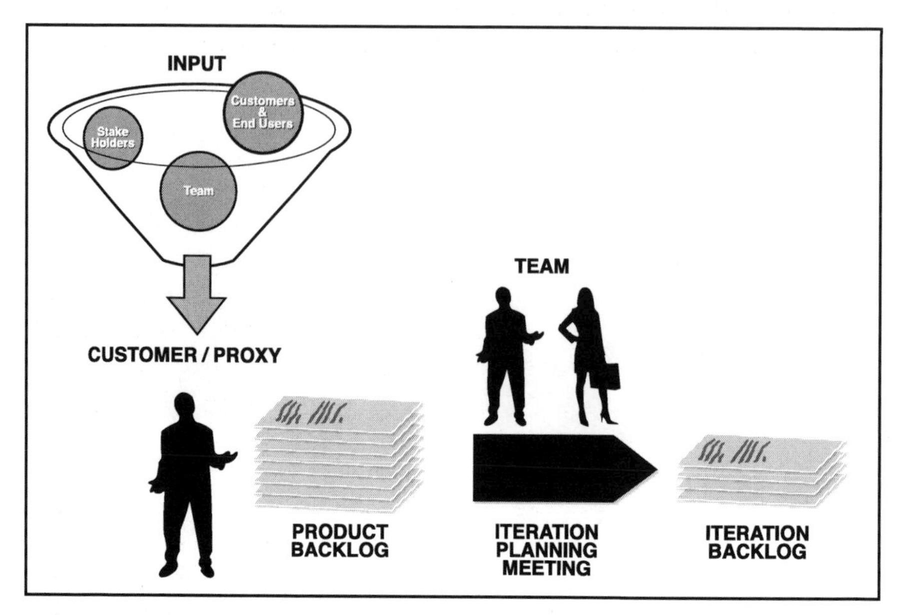

Figure 3.5 | *Iteration Backlog*

"What I want you to build is just a rough cut, a wire frame, of this part of the solution because I need to show it to some customers and get their feedback. Then, while you're working on other pieces that I am certain about in the next two Iterations, I will define detailed Stories of what should or should not be included based on the customer feedback."

Another common occurrence during the discussion is that the Team will say, "Wait a minute, Story number 3 is a good priority, but we can't build it without that infrastructure piece that you've prioritized as number 19 and left behind. So do you want to pull number 19 into this Iteration, and take something the same size out of the proposed Iteration Backlog or do you want to put number 3 back and wait until number 19 reaches the top of the stack?" The discussion is a collegial effort to figure out what can actually be built during the Iteration that will drive the most value because of the insight it will create for the customer. We call that, "Actionable insight!"

This process of developing subassemblies of the solution for the customer to see is particularly powerful with customers who do not understand perfectly clearly what they need and want. Those customers who say, "I don't know what I need, but I will know it when I see it." I will know it when I see it is referred to as "IKIWISI" (pronounced, "icky-whizzy"). Customers are not trying to be difficult when they say or imply IKIWISI, they are just being human. They don't know exactly so they are searching for the right answer and seeing pieces of the puzzle helps them figure it out. Agile engages and enables the humanity of each member of the triad – the Customer, the Customer-Proxy and the Team.

Once a joint decision is made, the Team commits to what will be developed in this next Iteration and the Customer-Proxy, on behalf of the Customer and Organization, commits to not change the goal or size of the timebox. Typically the process is done in two steps. Step One is where the Team makes the "Soft Commit" and says, "Yes, we think we can do the proposed Iteration Backlog." Then after an hour or two of analysis where they tear apart the Stories and break them into Tasks, if they are confident they can do it, they make the "Hard Commit."

The Hard Commit creates the Reciprocal Commitment. As noted above, on behalf of the organization, the Customer-Proxy says, "We won't change the time period, you get the whole four weeks. We won't change the goal, we have now set in stone what you are going to build, and we also won't molest, harass or interrupt."

During presentations to many hundreds of audiences with many thousands of participants, two simple truths have surfaces universal. First, there is not one best way to do every project. Not Agile, not Traditional, not any one way. Second, for every project Team there is one best way to execute any particular project based on the goal, the resources available, the constraints, and the context of the project. The process goal is to figure out the one best way for this Team to use the next Iteration to make measurable progress towards the project goal.

Crystalizing and freezing the Iteration goal creates an environment where the priorities don't change weekly, which is the only way to succeed. One of the reasons many teams love Agile is because they get to focus and deliver something, a concrete outcome, and then stand up and say, "Hey we succeeded!" For the Team, it feels like standing up in front of the room and singing like rock stars, "We are the champions!"

So when that Reciprocal Commitment happens, the Iteration begins (Figure 3.6). During that timebox, the Team completes Tasks and has a 15-minute meeting to stay synchronized. The meeting can be called a Daily Stand-up Meeting, Daily Meeting or Scrum Meeting.

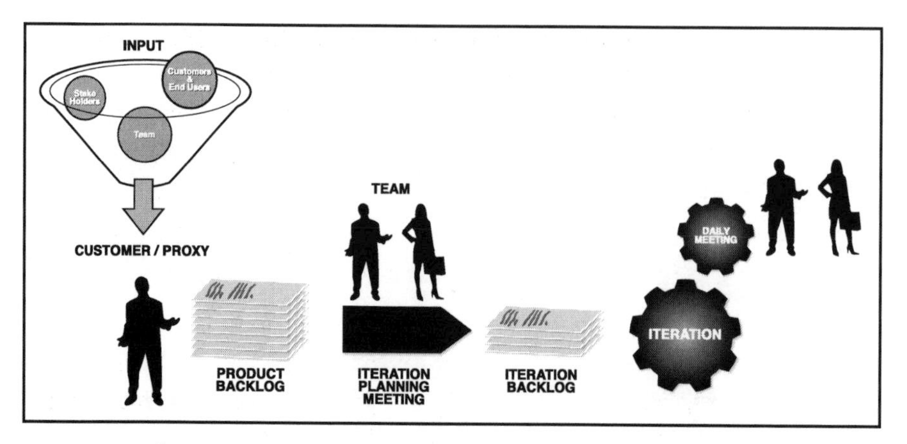

Figure 3.6| *Iteration Begins*

The meeting helps insure progress keeps moving forward by having each Team member answer three questions. "What have I worked on since yesterday?" "What will I work on today?" Those two answers synchronize the team. Then the third question, "What obstacles, if any, are impeding my ability to move forward?" alerts the team facilitator about obstacles outside of the team's authority that are slowing or stopping progress towards the Iteration goal. The team facilitator, usually a Scrum Master or Project Manager, accepts responsibility for removing the obstacle.

One core Lean principle is that development processes have work periods and wait periods, and wait periods are an avoidable type of waste. Work gets completed by one person then waits in the next person's inbox. Work period. Wait period. Work and wait over and over again until it is finished. The daily synchronization meeting limits, minimizes, or even eliminates a lot of wait time, eliminating a lot of waste.

Consider this simple analogy. If you are running a Traditional project and you do your Status Report meetings on the 15th and the 30th of the month, what are the two most productive days of the month for your team?" The 14th and 29th, right?! If you do your status report meeting on Friday, what is the most productive day of the week? Thursday is the most productive without fail. When you were a student in college, what were the most productive days of the semester? Right before the exam and right before the paper was due.

So waiting is an innately human thing. When we do our status report meetings infrequently there is a big spike then a lull, a big spike then a lull. It's a cycle. If Randy and I have our Status Report Meeting every Friday, and on

Monday I realize I need something from Randy, what do you think is likely to happen? Whether his cubicle is a hundred feet down the hallway, a floor or two away, across the parking lot, across town, or across country, I'll wait until Friday to ask for what I need. The further the distance, the higher the probability that our project and my deliverable will stay in the inbox until Friday and at Friday's Status Meeting I'll report, "I needed a thingy-bob from Randy so I didn't get anything done this week." Now, the project schedule just got hammered with a week of wait time!

Daily meetings eliminate a lot of wait time waste. They are very effective and can be done in 15 minutes with the right rules and techniques for managing them. We'll share those rules and techniques with you later.

The outcome of this process at the end of the Iteration is referred to as a Potentially Shippable Product (Figure 3.7). Please notice the word Potentially. It doesn't mean that it's actually shippable. But it does mean that we can show it to the customer or present it to the stakeholders so they can give feedback and input. That actionable insight keeps progress focused and on target. It helps resolve IKIWISI. That's really where agility comes from. That's really what Agile is striving for, to eliminate waste.

As the Potentially Shippable Product is being developed, the Team is sharing their progress with the Customer-Proxy. The final delivery of the Potentially Shippable Product is not a surprise to the Customer-Proxy at the end. Development has been receiving guidance from the Customer-Proxy during on-going conversations with the Team. The Customer-Proxy is giving feedback to questions from the Team. Questions such as, "Is this what you meant?" "Did that fit?" "Is this right?"

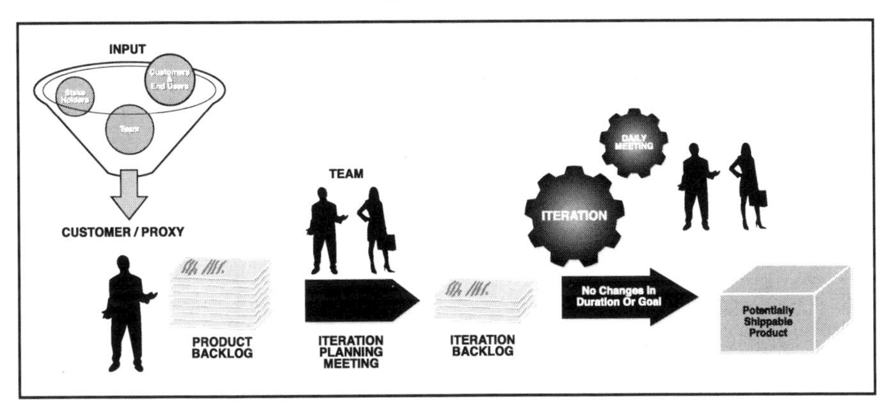

Figure 3.7 | *Potentially Shippable Product is delivered*

When the Iteration ends, the Customer-Proxy and Team are in agreement that either the delivery is the Potentially Shippable Product promised during the Iteration planning meeting or not. Sometimes a Story couldn't be developed, and even though that's an exception, everyone admits to that being the outcome.

The Iteration ends with the Customer-Proxy and Team presenting the completed deliverable at the Review Meeting (Figure 3.8). The ***Review Meeting*** is a product-centric meeting where any interested or impacted stakeholder can come and see what was just finished as the next piece of the project puzzle. They give feedback and ask questions that produce actionable insight for the Customer-Proxy to use to groom the Product Backlog.

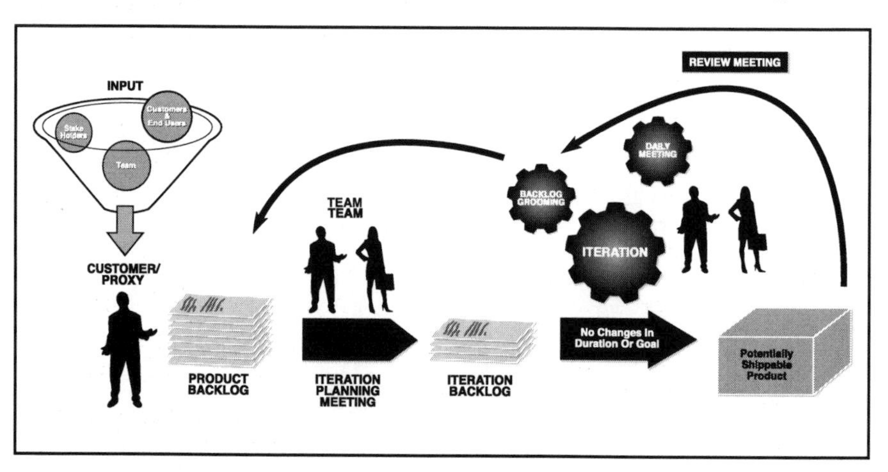

Figure 3.8| *Review meeting*

Following the Review Meeting, the Team holds a closed-door meeting just for them called a Retrospective Meeting (Figure 3.9). The ***Retrospective Meeting*** is a process-centric meeting where the Team, with nobody else present, talks about the development process. It is the application of the Lean principle of continuous improvement. Essentially the Team asks itself, "How could we improve our process so that we could deliver more results easier, faster, better, cheaper, and have a few more laughs along the way?"

One way to understand the Retrospective Meeting is to compare it to a Lessons Learned meeting done for a Traditional project at the end of 12, 18, or 24 months. The meetings that are commonly referred to as a "Project Post-mortem." What a great term! It reflects the feeling that the Team will cut the project cadaver open, find stinky stuff to blame on others, and stick it on them and ruin their career. We all know that knowledge is power. But

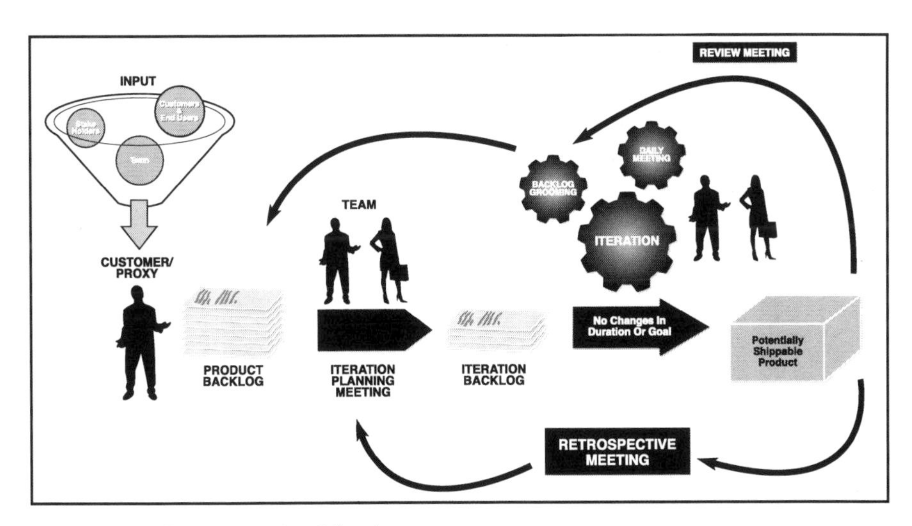

Figure 3.9| *Retrospective Meeting*

knowledge is only power if it's applied and shared. Teams don't get applied knowledge if they wait a year or two to do Lessons Learned. It does not generate shared learning if it is understood as a blaming session. That process simply doesn't work.

A process that does work is Retrospective Meetings. At the end of every Iteration, usually every 4 weeks or less, while the Team's memories are still fresh, they have a Retrospective Meeting. They identify, discuss and select ideas that they like and think will improve the process and start using those things the very next day. This creates a very big WIIFM. The big "What's in it for me (WIIFM)?" for the Team is that they get to use those ideas immediately to improve their environment.

Agile's micro-dynamic Team-level workflow, as just described, is a model that provides amazing power and results when dealing with project environments containing high degrees of complexity and uncertainty. One simple, yet brilliant, key that makes it powerful is that it creates and maintains a focus on measuring actual progress towards the goal. It defines actual progress as completed Potentially Shippable increments, so that is the unit of measure. It avoids the trap of trying to measure effort or cost or some other variable as a corollary of progress because other units of measure have all proven to be unreliable and flawed.

A second, brilliant key to its success is that it maintains flexibility regarding the logical flow being used for setting the order of development steps while honoring the rigid boundaries of the contract and the need for a stable work environment for the Team. This elegant integration of embracing change while enforcing stability is often misunderstood and poorly explained. But that elegant integration is still a dazzling insight!

Micro-Dynamic Roles

To best understand the roles involved in the Agile micro-dynamic team-level workflow it is useful to begin by comparing them to the various projects roles in a Traditional project.

The highest-level roles in both Traditional and Agile methodologies are Stakeholders and Sponsors. They define the business case that sets the project objectives, explain how it is aligned to the organization's strategic intent, and most importantly, control the funding.

At the next level down in Traditional methods the role is a Senior Project Manager or Program Manager, which is comparable to a Customer-Proxy in Agile methods. The roles are not exactly the same, but they have a rough approximation of the same responsibilities. What the roles share in common is the focus on answering the question, "What does the project have to do to deliver value to the customer and to the organization?"

The third-level role in Traditional methods is Technical Lead or Team Lead, which is comparable to a Scrum Master in Agile methods. Again, they have approximately the same duties and interest. What the roles share in common is the focus on solving the technical challenge, putting together the next piece of the technical puzzle, and doing it one Iteration after another. Focusing on how to create the next Potentially Shippable deliverable keeps the work results moving towards the solution.

At the fourth level in both Traditional and Agile methods, is the role of Team members who are Subject Matter Experts (SMEs). These are the people who do the tasks required to complete the development work of the project.

Finally, below that is the role for anyone else who is impacted by or interested in the project outcome, but do not set the objectives or control the funding.

Whether a project is being managed using a Traditional, Agile or Hybrid approach, the people who inhabit the world of the project don't change. And since it's really true that the people drive the complexity and the uncertainty, learning to leverage and take advantage of that humanity instead of trying to contain it is one of the biggest keys to success.

And that's why the popular notion that everybody's got to be a generalist not a specialist, able to do everything and be perfectly interchangeable does not pass the sniffer test. Can you imagine a National Basketball Association coach, a Major League Baseball coach or a World Cup soccer coach saying, "Just send in a player! They are all the same. Any player will do." In the real world it doesn't work that way.

What makes far more sense is not for a Developer to become a QA person, and vice-versa, but instead to recognize that the Team is running a relay race. In a relay race, strengthening the hand-offs is the key to success. This leverages human potential instead of constraining it!

Take a moment and think of a relay race at the Olympics. It is not always the team with the fastest runners that wins, but it is always a team that didn't drop the baton. So Developers and QA teammates need to be in enough conversation about their process so that the depth and strength of the interface, the point where the baton hand off happens, is being continuously improved. As the Developer becomes more QA aware and the QA person becomes more development aware, the strength and depth of the hand off grows.

People are hired based on their expertise and experience that can be defined as tacit knowledge. The tacit knowledge in their head is an asset that we hire, but then becomes a liability for the organization if that person wins the lottery or gets hit by a bus and never comes back to work. That is especially true if that person is an information hoarder.

When we treat the team process as running a relay race and the strength of the hand-off, that is the depth of interface between the Developer and QA person increases, then that tacit knowledge becomes tribal knowledge. Tribal knowledge means that when a new Developer is hired, the QA person who knows more because of the stronger interface can integrate and onboard the Developer so the team returns to productivity more quickly. That tribal knowledge reduces the liability that is otherwise inherent in the system. The goal is not generalists, but better integrated experts.

Micro-Dynamic Environment

The need for an Iterative Development Framework and an integrated, cross-functional team of experts is driven by the complexity and uncertainty that fill the micro-dynamic environment. That high level of complexity and uncertainty presupposes that an accurate understanding of the problem and its solution cannot exist in advance.

Millennia of human experience have shown that complexity and uncertainty also amplify the unavoidable and inevitable effect of time as planning attempts to peer into the future. The farther into the future planning attempts to peer, the more inexact, vague, and unreliable perceptions and forecasts get because more and more complexity and uncertainty are unavoidably introduced.

Regardless of how much time and money is spent on creating highly precise descriptions and highly engineered estimates, it all proves to be part of the waste stream, as far as Lean is concerned, because it does not increase the accuracy or reliability of planning activities.

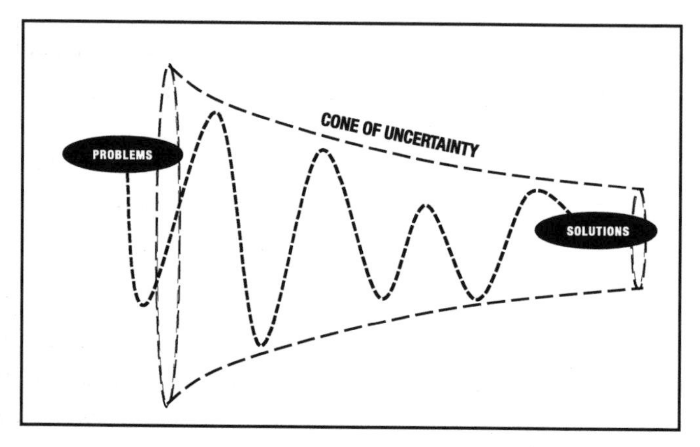

Figure 3.10| *Cone of Uncertainty*

Despite the dire sounding challenge of the micro-dynamic environment, there is an answer. The answer is to integrate the inescapable need for discovery and learning into the development process. The process must be designed to make progress through the unknown and unexpected challenges of development that is called the Cone of Uncertainty (Figure 3.10).

Cone of Uncertainty refers to the concept of how unknown facets of a problem decrease over time as customers traverse through an unavoidable, ambiguous process where discovery and learning occur.

The Cone of Uncertainty shows that at the beginning of development, the degree of uncertainty is very large and a straight line of development cannot be defined. Instead, development must begin with what little is known for certain and begin producing deliverables that can be inspected by the customer or exposed to tests that will produce actionable insight into how to

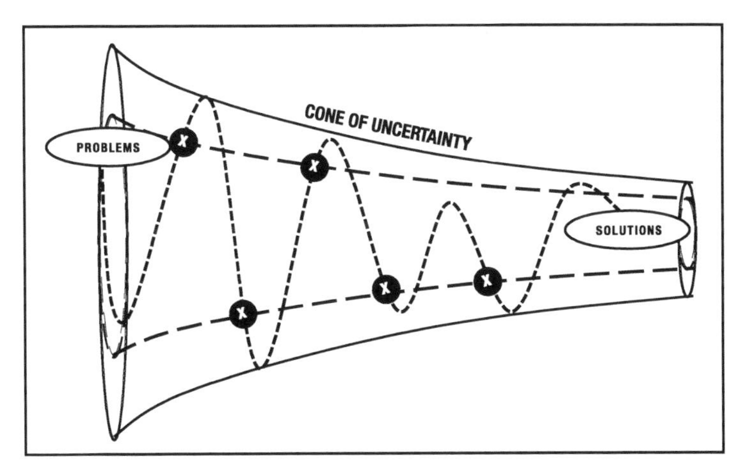

Figure 3.11 | *Narrowing the Cone of Uncertainty*

make the next move towards the solution. This method of development applies the scientifically validated empirical process control approach – transparency, inspection, and adaptation.

The goal is to narrow the Cone of Uncertainty by leveraging discovery and learning at each of the points marked with an "X" in Figure 3.11. Inspecting and adapting at those points will pivot decision-making towards the solution instead of continuing on the standard trajectory towards the outer limit of the Cone of Uncertainty.

Conceptually this is quite simple to understand, but that does not mean that the practical application is easy. It requires transparency in admitting what is unknown or uncertain followed by sometimes-vigorous debate about how to best inspect or test the deliverable. And finally it requires the courage to adapt development or customer expectations to the reality that is discovered.

Evidence from many projects suggests that most customers need an opportunity to interact with the solution in order to clarify their own understanding of the problem and accurately define the best solution.

While customers interact with the periodic Potentially Shippable deliverables, their understanding of the best solution moves from what they thought at the beginning to what they really need. Stakeholders, because of the limits of their humanity, need to be meaningfully engaged with the deliverables in order to move through the Cone of Uncertainty and find the optimal solution.

Micro-Dynamic Work Practices

Various Agile and Traditional frameworks have common Work Practices even when they use a different lexicon to name or describe them. This section will explain the most prominent ones and when each Framework is covered in depth, this content will be referenced. By explaining it here and reminding you later it will save you from having to read the same content over and over in each Deep Dive section.

Stakeholders and Minimal Marketable Features (MMF)

Establishing the project goal focuses all the trade-off and resource management decisions on making actual, measurable progress within a reasonable time. The key Stakeholders and the Sponsor define the goal in terms of the Minimal Marketable Features (MMF) that must be included. Ideally, they also prioritize them so that customer value drives the development schedule first, and efficiency of development drives it second.

For many Sponsors and Stakeholders a primary goal is to create a competitive advantage, often by being first to market. Being a first mover creates the opportunity to capture massive market share, generate premium pricing margins, and possibly enjoy cost savings. In order to achieve the goal of being first to market it is often necessary to tightly focus the project on quickly delivering an important set of MMFs.

Identifying and refining the project focus down to the MMFs also provides an early and important opportunity to engage Stakeholders in the participatory decision-making style that is central to Agile.

Minimum Marketable Features are defined as the smallest set of features providing enough functionality to fulfill the customer's expectations and create a desired level of engagement (i.e., consumer purchases or constituent votes).

Consider this analogy. Ford could build and sell a car more cheaply by not including a steering wheel or a transmission. But they probably wouldn't sell very many because, for most consumers, a steering wheel and a transmission are part of the MMFs of any car they want to buy. Conversely, Ford could produce and sell a car for less money if it had no body and no windshield. The car would have a chassis, transmission, steering wheel, seats, and engine, but no body or glass. It would function, but would they sell any? Interestingly, such vehicles are called dune buggies and are used for riding in the desert. In order to ride on the sand and not sink, dune buggies need to be light so not having a body is part of the MMFs because it reduces weight.

The key to defining MMFs is to understand the market, understand who the customer is, and help that customer define what is in their MMF.

The process that the Stakeholders and Sponsors use to define the MMFs often precedes and is separate from the project management process. However, in both Traditional and Agile Frameworks, an initial activity is to integrate it. That activity is called Project Chartering or Visioning, in Traditional and Agile Frameworks, respectively.

The Customer-Proxy uses the MMFs, in part, to understand what the customer wants. Then based on that understanding, the Customer-Proxy defines a Product Roadmap that expresses what is most important and schedules it to be developed first because it is the most important. Depending on the level of granularity, a Roadmap is equivalent to a Program plan or a Project plan in Traditional Frameworks.

Identifying and refining the project focus down to the MMFs provides an early and important opportunity to engage Stakeholders in participatory decision-making.

Value-Driven Deliverables

Defining MMFs is one approach used to help stakeholders clarify and articulate their goal. Another method used to help stakeholders identify desirable objectives is ***Value Stream Mapping,*** a technique developed in Lean manufacturing.

Value Stream Mapping is a process that analyzes, and potentially redesigns, the flow of materials and information used to deliver a product or service to the customer in order to reduce the total time required from beginning to end of the production stream without taking shortcuts at the expense of future opportunities.

While there are various permutations, the basic Value Stream Mapping process consists of the following steps:

- ***Identify the Value Stream Target.*** The target is a particular product or service (sometimes a product or service group, family or category) where improvement can provide strategic and competitive advantage.

- ***Define the Current State.*** Identifying the current state of the Value Stream is accomplished by creating a "map" or diagram showing the current process. The map illustrates the productive steps and accompanying information inputs required to deliver the product or service. It also identifies unproductive steps such as lead-time, delays, queuing time, or holds. For tangible products, the flow will show everything from acquiring the raw materials to customer receipt of the product. For intangible products, the flow will show everything from design concept to launch of the service or delivery of the product, such as a financial instrument or software.

- ***Clarify the Current Opportunity.*** Opportunities to eliminate waste (e.g., waiting time, delays, queuing, or holds) and thereby raise customer satisfaction and enhance competitive advantage with faster delivery and better quality and fit are clarified by analyzing the current-state Value Stream Map.

- ***Depict the Desired Future State.*** Once the current state has been properly analyzed, a desired future-state value stream map is documented. Then that map is used to implement a plan to transform the current workflow into the desired future state.

Value Stream Mapping is part of the recognized Six Sigma methodologies. While in the past Value Stream Mapping was most often associated with manufacturing, it has begun to see widespread use in industries as varied as logistics, healthcare, and software development for establishing Value-Driven delivery processes.

Value Stream Mapping can also be linked to high-level architectural outlines. Such outlines may be needed to facilitate planning for the initial Iteration (aka "Just Enough"), guide architectural and engineering activities during subsequent Iterations (aka "Just In Time"), and meet any regulatory requirements (aka "Just Because"). Architectural outlines must be adequate to guide emergent design and incremental delivery of business value.

The test of Value-Driven deliverables is whether a releasable product reflects the product vision and meets the acceptance criteria (and related metrics) defined by the Customer-Proxy.

At Intel®, where such a process has been successfully institutionalized to create a continuous flow of innovative breakthroughs for multiple decades, they call it "MAPP Day." ***MAPP*** stands for ***Make A Project (or Program) Plan.*** It is so important that Intel® has dedicated facilitators who guide the MAPP Day process.[11]

Intel® has demonstrated that establishing a Value-Driven delivery process, while neither quick nor painless, is well worth the investment. While it is not easy, it is amazingly effective when the right tools are employed and accompanied by adequate training and process standards.

The purpose of a value-driven development process is to help stakeholders clarify and articulate their priorities early in the project management process. Three additional tools commonly used are the ***Product Vision Box,*** the ***Project Data Sheet,*** and the ***Flexibility Matrix.***[12]

Product Vision Boxes are a graphical expression of the solution that includes whatever images and narrative content is necessary to convey what the customer expects from the product. The content is expressed in end user language and not techno-jargon.

Project Data Sheets (PDS) capture a project's objectives in a one-page summary of the key objectives, capabilities, and information needed to understand the purpose and progress of the project. The PDS is a minimalist document.[13]

Flexibility Matrices are a simple tool that help the Customer-Proxy communicate to the Team how to handle the unavoidable tradeoffs arising during solution development. The matrix clarifies which constraints are flexible and which are not, hence the name. It is a top-level decision-making tool for guiding tradeoff decisions when resource, time, or cost conflicts arise during execution.

Test-Driven Development (TDD)

The experience of teaching thousands of students has shown that sharing a couple of quick, common, everyday examples of Test Driven Development (TDD) creates a useful mental map for applying it in greater depth. Of course, the challenge with familiar examples is that they are not perfect analogies. They get your thinking started in the right direction, but they inherently fall victim to the pitfalls of oversimplifying complexity. Nonetheless, these three examples will help kick start the thinking process. If you already understand TDD then you should skip these examples because they might muddy the expertise you have already acquired.

Example #1

You are considering going out to dinner with your friends. You define a test such as, "Is my appetite satisfied?" For this example we will assume the answer is no because you are hungry. Failing that test means you need to do something. You decide to meet your friends at your favorite place and have a meal. Afterwards you run the test again, "Is my appetite satisfied?" and the answer is yes. You have passed the test so the solution worked.

Example #2

You are considering buying a car. You define a test such as, "Is my current mode of transportation satisfactory?" Since the answer is no, failing that test means you need to do something. You decide to go car shopping and after 13 grueling hours of searching, negotiating and getting a loan, you drive off in the perfect new car. Afterwards you run the test again, "Is my current mode of transportation satisfactory?" and the answer is yes. You have passed the test so the solution worked.

Example #3

You buy a book to study TDD and want to validate that you actually learn something. To do so you create a quiz by writing questions on the material you want to learn about TDD. Examples could include "What does TDD stand for?" or "What profession typically uses TDD?" Then you take the counter-intuitive step that is at the heart of TDD. You actually take the quiz you just developed. "Wait, what?" you say. That's right, you take the quiz and fail, but that's okay (excellent even) because you weren't suppose to know the answers! Next, you read the book you bought. Afterwards you take the quiz again and pass. Voila! You just used TDD to learn about TDD. (And who said you aren't one sharp cookie?)

For the average student, the most confusing concept of TDD is only confusing because of the awkward way it is usually stated. When TDD is described it is usually some form of, "Define a test, fail the test, and then write code until the test is passed." To which the average person says, "Huh?!? Come again! Write a test just to fail it!?!"

The first two examples above showed TDD in familiar, everyday situations. And the third example illustrated TDD using the formula [Create Well-Defined Test] then [Take Test and Fail] then [Do Something] then [Take Test and Pass]. Of course, if the step after [Do Something] turns out to be [Take

Test and Fail] then you must [Do Something (Again)] until you reach [Take Test and Pass]. (Figure 3.12)

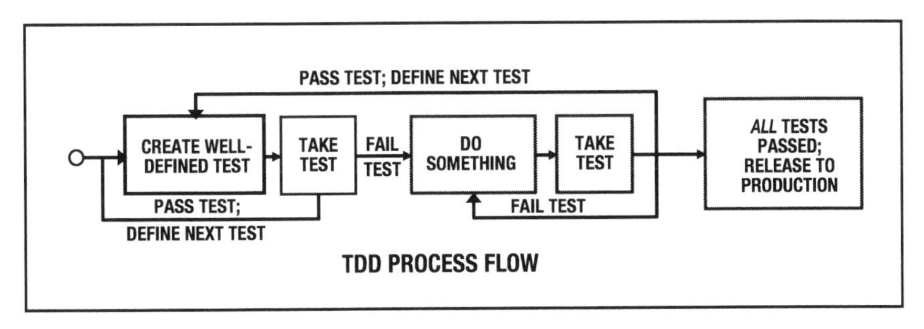

Figure 3.12| *Test-Driven Development (TDD)*

Test-driven development (TDD) is a four-step process that begins with creating a well-defined test, then invoking an operation to take the test and having a "fail" outcome, followed by doing something to change the operation, and finally invoking the modified operation to take the test and having a "pass" outcome.

Once the common confusion just described has been overcome, the challenging part of TDD comes to the surface. Applying it becomes challenging in situations that seem to have a large number of variables, which describes a great many projects. But TDD can be used for projects because it can be extended as a series of tests in situations with high complexity. In those situations, defining a testing architecture as a decision tree can be useful. However choosing the first test questions can be very challenging. It will require enough subject matter expertise to prioritize the tests so they align with the overall project objectives and cost-effectively reduce risks.

Luckily, the power of self-directed, cross-functional teams helps a great deal. As the possible schema for prioritizing the test questions is discussed, it is not uncommon to hear someone say, "Why didn't I think of that approach as an option?" Or, "Hey you can't use that tactic because of the F.D.A. regulations." The good news is that as the Team develops expertise in choosing testing schema appropriate to their environment, TDD becomes rather intuitive and moves the Team through the Cone of Uncertainty surrounding the project.

Drawing on its Lean roots, Agile Project Management takes the "Plan-Do-Check-Act" (PDCA) cycle and implements it using test-driven practices. PDCA requires teams to work using a defined plan of execution based on solid principles, guided by experience, and continuously refined with lessons learned. Thus, the most desirable solutions emerge from the disciplined process.

Test-driven practices support the emergent designs that validate or challenge the accuracy of the assumptions about the work that were made during planning. One key to get TDD adopted by an organization is to identify the general and specific benefits expected from applying emergent design techniques. Emergent design is the Team's internal creative work process that delivers design artifacts that are more than the sum of the parts.

Using an emergent design strategy aligns with the choice to acknowledge the reality of a Cone of Uncertainty and the need for a dynamic team process to move through it to find the best solutions. That is the starting point for identifying the benefits of emergent design. How important is it to find the best solutions and how much of a competitive advantage will that create?

Another source for identifying the benefits of emergent design is quantifying the value of moving from quality control (QC) to quality assurance (QA). How valuable is it to prevent defects not merely catch them? How many dollars and days can test-driven practices save by minimizing or eliminating rework?

By moving QA to the front of the build process, the Team eliminates many of the communication disconnects that cause delays, defects, and waste. Understanding and applying TDD practices enables the team to design change-tolerant architecture. Test-driven practices help developers recognize how their work will perform and integrate into the final solution so they can insure high quality results with minimal waste. Test-driven practices give the Team the confidence to embrace needed, even aggressive, design changes when circumstances demand it because they know the architecture can support it. But, test-driven practices will also require the organization to commit to automated testing tools in order to allow the extensive verification and validation needed as changes emerge and adjustments are implemented.

Product and Iteration Backlogs

The Customer-Proxy, also referred to as the Voice-of-the-Customer or Product Owner, is responsible for receiving, analyzing, and prioritizing information about the features and functionality required to successfully fulfill the customer's expectations with the solution being developed. That work is documented as the **Product Backlog.**

Product Backlogs are a prioritized collection of short descriptions of features, functions and capabilities included in the solution being developed.

The Product Backlog is equivalent to the product specification or requirements list in Traditional Project Management. It is, however, significantly different because the customer-proxy is continuously grooming it based on information received from internal and external sources. As priorities change, system features can be promoted or demoted within the overall scope or contract governing the project. So, the total project scope is stable, but the order of development within the Product Backlog is in a state of flux because feature ranking can change.

At the beginning of each Iteration, Features from the Product Backlog are selected for inclusion in the **Iteration Backlog.**

Iteration Backlogs are the specific subset of Product Backlog items the Team has committed to develop in a particular timebox period. Once the specific subset of items for the Iteration Backlog are agreed upon and fully committed to, they are not changed.

As the goal of that Iteration, the Team has committed to doing whatever is necessary to change the current condition of the Features in the Iteration Backlog into the desired future state. That is their sole focus. The desired future state of those Features is, by definition, the Potentially Shippable Product increment, which is the goal of that Iteration. The team will focus all of its energy on developing that part of the solution and at the end of the Iteration will demonstrate it for all interested stakeholders during a Review Meeting.

Grooming the Product Backlog

If we use a UPS delivery person as a metaphor, Product Backlog grooming is the "steering wheel" insuring the "Agile truck" is headed in the right direction and stops to deliver packages at the right time and location. Backlog grooming is important because research indicates that, for example, the cost of a $250,000 IT development project can have a negative variance of as much as $130,000 to achieve targeted functionality. The amount of the variance correlates to the maturity of the requirements[14]. Because Backlog grooming continuously improves project requirements it has a direct, quantitative positive financial impact.

Backlog grooming, sometimes referred to as Backlog Management, is a process that prioritizes and clarifies Backlog items as they move from the long-term edge of the time horizon into a time horizon that is more near-term.

Backlog items typically start with descriptions that are large, low resolution, identifiers of features, functions and capabilities. As they move through the grooming process, they are transformed from low granularity descriptions with Affinity estimates (explained in chapter 9) on the Roadmap, to Stories with Story Point estimates on the Release plan, to Tasks with detailed estimates when they are included in the Iteration plan. As they progress, they are refined by the customer's insight and learning during discussions with the Team.

The information about each specific Backlog item increases as it nears likely development. Grooming avoids waste by only gathering detailed information as it is needed and usable. As development progresses, design choices emerge, and the customer gains insight, any resources spent prematurely to create detailed information have a high probability of ending up as waste because most items will change, some of them quite dramatically.

An important responsibility for the customer-proxy is to articulate the business value being created by Backlog grooming in customer-facing, non-technical terms. In order to do this, the customer-proxy will lead customer collaboration by driving activities like product visioning exercises, focus group discussions, and marketing studies. Using those experiences, the customer-proxy will discern how to create both incremental and long-term value.

The Backlog is the tangible expression of the Product Vision and grooming is a real-time, iterative process that guides the project through an evolutionary requirements elaboration process.

A best practice for identifying and defining Backlog items is to have the customer-proxy discuss each of the following elements with the Team.

- ***Process elements*** – The definition, usage, and management of procedures discussed in the Business Case and Value Stream Map.
- ***Organizational elements*** – The infrastructure support for the current business practices and the support needs that must be developed for the future-state practices.
- ***Human elements*** – The knowledge and skills applied by the users in the current business practices and the additional user training needs for the future-state practices.
- ***Risk and Regulatory Compliance elements*** – What provisions are needed "just because" of the need for risk mitigation or regulatory compliance?

- ***Automation and Technology elements*** – How will the organization's approach to fulfilling required value-creation processes use a different model, such as queries replacing reports, pull replacing push inventory management, or automated replies replacing manual responses?

Backlog grooming along with planning Roadmaps, Releases, and Iterations is part of a bigger process goal. The goal is to transform a product vision into a Product Backlog that can be estimated then measured to predict the timing for delivering Releases.

Reducing waste is a Lean principle imbedded in Agile Frameworks. That means the frequency and level of detail in estimates must be tied to the business benefits of doing so. Elaboration for the sake of elaborating, or estimating for the sake of estimating, is waste. Elaborating and estimating to create insight, plan the future, and guide execution to create business value is not waste.

Operational Ceremonies

Almost all of Agile's various Frameworks use three core operational meetings, commonly referred to in Agile as ceremonies. Some have additional ceremonies not shared by others. The three common ceremonies are the Daily Stand-up Meeting, the Review Meeting, and the Retrospective Meeting. And yes, ceremonies could be called meetings, but as everyone knows, engineers and technical professionals hate meetings!

Daily Stand-up Meeting

Daily Meetings are held primarily to synchronize the Team members' activities and secondarily, to provide information for reporting work progress towards the Iteration Goal. The Daily Meeting is sometimes referred to as a Daily Stand-up or Scrum meeting.

Each day, each member of the Team is expected to make reasonable progress towards the committed, agreed-upon Iteration goal. Sometimes discoveries or insights will come out of the Daily Meeting. Those discoveries and insights are used by the Customer-proxy to improve Product Backlog grooming.

Because the core purpose of the meeting is to synchronize the Team members' activities, the meeting has a lightweight structure. That lightweight structure has only a few rules and they are intended to help adapt the dialogue about development to meet the Team's need to coordinate work.

It is commonly called a "Stand Up" meeting because of the practice of having collocated teams stand around the Task Board for the discussion. The belief is that standing up helps maintain brevity and keeps the discussion focused.

The structure for the meeting provides that it is self-directed by the Team and done in a 15 minute timebox. For new teams, facilitation by the Scrum Master or another appropriate person may occur until the Team becomes self-directed. The structure also requires that it be scheduled at the same time and place every day. Additionally, the structure makes it mandatory for every team member to attend and participate. Although others can attend to observe, they may not participate.

Finally, the structure provides a pattern for the ceremony where the Team gathers around the Task Board, speaks to each other, and responds to three questions. The three questions prompt and guide each team member's remarks. They are:

- What have I done since the last daily meeting?
- What will I do before the next daily meeting?
- What obstacles are impeding my work performance?

Self-directed teams employ a variety of methods to decide who speaks first. Some common approaches include Last In, First Up, "911" (aka I have an emergency/impediment and need to go first), Round Robin, Pass the Token, and Draw Straws. Using a variety keeps things from going rote and losing focus.

The meeting dynamic is working well when the Team stays focused on the work and not personalities, everyone arrives on time, and the meeting begins and ends on time. The dynamic is effective when work progress is honestly articulated and obstacles addressed are removed in a timely fashion.

Review Meeting

Review Meetings are ***product-centric*** meetings where any interested stakeholder can offer insights and concerns about the deliverables, as well as considerations for future enhancements.

Review Meetings occur at the end of each Iteration. They are a forum to present the most recently completed work products to all interested stakeholders so they can give feedback on how well it aligns with their needs and expectations. Secondarily, it provides transparency between the stakeholders' needs and the Team's work, allowing adjustments to the order of development to occur when needed.

Before the Review Meeting, the Customer-proxy approves or accepts the completed components of the Team's work. If all work is completed, the Iteration goal is reached.

The structure for the meeting provides for an appropriate sized timebox and facilitation by the Customer-Proxy. It is mandatory that the Team present only work that has been completed and accepted by the Customer-proxy.

The Review Meeting is a collaborative, collective information-sharing forum, as well as a review of project metrics and progress. The Review Meeting requires minimal preparation because only products that are completed, tested, and meet the acceptance criteria as set forth during Iteration planning are demonstrated. No smoke, no mirrors, no PowerPoint presentations about what it will do – just working, potentially shippable increments of the solution.

The meeting begins with the Customer-Proxy briefly describing the Iteration Goal and how it measures progress towards the project objective. The Customer-Proxy is responsible for clarifying what was set as the ***Definition of Done*** during iteration planning.

Definition of Done is the definition of all the activities to finish and tests to fulfill before a Story or Task is considered complete. It is an agreement between the Team and Customer-Proxy appropriate to the context of a project.

The Team then provides a demonstration of the completed work and discloses any of planned work that was not completed. Optionally, the presentation may include a review of Burn Charts, velocity metrics, and testing results to help the stakeholders get a clearer picture of the state of the project.

The attendees then ask questions of the Team about the work products. That interaction results in product feedback, potential updates to the Product Backlog, and sometimes updates to the Release plan.

Retrospective Meeting

Retrospective Meetings are ***process-centric*** meetings where the Team identifies how it can improve its process of creating Potentially Shippable Products. Typically, the Review Meeting and the

Retrospective Meeting are the first and second halves of a single day for the Team. The Team and possibly the Customer-proxy, but no one else, attend the Retrospective Meeting.

Retrospective Meetings occur at the end of each Iteration. The primary purpose is to create a shared understanding of how the Team worked together and how that interaction could be improved. Additionally, it provides the Team with insight into the different ways they each saw things, how they had different experiences, and ended up with different perspectives of the same Iteration.

As a best practice, GR8PM advises clients to ask their teams to seek a one percent improvement to their process. The reason for setting the "1% Expectation" is that nobody is intimidated by that request. Making it very approachable for the Team sets them up for success by reducing stress. However, we often find that clients are skeptical, initially, saying something like, "Why bother? What's the big deal if it is only a one percent improvement?" In order to understand, try to think about the "1% Expectation" as a financial instrument. If you could put your money into a financial instrument and it would earn one percent this month, two percent next month, three percent the third month, four percent the fourth month, and so on, would you put your money in? Would you keep it in? Of course you would! You'd end up wildly wealthy, right? So the "1% Expectation" leverages the magic of compound interest. And, by the way, sometimes the Team will make a change expecting a one percent improvement, and lo and behold, it unlocks a chain of events and turns out to be a five or ten percent improvement.

We learned from Lean that continuous improvement is important. Many Project Managers using Traditional approaches have had Lessons Learned sessions fail for many years. The key recurrent mistake being made is waiting too long to have the meeting and making it too serious. Agile approaches overcome that recurrent mistake by applying Lean's continuous improvement dictate and doing Lessons Learned – that is a Retrospective Meeting – at the end of every Iteration. That means that every 3 or 4 weeks, while it is fresh in the Team's mind, they review what they could do, starting tomorrow, to improve results and have more fun! The focus on fun unlocks the power of the prefrontal cortex at a physiological level and the immediacy of tomorrow creates a huge WIIFM for the Team. Doing that drives a lot of the big value Agile creates.

The structure for the meeting provides an appropriate sized timebox and a meeting facilitator. While it is a common practice for the Scrum Master to facilitate the meeting, the best practice is to have an outside facilitator, such as a Scrum Master from a different team at the same organization.

In order for the Retrospective to avoid the pitfall of each person staking out their territory to defend, it is critical that the meeting start with the best available facts. Notice that it is the best available, not perfect, data about the Iteration metrics. How many Stories were completed versus how many were committed to? What was the Team's velocity and how did it compare to the average? Were there changes in team membership? Were any new technologies tested or deployed? Was Daily Meeting attendance 100%? 100% on time? 100% committed and participating? What do the Burn Charts show? The point is to encourage the Team to refer to artifacts, creating a shared picture of what actually happened. Creating a visual reference makes it is easier to see patterns and identify linkages.

Then, the Team will do the serious lifting of interpreting the picture. How did the event pattern impact their ability to strive for more productivity? What feelings occurred – both positive and negative – because of specific aspects of the pattern? How did the Team unite in productive ways or divide in unproductive ways? When was the Iteration just a job versus exciting as hell versus being caught in hell?

The observations are usually recorded on a whiteboard or flipchart in a three column format. Some of the more common configurations are:

- What Went Well – What To Improve – What Could Be Changed
- Try – Keep – Stop
- ☺ ☹ ?
- Fears – Hopes – Expectations
- Do the Same – Do More – Do Less
- Enjoyable – Frustrating – Puzzling

The Retrospective Meeting is a cooperative, concerted effort to identify opportunities for significant and incremental progress in the Team's process. Saying significant and incremental progress sounds like an oxymoron, but it is the key to the power of the Retrospective. The meeting is an invitation to experiment with changes during the next Iteration that can achieve a figurative 1% goal. One percent is definitely incremental, but when it is compounded every 3 or 4 weeks, it becomes an immensely significant return on investment!

It is critical to master the science and art of Retrospectives. The worst possible outcome is the "Ho Hum Nothing New" event. The basic structure of the Retrospective is solid and predictable, but the delivery of the event has to be refreshed often enough to keep the Team engaged.

Before we can keep them engaged however, we must get them engaged and that brings us to the topic of kicking off the Agile project.

Kicking Off Agile Projects

In Traditional approaches, most projects start with a kickoff meeting. With Agile approaches, it is necessary to do likewise however, because of the immediacy with which the Team must embrace and begin the work, the way the meeting is conducted and its goal are more intense. An Agile project kick-off meeting has several key objectives. The agenda is designed to develop those key areas, typically including:

- Clarify the product vision and Roadmap. Best if presented by the Sponsor or Customer-Proxy.
- Review the business case.
- Review (or document) the most important one- or two-dozen features.
- Establish ground rules (aka Rules of Engagement).
- Document a Release plan.
- Do (or schedule) the first Iteration planning session.

Clarifying the product vision and Roadmap is one rather interesting difference between an Agile kick-off meeting and a more Traditional one because the Team engages through discussions and important group exercises. The exercises can include developing the Product Vision Box, the Flexibility Matrix, and the Project Data Sheet that were described previously. It might also include writing an **Elevator Statement.**

Elevator Statements are an uncomplicated way to define the product vision in a short statement using language everyone can understand.

Elevator statements are concise descriptions with a format driven by the research first developed by Geoffrey Moore and included in his book *Crossing the Chasm.* Elevator statements draw their name from the idea that they are brief enough to be shared during a short elevator ride.

The goal of the kick-off meeting is to get every team member aligned with a clearly defined scope documented at a very high level with a dozen or two key features. Those features are all very large pieces of information with minimal detail, but clear connections to one another and to the strategic objective embodied in the business case. Typically, the farther out on the time horizon the feature is, the lower the granularity in the description. The purpose is to orient the new project team to the business reasons driving the project.

Roadmap and Release planning focuses on identifying any required proof-of-concept work as well as laying out logical sequence Iteration goals. Defining the probable number of Iterations required to achieve a Release allows the Customer-proxy to make needed future planning decisions regarding the priority of the various features, functions and capabilities.

When teams are not collocated, every effort should be made to bring them together for the kick-off meeting. Agile emphasizes face-to-face communication because of its many benefits. Despite the reality of remote teams and budget constraints, this is the time for intelligent use of available resources. The kick-off meeting should receive high priority because the shared decisions will guide and focus the Team throughout the rest of the project.

It is useful to link these ceremonies to producing actionable reports.

Actionable Reports

There are many reports Agile uses to promote a value-oriented perspective with the Stakeholders, Sponsor and Team. The reports refine and reinforce the focus on prioritizing the highest value creation opportunities. Not every report Agile uses conforms to the common definition that conjures up pages of laser printed output. However, whether the report is being spit out of a printer, hanging on a wall or included on a Wiki page, they are guided by two key concepts. Those concepts are Information Radiators and Visual Controls.

Information Radiators are a visible display of the current work status, typically in the project workspace, that consolidates key information so stakeholders can evaluate it.

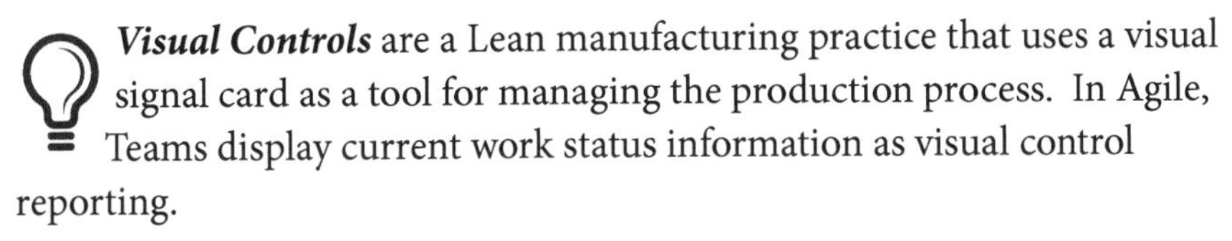

Visual Controls are a Lean manufacturing practice that uses a visual signal card as a tool for managing the production process. In Agile, Teams display current work status information as visual control reporting.

Let's look at some common ones.

Burn-Down and Burn-Up Charts

Burn charts come in two basic forms, Burn-down and Burn-up.

Burn-down Charts show the work remaining, like number of Story Points in the Iteration. Burn-Down Charts are used most often to reflect the results of the Team's Daily Meeting.

Burn-up Charts show the work completed, usually in terms of completed Iterations in the Release. Burn-up charts are used to show progress completing Features, Functions, and Capabilities so the probability of on-time delivery of the Release can be assessed.

Burn charts rarely reflect smooth curves because they reflect the Team's actual progress. Because of breakthroughs or unexpected technical challenges, for example, a Burn-Down Chart may show progress staggering ahead and falling back during various portions of the Release or Iteration.

The two most common ways to create and manage a Burn-Down Chart are manually, for collocated teams, and using Excel for remote, distributed teams. The most common mistake made on Burn-Down charts is overcomplicating them. A Burn-Down simply reports the sum of Story Points for the remaining User Stories, typically on a daily basis.

The standard Iteration Burn-Down Chart plots time on the horizontal X-axis and work remaining on the vertical Y-axis. (Figure 3.13)

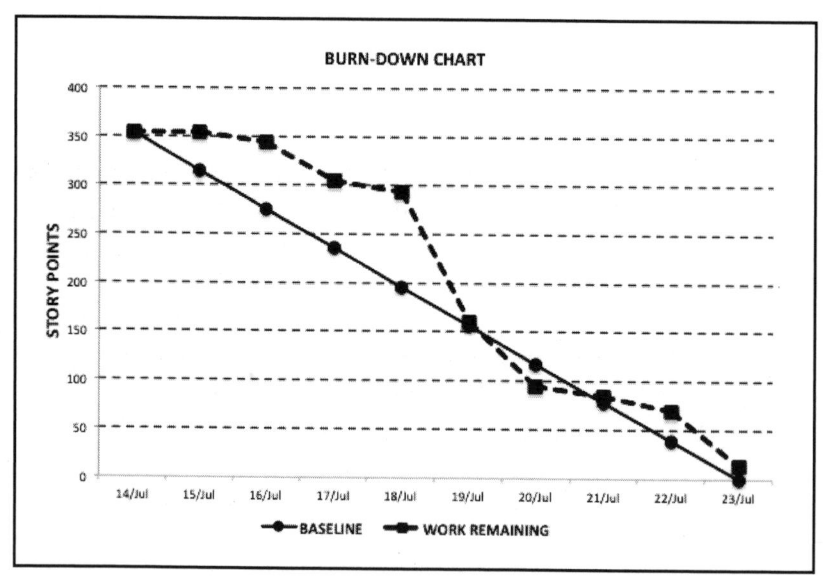

Figure 3.13| *Burn-down Chart*

During the Team's Daily Meeting each member reports if they have completed any User Stories. When they do, the Story Points for that Story are removed from the Work Remaining total and the Burn-Down Chart is updated to accurately show the reduction in work remaining.

Because the work remaining is measured in Story Points, if the Team identifies additional Tasks needed to complete the Story, that change will be reflected in Actual Cost reports, not on the Burn-Down Chart. The Burn-Down tracks work progress not work effort, cost or future expectations. Likewise, if the Team discovers a breakthrough that substantially decreases the hours required to complete the work remaining, it will be reflected in Actual Cost reports. The Burn-Down Chart will simply show that more Stories are completed because the remaining work on the chart will decrease.

The emerging work remaining line becomes a powerful visual communicator of the Team's progress towards the Iteration goal. The power of this simple chart lies in the clarity with which it articulates the project's two most important numbers – how much work remains and the net-net rate of progress towards the Iteration goal including all challenges, set-backs and victories.

Alternately, typical Burn-Up Charts show the completed Features, Functions, and Capabilities – that is deliverables – for the current Release, making the math required to forecast the probability of on-time delivery of the Release rather straightforward.

FFC, Story and Task Boards

All the various Boards contain information describing Features, Functions, Capabilities, Stories or Tasks. That information includes elements such as a description of the desired outcome (comparable to a Traditional requirement or specification) at a correlated level of granularity, the relative size (comparable to a Traditional estimate) also at a correlated level of granularity, and conditions of satisfaction or acceptance criteria (comparable to Traditional quality constraints). The information is critical because it is used to determine the best approach for solution development.

Feature, Function & Capability (FFC) Boards contain information, typically a collection of cards, describing attributes and traits with low-level granularity and long time horizons.

Story Boards contain a collection of User Stories describing specific deliverables with medium-level granularity detailed to support effective Iteration planning.

Task Boards hold a collection of cards with high-granularity descriptions of the work that must be completed in order to develop User Stories committed for completion during the current Iteration.

It is worth noting that the definitions for Story Boards and Task Boards are very specific as far certification exams are concerned, in common usage the names are frequently used as synonyms. Story Boards contain Stories and Tasks and Task Boards contain Tasks and Stories.

Notice that the granularity of the details increases as FFCs are decomposed into Stories and Stories are decomposed into Tasks. The Team uses Story and Task Boards during their Daily Meetings to focus discussion on the topics needed to synchronize their work efforts. The boards also provide a convenient visual radiator of the Iteration's work organization as well as how much work is left.

Because the primary duty of the board is to enable team synchronization, it must be designed with the flexibility to allow self-organization of the Team's work. When a team member finishes a Task, they select another Task to work on. Typically they explain their planned choice so other team members can express concurrence or make alternate suggestions until a mutually agreeable decision is made. By being easily visible and flexible, the board helps the Team see which Tasks are being worked and which are waiting.

The central design element of the board is the column. Columns define the process steps or development stages that Tasks or Stories pass through from Backlog to completion. Boards can be constructed on corkboards, whiteboards, flipcharts, walls, windows, cubicle dividers or even the backs of files cabinets with columns delineated using a marker, masking tape or any other medium.

The Tasks or Stories are written on sticky notes or cards and they are fixed, taped or pinned in a Backlog column. Then they move, in the western or American convention, from left to right as they progress towards completion. If they encounter difficulties, they can be moved in the opposite direction and return to a prior process step for rework.

Many enhancements can be added to the basic card convention including, for example, color-coded cards to signify specific feature groups or development swim lanes, noting Sizing or estimate information, and recording prioritization information.

In Figure 3.14, the board shows columns for Backlog, Development, Test, User Acceptance Testing (UAT), and Completed. The Development, Test, and UAT columns contain the in-progress work. For this team and this project, those categories enable proper synchronization and self-organized planning. They also represent a continuum of progress that the average Stakeholder can decipher to understand the state of the Iteration and correlate it to the Burn-Down chart usually displayed nearby.

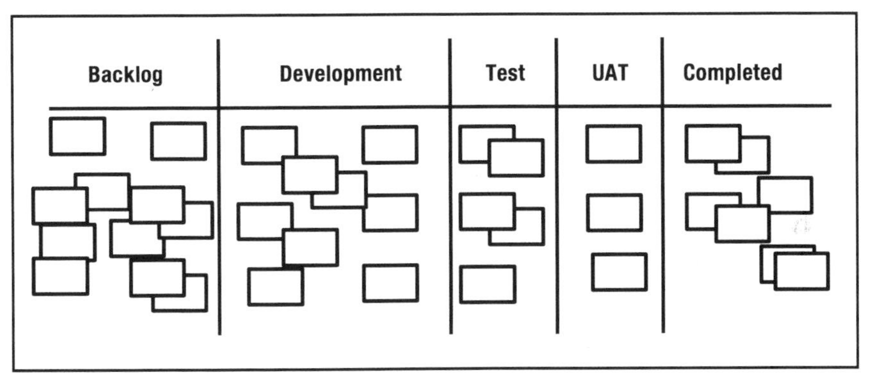

Figure 3.14| *Story or Task Board*

Because User Stories can have a one-to-many relationship with Tasks, some teams will choose to have Stories in the Backlog, but more detailed Tasks in the other columns. When they do this, some teams include numbering or color-coding to identify the Task to the Story or person doing the work. Other teams use nested naming conventions and initials on the in-progress Tasks. The key is to create visibility into work that is not started (in the Backlog), in process, or completed.

Electronic Task Boards for remote, distributed, and virtual teams accomplish the same purpose as their physical counterparts, and can often be facilitated using a conference call and a spreadsheet such as Excel. Typically the Task list (i.e., Task Board) and Story Point values are maintained on one tab and the graph is on a second tab. The results can then be easily published as a daily PDF, posted in a Team repository, printed if desired, and archived for future reference.

Of course, to have any value at all, the reports must contain accurate useful data and that implies reliance on another Agile concept, Osmotic communication.

Osmotic Communication

In order for a cross-functional team of experts to be self-directed and productive it must optimize communication bandwidth. Agile maintains that whenever possible, teams should be collocated in order to maximize communication bandwidth because that greatly enhances the opportunity to identify issues, find solutions, and reduce risk. High levels of osmotic communication are strongly correlated to dramatically improving the probability of a successful project outcome.

Osmotic communication means team members pick up pieces of information from conversations occurring near them and link that information to insights they can contribute to the discussion. The name is drawn from the perception that the relevant information was acquired in a fashion similar to minerals dissolving into a solution by osmosis.

It is worth noting that osmotic communication is critical to problem solving, an activity that is significantly more complex than synchronization or coordination. Synchronization can be achieved with a 15-minute Daily Meeting. Coordination of Task assignments can be achieved with periodic working group meetings. Problem solving, however, requires significantly higher idea transfer rates and collaboration time and that level of bandwidth is often only available when teams are collocated.

Agile acknowledges that projects benefit when people with a high need to communicate are in close proximity where they can overhear communications between all parties. This heightens awareness of issues that are current and important so they can be responded to quickly. Osmotic communication is powerfully good communication and it does not occur automatically or by accident. It must be chosen and cultivated.

The key implication is that Team members should be collocated to take advantage of the improved information flow. There is an opportunity cost associated with team members not asking questions. When a team is collocated, their very proximity leads them to ask more questions and discover unexpected answers. Direct communication lowers the cost of information transfer and ultimately saves time!

This principle has been applied in Traditional Project Management for many decades when critical projects become troubled. In those cases, the common and best practice is to create a "war room" and collocate all the needed experts to rescue the project or address the threat. In fact, the movie *Apollo 13*, a 1995 American docudrama film, pivoted on the tension that occurred when the crew appeared doomed to almost certain death because a liquid oxygen tank exploded unexpectedly. The crew is saved because Mission Controller Commander, Gene Kranz, immediately collocates his team in a war room and rallies them to get the astronauts home safely, declaring, "Failure is not an option!"

Osmotic communication and collocation are not without some limitations however. Foremost among those limits is team size. Both concepts work best with relatively small teams, but that can be a problem if a large project is involved. The next limitation is personal needs and preferences when doing tasks that require serious unbroken concentration. A best practice for mitigating this challenge is the workspace design concept called, "Caves and Commons." Most of the time the team members work in the Common area, but when the need for privacy arises, an individual moves into a Cave. They may do this to concentrate on solving a problem, handle a personal matter, or to complete legally mandated job duties or disclosures.

The forgoing does not mean that Agile denies the reality that many projects are delivered by distributed teams. Instead, it recognizes the challenges and risks associated with teams that cannot attain the high trust and communication levels fostered by collocation.

Osmotic communication is just one of the key elements that must be addressed in order to cultivate Agile leadership.

Agile Leadership

Amongst some, perhaps many, Agile aficionados, a grossly over-simplified characterization contrasting leadership in Traditional and Agile environments is popular. While it carries all of the drawbacks of any characterization, it may be helpful with comparing and contrasting the two methodologies. And for the purpose of passing the PMI-ACP® and CSP exams, it can be accepted as true.

In Traditional approaches, the Project Manager is characterized as often utilizing directive, command-and-control tactics such as assigning tasks to team members to administer the project and that is negative or bad.[15] By way of contrast, in Agile approaches, leaders seek to empower the Team to achieve the Iteration goal. The dichotomy defines the Project Manager negatively, as someone who controls the tasks, milestones and dates in the plan and resists change while pursuing inflexible objectives. The same dichotomy defines the Agile leader positively, as someone who pursues outcomes by influencing the Team as it embraces ambiguity and change while pursuing desirable outcomes. Both approaches have as their goal to deliver results effectively, but each is based on a very different set of assumptions. The assumptions that underpinned the Agile approach are embodied in what is commonly referred to as servant leadership.

Servant leadership is a philosophy emphasizing awareness, listening, persuasion, relationship building, and commitment to others' growth as the path to creating value. Servant leadership is embodied in practices such as embracing the energy and intelligence of others, developing colleagues, influencing teams, and inverting the power-pyramid.
One easily identifiable metric of how well an Agile leader embodies servant leadership is the existence of an environment of personal safety.

Personal safety[16] is when team members feel support for each individual as they work through the productive tension and respectful disagreements that accompany developing solutions to complex problems when uncertainty is unavoidable.

Being a servant leader and cultivating an environment of personal safety requires the Agile leader to develop a capability commonly described as emotional intelligence.

Emotional intelligence is the ability to identify, assess, and manage one's own emotions, and also the ability to identify, assess, and influence the emotions of others.

Jim Highsmith points out, "Management research shows that mood or "emotional intelligence" in leaders has a much larger impact on performance than we may have imagined."[17] So it is important for an Agile leader not to be distracted by the use of a term that has become a cliché and instead embrace the important issue it addresses.

Because the Team will experience both highs and lows during the Iteration, quite often with unexpected volatility, supporting appropriate responses and discouraging inappropriate ones is critical. Being able to induce group dynamics conducive to creating desirable, emergent results at the edge of chaos, where most teams must work, is as fundamental to producing optimal results as writing good User Stories. Therefore, the Agile leader must recognize that their emotional intelligence will dramatically impact the Team's success and takes the steps needed to refine and improve it.

Agile leaders help create an environment where emotional intelligence can flourish by applying the best practice of having the Team define its rules of engagement.

Rules of engagement establish norms and expectations for team member interactions, and are sometimes referred to as ground rules.

By demonstrating that the treatment of one another is an important area for the Team to discuss, develop, and define, the Agile leader can guide the Team to document common expectations and assumptions so misunderstandings are avoided. By posting the rules in a prominent place to act as a reminder, the Agile leader supports interdependent accountability even as the rules are adapted over time to improve team self-direction.

The rules foster and direct the healthy and necessary contention of emergent design in positive ways. Great teams feed on the energy of diverse ideas in contention to produce the highest quality results. And at the same time, they need positive guidance to avoid accidental negative interactions.

Examples of common Rules of Engagement include:

- Everyone participates
- Respect differences
- Attack issues, not people
- Everyone has an equal voice
- Everyone has a valuable contribution to make
- Honor confidentiality and privacy within the Team

Cultivating an Agile team spirit enables exciting productivity. It does so in part because the healthy contention of emergent design brings important risks into focus so the Team can mitigate and resolve them.

Servant leadership relies on a number of skills and techniques, all aimed at developing and facilitating the Team. They include:

- Mentoring team members on the Agile Framework as well as on general management and technical skills.
- Allowing the cross-functional team to become self-directed and fully accountable.

- Facilitating team meetings including, Release planning meetings, Daily Stand-ups, Demonstration meetings, Reflection Workshops, Review meetings, and Retrospective meetings.
- Guiding the Team as they foster appropriate, value-based decisions.
- Removing obstacles that impede progress, or facilitating the Team to do so.

As the Team matures, it moves along a continuum from being a highly directed Traditional team to a self-directing, highly motivated Agile team. When the Team reaches this state, the Agile leader acts largely as a consultant, serving the Team as a facilitator only when called upon.

A best practice for the Agile leader is to avoid conducting individual performance reviews for members of the Team as this creates a conflicting frame of reference for the team members and the appearance of violating the servant leadership role.

Another valuable thing to remember is that collocated teams enjoy a host of communication advantages and require only normal levels of support, whereas there is a very real challenge in supporting communication for virtual teams. That challenge is part of Agile leadership.

Key factors that must be considered include:

- Synchronizing communication through Daily Meetings
- Supporting collaboration through working group meetings
- Aiding problem solving by providing sufficient communication bandwidth to enable high-volume idea transfer rates

Remember that the foremost purpose of the Daily Meeting is to synchronize the Team's work, which requires clear communication. The most common challenges for virtual teams are language and accent issues due to the lack of visual clues. Because so much communication is non-verbal, the lack of visual clues creates a huge risk of misunderstanding.

Two best practices address this challenge. First, invest in a good headset because vocal clues are very subtle. Second, establish a Rule of Engagement stating each team member will provide detailed written answers to the three questions in an email preceding the call and that they will start by reading their written answers, verbatim. Because English is the lingua franca of many teams, but not everyone has a good "ear" for hearing past the accents of those speaking English as a second language, having the read-verbatim-first rule helps the other teammates by letting their "eyes train their ears" for the spoken words. This simple practice vastly increases the quality of communication.

Whatever tools or techniques are used it is a primary responsibility for the Agile leader to ensure that true problem solving – not just synchronization or collaboration – occurs.

That means participatory decision-making is critical.

Participatory Decision-Making

Agile leaders seeking to optimize team performance need to use a participatory decision-making model in order to make sure each Stakeholder and team member voice is heard.

Participatory Decision-Making is a creative process for finding effective options and cultivating collective ownership of decisions so that everyone can support those decisions.

Over the last ten years, Agile Frameworks have enjoyed a meteoric rise in interest because of the way they improved operating outcomes for so many organizations. One of the variables easily identified as a significant contributor to that success is participatory decision making. Agile recognizes that simply having human beings act like biological machines cannot solve the significant, complex problems faced by most organizations.

Organizations need the creative, non-linear, and imaginative insights that only come from fully engaged knowledge workers.

Knowledge workers are persons who combine various forms of structured and unstructured data and use creative thinking to solve mostly non-routine problems. They are commonly described as thinking for a living and examples include engineers, architects, scientists and lawyers.

Flexibility is an absolute requirement for achieving success on today's projects. Only the knowledge workers dealing with the challenges of developing the Iteration goal fully understand how to solve the problem. Remember the process is dynamic, always changing to meet an evolving challenge, as the Team moves through the Cone of Uncertainty.

In 1999, Peter Drucker emphasized the need for organizations to empower the knowledge worker to make decisions that they – more so than management – are in the best position to make; and also to avoid having the knowledge workers leave, damaging the organization.[18] In Jim Collins's famous book, *Good to Great*[19], the great organizations he describes engage in rigorous debate, often over extended periods of time, using dialogue, not coercion, to interrogate the truth down to the brutal facts, in a way that allows individuals to be extremely interactive, until the best solution is identified. Lastly, Roger Martin's article, T*he Opposable Mind: How Successful Leaders Win Through Integrative Thinking*[20] , describes how real leaders, great leaders, tolerate and embrace ambiguity as long as necessary during discussion because they refuse to be limited by "either/or" choices.

The Agile methodology and its many Frameworks embrace participatory decision making as the best alternative to old school industrial thinking. Experience has also shown that it is difficult to develop the sophisticated leadership skills needed to facilitate, influence, and coach a team into the healthy, durable relationships required for participatory decision making, so be patient with yourself and others.

Participatory decision-making either helps the Team operate smoothly or mires it in a swamp of indecision, and the difference is largely dependent on the actions of the leader. If the leader shies away from the discussion necessary to get the structural engineer to challenge the architect, then the building can't be built cost-effectively. If the construction manager has to attend too many meetings, in the name of "coordination", the project gets hopelessly behind schedule because the Team doesn't have access to the Customer-proxy when needed. The ends of the continuum – too little and too much – can both cripple participatory decision-making.

Leadership is critical to effective decision making in an Agile project environment where thousands of decisions must be made using information that is often vague. Customer desires are unclear. Technology is untried in the exact situation. Eight or nine out of ten decisions can paralyze the Team because the fuzziness makes them oscillate between choices. Often times, once the required, healthy, vigorous debate has occurred and the Team has reached an impasse because the ambiguity engulfs them, the leader has to step forward. An effective leader acknowledges the ambiguity, takes responsibility for the impact of the decision – whatever it may be – and enables the Team to resume productivity by making the decision.

This brings us to the basic assumption of participatory decision-making that the right team is executing the project.

The Right Team

It somehow seems necessary to reiterate that Agile is not a magic potion or a silver bullet because many Agile evangelists act as if it is. Without the right skills on the Team, nothing can help, not even Agile. So the Agile leader must communicate that it is not optional to have a cross-functional team with the right skills. The common question however is, "How do we go about getting that particular team?"

The first part of the answer is actually a reality check. If the project is number 103 on the company's priority list, the Agile leader must frame the Team requirements within that reality. The crucial key is to solicit the level of sponsorship needed to clarify the tactical reality with the Customer-proxy.

The second part of getting the particular team the project needs is evaluating (potential or assigned) team members according to key factors such as:

- **Ability** – What specific competencies do they provide?
- **Availability** – What is their availability and what are their competing commitments? Are they local or remote?
- **Cost** – How appropriate is their cost given the budget constraint?
- **Chemistry** – How well do their work style preferences align with the team culture and environment?
- **Experience** – What similar or related work have they done? Under what time and quality constraints?

In many, if not most organizations, whether they use a Traditional or Agile approach, one of the biggest challenges to getting the proper team is **pre-assignment.**

Pre-assignment means that someone in the organization has allocated, appointed, or designated the specific persons who will make up the Team without the Agile leader's involvement.

Pre-assignment is a common practice in large organizations and can actually help when the project is dependent on specific expertise that is in short supply and the correct person is pre-assigned. Sometimes pre-assignment involves specific individuals who were identified as a part of contract negotiation and so must be on the Team. But pre-assignment also happens many other times when there is limited rationale for the choices made and that is when the Agile leader must evaluate before accepting it. In those circumstances, the Agile leader must carefully evaluate whether critical skills are missing from the Team and take steps to correct the problem.

It may also be necessary for the Agile leader to act in order to insure the project receives competent staff on a timely basis, and team members don't have their bandwidth constricted due to other work assignments. A professional Agile leader must be willing and able to negotiate as toughly as required to ensure project success.

The desired result is the right person in the right role at the right time. Until the team has that result, the Agile leader must continue to negotiate to secure those people for the project team.

Recommended Reading

- *The Software Project Manager's Bridge to Agility*, by Michele Sliger and Stacia Broderick (Addison-Wesley Professional; May 2008)
- *Coaching Agile Teams: A Companion for ScrumMasters,* Agile Coaches, and Project Managers in Transition, by Lyssa Adkins (Addison-Wesley Professional; May 2010)

Chapter Close-Out

Practice Test

1. The foundation for organizing Agile Frameworks can be described as ___________.

   A. Processes
   B. Approaches
   C. Methodologies
   D. Philosophies

2. ______________________ are context-specific foundations that have a set of Processes that are used to execute work in a defined way.

   A. Frameworks
   B. Processes
   C. Methodologies
   D. Philosophies

3. Practical "how to" protocols used to direct things like sponsoring, organizing, funding, and controlling solution development can be described as _____________.

   A. Frameworks
   B. Processes
   C. Methodologies
   D. Philosophies

4. The person who prioritizes the Backlog by sorting the most important ones to the top of the stack, and pushing the less important ones to the bottom of the stack is the ______________________.

   A. Project Manager
   B. Scrum Master
   C. Sponsor
   D. Customer-Proxy

5. During Iteration planning, the __________________ creates the Reciprocal Commitment.

   A. Soft Commitment
   B. Hard Commitment
   C. Signed contracts
   D. Iteration Backlog

6. A ________________ is a product-centric meeting where any interested or impacted Stakeholder can come and see what was just finished.

   A. Stakeholder Workshop
   B. Daily Stand-Up
   C. Review Meeting
   D. Retrospective Meeting

7. A process-centric meeting where the Team, with nobody else present, talks about the development process is called the ______________.

   A. Stakeholder Workshop
   B. Daily Stand-Up
   C. Review Meeting
   D. Retrospective Meeting

8. ______________________ refers to the concept of how unknown facets of a problem decrease over time.

A. Iterative Development
B. Cone of Uncertainty
C. Progressive Elaboration
D. Rolling Wave Planning

9. _________________________ are defined as the smallest set of features that provide enough functionality to fulfills the customer's expectations.

A. Minimal Marketable Features
B. Contract Requirements
C. Minimal Marketable Specifications
D. Minimal Elicited Features

10. A process that analyzes, and potentially redesigns, the flow of materials and information used to deliver a product or service is called _________________________.

A. Roadmap Planning
B. Logic Network Diagramming
C. Value Stream Mapping
D. Participatory Decision Making

11. The Team creates a graphical expression of the solution that includes whatever images and narrative content is necessary to convey what the customer expects. This is called the ___________.

A. Project Data Sheet
B. Product Vision Box
C. Project Vision Box
D. Product Data Sheet

12. A _______________________ presents a project's objectives in a one-page summary of the key objectives and capabilities.

A. Project Data Sheet
B. Product Vision Box
C. Project Vision Box
D. Product Data Sheet

13. A simple tool used to communicate how to handle the unavoidable tradeoffs that will arise during solution development is called a _______________________.

A. Project Data Matrix
B. Product Flexibility Grid
C. Project Flexibility Matrix
D. Flexibility Matrix

14. A four-step process that begins with creating a well-defined test, then invoking an operation to take the test is referred to as a _______________________.

A. QA/QC Planning
B. Regression Testing
C. TDD
D. Product Refactoring

15. A(n) _________________ is an uncomplicated way to prioritized a collection of short descriptions of features, functions and capabilities.

A. Product Backlog
B. Feature List
C. Elevator statement
D. Iteration Backlog

16. The specific subset of Product Backlog items the Team has committed to develop is referred to as a(n) _________________________.

A. Product Backlog
B. Feature List
C. Elevator statement
D. Iteration Backlog

17. ______________________ is the process that prioritizes and clarifies Backlog items as they move from the long-term to a more near-term time horizon.

A. Roadmap Planning
B. Release Planning
C. Backlog Grooming
D. Iteration Grooming

18. A meeting held primarily to synchronize the team members' activities is called a _____________________.

A. Demonstration Meeting
B. Daily Meeting
C. Review Meeting
D. Retrospective Meeting

19. A meeting where any interested stakeholder can offer insights and concerns is called a _____________________.

A. Demonstration Meeting
B. Daily Meeting
C. Review Meeting
D. Retrospective Meeting

20. ________________ is the definition of all the activities to finish and tests to fulfill before the work is complete.

A. Refactoring
B. Definition of Done
C. Acceptance Criteria
D. Conditions of Satisfaction

21. A meeting where the Team identifies how it can improve its process of creating Potentially Shippable Products is called a

________________.

A. Demonstration Meeting
B. Daily Meeting
C. Review Meeting
D. Retrospective Meeting

22. An information radiator that shows the work remaining, like number of Story Points in the Iteration is called a (n)

________________.

A. Agile Report
B. Burn-down Chart
C. Burn-up Chart
D. Visual Control

23. A visual control that shows the work completed, usually in terms of completed Iterations is called a (n) ________________.

A. Information Radiator
B. Burn-down Chart
C. Burn-up Chart
D. Agile Report

24. An Agile report that is a visible display of the current work status, typically in the project workspace is called a (n) ___________________.

A. Information Radiator
B. Burn-down Chart
C. Burn-up Chart
D. Visual Control

25. An Agile report that uses a visual signal card as a tool for managing the production process is called a (n) ___________________.

A. Information Radiator
B. Burn-down Chart
C. Burn-up Chart
D. Visual Control

26. An information radiator that contains a collection of User Stories describing specific deliverables is called a (n) ___________________.

A. Burn-down Chart
B. Story Board
C. Burn-up Chart
D. Task Board

27. An information radiator that contains high-granularity descriptions of the work that must be completed in order to develop User Stories is called a (n) ___________________.

A. Burn-down Chart
B. Story Board
C. Burn-up Chart
D. Task Board

28. A philosophy that emphasizes awareness, listening, and relationship building as the path to creating value is called

_____________________.

A. Servant Leadership
B. Serving Leaders
C. Leadership Service
D. Agile Leadership

29. The condition when team members feel support for each individual as they work through the productive tension is called

_____________________.

A. Osmotic Communication
B. Personal Integrity
C. Personal Safety
D. Disagree and Commit

30. When team members pick up pieces of information from conversations occurring near them and link that information to insights it is called _____________________.

A. Osmotic Communication
B. Personal Integrity
C. Personal Safety
D. Disagree and Commit

Fill-in-the-Blank Challenge

1. When organizing Frameworks, the philosophical foundations are called ________________________________.

2. ________________________ are context-specific foundations created to support particular industry settings, such as aerospace or automotive.

3. ________________________ are practical "how to" protocols used to guide work to follow or align with context-specific best practices.

4. The person who continuously grooms the Backlog is the ________________________.

5. During Step Two of Iteration planning, the Team makes the ________________________.

6. A product-centric meeting where stakeholders give feedback and ask questions that produce actionable insight is called the ________________________.

7. A process-centric meeting where the Team applies the Lean principle of continuous improvement to the development process is called the ________________________.

8. ________________________ refers to problems decreasing over time as customers traverse through an unavoidable, ambiguous process.

9. The smallest set of features that provide the level of functionality required to fulfill customer expectations are called ________________________________.

10. A process that reduces the total time required from the beginning to end of the production stream without taking shortcuts at the expense of future opportunities is called ________________________.

11. When the Team creates a graphical expression to convey what the customer expects from the product it is called the ________________________.

12. A ____________________ presents a one-page summary of information needed to understand the purpose and progress of the project.

13. A simple, top-level decision-making tool for guiding tradeoff decisions when resource, time, or cost conflicts arise during execution is called a ____________________.

14. A four-step process where invoking an operation to take a test and having a "fail" outcome is followed by doing something to change the operation is referred to as ____________________________.

15. A ____________________ is an uncomplicated way to prioritize short descriptions of Features, Functions and Capabilities included in the solution.

16. The specific subset of Product Backlog items the Team has fully committed to develop and cannot be changed is referred to as a(n) ____________________________.

17. ____________________________ is the process that prioritizes and clarifies Backlog items as they move from the long-term to a more near-term time horizon.

18. A meeting held primarily to synchronize the team members' activities is called a ______________________.

19. A meeting where any interested stakeholder can offer considerations for future enhancements is called a ______________________.

20. ______________________ is an agreement between the Team and Customer-Proxy, appropriate to the context of a project.

21. A meeting where the Team and possibly the Customer-proxy, but no one else, attend is called a ________________________.

22. An information radiator that shows the work remaining, like number of Story Points in the Iteration is called a ______________________.

23. A visual control that shows the work completed, usually in terms of completed Iterations is called a ______________________.

24. An Agile report that is a visible display of the current work status, typically in the project workspace is called a(n) ________________________.

25. An Agile report using a visual signal card as a tool for managing the production process is called a ________________________.

26. An information radiator that contains a collection of User Stories describing specific deliverables is called a ____________________.

27. An information radiator containing high-granularity descriptions of the work that must be completed in order to develop User Stories is called a __________________.

28. A philosophy that emphasizes awareness, persuasion, and commitment to others' growth as the path to creating value is called ________________________.

29. The condition when team members engage the productive tension and respectful disagreements that accompany developing solutions to complex problems is called ____________________.

30. When team members pick up pieces of information and link that information to insights they can contribute to the discussion it is called ________________________.

Terminology Matching Exercise

In the blank column to the left of the Term, fill in the letter that identifies the correct Definition or Description.

	TERM		DEFINITION / DESCRIPTION
	1. Methodologies	A	A process that analyzes the flow of materials and information to reduce the total time required for production.
	2. Frameworks	B	Prioritizes the Backlog by sorting the most important ones to the top of the stack, and then continuously grooms the Backlog. This sorting process is an important step that precedes the planning session occurring at the beginning of each Iteration or Sprint.
	3. Processes	C	During Step Two of Iteration planning it creates the Reciprocal Commitment.
	4. Customer-Proxy	D	Context-specific foundations created to support particular industry settings with a set of Processes used to execute work in a defined way.
	5. Hard Commit	E	A prioritized collection of short descriptions of features, functions and capabilities in the solution being developed.
	6. Review Meeting	F	A process-centric meeting where the Team talks about the development process and applies the Lean principle of continuous improvement.
	7. Retrospective Meeting	G	Refers to the concept of problems decreasing over time as customers experience discovery and learning.
	8. Cone of Uncertainty	H	A product-centric meeting where stakeholders see what was just finished, give feedback and ask questions.
	9. MMF	I	The philosophical foundation for organizing Frameworks.
	10. Value Stream Mapping	J	Graphical expressions of the solution that include whatever images and narratives needed to convey what the customer expects.

	TERM		DEFINITION / DESCRIPTION
	11. Product Vision Box	K	The smallest set of features that provide enough functionality and create a desired level of engagement.
	12. PDS	L	A simple tool used to communicate how to handle unavoidable tradeoffs during solution development.
	13. Flexibility Matrix	M	Practical "how to" protocols used to direct and guide work to follow or align with context-specific best practices.
	14. TDD	N	A one-page summary of a project's the key objectives and capabilities.
	15. Product Backlog	O	A four-step process that identifies a "fail" outcome to change an operation and create a "pass" outcome.

Answers - Practice Test

1. **C.** The foundation for organizing Agile Frameworks can be described as **METHODOLOGIES.**

   Methodologies provide the philosophical foundation for organizing Frameworks. In project management the two dominant choices are Traditional, as embodied in the PMBOK® Guide, and Agile. Methodologies contain and define various Frameworks as context-specific logical foundations.

2. **A. FRAMEWORKS** are context-specific foundations that have a set of Processes that are used to execute work in a defined way.

   Frameworks are context-specific foundations created to support particular industry settings, such as aerospace or automotive, or particular categories of activities, such as software or product development. Frameworks have a set of Processes used to execute work in a defined way.

3 **B.** Practical "how to" protocols used to direct things like sponsoring, organizing, funding, and controlling solution development can be described as **PROCESSES.**

   Processes are practical "how to" protocols used to direct things like sponsoring, organizing, funding, and controlling solution development projects. The Processes guide work to follow or align with context-specific best practices.

4. **D.** The person who prioritizes the Backlog by sorting the most important ones to the top of the stack, and pushing the less important ones to the bottom of the stack, is the **CUSTOMER-PROXY.**

   The Customer-Proxy prioritizes the Backlog by sorting the most important ones to the top of the stack, and pushing the less important ones to the bottom of the stack. The idea is that the Customer-Proxy will continuously groom the Backlog. This sorting process is an important step that precedes the planning session and occurs at the beginning of each Iteration or Sprint.

5. **B.** During Iteration planning, the **HARD COMMIT** creates the Reciprocal Commitment.

   The Hard Commit creates the Reciprocal Commitment. During Step One of Iteration planning the Team makes the "Soft Commit" meaning they think they can fulfill the proposed Iteration Backlog." In Step Two, after some analysis, if they are confident they can do it, they make the "Hard Commit."

6. **C. A REVIEW MEETING** is a product-centric meeting where any interested or impacted stakeholder can come and see what was just finished.

   The Review Meeting is a product-centric meeting where any interested or impacted stakeholder can come and see what was just finished as the next piece of the project puzzle. They give feedback and ask questions that produce actionable insight for the Customer-Proxy to use to groom the Product Backlog.

7. **D.** A process-centric meeting where the Team, with nobody else present, talks about the development process is called the **RETROSPECTIVE MEETING.**

   The Retrospective Meeting is a process-centric meeting where the Team, with nobody else present, talks about the development process. It is the application of the Lean principle of continuous improvement.

8. **B. CONE OF UNCERTAINTY** refers to the concept of how unknown facets of a problem decrease over time.

   Cone of uncertainty refers to the concept of how unknown facets of a problem decrease over time as customers traverse through an unavoidable, ambiguous process where discovery and learning occur.

9. **A. MINIMAL MARKETABLE FEATURES** are defined as the smallest set of features that provide enough functionality to fulfill the customer's expectations.

   Minimum Marketable Features are defined as the smallest set of features that provide enough functionality to fulfill the customer's expectations and create a desired level of engagement (i.e., consumer purchases or constituent votes).

10. **C.** A process that analyzes, and potentially redesigns, the flow of materials and information used to deliver a product or service is called **VALUE STREAM MAPPING.**

    Value Stream Mapping is defined as a process that analyzes, and potentially redesigns, the flow of materials and information used to deliver a product or service to the customer in order to reduce the total time required from the beginning to end of the production stream without taking shortcuts at the expense of future opportunities.

11. **B.** When the Team creates a graphical expression of the solution that includes whatever images and narrative content is necessary to convey what the customer expects. This is called the **PRODUCT VISION BOX.**

    Product vision boxes are a graphical expression of the solution that includes whatever images and narrative content is necessary to convey what the customer expects from the product. The content is expressed in end user language and not techno-jargon.

12. **A. A PROJECT DATA SHEET** presents a project's objectives in a one-page summary of the key objectives and capabilities.

    Project data sheets (PDS) capture a project's objectives in a one-page summary of the key objectives, capabilities, and information needed to understand the purpose and progress of the project. The PDS is a minimalist document.

13. D. A simple tool used to communicate how to handle the unavoidable tradeoffs that will arise during solution development is called a **FLEXIBILITY MATRIX.**

    Flexibility Matrices are a simple tool that help the Customer-proxy communicate to the Team how to handle the unavoidable tradeoffs that will arise during solution development. The matrix clarifies which constraints are flexible and which are not, hence the name. It is a top-level decision-making tool for guiding tradeoff decisions when resource, time, or cost conflicts arise during execution.

14. **C.** A four-step process that begins with creating a well-defined test then invoking an operation to take the test is referred to as a **TDD (TEST-DRIVEN DEVELOPMENT)**

    Test-driven development (TDD) is a four-step process that begins with creating a well-defined test, invoking an operation to take the test and having a "fail" outcome, followed by doing something to change the operation, and finally invoking the modified operation to take the test and having a "pass" outcome.

15. **A. A PRODUCT BACKLOG** is an uncomplicated way to prioritize a collection of short descriptions of features, functions and capabilities.

    Product Backlogs are a prioritized collection of short descriptions of features, functions and capabilities included in the solution being developed.

16. **D.** The specific subset of Product Backlog items the Team has committed to develop is referred to as an **ITERATION BACKLOG.**

    Iteration Backlogs are the specific subset of Product Backlog items the Team has committed to develop in a particular timebox period. Once the specific subset of items for the Iteration Backlog are agreed upon and fully committed to, they are not changed.

17. **C. BACKLOG GROOMING** is the process that prioritizes and clarifies Backlog items as they move from the long-term to a more near-term time horizon.

    Backlog Grooming, sometimes referred to as Backlog Management, is a process that prioritizes and clarifies Backlog items as they move from the long-term edge of the time horizon into a time horizon that is more near-term.

18. **B.** A meeting held primarily to synchronize the team members' activities is called a **DAILY MEETING.**

    Daily Meetings are held primarily to synchronize the team members' activities and secondarily, to provide information for reporting work progress towards the Iteration Goal. The Daily Meeting is sometimes referred to as a Daily Stand-up or Scrum meeting.

19. **C.** A meeting where any interested stakeholder can offer insights and concerns is called a **REVIEW MEETING.**

    Review Meetings are product-centric meetings where any interested stakeholder can offer insights and concerns about the deliverables, as well as considerations for future enhancements.

20. **B. DEFINITION OF DONE** is the definition of all the activities to finish and tests to fulfill before the work is complete.

    Definition of Done is the definition of all the activities to finish and tests to fulfill before a Story or Task is considered complete. It is an agreement between the Team and Customer-Proxy appropriate to the context of a project.

21. **D.** A meeting where the Team identifies how it can improve its process of creating Potentially Shippable Products is called a **RETROSPECTIVE MEETING.**

    Retrospective Meetings are process-centric meetings where the Team identifies how it can improve its process of creating Potentially Shippable Products. Typically, the Review Meeting and the Retrospective Meeting are the first and second halves of a single day for the Team. The Team and possibly the Customer-proxy, but no one else, attend the Retrospective Meeting.

22. **B.** An information radiator that shows the work remaining, like number of Story Points in the Iteration, is called a **BURN-DOWN CHART.**

    Burn-Down Charts show the work remaining, like number of Story Points in the Iteration. Burn-Down charts are used most often to reflect the results of the Team's daily meeting.

23. **C.** A visual control that shows the work completed, usually in terms of completed Iterations, is called a **BURN-UP CHART.**

    Burn-Up charts show the work completed, usually in terms of completed Iterations in the Release. Burn-Up charts are used to show progress completing features, functions, and capabilities so the probability of on-time delivery of the Release can be assessed.

24. **A.** An Agile report that is a visible display of the current work status, typically in the project workspace, is called an **INFORMATION RADIATOR.**

    Information radiators are a visible display of the current work status, typically in the project workspace, that consolidates key information so stakeholders can evaluate it.

25. **D.** An Agile report that uses a visual signal card as a tool for managing the production process is called a **VISUAL CONTROL.**

    Visual Controls are a Lean manufacturing practice that uses a visual signal card as a tool for managing the production process. In Agile reporting, teams display current work status information as a visual control.

26. **B.** An information radiator that contains a collection of User Stories describing specific deliverables is called a **STORY BOARD.**

    Story Boards contain a collection of User Stories describing specific deliverables with medium-level granularity detailed to support effective Iteration planning.

27. **D.** An information radiator containing high-granularity descriptions of the work that must be completed in order to develop User Stories is called a **TASK BOARD.**

    Task Boards hold a collection of cards with high-granularity descriptions of the work that must be completed in order to develop User Stories that are committed for completion during the current Iteration.

28. **A.** A philosophy that emphasizes awareness, listening, and relationship building as the path to creating value is called **SERVANT LEADERSHIP.**

    Servant leadership is a philosophy that emphasizes awareness, listening, persuasion, relationship building, and commitment to others' growth, as the path to creating value. Servant leadership is embodied in practices such as embracing the energy and intelligence of others, developing colleagues, influencing teams, and inverting the power-pyramid.

29. **C.** The condition when team members feel support for each individual as they work through the productive tension is called **PERSONAL SAFETY.**

    Personal safety is when team members feel support for each individual as they work through the productive tension and respectful disagreements that accompany developing solutions to complex problems when uncertainty is unavoidable.

30. **A.** When team members pick up pieces of information from conversations occurring near them and link that information to insights it is called **OSMOTIC COMMUNICATION.**

    Osmotic communication means team members pick up pieces of information from conversations occurring near them and link that information to insights they can contribute to the discussion. The name is drawn from the perception that the relevant information was acquired in a fashion similar to minerals dissolving into a solution by osmosis.

Answers - Fill-in-the-Blank Challenge

1. When organizing Frameworks, the philosophical foundations are called **METHODOLOGIES.**

   Methodologies provide the philosophical foundation for organizing Frameworks. In project management the two dominant choices are Traditional, as embodied in the PMBOK® Guide, and Agile. Methodologies contain and define various Frameworks as context-specific logical foundations.

2. **FRAMEWORKS** are context-specific foundations created to support particular industry settings, such as aerospace or automotive.

   Frameworks are context-specific foundations created to support particular industry settings, such as aerospace or automotive, or particular categories of activities, such as software or product development. Frameworks have a set of Processes that are used to execute work in a defined way.

3. **PROCESSES** are practical "how to" protocols used to guide work to follow or align with context-specific best practices.

   Processes are practical "how to" protocols used to direct things like sponsoring, organizing, funding, and controlling solution development projects. The Processes guide work to follow or align with context-specific best practices.

4. The person who continuously grooms the Backlog is the **CUSTOMER-PROXY.**

   The Customer-Proxy prioritizes the Backlog by sorting the most important ones to the top of the stack, and pushing the less important ones to the bottom of the stack. The idea is that the Customer-Proxy will continuously groom the Backlog. This sorting process is an important step that precedes the planning session and occurs at the beginning of each Iteration or Sprint.

5. During Step Two of Iteration planning the Team makes the **HARD COMMIT.**

   During Step One of Iteration planning, the Team makes the "Soft Commit" meaning they think they can fulfill the proposed Iteration

Backlog. In Step Two, after some analysis, if they are confident they can do it they make the "Hard Commit." The Hard Commit creates the Reciprocal Commitment.

6. A product-centric meeting where stakeholders give feedback and ask questions that produce actionable insight is called the **REVIEW MEETING.**

   The Review Meeting is a product-centric meeting where any interested or impacted stakeholder can come and see what was just finished as the next piece of the project puzzle. They give feedback and ask questions that produce actionable insight for the Customer-Proxy to use to groom the Product Backlog.

7. A process-centric meeting where the Team applies the Lean principle of continuous improvement to the development process is called the **RETROSPECTIVE MEETING.**

   The Retrospective Meeting is a process-centric meeting where the Team, with nobody else present, talks about the development process. It is the application of the Lean principle of continuous improvement.

8. **CONE OF UNCERTAINTY** refers to problems decreasing over time as customers traverse through an unavoidable, ambiguous process.

   Cone of uncertainty refers to the concept of how unknown facets of a problem decrease over time as customers traverse through an unavoidable, ambiguous process where discovery and learning occur.

9. The smallest set of features that provide the level of functionality required to fulfill customer expectations are called **MINIMAL MARKETABLE FEATURES.**

   Minimum Marketable Features are defined as the smallest set of features that provide enough functionality to fulfill the customer's expectations and create a desired level of engagement (i.e., consumer purchases or constituent votes).

10. A process that reduces the total time required from the beginning to end of the production stream without taking shortcuts at the expense of future opportunities is called **VALUE STREAM MAPPING**

    Value Stream Mapping is defined as a process that analyzes, and potentially redesigns, the flow of materials and information used to deliver a product or service to the customer in order to reduce the total time required from the beginning to end of the production stream without taking shortcuts at the expense of future opportunities.

11. When the Team creates a graphical expression to convey what the customer expects from the product it is called the **PRODUCT VISION BOX.**

    Product vision boxes are a graphical expression of the solution that includes whatever images and narrative content is necessary to convey what the customer expects from the product. The content is expressed in end user language and not techno-jargon.

12. **A PROJECT DATA SHEET** presents a one-page summary of information needed to understand the purpose and progress of the project.

    Project data sheets (PDS) capture a project's objectives in a one-page summary of the key objectives, capabilities, and information needed to understand the purpose and progress of the project. The PDS is a minimalist document.

13. A simple top-level decision-making tool for guiding tradeoff decisions when resource, time, or cost conflicts arise during execution is called a **FLEXIBILITY MATRIX.**

    Flexibility Matrices are a simple tool that help the Customer-proxy communicate to the Team how to handle the unavoidable tradeoffs that will arise during solution development. The matrix clarifies which constraints are flexible and which are not, hence the name. It is a top-level decision-making tool for guiding tradeoff decisions when resource, time, or cost conflicts arise during execution.

14. A four-step process where invoking an operation to take a test and having a "fail" outcome is followed by doing something to change the operation is referred to as a **TEST-DRIVEN DEVELOPMENT (TDD).**

    Test-driven development (TDD) is a four-step process that begins with creating a well-defined test, then invoking an operation to take the test and having a "fail" outcome, followed by doing something to change the operation, and finally invoking the modified operation to take the test and having a "pass" outcome.

15. A **PRODUCT BACKLOG** is an uncomplicated way to prioritize short descriptions of features, functions and capabilities included in the solution.

    Product Backlogs are a prioritized collection of short descriptions of features, functions and capabilities included in the solution being developed.

16. The specific subset of Product Backlog items the Team has fully committed to develop that cannot be changed is referred to as an **ITERATION BACKLOG.**

    Iteration Backlogs are the specific subset of Product Backlog items the Team has committed to develop in a particular timebox period. Once the specific subset of items for the Iteration Backlog are agreed upon and fully committed to, they are not changed.

17. **BACKLOG GROOMING** is the process that prioritizes and clarifies Backlog items as they move from the long-term to a more near-term time horizon.

    Backlog Grooming, sometimes referred to as Backlog Management, is a process that prioritizes and clarifies Backlog items as they move from the long-term edge of the time horizon into a time horizon that is more near-term.

18. A meeting held primarily to synchronize the team members' activities is called a **DAILY MEETING.**

    Daily Meetings are held primarily to synchronize the team members' activities, and secondarily, to provide information for reporting work progress towards the Iteration goal. The Daily Meeting is sometimes referred to as a Daily Stand-up or Scrum meeting.

19. A meeting where any interested stakeholder can offer considerations for future enhancements is called a **REVIEW MEETING.**

    Review Meetings are product-centric meetings where any interested stakeholder can offer insights and concerns about the deliverables, as well as considerations for future enhancements.

20. **DEFINITION OF DONE** is an agreement between the Team and Customer-Proxy appropriate to the context of a project.

    Definition of Done is the definition of all the activities to finish and tests to fulfill before a Story or Task is considered complete. It is an agreement between the Team and Customer-Proxy appropriate to the context of a project.

21. A meeting where the Team and possibly the Customer-Proxy, but no one else, attend is called a **RETROSPECTIVE MEETING.**

    Retrospective Meetings are process-centric meetings where the team identifies how it can improve its process of creating Potentially Shippable Products. Typically, the Review Meeting and the Retrospective Meeting are the first and second halves of a single day for the Team. The Team and possibly the Customer-proxy, but no one else, attend the Retrospective Meeting.

22. An information radiator that shows the work remaining, like number of Story Points in the Iteration, is called a **BURN-DOWN CHART.**

    Burn-Down charts show the work remaining, like number of Story Points in the Iteration. Burn-Down charts are used most often to reflect the results of the Team's daily meeting.

23. A visual control that shows the work completed, usually in terms of completed Iterations, is called a **BURN-UP CHART.**

    Burn-Up charts show the work completed, usually in terms of completed Iterations in the Release. Burn-Up charts are used to show progress completing features, functions, and capabilities so the probability of on-time delivery of the Release can be assessed.

24. An Agile report that is a visible display of the current work status, typically in the project workspace, is called an **INFORMATION RADIATOR.**

    Information radiators are a visible display of the current work status, typically in the project workspace, that consolidates key information so stakeholders can evaluate it.

25. An Agile report that uses a visual signal card as a tool for managing the production process is called a **VISUAL CONTROL.**

    Visual controls are a Lean manufacturing practice that uses a visual signal card as a tool for managing the production process. In Agile reporting, Teams display current work status information as a visual control.

26. An information radiator that contains a collection of User Stories describing specific deliverables is called a **STORY BOARD.**

    Story Boards contain a collection of User Stories describing specific deliverables with medium-level granularity detailed to support effective Iteration planning.

27. An information radiator that contains high-granularity descriptions of the work that must be completed in order to develop User Stories is called a **TASK BOARD.**

    Task Boards hold a collection of cards with high-granularity descriptions of the work that must be completed in order to develop User Stories that are committed for completion during the current Iteration.

28. A philosophy that emphasizes awareness, persuasion, and commitment to others' growth as the path to creating value, is called **SERVANT LEADERSHIP.**

    Servant leadership is a philosophy that emphasizes awareness, listening, persuasion, relationship building, and commitment to others' growth, as the path to creating value. Servant leadership is embodied in practices such as embracing the energy and intelligence of others, developing colleagues, influencing teams, and inverting the power-pyramid.

29. The condition when team members engage the productive tension and respectful disagreements that accompany developing solutions to complex problems is called **PERSONAL SAFETY.**

    Personal safety is when team members feel support for each individual as they work through the productive tension and respectful disagreements that accompany developing solutions to complex problems when uncertainty is unavoidable.

30. When team members pick up pieces of information and link that information to insights they can contribute to the discussion, it is called **OSMOTIC COMMUNICATION.**

    Osmotic communication means team members pick up pieces of information from conversations occurring near them and link that information to insights they can contribute to the discussion. The name is drawn from the perception that the relevant information was acquired in a fashion similar to minerals dissolving into a solution by osmosis.

Answers - Terminology Matching

1:I, 2:D, 3:M, 4:B, 5:C, 6:H, 7:F, 8: G, 9:K, 10:A, 11:J, 12:N, 13:L, 14:O, 15: E

Chapter End Notes

[10]Copyright© 2001 Kent Beck, Mike Beedle, Arie van Bennekum, Alistair Cockburn, Ward Cunningham, Martin Fowler, James Grenning, Jim Highsmith, Andrew Hunt, Ron Jeffries, Jon Kern, Brian Marick, Robert C. Martin, Steve Mellor, Ken Schwaber, Jeff Sutherland, and Dave Thomas; this declaration may be freely copied in any form, but only in its entirety through this notice.

[11]One of the best known Intel© MAPP Day facilitators in Jeff Hodgkinson who can be found on LinkedIn©.

[12]Highsmith, J. (2010). *Agile project management creating innovative products, Second edition.* Upper Saddle River, NJ: Pearson Education.

[13]Ibid.

[14]Source: 2009 Business Analysis Benchmark Report, IAG Consulting, 42 Reads Way, New Castle, DE

[15]Sliger, M., & Broderick, S. (2008).*The software project manager's bridge to agility.* Upper Saddle River, NJ: Addison-Wesley.

[16]Cockburn, A. (2007). *Agile software development: The cooperative game, Second edition.* Upper Saddle River, NJ: Addison-Wesley.

[17]Highsmith, J. (2010). *Agile project management creating innovative products, Second edition.* Upper Saddle River, NJ: Pearson Education.

[18]Drucker, P. F. (1999). *Management challenges for the 21st century.* New York: HarperCollins.

[19]Collins, J. (2001). *Good to great: Why some companies make the leap... and others don't.* New York: HarperCollins.

[20]Martin, R. (2007). *The opposable mind: How successful leaders win through integrative thinking.* Boston: Harvard Business School Press.

PART TWO
THE "BIG 5" DEEP DIVE

Scrum Deep Dive

Chapter Highlights

In this chapter you will find an overview of Scrum as well as a detailed description of its key elements. Those elements are broken out as the Roles, Workflow, Ceremonies and Artifacts. The people who work in the Scrum Framework are identified by the Roles they fulfill. The Workflow details how those people work together and produce the planned results. Lastly, the Artifacts are the electronic or printed evidence of the results.

Overview of Scrum

The Scrum Alliance is the largest professional user group in the Agile world. Its flagship certification, the Certified ScrumMaster® (CSM), has the highest name recognition and largest market share of any Agile certification at the time of this writing (July 2015). The Scrum Alliance also offers the Certified Product Owner® (CSPO), Certified Scrum Developer® (CSD), Certified Scrum Professional® (CSP), Certified Scrum Coach® (CSC), and Certified Scrum Trainer® (CST) designations.

The vast majority of Scrum Alliance members and certification holders are in the software industry, and that is the greatest strength and weakness of the Scrum Alliance. It generated a lot of the early energy and interest in Agile as well as defining and documenting most of the early ideas and practices however, its credibility is somewhat limited as Agile moves into other fields such as construction, shipbuilding, medical devices and pharmaceutical organizations.

The seeds of Scrum were planted in 1986 when Hirotaka Takeuchi and Ikujiro Nonaka wrote about a new approach to product development that increased speed and flexibility.[21] They described a holistic approach of one cross-functional development team moving through multiple overlapping phases, similarly to rugby players passing the ball back and forth in a rugby scrum.

However, the Scrum name first appeared in 1991 when Peter DeGrace and Leslie Stahl referred to this as the "Scrum approach" in their book *Wicked Problems, Righteous Solutions.*[22] But Jeff Sutherland, John Scumniotales and Jeff McKenna were the first to refer to it using the single word "Scrum" as the name of the approach they developed at the Easel Corporation.

In 1995, Jeff Sutherland and Ken Schwaber, another early luminary, collaborated in writing, sharing experiences and suggesting industry best practices. Their work became the first public presentation of what is now known as Scrum. A third luminary who was significant in advancing Scrum and is considered by many to be its most articulate thought leader is Mike Cohn. The three of them have been the source of many of the practices and processes related to the Scrum Framework.

In 2014, the Scrum Alliance announced its collaborative adoption of the Scrum Guide created by Jeff Sutherland and Ken Schwaber. It documents *"Scrum's roles, artifacts, events, and rules…".* The Scrum Guide also says, in part, that those rules, *"…are immutable…"* and that *"Scrum exists only in its entirety and functions well as a container for other techniques, methodologies, and practices."* That dogmatic position is both true and also the reason so many organizations that start with Scrum grow beyond it and begin using a customized approach referred to as Hybrid Project Management.

The most recent version of the Scrum Guide (2013) is available as a free download. It defines Scrum as a *"Framework within which people can address complex adaptive problems, while productively and creatively delivering products of the highest possible value."* It goes on to describe Scrum as being, *"Lightweight, Simple to understand, and Difficult to master."* Lastly, it says that it provides the rules of Scrum and that, *"Specific tactics for using the Scrum framework vary and are described elsewhere."*

The Organization and the Development Team exchanging mutual commitments as the gateway to progress is the central doctrine of Scrum. The Organization agrees that the size of the timebox for all Sprints[23], and the Increment[24] that is the Sprint Goal[25] will be stable and not changed. In exchange for the Organization's promise to allow the Development Team to work uninterrupted and without harassment to achieve the Sprint Goal, the Development Team promises to produce the Increment regardless of any obstacles, expected or unexpected, that it may encounter. In essence, the Organization promises to be reliable, giving the Development Team a stable work environment during the Sprint and the Development Team promises to be as creative as necessary to solve problems and conquer the unknown.

Scrum relies on the power of self-organizing, self-directing teams to deliver those results. Because of that dependence on team-power, Scrum strongly prefers collocation of all Scrum Team members to enable immediate, direct communication, as well as osmotic communication.

One key principle in Scrum is that customers are free to change their minds about the importance of User Stories[26] in the Product Backlog[27]. That freedom is reflected in the Backlog Grooming process exercised by the Product Owner. During Backlog Grooming, the Product Owner adds, edits, removes and prioritizes the User Stories to define the logical order of development work to reflect the customer's thinking. Two important things to note are that Backlog Grooming is applied to requirements that are within the boundaries of the contract and that it does not affect the Sprint Goal or Stories that have been committed to in the current Sprint.

This creates an environment that embraces emerging needs with flexibility outside the Sprint timebox while providing stability for the Development Team within the Sprint. Scrum accepts the principle that complex problems cannot be fully defined in advance and are better solved using a scientifically validated empirical process control approach – transparency, inspection, and adaptation. That process focuses the Scrum Team on quickly delivering results that proceed through the Cone of Uncertainty towards a solution in the midst of emerging requirements.

Roles

In Scrum, the three roles are Product Owner, Scrum Master, and Development Team. The three roles together are referred to as the Scrum Team. The Development Team is self-directing and cross-functional. Self-directing means it chooses how best to accomplish the committed work of the Sprint Goal. Cross-functional means it has all the expertise needed to accomplish the work and that is why Development Team members are often referred to as Subject Matter Experts (SMEs). This approach optimizes flexibility and creativity, which in turn, enhances productivity.

Product Owner

The **Product Owner** (PO) is the "voice of the customer" representing the stakeholders and the business, and setting the logical order of development priorities for Increments. **Certified Scrum Product Owner®** (CPO) is a designation granted by the Scrum Alliance.

The Product Owner's primary responsibility is to maximize the value of the product, for both the customer and organization, by optimizing the work of the Development Team. The Product Owner is critical to success because their decisions direct the course of development. Therefore, the Product Owner is always a person, not a group or committee, even if the Product Owner represents a customer group or executive committee.

The Product Owner's biggest tool for achieving the interrelated goals of maximizing value and optimizing the work is managing the Product Backlog. Backlog management requires defining the logical order of development with Stories that clearly express the work the Development Team needs to perform. Therefore, the Product Owner controls all changes to the priority of a Product Backlog item.

For the project to succeed, the entire organization must respect the decisions made by the Product Owner.

Scrum Master

The ***Scrum Master*** (SM) ensures the process is understood and followed, shielding the Development Team from outside interference and removing impediments. ***Certified ScrumMaster®*** (CSM) is a designation granted by the Scrum Alliance.

The Scrum Master's primary responsibility is to ensure the Scrum Team understands the principles of Scrum so they can properly apply its rules and practices. As a servant-leader, the Scrum Master guides the Scrum Team's interactions to maximize the value they create and coaches stakeholders so they understand how to interact with the Scrum Team in helpful and effective ways.

The Scrum Master's effectiveness and efficiency is a result of interacting with the Product Owner, Development Team, and Organization. The Scrum Master and Product Owner work together to ensure desirable Product Backlog management with clear and concise Stories that maximize value. They work together to communicate the empirical planning environment and data to all stakeholders.

The Scrum Master and Development Team work together to create a self-organized and cross-functional environment, construct high-value Increments, remove impediments, and find ways to more fully adopt and implement Scrum.

The Scrum Master and Organization work together to create an understanding of Scrum with appropriate training and coaching. Together, they work together to identify and plan opportunities to implement Scrum and apply empirical product development best practices.

Development Team

The **Development Team** is a cross-functional group, which creates solutions by analyzing, designing, developing, testing, and implementing deliverables. It is assumed that it has all the needed skills, is highly trusted and self-managing.

The Development Team's primary responsibilities are to structure and manage the development work of an Increment that fulfills the Definition of Done committed to during Sprint Planning and to have that work completed by the end of the Sprint.

The Development Team's effectiveness and efficiency is a result of being self-directed and cross-functional. Because they are empowered by the organization to decide for themselves how to turn the Stories into an Increment, their only limits are self-imposed. Because they are cross-functional, they have all of the skills necessary to complete the product increment by the end of each Sprint and are accountable, as a whole, for the results, good or bad.

Developer is the only title that Scrum recognizes for members of the Development Team. Regardless of the work the person performs they are called a Developer without exception. Also, Scrum does not recognize sub-teams or other divisions within the Development Team, again without exception. These rules are rigid and have both positive and negative consequences. On the positive side, they create an environment of equality intended to foster robust problem solving in an environment of personal safety. On the negative side, they can cause confusion among stakeholders with limited knowledge of Agile and Scrum, and also inhibit Scrum's scalability for larger programs, portfolios and enterprise initiatives.

The Scrum Guide says, *"Optimal Development Team size is small enough to remain nimble and large enough to complete significant work within a Sprint."* The generally accepted best practice from the leadership body of knowledge is that team size should be "seven plus or minus two". In other words, the Team should be between five and nine members. Since the Development Team, by definition, includes a Product Owner and Scrum Master, they should have between three and seven Developers.

On the positive side, that means they avoid having too much complexity for an empirical process to manage. On the negative side, they sometimes lack the skills and creative interaction needed to deliver Increments that the stakeholders and organization recognize as important.

However, the Scrum Guide also says, *"The Product Owner and Scrum Master roles are not included in this count* (i.e., team size) *unless they are also executing the work of the Sprint Backlog."* This seems to violate the generally accepted best practice that it is risky and counter-productive to have anyone mixing Developer duties with Product Owner or Scrum Master responsibilities or even to have someone mixing the duties of the Product Owner and Scrum Master. As one team we worked with said, "We didn't know if 'Bad Dave' the Product Owner was coming in to challenge us or 'Good Dave' the Scrum Master or Developer was coming to help us. We all felt schizophrenic!"

Scrum supports self-organizing teams by preferring collocation of all Scrum Team members to promote immediate, verbal communication between all the subject matter experts on the Development Team. Sometimes this preference is misinterpreted or misrepresented to mean that Scrum cannot be used with remote, distributed or virtual teams, or that it cannot be used with team members who are fractionalized across multiple projects. Both assumptions are incorrect. However, both situations will raise the complexity and risk associated with the project so using Scrum in those environments requires more careful management and structure in order to set the Development Team up for success.

Workflow

The Scrum framework is intended to be lightweight and contain a minimal set of practices and roles that can be customized after it has been learned and implemented.

As described in Chapter 3, Scrum shares in common with all Agile Frameworks, a theoretical approach founded on empirical process control theory. The theory states that knowledge comes from experiential data and decisions should be based on what is known from that data. Using empirical data within an iterative, incremental process allows Agile approaches, including Scrum, to reduce risk by optimizing predictability. Empirical process control applies three concepts – transparency, inspection, and adaptation.

Transparency is defined as making important aspects of the process visible using an understood standard, such as the Definition of Done, for those making decisions about the outcome, such as the Increment, to enable a shared understanding of what has occurred.

Inspection is defined as frequently examining work products, called Artifacts, to detect undesirable variances that could negatively impact progress toward a desired outcome, such as the Sprint Goal. It is optimal to inspect as near as possible to the point the work is being done. Care must be exercised to prevent the frequency from negatively impacting progress.

Adaptation is defined as adjusting a process input or the development process to correct unacceptable deviations from the defined standard that were detected during inspection. Adjustment should be done quickly to minimize the negative impact or the occurrence of further deviation.

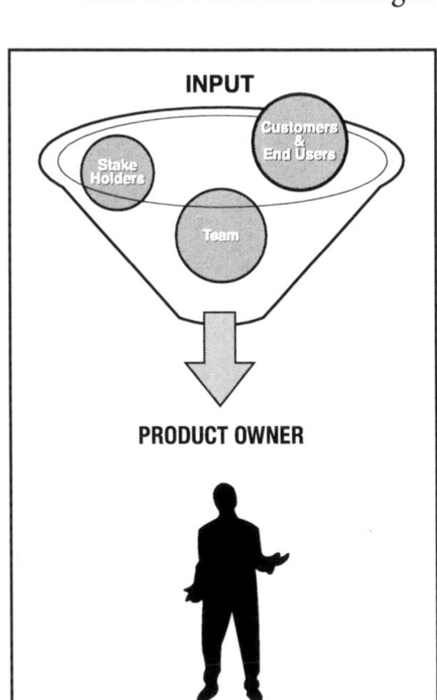

Figure 4.1 | *Product Owner*

In Chapter 3, the generic Agile micro-dynamic workflow was described. In Scrum, the specific description of the team-level workflow starts with all product information being directed to the Product Owner (Figure 4.1). The Product Owner is responsible for knowing what the customer wants, putting it in the Product Roadmap (reference Figure 4.2) and deciding what is most important and will be developed first.

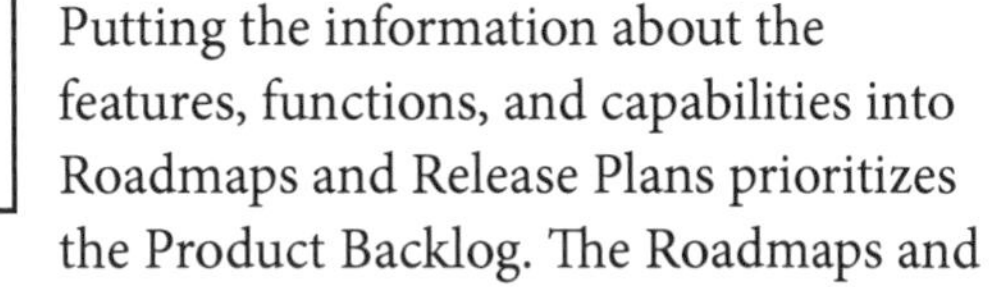

Putting the information about the features, functions, and capabilities into Roadmaps and Release Plans prioritizes the Product Backlog. The Roadmaps and

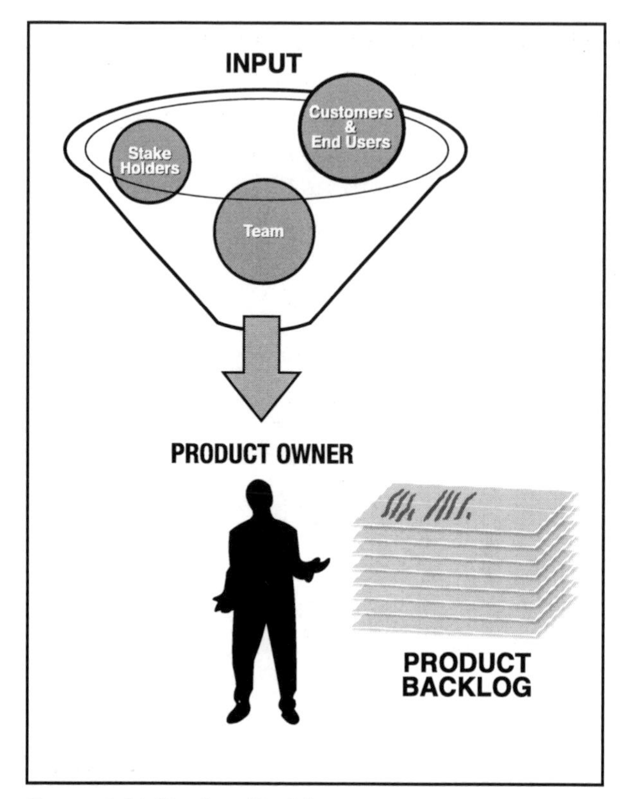

Figure 4.2 | *Product Backlog*

Release Plans show what needs to be developed in order to successfully deliver the final outcome. Each requirement, function or capability is recorded as a User Story or Epic so that the Product Owner can prioritize them. The Product Owner continuously grooms the Product Backlog as an important step preceding the planning session occurring at the beginning of each Sprint. That planning session is the next step in the process.

The Product Owner submits the next piece of the puzzle to be developed to the Development Team and they negotiate an outcome that is both valuable and doable. The outcome is called the Sprint Goal. The Goal is documented with Stories in the Sprint Backlog (reference Figure 4.3). The Product Owner takes the most important Product Backlog Stories to the Development Team where they ask clarifying questions..

The clarifying questions make sure the Development Team and Product Owner share a clear idea of what will be built. The discussion is a collegial effort to figure out what can actually be built during the Sprint that will drive the most value because of the customer insight it will create. It leads to a joint decision about the Sprint Goal.

Typically the process is done in two steps. Step One is where the Development Team makes the "Soft Commit" to the proposed Sprint Backlog. Then, after analysis, if they are confident they can do it, they make the "Hard Commit" to the Sprint Goal. The Hard Commit creates the Reciprocal Commitment.

The goal of the Sprint Planning process is to figure out the best way for the Development Team to make measurable progress towards the Sprint Goal. Crystallizing the Sprint Goal creates an environment where the priorities don't change every week, enabling the Development Team to succeed.

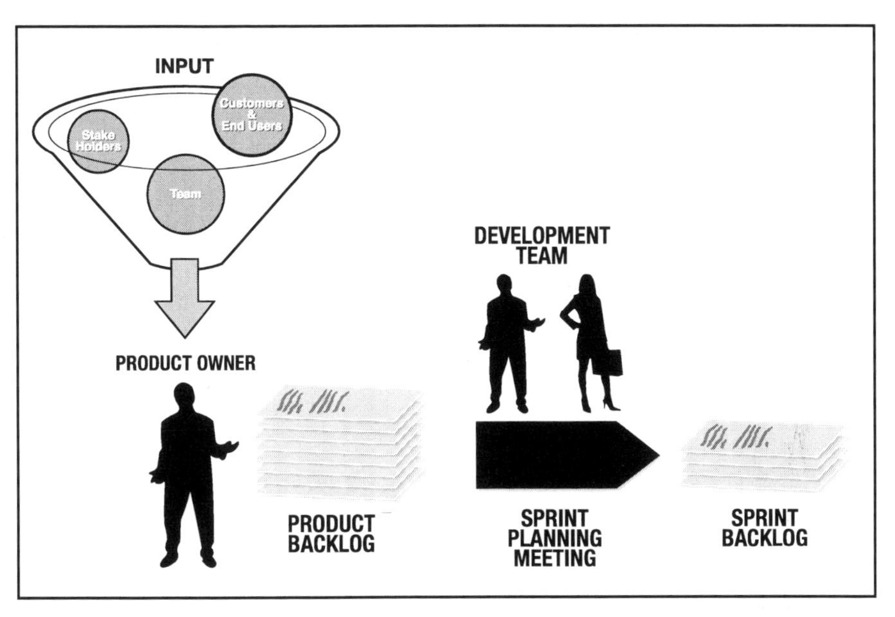

Figure 4.3| *Sprint Backlog*

When that Reciprocal Commitment happens, when the Hard Commit happens, the Sprint begins (reference Figure 4.4). During the Sprint the Development Team completes Tasks and has a daily, 15-minute Scrum Meeting to stay synchronized. The meeting helps insure progress keeps moving forward by having each Development Team member answer the

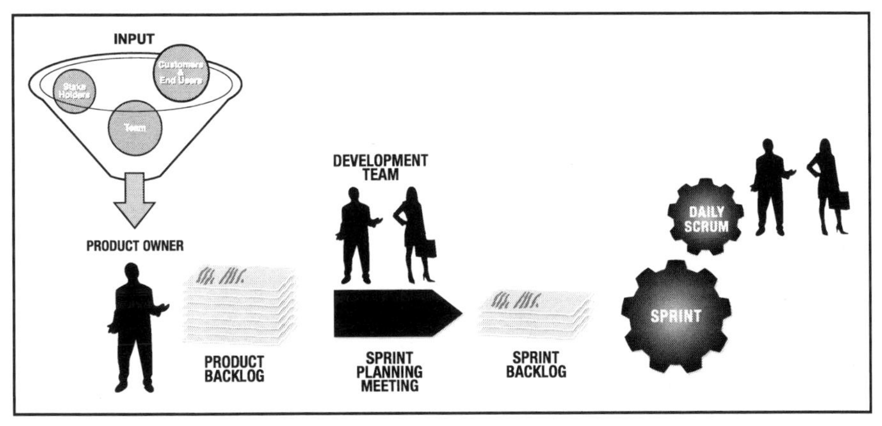

Figure 4.4| *Sprint Begins*

…tions that were explained in Chapter 3. The Scrum Master …es the Development Team and removes impediments.

…he outcome of the Sprint is an Increment (reference Figure 4.5). As it is being developed, the Development Team is sharing their progress with the Product Owner. The final delivery of the Increment is not a surprise to the Product Owner at the end. The Product Owner and Development Team are in agreement that when the Sprint ends, either the Increment is delivered as promised or not. Sometimes a Story couldn't be developed, and even though that's an exception, everyone admits to that being the outcome.

Figure 4.5| *Sprint Increment*

The Sprint ends with the Scrum Team presenting the completed deliverable at the Review Meeting (Figure 4.6). The product-centric meeting gives any interested stakeholder a chance to see the Increment, give feedback and ask questions.

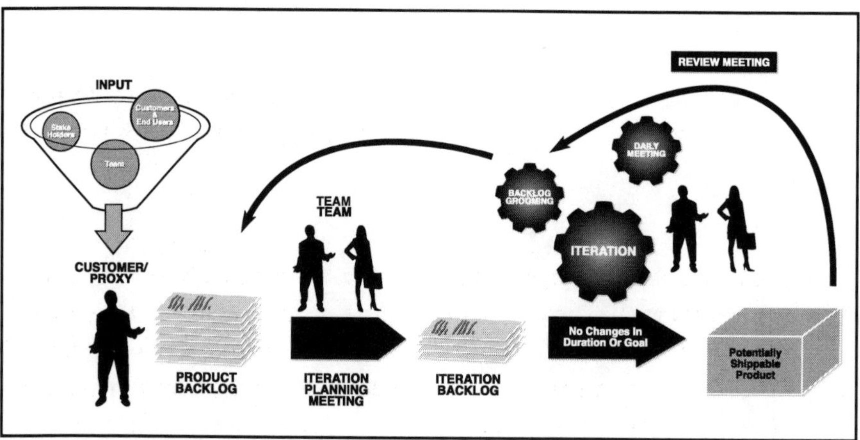

Figure 4.6| *Sprint Review*

Following the Review Meeting, the Scrum Team holds a closed-door Sprint Retrospective (reference Figure 4.7). This process-centric meeting is where the Scrum Team talks about continuous improvement and their development process. It generates a shared understanding and is not a blaming session. The process occurs while the Scrum Team's memories are still fresh so they can identify and select ideas that will improve their process. They start using those ideas the very next day.

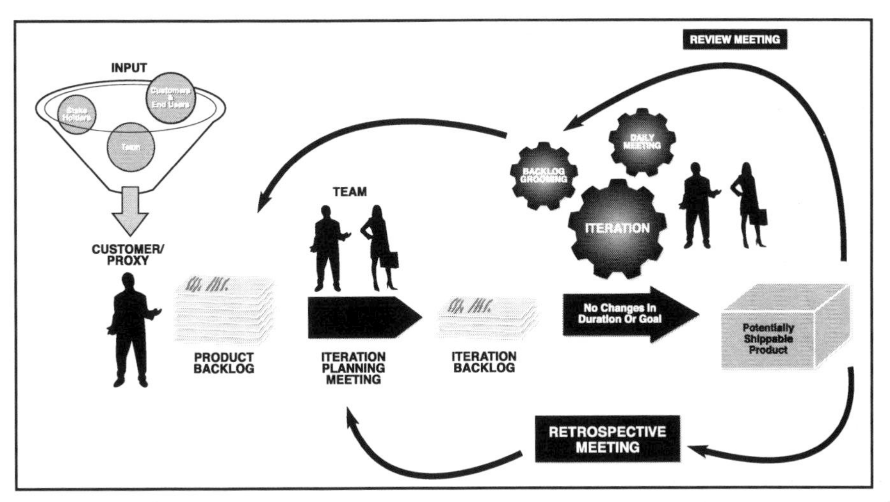

Figure 4.7 | *Sprint Retrospective*

Ceremonies

The Scrum Guide says, *"Prescribed events are used in Scrum to create regularity and to minimize the need for meetings not defined in Scrum."* Scrum's "events" include the Sprint as well as the three core operational meetings commonly referred to in Agile as ceremonies.

The Scrum Guide also says, *"Other than the Sprint itself, which is a container for all other events, each event in Scrum is a formal opportunity to inspect and adapt something."*

The Sprint

The Sprint is the core process of Scrum. It uses a timebox with a consistent duration to create a cadence or pace for the Development Team throughout development. Each Sprint starts immediately following the previous Sprint with a Sprint Planning ceremony. During the Sprint, no scope changes are made and the quality standard that was used for the Definition of Done is maintained as the Sprint Goal is pursued.

The Product Owner may cancel a Sprint, but would normally only do so if the Increment or the project as a whole became unneeded due to an organizational decision to change strategic or tactical direction caused by factors like competitive or technological conditions. When that happens, it is referred to as an Abnormal Termination because cancellation is rare and seldom makes sense. Sprint cancellations are traumatic for the Development Team and should be avoided if at all possible.

The Sprint is planned in a creative, collaborative Development Team ceremony called Sprint Planning. The Scrum Guide describes Sprint Planning as not exceeding eight hours for a one-month Sprint. It also says the Scrum Master facilitates Sprint Planning so that it answers two questions. First, what can be delivered in the upcoming Sprint? And second, how will the Development Team achieve the work needed to deliver the Potentially Shippable Product? The answer to the first question defines the Potentially Shippable Product. The answer to the second question is decided before the Hard Commit is made.

Interestingly, the Scrum Guide states, *"Scope may be clarified and re-negotiated between the Product Owner and Development Team as more is learned."* It continues with, *"Each Sprint may be considered a project with no more than a one-month horizon."* And lastly, *"Sprints are limited to one calendar month."* The first statement seems to violate the generally accepted best practice that scope is fixed during Sprint. The second demonstrates a major misunderstanding of the universally accepted definition of a project. And the third clearly demonstrates a perspective limited to software development even thought Scrum is being extended into many other fields, such as shipbuilding, where Sprints of six to eight weeks are not uncommon. Therefore, the wording in the Scrum Guide is somewhat vague and even counter-productive to some people trying to understand and apply Scrum[28].

Daily Scrum

Daily Scrums are time-boxed to 15-minutes. The Scrum Master and Development Team use them to synchronize activities. Because the core purpose of the meeting is to synchronize their activities, the meeting has a lightweight structure. That lightweight structure has only a few rules and they are intended to help adapt the dialogue about development to meet the need to coordinate work.

The meetings are held at the same time and place each day. During the meeting, each Development Team member answers the three questions described in Chapter 3. What did I do yesterday? What will I do today? Are any impediments preventing me from meeting the Sprint Goal?

The Scrum Master ensures Daily Scrum occurs, but the Development Team is self-organized and responsible for running it. The Scrum Master coaches the Development Team to keep the Daily Scrum within the 15-minute timebox.

One particularly effective technique that Scrum Masters can teach teams to help self-manage the meeting and keep it within the 15-minute timebox is The Seven-Second Rule[29]. The Seven-Second Rule states that the only problems that are solved in daily meetings are ones that can be solved in seven seconds or less. Since exactly zero problems can be solved in seven seconds, the purpose of teaching the Development Team this rule is that whenever the discussion diverts away from the three questions and into problem solving, the first member to realize it calls out, "Seven-Second Rule!" At that point the other members acknowledge that a working group or problem-solving meeting needs to be scheduled and everyone returns to the focus of synchronizing. A best practice for this rule is to teach it to teams at the very beginning of their formation before it is needed so no one feels singled out when it is used.

Each day, each member of the Development Team is expected to make reasonable progress towards the committed, agreed-upon Sprint Goal. Sometimes discoveries or insights will come out of the Scrum Meeting. Those discoveries and insights are used by the Product Owner to improve Product Backlog grooming.

Sprint Review

The Scrum Guide says, *"A Sprint Review is … an informal meeting, not a status meeting, and the presentation of the Increment is intended to elicit feedback and foster collaboration."* It goes on to say, *"This is a four-hour time-boxed meeting for one-month Sprints."*

Sprint Reviews are product-centric meetings where any interested stakeholder can offer insights and concerns about the deliverables, as well as considerations for future enhancements. They occur at the end of each Sprint and are a forum to present the most recently completed work products to all interested stakeholders. They also provide transparency between the stakeholders' needs and the Development Team's work, allowing adjustments to occur when needed.

To start the Sprint Review, the Product Owner explains what has and has not reached the Definition of Done. Next, the Development Team briefly explains what went well, what problems occurred, and how challenges were resolved. It then demonstrates the work completed and answers questions about the Increment (i.e., Potentially Shippable Product). Finally the Product Owner explains the state of the Product Backlog and may forecast likely completion dates for the Release Plan and Roadmap.

With that understanding established, the participants discuss what the priorities should be for the next Sprint Planning meeting and its relationship to changes in the competitive marketplace or internal use of the product. They may also review the impact of changes to the forecast timeline on budgets and customer expectations about features, functions and capabilities.

The interactions during the Sprint Review results in product feedback, potential updates to the Product Backlog, and sometimes updates to the Release plan.

Sprint Retrospective

The Scrum Guide states, *"A Sprint Retrospective occurs after the Sprint Review and prior to the next Sprint Planning. This is a three-hour time-boxed meeting for one-month Sprints. ... The Scrum Master participates as a peer team member in the meeting..."* Sprint Retrospectives are process-centric meetings where the Scrum Team identifies improvements it can make to its process of creating Increments then makes a plan to implement those improvements. It accomplishes this process by creating a shared understanding of how the Development Team worked together and how that interaction could be improved.

The Scrum Master encourages the Development Team to focus its inspection on the actual process it has used and to plan adaptations it can implement in the next Sprint. While it is a common practice for the Scrum Master to facilitate the meeting, the best practice is to have an outside facilitator, such as a Scrum Master from a different team at the same organization, do it.

The Retrospective is a formal application of continuous improvement, imbued with the power of fun, to unlock the prefrontal cortex so it creates a huge WIIFM for the Scrum Team. It is a cooperative, concerted effort to identify opportunities for improvements in the Team's process.

Artifacts

The Scrum Guide says, *"Scrum's Artifacts are specifically designed to maximize transparency of key information so that everybody has the same understanding of the artifact."* It then specifically describes the Product Backlog, Sprint Backlog and Increment.

Product Backlog

The Product Backlog is a prioritized collection of cards or a list of all the features, functions and capabilities that are envisioned as possibly needed in the final product. It is a comprehensive expression of the requirements held in a specific place, physical or electronic, by the Product Owner. Each item in the Product Backlog has a description, prioritization, approximation of development cost and assessment of customer value.

The Product Backlog changes dynamically during product development in order to keep the product relevant and useful even as the external competitive or internal operational context changes. The Scrum Guide says, *"As long as a product exists, its Product Backlog also exists."* However, it might be more accurate to say that as long as a product remains in development, its Product Backlog continues to exist.

Grooming, or as the Scrum Guide calls it, Product Backlog refinement, is an ongoing activity facilitated by the Product Owner in collaboration with the Development Team. Together, they increase the granularity of the details about Product Backlog items as they move from a more distant time horizon to a more current time horizon and the likelihood of understanding what will actually be developed increases.

The Scrum Guide says, *"The Scrum Team decides how and when refinement is done. Refinement usually consumes no more than 10% of the capacity of the Development Team. However, Product Backlog items can be updated at any time by the Product Owner or at the Product Owner's discretion."* The key idea is that Grooming is an ongoing process that involves both the Development Team and the Product Owner.

Product Backlog items for the upcoming Sprint must be refined enough to have a clear and reasonable Definition of Done. Any item that has not reached that level of refinement is not ready for the next Sprint and should not be selected for inclusion in Sprint Planning.

The Scrum Guide says, *"The Development Team is responsible for all estimates. The Product Owner may influence the Development Team by helping it understand and select trade-offs, but the people who will perform the work make the final estimate."* This is an important and true statement. However, it does not imply nor support the commonly heard assertion that Scrum only estimates the work in the very next Sprint. As the details are refined during Grooming and granularity is increased, so does the estimate associated with it. The continuum goes from Affinity estimates to Planning Poker estimates (explained in chapter 10) to final or engineering estimates[30].

Lastly, defining the Product Backlog as an artifact is interesting because it is in a continuous state of change as the product is being developed and only becomes fixed, in the traditional sense of an artifact, after development of a specific piece of the product is complete.

Sprint Backlog

The Scrum Guide says, *"The Sprint Backlog is the set of Product Backlog items selected for the Sprint, plus a plan for delivering the product Increment and realizing the Sprint Goal."* A common misunderstanding is to think of the Sprint Backlog as only containing descriptions of the items to be developed. It is also the Development Team's plan for developing the Increment that fulfills the Sprint Goal. However, it is not a plan in the sense commonly used in Traditional Project Management because the Development Team is self-directing and responds to change by integrating what it learns as it develops.

The Sprint Backlog creates transparency so the work that the Development Team plans to complete is visible for all stakeholders. It also provides enough detail to enable the Development Team to make adjustments during the Daily Scrum as progress is better understood. The adjustments are part of the iterative cycle of discovery where the Development Team modifies the Sprint Backlog, causing a clearer understanding to emerge, and leading to additional adjustments. This micro-cycle of plan, build, check and adjust is an application of the empirical process control approach – transparency, inspection, and adaptation – discussed earlier.

The Scrum Guide says, *"As new work is required, the Development Team adds it to the Sprint Backlog. As work is performed or completed, the estimated remaining work is updated."* A common point of confusion caused by this wording is that the scope of the work can be changed or expanded during the Sprint. A more correct interpretation would be that the amount of granularity, the depth of the detail, the exactness of the description of the work increases and specific tasks are delineated and "added" to the Sprint Backlog. However, the overall scope of the work that was committed to as the Sprint Goal does not change or increase during a Sprint. That is why the Scrum Guide's next statement says, *"Only the Development Team can change its Sprint Backlog during a Sprint. The Sprint Backlog is a highly visible, real-time picture of the work that the Development Team plans to accomplish during the Sprint, and it belongs solely to the Development Team."*

Progress towards the Sprint Goal is tracked and monitored using Velocity. Each day, as part of the Daily Scrum, the total work remaining is recorded by summing up the quantity of work remaining for each uncompleted Backlog item. That quantity is expressed in whatever unit of measure was agreed upon and used to size or estimate the User Stories and Tasks. It is commonly plotted on a Burn-Down Chart in order to see the probability of achieving the Sprint Goal.

The Scrum Guide updated the phrase Potentially Shippable Product to the word "Increment." Potentially Shippable Product originated with Scrum and became the generic Agile expression. Using the word Increment is, in our opinion, an improvement on the older, more common term because stakeholders in the industries in which Scrum is growing more easily understand it.

Increment is defined as, *"the sum of all the Product Backlog items completed during a Sprint and the value of the increments of all previous Sprints"* by the Scrum Guide.

Potentially Shippable Product is defined as the deliverable(s) at the end of the Sprint that adds value to the customer's understanding project progress.

The two terms are closely aligned and used as synonyms.

The Scrum Team works together with stakeholders to identify and create the artifacts needed to increase the probability of successfully reaching the Sprint and Release Goals. Because Scrum relies on empirical process control, the need for transparency is very important. In order to maximize customer and business value and reduce risk, every artifact must be as transparent as possible. As transparency rises, so does the likelihood of making sound decisions. The inverse is also true.

The Scrum Guide uses the phrase, "*... an Increment is described as "Done"...*" in the same way generic Agile uses the more common phrase, "Definition of Done." It is also not uncommon at Scrum and Agile gatherings to hear practitioners actively debating whether the idea of Done, Done-Done or the 4-Levels of Done is more correct. No matter what your position in that conundrum might be, the Scrum Guide is absolutely correct when it says, "*When a Product Backlog item or an Increment is described as "Done", everyone must understand what "Done" means.*"

Done, when used to describe the completion of an Increment, is defined as a mandatory *"shared understanding of what it means for work to be complete, (and) to ensure transparency. This is the definition of "Done" for the Scrum Team and is used to assess when work is complete on the product Increment"* according to the Scrum Guide.

Definition of Done is defined as the description of all the activities to finish and tests to fulfill before a Story or Task is considered complete. It is an agreement between the Development Team and Product Owner, appropriate to the context of a project.

The two terms are closely aligned and used as synonyms. They focus on a single core concept. To succeed, everyone must understand and accept whatever Definition of Done is being used to guide the work of the Sprint.

Although Scrum has not been explicitly extended from the micro-dynamic team level into the macro-dynamic enterprise level, the Scrum Guide does note, "*If the definition of "done" for an increment is part of the conventions, standards or guidelines of the development organization, all Scrum Teams must follow it as a minimum.*" As Scrum continues to grow, if it really wants to fulfill its mission to transform the world of work, it will need more practitioners to embrace more formalized standards as the above quote implies.

Recommended Reading

- *Agile Product Management with Scrum: Creating Products that Customers Love,* by Mike Cohn (Addison-Wesley Professional; April 2010)
- *Exploring Scrum: The Fundamentals,* by Dan Rawsthorne and Doug Shimp (CreateSpace Independent Publishing Platform; July 2011)

Chapter Close-Out

Practice Test

01. The Scrum Alliance is the largest professional user group in the Agile world and its best known certifications is:

    A. Certified ScrumMaster® (CSM)
    B. Certified Product Owner® (CSPO)
    C. Certified Scrum Professional® (CSP)
    D. Certified Scrum Trainer® (CST)

02. The seeds of Scrum were planted in 1986 when Hirotaka Takeuchi and Ikujiro Nonaka wrote ________________________________.

    A. PMBOK Guide®
    B. The New New Product Development Game
    C. Wicked Problems, Righteous Solutions
    D. The Scrum Guide

03. Peter DeGrace and Leslie Stahl first referenced the "Scrum approach" in their book ________________________________.

    A. PMBOK Guide®
    B. The New New Product Development Game
    C. Wicked Problems, Righteous Solutions
    D. The Scrum Guide

04. Jeff Sutherland and Ken Schwaber created ____________________ and made it available as a free download.

    A. PMBOK Guide®
    B. The New New Product Development Game
    C. Wicked Problems, Righteous Solutions
    D. The Scrum Guide

05. During Sprint Planning, the ___________________ creates the Reciprocal Commitment.

A. Soft Commit
B. Hard Commit
C. Signed contracts
D. Sprint Backlog

06. The Product Owner sets the logical order of ___________________ ___________________ for Increments.

A. Stakeholder Expectations
B. Daily Tasks
C. Development Priorities
D. Testing Procedures

07. The Product Owner's primary responsibility is to _____________ _____________________ of the product by optimizing the work of the Development Team.

A. Maximize the Deliverables
B. Maximize the Value
C. Maximize the Quality
D. Maximize the Scope

08. A process-centric meeting where the Development Team applies continuous improvement to its process of creating Increments is called the _______________.

A. Stakeholder Workshop
B. Daily Stand-Up
C. Sprint Review
D. Sprint Retrospective

09. A ________________ is a product-centric meeting where any interested or impacted stakeholder can come and see what was just finished.

A. Stakeholder Workshop
B. Daily Stand-Up
C. Sprint Review
D. Sprint Retrospective

10. The Scrum Master ensures the process is understood, shields the Development Team from outside interference and ________________________ for the Development Team.

A. Supports Roadmap Planning
B. Removes Obstacles
C. Leads Release Planning
D. Participates in Customer Decision Making

11. The ____________________________'s primary responsibility is to structure and manage the development work that fulfills the Definition of Done.

A. Scrum Team
B. Product Owner
C. Scrum Master
D. Development Team

12. Scrum use empirical process control – transparency, inspection, and adaptation. ________________________ means making important aspects of the process visible.

A. Adaptation
B. Inspection
C. Transparency
D. Adoption

13. Scrum use empirical process control – transparency, inspection, and adaptation. ______________________________ means frequently examining work products to detect undesirable variances.

A. Adaptation
B. Inspection
C. Transparency
D. Adoption

14. Scrum use empirical process control – transparency, inspection, and adaptation. ______________________________ means adjusting a process input to correct unacceptable deviations.

A. Adaptation
B. Inspection
C. Transparency
D. Adoption

15. A(n) ______________is an uncomplicated way to prioritize a collection of short descriptions of features, functions and capabilities.

A. Product Backlog
B. Feature List
C. Elevator Statement
D. Sprint Backlog

16. The specific subset of Product Backlog items the Development Team has committed to develop is referred to as a(n) ____________________.

A. Product Backlog
B. Feature List
C. Elevator Statement
D. Sprint Backlog

17. ____________________ is the process that prioritizes and clarifies Backlog items as they move from the long-term to a more near-term time horizon.

A. Roadmap Planning
B. Release Planning
C. Grooming or Refinement
D. Sprint Grooming

18. A meeting held primarily to synchronize the Scrum Master and Development Team members' activities is called a ____________________.

A. Daily Demo
B. Daily Scrum
C. Daily Review
D. Stand-up Meeting

19. The core process of Scrum is called ____________________.

A. The Daily Scrum
B. The Sprint Review
C. The Product Demo
D. The Sprint

20. __________________ is the definition of all the activities to finish and tests to fulfill before the work is complete.

A. Refactoring
B. Definition of Done
C. Acceptance Criteria
D. Conditions of Satisfaction

21. A meeting where the Scrum Team identifies how it can improve its process of creating Potentially Shippable Products is called a ____________________.

    A. Sprint Demo
    B. Daily Meeting
    C. Sprint Review
    D. Sprint Retrospective

22. According to the Scrum Guide, a(n) ____________________ is defined as, "The sum of all the Product Backlog items completed during a Sprint."

    A. Potentially Shippable Product
    B. Increment
    C. Sprint Backlog
    D. Velocity

23. ____________________ is used to track and monitor progress towards the Sprint Goal.

    A. Velocity
    B. Burn-Down Chart
    C. Burn-Up Chart
    D. Agile Report

24. Summing up the quantity of work remaining for each uncompleted Backlog item is called ____________________.

    A. Information Radiator
    B. Burn-Down Chart
    C. Velocity
    D. Visual Control

25. When the Scrum Guide describes the completion of an Increment as a mandatory shared understanding of what it means for work to be complete, it is called ______________.

A. Done

B. Done-Done

C. Definition of Done

D. Four Levels of Done

Fill-in-the-Blank Challenge

1. In addition to the Certified ScrumMaster®, the Scrum Alliance certifications that apply to members of the Development Team are ____________________________ and ____________________________.

2. The seeds of Scrum were planted in 1986 when Hirotaka Takeuchi and Ikujiro Nonaka wrote ____________________________.

3. Peter DeGrace and Leslie Stahl first referenced the "Scrum approach" in their book ____________________________.

4. Jeff Sutherland and Ken Schwaber created the ____________________ and made it available as a free download.

5. During Step Two of Sprint Planning, the Development Team makes the ____________________.

6. The Product Owner sets the logical order of ________________________ for Increments.

7. The Product Owner's primary responsibility is to ________________________ of the product by optimizing the work of the Development Team.

8. A process-centric meeting where the Scrum Team applies continuous improvement to its process of creating Increments is called the ____________________________.

9. A ____________________ is a product-centric meeting where any interested or impacted stakeholder can come and see what was just finished.

10. The Scrum Master ensures the process is understood, shields the Development Team from outside interference and ____________________________ for the Development Team.

11. The ______________________________________'s primary responsibility is to structure and manage the development work that fulfills the Definition of Done.

12. Scrum uses empirical process control – transparency, inspection, and adaptation. ____________________________ means making important aspects of the process visible.

13. Scrum uses empirical process control – transparency, inspection, and adaptation. ________________________________ means frequently examining work products to detect undesirable variances.

14. Scrum uses empirical process control – transparency, inspection, and adaptation. ___________________________ means adjusting a process input to correct unacceptable deviations.

15. A ____________________ is an uncomplicated way to prioritize short descriptions of features, functions and capabilities included in the solution.

16. The specific subset of Product Backlog items the Development Team has fully committed to develop that cannot be changed is referred to as a ________________________________.

17. ________________________________ is the process that prioritizes and clarifies Backlog items as they move from the long-term to a more near-term time horizon.

18. A meeting held primarily to synchronize the Scrum Master and Development Team members' activities is called a ________________________.

19. The core process of Scrum is called ________________________.

20. ______________________ is an agreement between the Development Team and Product Owner appropriate to the context of a project.

21. A meeting where the Development Team, Scrum Master and possibly the Product Owner, but no one else, attend is called a ___________________________.

22. According to the Scrum Guide a(n) ______________________ is defined as, "The sum of all the Product Backlog items completed during a Sprint."

23. ________________ is used to track and monitor progress towards the Sprint Goal.

24. Summing up the quantity of work remaining for each uncompleted Backlog item is called ____________________.

25. When the Scrum Guide describes the completion of an Increment as a mandatory shared understanding of what it means for work to be complete it is called _________.

Terminology Matching Exercise

In the blank column to the left of the Term, fill in the letter that identifies the correct Definition or Description.

	TERM		DEFINITION / DESCRIPTION
	1. Hard Commit	A	A cross-functional group that creates solutions
	2. Product Owner	B	Product-centric meeting where interested or impacted stakeholders can see what was just finished
	3. Sprint Retrospectives	C	Shields the Development Team from outside interference and removes impediments
	4. Sprint Review	D	Represents the customer and stakeholders
	5. Scrum Master	E	Process-centric meetings where the Scrum Team applies continuous improvement
	6. Development Team	F	Making important aspects of the process visible for those making decisions
	7. Transparency	G	Creates the Reciprocal Commitment
	8. Inspection	H	Prioritized collection list of all the product features
	9. Adaptation	I	Descriptions of the items to be developed and the Development Team's plan to fulfill the Sprint Goal
	10. Product Backlog	J	Examining work products to detect undesirable variances
	11. Sprint Backlog	K	Adjusting the development process to correct unacceptable deviations
	12. Refinement	L	A 15-minute time-boxed meeting the Scrum Master and Development Team use
	13. Daily Scrum	M	The sum of all the Product Backlog items completed during a Sprint and the value of the Increments of all previous Sprints
	14. Sprint	N	Ongoing activity that increases the granularity of items as they move to the current time horizon
	15. Increment	O	The core process of Scrum

Answers - Practice Test

1. **A.** The Scrum Alliance is the largest professional user group in the Agile world and its best known certifications is the **CERTIFIED SCRUMMASTER® (CSM)**

   The Scrum Alliance is the largest professional user group in the Agile world. Its flagship certification, the Certified ScrumMaster® (CSM), has the highest name recognition and largest market share of any Agile certification at the time of this writing (July 2015).

2. **B.** The seeds of Scrum were planted in 1986 when Hirotaka Takeuchi and Ikujiro Nonaka wrote **THE NEW NEW PRODUCT DEVELOPMENT GAME.**

   The seeds of Scrum were planted in 1986 when Hirotaka Takeuchi and Ikujiro Nonaka wrote The New New Product Development Game. (Harvard Business Review).

3. **C.** Peter DeGrace and Leslie Stahl first referenced the "Scrum approach" in their book **WICKED PROBLEMS, RIGHTEOUS SOLUTIONS.**

4. **D.** Jeff Sutherland and Ken Schwaber created the **SCRUM GUIDE** and made it available as a free download.

   The Scrum Guide was created by Jeff Sutherland and Ken Schwaber and the most recent version of the Scrum Guide (2013) is available as a free download.

5. **B.** During Sprint Planning the **HARD COMMIT** creates the Reciprocal Commitment.

   The Hard Commit creates the Reciprocal Commitment. During step one of Sprint Planning, the Development Team makes the "Soft Commit" meaning they think they can fulfill the proposed Sprint Backlog. In step two, after some analysis, when they are confident they can do it, they make the "Hard Commit."

6. **C.** The Product Owner sets the logical order of **DEVELOPMENT PRIORITIES** for Increments.

   The Product Owner is the "voice of the customer" representing the stakeholders and the business, and setting the logical order of development priorities for Increments.

7. **B.** The Product Owner's primary responsibility is to **MAXIMIZE THE VALUE** of the product by optimizing the work of the Development Team.

   The Product Owner's primary responsibility is to maximize the value of the product, for both the customer and organization, by optimizing the work of the Development Team. The Product Owner's biggest tool for achieving their goal is managing the Product Backlog by defining the logical order of development with clearly expressed stories.

8. **D.** A process-centric meeting where the Scrum Team applies continuous improvement to its process of creating Increments is called the **SPRINT RETROSPECTIVE.**

   Sprint Retrospectives are process-centric meetings where the Scrum Team applies continuous improvement to its process of creating Increments.

9. **C. A SPRINT REVIEW** is a product-centric meeting where any interested or impacted stakeholder can come and see what was just finished.

   The Sprint Review is a product-centric meeting where any interested or impacted stakeholder can come and see what was just finished as the next piece of the project puzzle. They give feedback and ask questions that produce actionable insight the Product Owner uses to groom the Product Backlog.

10. **B.** The **Scrum Master** ensures the process is understood, shields the Development Team from outside interference and REMOVES OBSTACLES for the Development Team.

    The Scrum Master (SM) ensures the process is understood and followed, shielding the Development Team from outside interference and removing impediments for the Development Team. The Scrum Master's primary responsibility is to ensure the Scrum Team understands and applies the principles of Scrum properly.

11. **D.** The **DEVELOPMENT TEAM'S** primary responsibility is to structure and manage the development work that fulfills the Definition of Done.

    The Development Team is a cross-functional group, which creates solutions by analyzing, designing, developing, testing, and implementing deliverables. The Development Team's primary responsibility is to structure and manage the development work that fulfills the Definition of Done committed to during Sprint Planning.

12. **C.** Scrum uses empirical process control – transparency, inspection, and adaptation. TRANSPARENCY means making important aspects of the process visible.

    Scrum uses empirical process control – transparency, inspection, and adaptation. Transparency is defined as making important aspects of the process visible for those making decisions about the outcome to enable a shared understanding of what has occurred.

13. **B.** Scrum uses empirical process control – transparency, inspection, and adaptation. **INSPECTION** means frequently examining work products to detect undesirable variances.

    Scrum uses empirical process control – transparency, inspection, and adaptation. Inspection is defined as frequently examining work products to detect undesirable variances that could negatively impact progress toward a desired outcome.

14. **A.** Scrum uses empirical process control – transparency, inspection, and adaptation. **ADAPTATION** means adjusting a process input to correct unacceptable deviations.

    Scrum uses empirical process control – transparency, inspection, and adaptation. Adaptation is defined as adjusting a process input or the development process to correct unacceptable deviations from the defined standard that were detected during inspection.

15. **A. A PRODUCT BACKLOG** is an uncomplicated way to prioritize a collection of short descriptions of features, functions and capabilities.

    The Product Backlog is a prioritized collection of cards or a list of all the features that are envisioned in the final product. The Product Owner holds it in a specific place, physical or electronic, and each item has a description, prioritization, approximation of development cost, and assessment of customer value.

16. **D.** The specific subset of Product Backlog items the Development Team has committed to develop is referred to as a **SPRINT BACKLOG.**

    The Sprint Backlog contains descriptions of the items to be developed and the Development Team's plan for development that fulfills the Sprint Goal. It creates transparency and also provides enough detail to enable the Development Team to make adjustments during the Daily Scrum as progress is better understood.

17. **C. GROOMING** or **REFINEMENT** is the process that prioritizes and clarifies Backlog items as they move from the long-term to a more near-term time horizon.

    Grooming, or as the Scrum Guide calls it, Product Backlog refinement, is an ongoing activity that increases the granularity of the details about Product Backlog items as they move from a more distant time horizon to a more current time horizon and the likelihood of understanding what will actually be developed increases.

18. **B.** A meeting held primarily to synchronize the Development Team members' activities is called a **DAILY SCRUM.**

    The Daily Scrum is time-boxed to 15-minutes. The Scrum Master and Development Team use it to synchronize activities. The meetings are held at the same time and place each day. Every Development Team member answers three questions.

19. **D.** The core process of Scrum is called **THE SPRINT.**

    The Sprint is the core process of Scrum. It uses a time-box with a consistent duration throughout development. Each Sprint starts immediately following the previous Sprint with a Sprint Planning ceremony.

20. **B. DEFINITION OF DONE** is the definition of all the activities to finish and tests to fulfill before the work is complete.

    Definition of Done is defined as the description of all the activities to finish and tests to fulfill before a Story or Task is considered complete. It is an agreement between the Development Team and Product Owner appropriate to the context of a project.

21. **D.** A meeting where the Scrum Team identifies how it can improve its process of creating Increments is called a **SPRINT RETROSPECTIVE.**

    Sprint Retrospectives are process-centric meetings where the Scrum Team applies continuous improvement to its process of creating Increments.

22. **B.** According to the Scrum Guide, a(n) **INCREMENT** is defined as, "The sum of all the Product Backlog items completed during a Sprint."

    Increment is defined as, "the sum of all the Product Backlog items completed during a Sprint and the value of the increments of all previous Sprints" by the Scrum Guide.

23. **A. VELOCITY** is used to track and monitor progress towards the Sprint Goal.

    Velocity is used to track and monitor progress towards the Sprint Goal. Velocity is recorded by summing up the quantity of work remaining for each uncompleted Backlog item.

24. **C.** Summing up the quantity of work remaining for each uncompleted Backlog item, is called **VELOCITY.**

    Velocity is used to track and monitor progress towards the Sprint Goal. Velocity is recorded by summing up the quantity of work remaining for each uncompleted Backlog item.

25. **A.** When the Scrum Guide describes the completion of an Increment as a mandatory shared understanding of what it means for work to be complete, it is called **DONE.**

    Done, when used to describe the completion of an Increment, is defined as a mandatory "shared understanding of what it means for work to be complete, (and) to ensure transparency. This is the definition of "Done" for the Scrum Team and is used to assess when work is complete on the product Increment" according to the Scrum Guide.

Answers - Fill-in-the-Blank Challenge

1. In addition to the Certified ScrumMaster®, the Scrum Alliance certifications that apply to members of the Development Team are **CERTIFIED PRODUCT OWNER®** and **CERTIFIED SCRUM DEVELOPER®.**

   The Scrum Alliance certifications that apply to members of the Development Team are Certified Product Owner® and Certified Scrum Developer®, at the time of this writing (July 2015).

2. The seeds of Scrum were planted in 1986 when Hirotaka Takeuchi and Ikujiro Nonaka wrote **THE NEW NEW PRODUCT DEVELOPMENT GAME.**

   The seeds of Scrum were planted in 1986 when Hirotaka Takeuchi and Ikujiro Nonaka wrote The New New Product Development Game. (Harvard Business Review).

3. Peter DeGrace and Leslie Stahl first referenced the "Scrum approach" in their book **WICKED PROBLEMS, RIGHTEOUS SOLUTIONS.**

4. Jeff Sutherland and Ken Schwaber created the **SCRUM GUIDE** and made it available as a free download.

   The Scrum Guide was created by Jeff Sutherland and Ken Schwaber and the most recent version of the Scrum Guide (2013) is available as a free download.

5. During Step Two of Sprint Planning the Development Team makes the **HARD COMMIT.**

   During Step One of Sprint Planning, the Development Team makes the "Soft Commit" meaning they think they can fulfill the proposed Sprint Backlog." In Step Two, after some analysis, when they are confident they can do it, they make the "Hard Commit." The Hard Commit creates the Reciprocal Commitment.

6. The Product Owner sets the logical order of **DEVELOPMENT PRIORITIES** for Increments.

   The Product Owner is the "voice of the customer" representing the stakeholders and the business, and setting the logical order of development priorities for Increments.

7. The Product Owner's primary responsibility is to **MAXIMIZE THE VALUE** of the product by optimizing the work of the Development Team.

   The Product Owner's primary responsibility is to maximize the value of the product, for both the customer and organization, by optimizing the work of the Development Team. The Product Owner's biggest tool for achieving their goal is managing the Product Backlog by defining the logical order of development with clearly expressed Stories.

8. A process-centric meeting where the Scrum Team applies continuous improvement to its process of creating Increments is called the **SPRINT RETROSPECTIVE.**

   Sprint Retrospectives are process-centric meetings where the Scrum Team applies continuous improvement to its process of creating Increments.

9. A **SPRINT REVIEW** is a product-centric meeting where any interested or impacted stakeholder can come and see what was just finished.

   The Sprint Review is a product-centric meeting where any interested or impacted stakeholder can come and see what was just finished as the next piece of the project puzzle. They give feedback and ask questions that produce actionable insight for the Product Owner to use to groom the Product Backlog.

10. The Scrum Master ensures the process is understood, shields the Development Team from outside interference and **REMOVES OBSTACLES** for the Development Team.

    The Scrum Master ensures the process is understood and followed, shielding the Development Team from outside interference and removing impediments. The Scrum Master's primary responsibility is to ensure the Scrum Team understands and applies the principles of Scrum properly.

11. The **DEVELOPMENT TEAM'S** primary responsibility is to structure and manage the development work that fulfills the Definition of Done.

    The Development Team is a cross-functional group, which creates solutions by analyzing, designing, developing, testing, and implementing deliverables. The Development Team's primary responsibility is to structure and manage the development work that fulfills the Definition of Done committed to during Sprint Planning.

12. Scrum uses empirical process control – transparency, inspection, and adaptation. **TRANSPARENCY** means making important aspects of the process visible.

    Scrum uses empirical process control – transparency, inspection, and adaptation. Transparency is defined as making important aspects of the process visible for those making decisions about the outcome to enable a shared understanding of what has occurred.

13. Scrum uses empirical process control – transparency, inspection, and adaptation. **INSPECTION** means frequently examining work products to detect undesirable variances.

    Scrum uses empirical process control – transparency, inspection, and adaptation. Inspection is defined as frequently examining work products to detect undesirable variances that could negatively impact progress toward a desired outcome.

14. Scrum use empirical process control – transparency, inspection, and adaptation. **ADAPTATION** means adjusting a process input to correct unacceptable deviations.

    Scrum uses empirical process control – transparency, inspection, and adaptation. Adaptation is defined as adjusting a process input or the development process to correct unacceptable deviations from the defined standard that were detected during inspection.

15. A **PRODUCT BACKLOG** is an uncomplicated way to prioritize short descriptions of features, functions and capabilities included in the solution.

    The Product Backlog is a prioritized collection of cards or a list of all the features that are envisioned in the final product. The Product Owner holds it in a specific place, physical or electronic, and each item has a description, prioritization, approximation of development cost, and assessment of customer value.

16. The specific subset of Product Backlog items the Development Team has fully committed to develop that cannot be changed is referred to as a **SPRINT BACKLOG.**

    The Sprint Backlog contains descriptions of the items to be developed and the Development Team's plan for development that fulfills the Sprint Goal. It creates transparency and also provides enough detail to enable the Development Team to make adjustments during the Daily Scrum as progress is better understood.

17. **GROOMING** or **REFINEMENT** is the process that prioritizes and clarifies Backlog items as they move from the long-term to a more near-term time horizon.

    Grooming, or as the Scrum Guide calls it, Product Backlog refinement, is an ongoing activity that increases the granularity of the details about Product Backlog items as they move from a more distant time horizon to a more current time horizon and the likelihood of understanding what will actually be developed increases.

18. A meeting held primarily to synchronize the Scrum Master and Development Team's activities is called a **DAILY SCRUM.**

    The Daily Scrum is time-boxed to 15-minutes. The Scrum Master and Development Team use it to synchronize activities. The meetings are held at the same time and place each day. Every team member answers three questions.

19. The core process of Scrum is called **THE SPRINT.**

    The Sprint is the core process of Scrum. It uses a time-box with a consistent duration throughout development. Each Sprint starts immediately following the previous Sprint with a Sprint Planning ceremony.

20. **DEFINITION OF DONE** is an agreement between the Team and Product Owner appropriate to the context of a project.

    Definition of Done is defined as the description of all the activities to finish and tests to fulfill before a Story or Task is considered complete. It is an agreement between the Development Team and Product Owner appropriate to the context of a project.

21. A meeting where the Development Team, Scrum Master and possibly the Product Owner, but no one else, attend is called a **SPRINT RETROSPECTIVE.**

    Sprint Retrospectives are process-centric meetings where the Scrum Team applies continuous improvement to its process of creating Increments.

22. According to the Scrum Guide a(n) **INCREMENT** is defined as, "The sum of all the Product Backlog items completed during a Sprint."

    Increment is defined as, "The sum of all the Product Backlog items completed during a Sprint and the value of the increments of all previous Sprints" by the Scrum Guide.

23. **VELOCITY** is used to track and monitor progress towards the Sprint Goal.

    Velocity is used to track and monitor progress towards the Sprint Goal. Velocity is recorded by summing up the quantity of work remaining for each uncompleted Backlog item.

24. Summing up the quantity of work remaining for each uncompleted Backlog item is called **VELOCITY.**

    Velocity is used to track and monitor progress towards the Sprint Goal. Velocity is recorded by summing up the quantity of work remaining for each uncompleted Backlog item.

25. When the Scrum Guide describes the completion of an Increment as a mandatory shared understanding of what it means for work to be complete, it is called **DONE.**

    Done when used to describe the completion of an Increment is defined as a mandatory "shared understanding of what it means for work to be complete, (and) to ensure transparency. This is the definition of "Done" for the Scrum Team and is used to assess when work is complete on the product Increment" according to the Scrum Guide.

Answers - Terminology Matching

1:G, 2:D, 3:E, 4:B, 5:C, 6:A, 7:F, 8:J, 9:K, 10:H, 11:I, 12:N, 13:L, 14:O, 15:M

Chapter End Notes

[21]Takeuchi, H., & Nonaka, I. (1986, January-February). *The new new product development game.* Harvard Business Review, 64(1), 137-146.

[22]DeGrace, P., & Stahl, L. H. (1990). *Wicked problems, righteous solutions: A catalogue of modern software engineering paradigms.* New York: Prentice Hall.

[23]Sprint is the Scrum-specific term for Iteration.

[24]Increment became the Scrum-specific term that replaced the original Potentially Shippable Product and approximates the Traditional term deliverables.

[25]Sprint Goal is the Scrum-specific term that approximates the Traditional term milestone.

[26]User Stories is the Scrum-specific term that approximates the Traditional term requirement or specification and the *PMBOK Guide®* terms Work Package or Activity.

[27]Product Backlog is the Scrum-specific term that approximates the Traditional and *PMBOK Guide®* term Project Scope.

[28]Or perhaps those dogmatic positions are why so many organizations that start with Scrum grow beyond it and begin using a customized approach referred to as Hybrid.

[29]The Seven-Second Rule was developed by John Stenbeck and has been taught to many thousands of GR8PM students in classes around the world since 1998.

[30]This same continuum in Traditional project management is referred to as Rough Order of Magnitude (ROM), Budgetary and Definitive and is documented in the *PMBOK Guide®*.

CHAPTER

5

eXtreme Programming (XP) Deep Dive

Chapter Highlights

In this chapter you will find an overview of eXtreme Programming (XP) as well as a detailed description of its key elements. Those elements are broken out as the Roles, Workflow, Ceremonies and Artifacts. The people who work in the XP Framework are identified by the Roles they fulfill. The Workflow details how those people work together and produce the planned results. Lastly, the Artifacts are the electronic or printed evidence of the results.

Overview of eXtreme Programming (XP)

eXtreme Programming (XP) originated with Kent Beck while he was working on a Chrysler compensation system project in early 1996. For several years he created and refined a software-specific development method and in 1999 published *Extreme Programming Explained.* Chrysler cancelled the project in 2000 after being acquired by Daimler-Benz, but eXtreme Programming had been born!

Although many of XP's specific practices were new, it was founded on proven best practices and described its approach as "taking 'best practices' to extreme levels." One example was using the test-first development practices used and proven on NASA's Project Mercury in the early 1960s and taking it to the extreme, automating the tests to validate small sections of software code and thereby shorten total development time.

While Kent Beck was working at Chrysler, software development practices were being reshaped by both object-oriented programming, which replaced procedural programming, and the growth of the Internet, as a competitive arena, driven by a critical need for speed-to-market. He seized the opportunity to champion practice changes at Chrysler. Serendipitously, Beck also invited Ron Jeffries, who has become well recognized throughout the XP domain, to get involved to help refine them.

A large community of software developers adopted XP and as it grew, XP moved into many development environments not envisioned at its origin. For example, the high discipline of daily integration testing required by the original practices got modified to allow development of more complex features over multi-day periods using periodic testing to detect non-compatible code before too much work was invested. The XP community's website *www.extremeprogramming.org* was launched in 1999 and continues to be a good source for information.

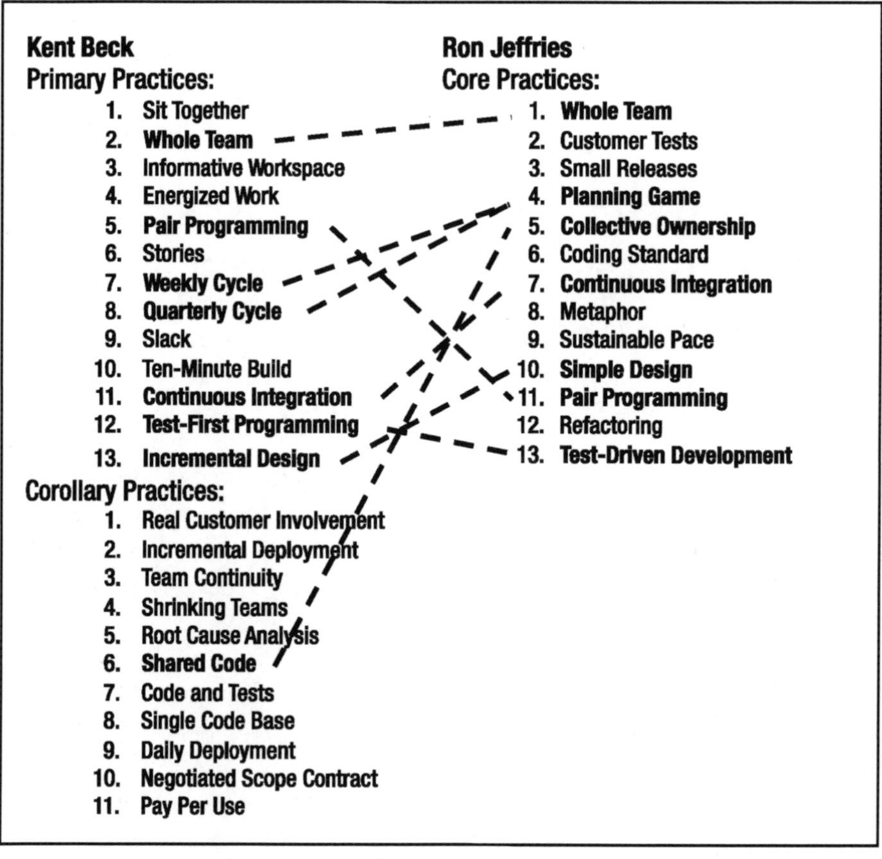

Figure 5.1 | *Kent Beck and Ron Jeffries' Practices*

During those early years, Kent Beck and Ron Jeffries became thought leaders in the eXtreme Programming world and remain so today. Beck has written a second edition of his book with an expanded array of values and practices. Jeffries has also written several books. Along the way, their explanations and interpretations have moved in different directions. Seeing these differences between Jeffries and Beck's outlines of XP practices explains why it is no surprise that XP practices are strongly debated. (Figure 5.1)

One of XP's important assumptions is that a unified client viewpoint exists. When that assumption is correct, XP is productive. Otherwise it is risky at best. That assumption drives the practice of having an on-site customer that proponents cite as providing needed flexibility while reducing cost. Critics claim it causes rework and scope creep.

Another point of controversy within XP surrounds the belief that requirements must be defined incrementally not in advance, and that those requirements must be expressed as acceptance tests not specifications. XP subscribes to the philosophy, "No Big Design Up Front" advocating for design activity starting with "the simplest thing that could possibly work" and adding complexity only to overcome failed tests. Critics claim this results in constant re-designing as requirements emerge.

Matt Stephens and Doug Rosenberg's book *Extreme Programming Refactored: The Case Against XP* (Apress 2003) questioned the value of the XP, arguing that XP's practices are interdependent and, because few organizations adopt all of them, fail entirely. They even went so far as to compare XP's "collective ownership" model to socialism and its evils.

Many practitioners believe the criticisms, while not entirely without merit, are driven more by misunderstandings than reality. Regardless, three things are certain. First, XP is here to stay. Second, XP's practices conform to Agile values and Lean principles. Third, as with Scrum, users of XP invariably tailor their process over time to meet organizational needs and the result is a Hybrid approach to managing projects.

For the remainder of this deep dive, because there isn't a single generally accepted authority for XP, like the *PMBOK® Guide* for Traditional approaches, the content presented will start with Kent Beck's work as the baseline and integrate other work as appropriate. That means, some points of information may disagree slightly, or even be in direct conflict with one another, not because it is mistakenly written but because there is disagreement within the

XP community. Please recall that the goal of this almanac is to serve the entire community by presenting best practices without advocating for any particular position or school of thought.

Roles

In XP, the Team is a group including some or all of the roles for an Architect, Coach, Customer, Interaction Designer, Product Manager, Programmer, Project Manager, Tester, Tracker, and even a super hero – Batman! The Team is self-directing and cross-functional in order to optimize flexibility and creativity, which in turn enhances productivity.

Architect

The ***Architect*** guides development through small, safe steps to modify the architecture without undermining its integrity so the best solution emerges as the product evolves. The Architect manages one of the biggest challenges for an XP team, maintaining stability while developing a complex solution in an uncertain environment. Architects partition systems along natural fracture lines into relatively independent parts so the Team can focus on developing a smaller, less complicated system. Then, the Architect uses large-scale refactoring and system level tests to validate the smaller systems as they are integrated successfully and expand into the full solution.

Coach

The ***Coach*** monitors the process and mentors the Team on XP processes and techniques, but is considered optional. The Coach helps the Team identify and focus on risks and optimization opportunities.

Customer

The ***Customer*** creates and prioritizes the Stories to be developed. Unlike other Agile Frameworks, the Customer can vary the release date by adding or removing Stories from the Backlog to be delivered in any given Release. Similar to other Frameworks, the Customer sets the development priorities.

Interaction Designer

The ***Interaction Designer*** chooses a simple description of the program vision as a metaphor that the Team uses to guide system development choices as they write Stories and evaluate progress towards the completed system. The Interaction Designer uses tools like Personas and goals to help the Team analyze and understand the user's world.

Product Manager

The ***Product Manager*** encourages communication about important customer concerns so the Team can respond to them. The Product Manager writes Stories and also prioritizes them in quarterly and weekly cycles, answering clarifying questions as the Team encounters Stories they don't understand. Because a plan in XP is considered an expression of what could happen, not a guarantee of what will happen, Product Managers groom the logical development sequence for business value, not technical efficiency. Their goal is to develop a system that meets the Customer's particular needs and is also valuable and competitive in the marketplace.

Programmer

The ***Programmer*** role is the simplest to describe, but that doesn't mean it is the easiest to fulfill. The Programmer estimates Stories, defines tests, writes code, usually working with a partner as a "pair", and accepts responsibility for completing the tasks that ultimately deliver a successful result. The Programmer is the engine that drives the rest of the XP value chain.

Project Manager

The ***Project Manager*** facilitates communication by keeping plans synchronized with reality because planning in XP is a continuous activity not a phase. Packaging that information so it is helpful to all stakeholders in an environment where the information changes frequently is an immense challenge with significant consequences when it is not done well.

Tester

The ***Tester*** coaches the Customer on selecting system-level tests that will define and validate acceptable functioning of the system before development and improve deployment of the system after development. Testers must be skilled at looking beyond what happens when things go right and asking the critical questions that uncover what will happen when something goes wrong. Testers also guide Programmers on implementing testing techniques that ensure the tests only succeed when Stories are correctly developed and can be implemented and deployed.

Tracker

The ***Tracker,*** another preferred but optional position, monitors team progress and warns when redistributing tasks might be required to adjust the schedule. Sometimes a Programmer "doubles" as Tracker for the same pair, and sometimes a Programmer serves as Tracker for a different pair.

Batman

The ***Batman*** is the super hero who must handle organizational emergencies and support requests so that the Programmers and Team aren't diverted from their work. While a mask and cape are optional, nerves of steel are mandatory!

Workflow

Unlike other Agile Frameworks that are intended to be lightweight, XP has a substantial structure and contains specific practices designed to work together as an integrated system.

At the highest-level, XP starts with a quarterly planning cycle focused on understanding and aligning the project goal within the organization's bigger objectives. The Release Plan is a quarterly plan that is progressively elaborated into a weekly cycle of plans.

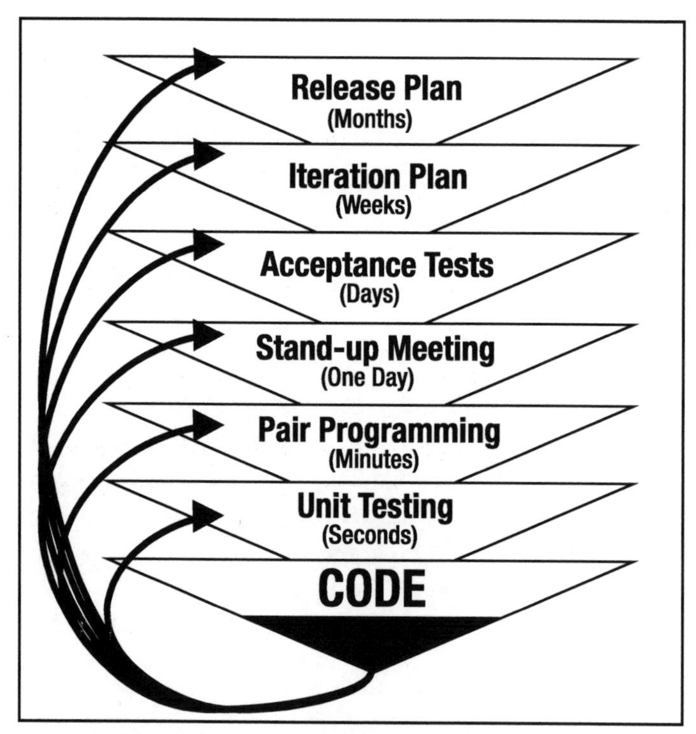

Figure 5.2| *XP Workflow and Feedback Loops*

At the start of each week, the Team reviews its progress by comparing actual Stories completed versus planned Stories for the prior week. With that information clarified, the Customer picks another group of Stories to be the current week's work for the Team. The Stories selected are expected to produce another specific step of progress towards to the project goal. (Figure 5.2)

Next, acceptance tests are defined with the Team members helping to develop and refine them. Once the Stories and acceptance tests are defined, the work and Daily Stand-up Meetings begin.

The work is done using the Pair Programming best practice. The Stories are decomposed into Tasks and an estimate of how long each Task is likely to take to complete is made. Then, team members take personal ownership of specific Tasks. Doing so creates internal team accountability as well as an opportunity to demonstrate individual technical mastery and succeed.

However, even though each Task is individually owned, the programming is done in pairs. That means the pair will choose a Task, decide how to develop it, negotiate who starts, clarify what they'll focus on first, and all the other details associated with two people working on one specific piece of code, the Task, together. Pair programming is an ongoing dialog of simultaneous programming and continuously improvement of the approach to programming.

In Pair Programming environments it is not uncommon to rotate partners frequently with some teams even using a timer to shift partners at regular intervals, such as sixty or ninety minutes. Programming with a new partner every couple of hours may sound counter-intuitive, but creating a cadence of natural breaks by switching partners resets and refreshes the mental focus and energy before productivity goes stale. It also reduces errors by continuously readjusting the perspective used to evaluate the work.

As code is written it is subject to Unit Testing as early, often, and automatically as possible. Testing is important because the goal of development is to reduce defect frequency to an economically desirable level that increases competitive advantage. Defects also destroy customer trust and undermine their confidence in the Team's progress reports. Quality increases stakeholder belief in the Team to a level that is reasonable and warranted.

Defects are expensive, but eliminating defects is also expensive. The belief that most defects cost more than preventing them is widely held. Certainly the principle of double-checking, first by stating in a test what the code is supposed to do, then running the code against the test, is reliable and cost effective. If both expressions of code behavior match, then the code is likely to be correct because the chance of making precisely offsetting errors is small.

However, the widely accepted principle of Defect Cost Increase (DCI) that states, "The sooner the defect is found, the cheaper it is to fix" has both proponents and critics. Because the idea is so intuitive the proponents exceed the critics by a significant number, but that does not mean they are automatically correct. (Figure 5.3)

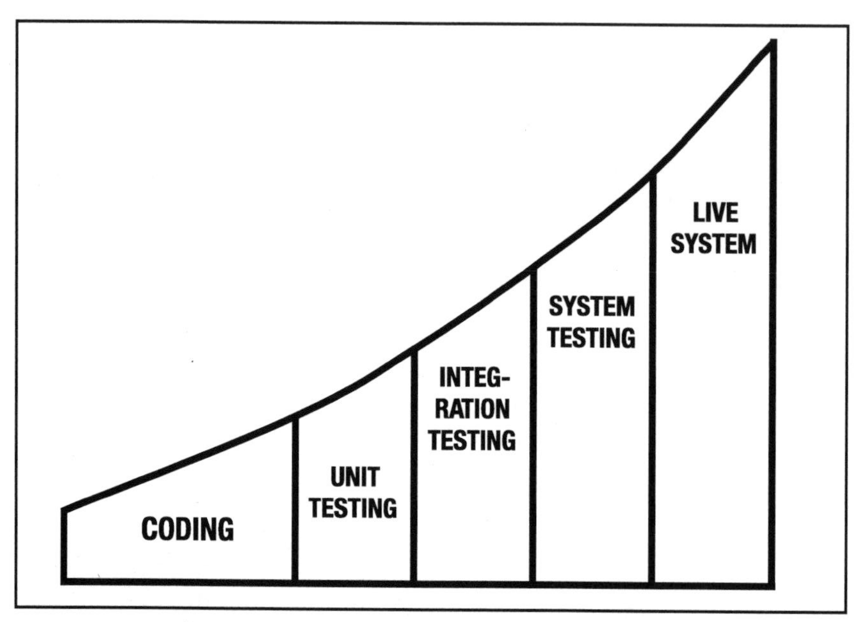

Figure 5.3| *Defect Cost Increase (DCI)*

Cost-per-defect data regarding the economic value of software quality has been around for more than three decades. Scores of articles and books have stated things like, "It costs 10 times (or even 100 times) as much to fix a defect after release as during development." The typical data varies depending on the study, but the pattern usually comes out something like fixing a defect identified during the Requirements Phase costs $250, during Design costs $500, and finally, after Release costs $5,000.

Even though that may be mathematically true, studies have shown the actual time required to repair a defect varies little regardless of when it is discovered. The real cause driving added cost is the potential cascade of additional issues associated with defects discovered late in the process, not the cost of fixing the specific defect.

The misunderstanding is caused by hidden assumptions that get overlooked. For example, the cost per defect (or anything else) is always cheapest where the greatest numbers are found. Therefore, because bugs are more plentiful at the beginning than at the end of development, the purported increased cost is artificial. The cost per defect will always get higher until it reaches to infinity when zero defects are produced.

So even though cost-per-defect may be an urban legend when it is used to justify early detection and removal, what is far more important is the economic value of improved software quality. Improved quality drives shorter development schedules, reducing development costs as well as potentially creating a competitive advantage in the marketplace for the Organization. That is the correct reason to support testing as early, often, and automatically as possible.

In summary, the XP workflow is Agile because it uses a Lean engineering process to produce software.

Ceremonies

In the previous chapter, the four ceremonies of Scrum – Sprint, Daily Scrum, Sprint Review and Sprint Retrospective – were described. However, describing the ceremonies of XP is difficult because it varies, as Figure 5.1 demonstrated, depending on which source is used – Kent Beck, Ron Jeffries, or another thought leader. After considering the various points of agreement and divergence, three ceremonies at three levels were identified as the best expression of common ground. At the highest level, three Organizational ceremonies – Whole Team, Planning Game, and Test-Driven Development – establish the necessary environment for the Team. At the second level, three Team ceremonies – Incremental Architectural Design, Pair Programming, Collective Code Ownership – help the Team be as powerful and productive as possible. And finally, at the lowest level, three Technical ceremonies – Small Releases, Ten-Minute Build, and Continuous Integration – support the Team's work and ensure that software delivered is sturdy enough to handle current demands and robust enough to facilitate future improvements. (Figure 5.4)

Whole Team

The ***Whole Team XP*** ceremony directly addresses the issue that software development, at its core, is a complex challenge in an environment of high uncertainty. Therefore defining a "whole team" is a dynamic undertaking to assemble a variety of people that must interlink their perspectives to create the work that will make the project successful.

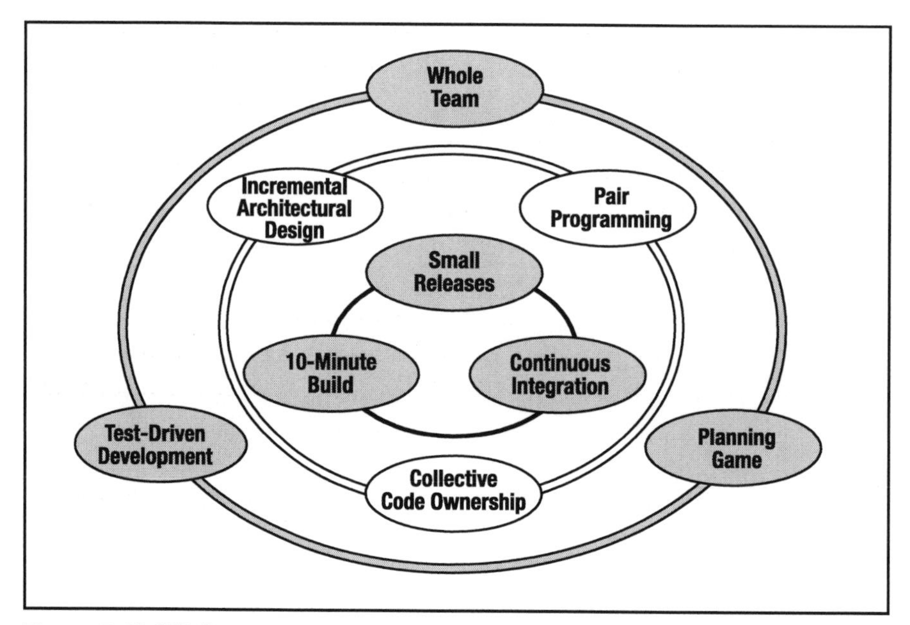

Figure 5.4| *XP Ceremonies*

That means each team member has to seek power through information sharing not information hoarding or else the very health of the project will be threatened. They must interact and identify with being part of the Team more so than with their department or function. They must see themselves as part of a relay team or mountain climbing expedition where every member is voluntarily "roped together" figuratively and literally as they race the competition or summit Mt. Everest. If they argue about who is running the most important lap or who gets to be first in the rope line then the whole team will fail.

Testers who help Customers choose tests are just as important and must be complementary partners with Interaction Designers, selecting personas to help the Team make sense of the world of the User. Likewise, the Architect working on large-scale system tests must be concerned with helping the Project Manager facilitate communication with the Stakeholders. By uniting, the Team gains power from caring for each other, which must be more important than other allegiances.

However, Whole Team means more than that. It means that the Organization must understand what an effective team looks like and embrace the XP philosophy to start where they are now and move toward the ideal. It means that defining new roles can be a bridge to learning new habits, but those changes must occur in an environment imbued with personal safety. It means having policies that support, even require, technical people to make technical decisions and business people to make business decisions, while also providing protection as they master those new responsibilities. It means accepting that conversation is integral to working together for XP teams, so loud raucous conversation is a sign of health whereas silence and avoiding fierce conversations is a sign of dysfunction.

Whole Team is a new paradigm for most organizations and presents challenges in both hiring and managing employees. The Whole Team interviewing and hiring process must take the next evolutionary step beyond behavior-based interviewing questions and require actual time working with an existing team for a day or two, or even a week. That is the best, and possibly only, way to test and evaluate both technical and social skills. After hiring, management of performance reviews and raises must be focused, first, on team performance, and second, on individual deliverables and achievements. This challenge can be addressed by leveraging XP's transparency, giving managers access to large amounts of information on which to base individual evaluations.

Whole Team management also means making a commitment to being team-centric. For example, it means creating workspace with physical and virtual Caves and Commons. Caves are small private spaces adjacent to or integrated with the large Team workspace, the Commons. Everyone shares the Commons area in order to facilitate instant or immediate communication. The Caves provide private space when Team members need to retreat and focus in order to solve a challenging issue.

Being team-centric also means, for instance, fracturing development not people. Team-centric development can be scaled up with multiple teams, but avoids requiring team members to be schizophrenic, constantly jumping back and forth between ten different projects. It means heeding the advice in *The Tipping Point* by Malcolm Gladwell to exercise caution at the two thresholds of discontinuity in team size, 12 and 150. Twelve is the limit of comfortable interaction for a team and 150 is the limit beyond which organizational units find the faces of everyone cannot be recognized. Across both of these thresholds it is harder to maintain trust. Trust is vital for XP. As a final illustration, it means keeping effective, well-functioning teams together while resisting the common urge in large organizations to abstract people into plug-and-pay objects. Ignoring the critical importance of relationships and trust in order to reduce scheduling challenges might maximize micro-efficiency, but it undermines macro-efficiency, known as organizational throughput. By keeping most teams stable while encouraging information sharing and a carefully evaluated amount of rotation-by-design, the Organization benefits from consistently high production and the spread of tribal knowledge.

Planning Game

The ***Planning Game*** ceremony enables organizations using XP to define a rough order of magnitude (ROM) plan for a project so the Team can refine it as the project progresses. It is a critical point of collaboration between Customer, Product Manager and Team where business value is defined by literally putting the cards on the table. The core purpose of this ceremony is to define the scope of the Release and the delivery order of features, functions and capabilities and discuss the technical impacts of choosing to implement the requirements in that order. The outcome is a shared understanding of the expected release dates and a collection of specific User Stories that will be broken down into Tasks so the Team can allocate its work.

Problems and questions are addressed by the people who understand what is needed and those doing the work, so the Planning Game produces a rough plan that is often a more accurate picture than any other approach could create. Connecting Customers and Programmers to meet a common goal using the simple, low-tech, high-touch tools of index cards or sticky notes is a very effective, proven technique. Using index cards or sticky notes is not mandatory, but it is highly recommended. It is mandatory that the Customer and each member of the Team accept responsibility for committing to give it their best.

Test-Driven Development

The ***Test-Driven Development*** ceremony used in XP is the same as the one described in Chapter 3. Test-driven development (TDD) is a four-step process that begins with creating a well-defined test, then invoking an operation to take the test and having a "fail" outcome, followed by doing something to change the operation, and finally invoking the modified operation to take the test and having a "pass" outcome. (reference Figure 3.11)

Because XP uses a rigorous TDD approach, it requires the test to be written before the code is developed and run frequently while the code is being written. Applying a rigid TDD discipline helps the Team limit scope creep because expectations are clearly and objectively stated. It also helps them develop robust designs because if a test is hard to write there is a likely design problem, like coupling and cohesion. It means that the code being written is clean, maybe even elegant, which fosters teammates' trust in one another. And lastly the process of test, code, and refactor is repeated over and over again creating a cadence that assists the twin goals of speed and quality.

Incremental Architectural Design

Saying incremental and architectural design may sound like an oxymoron, but it is the key to making XP powerful. Incremental progress within robust architecture is like the magic of compounded interest applied every week. It becomes an immensely significant return on investment! And since that's true, one might ask, "Why all the historical (and hysterical) confusion within the XP community about this topic?"

The cause seems to originate with those who are new to XP and the many who only have brief contact with XP interpreting the call for "No Big Design Up Front" to mean that software design must be put to death. The reality, however, is that XP requires serious architectural design that can be implemented incrementally using an evolutionary design strategy and practices. This approach raises new challenges and demands higher-level skills from Architects and Interaction Designers. The goal is to minimize waste caused by misunderstanding the real functionality needed on the Customer and Product Owner side and caused by redundant development and rework on the Team side.

As with the widely accepted principle of Defect Cost Increase (DCI) discussed previously, it has been a matter of software development orthodoxy for decades that the cost of changes increases over time. That assumption has received far too little scrutiny and may no longer be valid, especially if the right architecture is supporting incremental change. Without the right architecture, it is certain that the cost of changes will skyrocket, but more importantly, the outcome will be a brittle system that is difficult to adapt to changing Customer needs.

The ***Incremental Architectural Design*** ceremony means the Team works hard to create and apply a robust architecture where design investments are in proportion to system needs so the cost of changing during development doesn't rise exponentially. It entails defining an incremental design strategy where the system grows through gradual, predictable change, minimizing the cost of complexity and maximizing the probability that the simplest design will actually work. And it also means that the architecture provides enough design guidance to suit the current need without requiring the Team to do additional "what if" designing during development.

Because software can be endlessly replicated and extended at almost no cost, it is a game of insight, which means architecture and design are what make software inherently valuable. Comparing software development to construction makes this more tangible and understandable. It is unfeasible, if not outright impossible, to triple the size of a building by jacking it up to install a stronger foundation to create a skyscraper. But doing the same thing in software is close to a daily occurrence.

Software development is like starting with an apartment building and gradually replacing pieces until a skyscraper has been built, and doing it all with the tenants still living there. While that concept is ridiculous in the tangible world, it's the most sensible, low risk way to develop software. In fact, part of what makes the ceremony of Incremental Architectural Design so valuable is that development is often about writing new applications or extending old ones in ways that have not been done before. Designing and developing an increment that has just enough functionality to get actionable insight then using that feedback to improve the design of the next increment is why XP is, "design always" not, "design nothing." The price of the Incremental Architectural Design ceremony is the discipline to continuously invest in designs that make large changes in valuable functionality using small steps guided by robust architecture.

Pair Programming

The ***Pair Programming*** ceremony used in XP was briefly described above stating that Programmers take personal ownership of specific Tasks and that doing so creates internal team accountability. It also presents a personal opportunity to demonstrate technical mastery. However, even though each Task is individually owned, the programming pair chooses the Task, decides how to develop it, and negotiates who will code first as the Driver and who will peer review the code for errors as the Navigator. Pair programming is an ongoing dialog to continuously improve the approach to programming and the code being written simultaneously.

Although it may be counter intuitive, pair programming increases software quality without slowing down delivery and that increased quality often creates cost savings for the project. What's more, because it is common to pair experienced developers with junior developers so they can acquire tribal knowledge, it accelerates the growth of organizational competence.

Pairing experienced and junior developers does not mean, however, that it is a teacher-student relationship. It is a peer-to-peer cooperative working style that includes give and take from both partners. Pair programming is a social skill that takes time to learn. The best partners know when to say, "Let's try your idea first." The best approach to pair programming is for the partners to sit side-by-side in front of the computer and concentrate on the code being written as the Driver or Navigator and share observations.

Collective Code Ownership

Critics of XP have compared the "collective code ownership" model to socialism and its evils. But using that same logic, they'd also have to accuse the Toyota Production System of the same evil because everyone is empowered to stop the production line when a problem is identified.

The ***Collective Code Ownership*** ceremony used in XP means anyone on the Team can improve any part of the system at any time, as long as fixing it is not out of scope. Collective ownership encourages everyone to contribute improvement ideas, but the inherent risk is that everyone will become no one when responsibility for maintaining quality requires the courage to insist on disciplined adherence to standards. Quality will deteriorate if the Team hasn't developed a commitment to collective responsibility.

However, because today's software systems are so complex, it is impossible to imagine that one person, even the most amazing Chief Architect, can model and manage all of the details of the whole system in their mind. Also, because the size of teams working on systems are so large, without a commitment to Incremental Architectural Design there will invariably be Programmers changing the system without benefit of the Architect's vision. That means, in a certain sense, that Collective Code Ownership within the guidelines of Incremental Architectural Design may be the only option to successfully to distribute a cogent process among your team.

Another unavoidable aspect of this conundrum is that the only way to remove development bottlenecks is to empower the entire team to be responsible for system design. The Collective Code Ownership ceremony means every

Programmer creates unit tests as code is developed and every piece of code released into the source code repository includes the unit tests that ran at 100 percent. That requires every bit of code, from bug fixes to changes in legacy functionality, be subjected to automated testing as it is changed. Therefore, the test suite becomes the watchdog over the entire code repository. So ultimately, when combined with frequent integration, the practice of collective ownership is more reliable than having a single person responsible for controlling detailed design.

One final, often overlooked benefit of the Collective Code Ownership ceremony is that the test suite never sleeps, never takes a vacation, and especially never leaves the project for a better opportunity elsewhere.

Small Releases

The ***Small Releases*** ceremony used in XP is intrinsically linked to the Team's Incremental Architectural Design ceremony and the Organization's Planning Game ceremony.

XP teams apply the Small Releases ceremony by delivering operational, tested software at the end of every Iteration, creating the business value prioritized by the Customer. Whether the Customer chooses to use the software to solicit internal user feedback, demonstrate to their external customers or deploy it directly to production, the important consideration is that development progress and value creation are visible to the Customer frequently.

The Small Releases ceremony is technical and critical. It is technical because the software coding must be finished properly. It is critical because it is the only way to be absolutely sure the software being developed meets the Customer's expectations. The fact that the Release is small does not mean it can't deliver business value. As part of the continuous planning activity in XP, the Customer and Product Owner have collaborated with the Programmers to define the logical order of User Story development so that value is created. It is also critical because feedback is received early enough to have an impact on system development choices.

Another benefit of small releases is that estimating variances can be used validate or revise forecasts of future Releases closing the feedback loop to the Organization's Planning Game ceremony and flowing down to the Team's Incremental Architectural Design ceremony.

Ten-Minute Build

The ***Ten-Minute Build*** ceremony means that at all times during development, the system architecture and design is maintained in a way that allows for an automatic build of the whole system where all of the tests run in ten minutes or less.

The value of the Ten-Minute Build ceremony is that it facilitates many of the other ceremonies, including Test-Driven Development, Incremental Architectural Design and Collective Code Ownership. Given the likely complexity of the system being developed, having an automated and reliable build of the system that runs in ten minutes means it can be run many times a day thereby reducing risk. The build must run fast enough that Programmers will run it frequently. If the pair-programming partners can come up to clear their minds, grab a cup of coffee, and review the work just completed without having to wait too long for the build to finish before they can resume coding, they will run it and productivity will be optimized. If not, they won't run it and risk will rise as timely feedback decreases.

The Ten-Minute Build ceremony also supports the Continuous Integration ceremony that will be explained next. When the two ceremonies are both being used, developers establish a pattern of proactive habits that reinforce speed and quality happening simultaneously. Because they don't have to wait excessively, Programmers will consistently do a local clean build before committing changes to the repository. That habit will reduce integration errors that will otherwise occur as soon as the continuous integration build is run thereby optimizing team productivity.

One best practice to keep the build time focused on being under a ten minute maximum is to manage the build time from the beginning. Instead of making the mistake of letting the build get too long, the Team continuously prevents technical debt from piling up due to poorly written tests. For example, instead of writing end-to-end tests, they focus on unit and integration tests. They also apply standard metrics such as being able to run about 100 unit tests per second, limiting integration tests to less than fifteen percent of total tests, then leveraging dependency evaluation features of the build tool to avoid rebuilding any code or objects that haven't changed.

Continuous Integration

The ***Continuous Integration*** ceremony used in XP means integration is part of the daily workflow where Programmers integrate their code frequently and have it validated by an automated build tool using defined tests to detect errors so they can be fixed immediately. As a result, a team of Programmers can use a divide and conquer strategy, avoid integration problems and develop software that is cohesive and reliable. A common best practice is to integrate and test changes every hour or two. Without the Continuous Integration ceremony and an automated tool, integrating the work of multiple Programmers on a large team is unpredictable at best and often disastrous.

With continuous integration, the Programmer loads a copy of the source file onto the local development computer from a source code control system keeping all of the source code in a repository. This is referred to as "checking out" a working copy. Next, the Programmer modifies the working copy to do a new task or to do a task differently. This requires altering the working code and adding or editing automated tests. As the Programmer changes the code, periodic automated tests, called builds, are done to validate the new code works. When all of the changes are complete, a final build is done. If, and only if, the final build is error free is the new code considered ready to be committed to the repository.

The challenge that arises when a team of Programmers is working on a system is other Programmers have usually made simultaneous changes to the source code and those changes may clash. When that is the case it will show as a failure in the build or in the tests and the Programmer has two choices. Either take responsibility to edit the code and repeat the build until a working copy can be properly validated or roll back the changes.

When the Programmer has completed a working copy that is properly synchronized with the source code, the next step can be taken. The working copy goes through a build on an integration machine based on the source code. Only when the integration build succeeds are the changes are done. This final step ensures nothing was missed during the local build, such as the repository not having been properly updated.

Thus, each integration involves builds at two levels – the local machine and the integration machine – and both builds must finish and be error free before the Programmer can continue to another task because XP requires the build never be broken. The combination of double builds and automated testing means errors are detected rapidly so they can be fixed and a working build properly maintained.

With the Continuous Integration ceremony, the project never has a failed integration build for long. Good builds occur many times a day and bad builds are quickly fixed. The result is a stable software base and development that never gets too far off base so more time is spent generating additional valuable code and less time is spent finding and fixing bugs.

One final aspect of XP needs to be included under Ceremonies because it affects all of the other ceremonies even though it isn't a ceremony.

The environment where the Team works is one of immediacy and intimacy by design. In order to solve the challenging complex problems involved with producing serious software, the Team needs extremely high communication bandwidth. Being collocated in the Commons facilitates the necessary instant or immediate communication in a way that is referred to as osmotic communication. The name implies that Team members regularly pick up important data "by osmosis" which they otherwise might not get.

Acquiring the tribal knowledge vital to XP teams has been described as a practically effortless or unconscious assimilation of knowledge when teams are collocated. It is almost as if the mind becomes semi-permeable when it is engaged in solving a problem and, being immersed in an environment where team discussions are happening around the person whose mind is so engaged, causes information to flow in or act upon the mind. The result is often breakthrough ideas for solving design and coding problems.

Artifacts

Although XP has more ceremonial rigor than other Agile Frameworks, XP teams are expected to move fast and only maintain a few artifacts that are simple and valuable. The environment that XP works in is one of the drivers behind this philosophy. XP operates where designs emerge as insight grows, Customers choose a different outcome than originally envisioned, technologies suddenly appear, and the business climate shifts dramatically.

Artifacts are tangible or intangible output of development and production processes such as printed vision statements, elevator statements and team agreements or completed code files archived in a system repository.

In response, starting with the Planning Game ceremony, XP defines a quarterly Release Plan that produces a rough order of magnitude artifact. That quarterly plan is elaborated into a collection of weekly plans as artifacts with more granularity.

Those plans guide development that produces architectural and incremental designs as artifacts. The designs are documented with Stories that also become artifacts with tests that are related artifacts.

An often-overlooked artifact is documentation related to "throw away" code used for development Spikes that wasn't integrated and "checked in", or related to useful pieces of experiments and research.

Another category of artifacts are diagrams, abstractions and wall charts, often created on giant printers, that were important tools used to clarify design options and choices that led to the final, completed design. These artifacts come from the Architects and Designers, not the Programmers, but fill inevitable gaps when later discussions occur about how problems were discovered and solved.

And even though many of the artifacts are intangible and may have a short lifespan, they are still important project artifacts. The common best practice for recording and archiving the artifacts is a version control system with a central repository that provides a history of changes.

The core concept is that planning starts with units of customer-desired functionality that are approximately defined in Stories. The process is guided by the certainty that a system deployed with the right ten percent of functions will provide more business benefit than a system deployed with eighty percent of functions that were randomly, contractually or alphabetically chosen. As the right functions are created, maintaining that code and those tests as permanent artifacts is most important because Customers believe they are paying for what the system can do today as well as what it can be made to do tomorrow. Only the artifacts that contribute to providing those two sources of value are useful. Therefore the better development becomes at delivering business value, the more focused the artifacts should be also.

In conclusion, XP is explicitly defined as an Agile Framework for software development. That clear and narrow focus gives it the strength associated with doing one thing extremely well. As Agile continues to grow into many other fields, if XP maintains that singular focus, it will fulfill its mission to 'take "best practices" to extreme levels'.

Recommended Reading

- *Extreme Programming Explained: Embrace Change,* by Kent Beck with Cynthia Andres (Addison-Wesley; November 2004)

Chapter Close-Out

Practice Test

1. Because of work done by ________________, eXtreme Programming (XP) originated in early 1996 and was born in 1999 when he published *Extreme Programming Explained.*

   A. Matt Stephens
   B. Ron Jeffries
   C. Kent Beck
   D. Doug Rosenberg

2. One of XP's important assumptions is that ______________________ exists. Where that assumption is correct, XP is productive. Otherwise it is risky at best.

   A. Important *PMBOK Guide*® guidance
   B. A unified client viewpoint
   C. Wicked problems with a righteous solution
   D. XP solutions for software problems

3. The ______________ guides development through small, safe steps to modify the architecture without undermining its integrity so the best solution emerges as the product evolves.

   A. Architect
   B. Interaction Designer
   C. Programmer
   D. Tester

4. The ____________________ estimates Stories, defines tests, and writes code, usually working with a partner as a "pair".

   A. Architect
   B. Interaction Designer
   C. Programmer
   D. Tester

5. The ____________________ chooses a simple description of the program vision as a metaphor that the Team uses to guide system development choices.

   A. Architect
   B. Interaction Designer
   C. Programmer
   D. Tester

6. The ____________________ coaches the Customer on selecting system-level tests that will define and validate acceptable functioning of the system.

   A. Architect
   B. Interaction Designer
   C. Programmer
   D. Tester

7. The ____________________ encourages communication about important customer concerns so the Team can respond to them.

   A. Coach
   B. Customer
   C. Product Manager
   D. Project Manager

8. The _____________________ monitors the process and mentors the team on XP processes and techniques, but is considered optional.

A. Coach
B. Customer
C. Product Manager
D. Project Manager

9. The ________________________ facilitates communication by keeping plans synchronized with reality.

A. Coach
B. Customer
C. Product Manager
D. Project Manager

10. The ________________________ creates and prioritizes the Stories to be developed.

A. Coach
B. Customer
C. Product Manager
D. Project Manager

11. The ________________________________ monitors progress and warns when redistributing Tasks might be required to adjust the schedule.

A. Batman
B. Coach
C. Customer
D. Tracker

12. The ______________ is the super hero who must handle organizational emergencies and support requests so that the Programmers and Team aren't diverted from their work.

    A. Batman
    B. Coach
    C. Customer
    D. Tracker

13. At the highest-level, XP starts with a quarterly Release planning cycle that is focused on ______________________________.

    A. Picking Stories for each weekly Iteration
    B. Aligning the project goal within the Organization's bigger objectives
    C. Progressively elaborating it into a monthly cycle of plans
    D. Defining the Stories and acceptance tests for the work

14. At the start of each week, the Team reviews its progress with the Customer and __________________________.

    A. Picks Stories for the weekly Iteration
    B. Aligns the project goal with the Organization's bigger objectives
    C. Elaborates the monthly cycle
    D. Defines the Stories to review at the Stand-up Meeting

15. A(n) ______________ ceremony addresses the issue that software development, at its core, is a complex challenge in an environment of high uncertainty.

    A. Caves and Commons
    B. Planning Game
    C. Test-Driven Development
    D. Whole Team

16. The ______________________ ceremony is a critical point of collaboration between Customer, Product Manager and Team where business value is defined.

    A. Caves and Commons
    B. Planning Game
    C. Test-Driven Development
    D. Whole Team

17. The ____________________ ceremony helps the Team limit scope creep because expectations are clearly and objectively stated.

    A. Caves and Commons
    B. Planning Game
    C. Test-Driven Development
    D. Whole Team

18. The ______________________ ceremony defines the scope of the Release and the order of delivery of features, functions and capabilities.

    A. Caves and Commons
    B. Planning Game
    C. Test-Driven Development
    D. Whole Team

19. The goal of __________________ is to minimize waste caused by misunderstanding.

    A. Small Releases
    B. Incremental Architectural Design
    C. Pair Programming
    D. Collective Code Ownership

20. The __________________ ceremony means that Programmers take personal ownership of specific tasks.

A. Small Releases
B. Incremental Architectural Design
C. Pair Programming
D. Collective Code Ownership

21. A ceremony where anyone on the Team can improve any part of the system at any time is called ____________________.

A. Small Releases
B. Incremental Architectural Design
C. Pair Programming
D. Collective Code Ownership

22. The XP ____________________ ceremony is applied by delivering operational, tested software at the end of every Iteration.

A. Small Releases
B. Incremental Architectural Design
C. Pair Programming
D. Collective Code Ownership

23. The ____________________ ceremony means that, at all times during development, the system architecture and design is maintained.

A. Osmotic Communication
B. Continuous Integration
C. Pair Programming
D. Ten-Minute Build

24. Integrating code frequently and having it validated by an automated build tool that uses defined tests to detect errors is part of the ____________________ ceremony.

    A. Osmotic Communication
    B. Continuous Integration
    C. Pair Programming
    D. Ten-Minute Build

25. When a team member picks up pieces of a conversation in a common area and is then able to make a meaningful contribution it is called __________________________.

    A. Osmotic Communication
    B. Continuous Integration
    C. Pair Programming
    D. Ten-Minute Build

Fill-in-the-Blank Challenge

1. Because of work done by ________________, eXtreme Programming (XP) originated in early 1996 and was born in 1999 when he published *Extreme Programming Explained.*

2. One of XP's important assumptions is that ________________ exists. Where that assumption is correct, XP is productive. Otherwise it is risky at best.

3. The ________________ manages one of the biggest challenges for an XP team, maintaining stability while developing a complex solution in an uncertain environment.

4. The ________________ accepts responsibility for completing the Tasks that ultimately deliver a successful result.

5. The ________________ chooses a simple description of the program vision as a metaphor the Team uses as they write Stories and evaluate progress towards the completed system.

6. The ________________ guides Programmers on implementing testing techniques.

7. The ________________ writes Stories and also prioritizes them in quarterly and weekly cycles.

8. The ________________ helps the Team identify and focus on risks and optimization opportunities.

9. The ________________ packages information so it is helpful to all of the stakeholders.

10. Unlike other Agile Frameworks, the ________________ can vary the Release date by adding or removing Stories from the Backlog.

11. The ________________ monitors progress and warns when redistributing Tasks might be required to adjust the schedule.

12. The ________________ must handle organizational emergencies and support requests so that the Programmers and Team aren't diverted from their work.

13. At the highest-level, XP starts with a quarterly Release planning cycle that is focused on ______________________________.

14. At the start of each week, the Team reviews its progress with the Customer and ______________________________.

15. A ______________________ ceremony addresses the issue that software development, at its core, is a complex challenge in an environment of high uncertainty.

16. The ____________________ ceremony discusses the technical impacts of choosing to implement the requirements in a particular order.

17. The ____________________ ceremony occurs before the code is developed and run frequently while the code is being written.

18. The ____________________ ceremony creates a shared understanding of the expected release dates.

19. The goal of ____________________________ is to minimize waste caused by misunderstanding.

20. The ____________________ ceremony means that Programmers take personal ownership of specific tasks.

21. A ceremony where anyone on the Team can improve any part of the system at any time is called ______________________.

22. The XP ______________________ ceremony is applied by delivering operational, tested software at the end of every Iteration.

23. The ________________________ ceremony requires that the system architecture and design be maintained in a way that allows for an automatic build of the whole system.

24. When a team of Programmers can use a divide and conquer strategy, avoid integration problems and develop software that is cohesive and reliable, they are using a(n) ______________________________ ceremony.

25. When a team member picks up pieces of a conversation in a common area and is then able to make a meaningful contribution it is called ____________________________.

Terminology Matching Exercise

In the blank column to the left of the Term, fill in the letter that identifies the correct Definition or Description.

	TERM		DEFINITION / DESCRIPTION
	1. Continuous Integration	A	Planning cycle focused on aligning the project goal within the Organization's bigger objectives
	2. Small Releases	B	Defines the scope of the Release and the order of delivery of features, functions and capabilities
	3. Incremental Architectural Design	C	Helps the Team limit scope creep because expectations are clearly and objectively stated
	4. Planning Game	D	A ceremony applied by delivering operational, tested software at the end of every iteration
	5. TDD	E	One of XP's important assumptions
	6. Release	F	Monitors progress and warns when redistributing Tasks might be required to adjust the schedule
	7. Tracker	G	Integrating code frequently and having it validated by an automated build tool.
	8. Customer	H	Helps the Team identify and focus on risks and optimization opportunities
	9. Project Manager	I	Grooms the Backlog according to the logical development sequence for business value
	10. Coach	J	Can vary the release date by adding or removing Stories from the Backlog
	11. Product Manager	K	Facilitates communication by keeping plans synchronized with reality

TERM		DEFINITION / DESCRIPTION	
	12. Interaction Designer	L	Accepts responsibility for completing the tasks that ultimately deliver a successful result
	13. Programmer	M	Applying a robust architecture where design investments are in proportion to system needs
	14. Architect	N	Chooses a simple description of the program vision as a metaphor
	15. Unified Client Viewpoint	O	Guides development through small, safe steps so the best solution emerges

Answers - Practice Test

1. **C.** Because of work done by **KENT BECK,** eXtreme Programming (XP) originated in early 1996 and was born in 1999 when he published *Extreme Programming Explained.*

   eXtreme Programming (XP) originated with Kent Beck while working at Chrysler in early 1996. In 1999 he published Extreme Programming Explained and eXtreme Programming was born!

2. **B.** One of XP's important assumptions is that A **UNIFIED CLIENT VIEWPOINT** exists. Where that assumption is correct, XP is productive. Otherwise it is risky at best.

   That assumption drives the practice of having an on-site Customer that proponents cite as providing needed flexibility while reducing cost. Critics claim it causes rework and scope creep.

3. **A.** The **ARCHITECT** guides development through small, safe steps to modify the architecture without undermining its integrity so the best solution emerges as the product evolves. The Architect manages one of the biggest challenges for an XP team, maintaining stability while developing a complex solution in an uncertain environment.

4. **C.** The **PROGRAMMER** estimates Stories, defines tests, and writes code, usually working with a partner as a "pair", and accepts responsibility for completing the Tasks that ultimately deliver a successful result.

5. **B.** The **INTERACTION DESIGNER** chooses a simple description of the program vision as a metaphor that the Team uses to guide system development choices as they write Stories and evaluate progress towards the completed system.

6. **D.** The **TESTER** coaches the Customer on selecting system-level tests that will define and validate acceptable functioning of the system before development and improve deployment of the system after development. Testers also guide Programmers on implementing testing techniques.

7. **C.** The **PRODUCT MANAGER** encourages communication about important customer concerns so the Team can respond to them. The Product Manager writes Stories and also prioritizes them in quarterly and weekly cycles. Product Managers groom the logical development sequence for business value, not technical efficiency.

8. **A.** The **COACH** monitors the process and mentors the Team on XP processes and techniques, but is considered optional. The Coach helps the Team identify and focus on risks and optimization opportunities.

9. **D.** The **PROJECT MANAGER** facilitates communication by keeping plans synchronized with reality and packaging that information so it is helpful to all of the stakeholders.

10. **B.** The **CUSTOMER** creates and prioritizes the Stories to be developed. Unlike other Agile Frameworks, the Customer can vary the release date by adding or removing Stories from the Backlog to be delivered in any given Release. Similar to other frameworks, the Customer sets the development priorities.

11. **D.** The **TRACKER** monitors progress and warns when redistributing Tasks might be required to adjust the schedule.

    The Tracker, another preferred but optional position, monitors team progress and warns when redistributing Tasks might be required to adjust the schedule. Sometimes a Programmer "doubles" as Tracker for the same pair, and sometimes a Programmer serves as Tracker for a different pair.

12. **A.** The **BATMAN** is the super hero who must handle organizational emergencies and support requests so that the Programmers and Team aren't diverted from their work.

    While a mask and cape are optional, nerves of steel are mandatory!

13. **B.** At the highest-level, XP starts with a quarterly Release planning cycle that is focused on **ALIGNING THE PROJECT GOAL WITHIN THE ORGANIZATION'S BIGGER OBJECTIVES.**

    The quarterly plan is progressively elaborated into a weekly cycle of plans.

14. **A.** At the start of each week, the Team reviews its progress with the Customer and **PICKS STORIES FOR THE WEEKLY ITERATION.**

    At the start of each week, the Team reviews its progress and the Customer picks another group of Stories to be the current week's work. Next, acceptance tests are defined. Once the Stories and acceptance tests are defined, the work and daily Stand-up Meetings begin.

15. **D.** A **WHOLE TEAM** ceremony addresses the issue that software development, at its core, is a complex challenge in an environment of high uncertainty.

    The XP ceremony of Whole Team directly addresses the issue that software development at its core is a complex challenge in an environment of high uncertainty.

16. **B.** The **PLANNING GAME** ceremony is a critical point of collaboration between Customer, Product Manager and Team where business value is defined.

    The Planning Game defines a rough order of magnitude (ROM) plan for a project so the Team can refine it as the project progresses. It is a critical point of collaboration between Customer, Product Manager and Team where business value is defined. The core purpose is to define the scope of the Release and the order of delivery of features, functions and capabilities and discuss the technical impacts of choosing to implement the requirements in that order. The outcome is a shared understanding of the expected release dates and a collection of specific User Stories that will be broken down into Tasks so the Team can allocate its work.

17. **C.** The **TEST-DRIVEN DEVELOPMENT** ceremony helps the Team limit scope creep because expectations are clearly and objectively stated.

    The Test-Driven Development ceremony requires the test to be written before the code is developed and run frequently while the code is being written. Applying a rigid TDD discipline helps the Team limit scope creep because expectations are clearly and objectively stated. The process of test, code, and refactor is repeated over and over again, creating a cadence that assists the twin goals of speed and quality.

18. **B.** The **PLANNING GAME** ceremony defines the scope of the Release and the order of delivery of features, functions and capabilities.

    The Planning Game defines a rough order of magnitude (ROM) plan for a project so the Team can refine it as the project progresses. It is a critical point of collaboration between Customer, Product Manager and Team where business value is defined. The core purpose is to define the scope of the Release and the order of delivery of features, functions and capabilities and discuss the technical impacts of choosing to implement the requirements in that order. The outcome is a shared understanding of the expected release dates and a collection of specific User Stories that will be broken down into Tasks so the Team can allocate its work.

19. **B.** The goal of **INCREMENTAL ARCHITECTURAL DESIGN** is to minimize waste caused by misunderstanding.

    The goal of Incremental Architectural Design is to minimize waste caused by misunderstanding about the real functionality needed on the Customer and Product Owner side and caused by redundant development and rework on the Team side.

    The ceremony means the Team works hard to create and apply a robust architecture where design investments are in proportion to system needs so the cost of changing during development doesn't rise exponentially. It means defining an incremental design strategy where the system grows through gradual, predictable change, minimizing the cost of complexity and maximizing the probability that the simplest design will actually work.

20. **C.** The **PAIR PROGRAMMING** ceremony means that Programmers take personal ownership of specific tasks.

    The Pair Programming ceremony means that Programmers take personal ownership of specific Tasks and that doing so creates internal team accountability.

    The best approach to pair programming is for the partners to sit side-by-side in front of the computer and concentrate on the code being written as the Driver or Navigator and share observations.

21. **D.** A ceremony where anyone on the Team can improve any part of the system at any time is called **COLLECTIVE CODE OWNERSHIP.**

    The Collective Code Ownership ceremony means anyone on the Team can improve any part of the system at any time, as long as fixing it is not out of scope. It means every Programmer creates unit tests as code is developed and every piece of code released into the source code repository is subjected to automated testing as it is changed.

22. **A.** The **XP SMALL RELEASES** ceremony is applied by delivering operational, tested software at the end of every Iteration.

    XP teams apply the Small Releases ceremony by delivering operational, tested software at the end of every Iteration, creating the business value prioritized by the Customer.

    The Small Releases ceremony is technical and critical. It is technical because the software coding must be finished properly. It is critical because it is the only way to be absolutely sure the software being developed meets the Customer's expectations.

23. **D.** The **TEN-MINUTE BUILD** ceremony means that at all times during development, the system architecture and design is maintained.

    The Ten-Minute Build ceremony means that at all times during development, the system architecture and design is maintained in a way that allows for an automatic build of the whole system where all of the tests run in ten minutes or less.

    Having an automated and reliable build of the system that runs in ten minutes means it can be run many times a day, thereby reducing risk. If not, it won't be run and risk will rise as timely feedback decreases.

24. **B.** Integrating code frequently and having it validated by an automated build tool that uses defined tests to detect errors is part of the **CONTINUOUS INTEGRATION** ceremony.

    The Continuous Integration ceremony means integration is part of the daily workflow where Programmers integrate their code frequently and have it validated by an automated build tool that uses defined tests to detect errors so they can be fixed immediately. As a result, a team of Programmers can use a divide and conquer strategy, avoid integration problems and develop software that is cohesive and reliable.

Each integration involves builds at two levels – the local machine and the integration machine – and both builds must finish and be error free before the Programmer can continue to another Task because XP requires the build never be broken. The combination of double builds and automated testing means errors are detected rapidly so they can be fixed and a working build properly maintained.

25. **A.** When a team member picks up pieces of a conversation in a common area and is then able to make a meaningful contribution it is called **OSMOTIC COMMUNICATION.**

    Osmotic communication can be described as a team member picking up pieces of a conversation in a common area then being able to make a meaningful contribution even though he or she was not fully engaged in the discussion.

Answers - Fill-in-the-Blank Challenge

1. Because of work done by **KENT BECK**, eXtreme Programming (XP) originated in early 1996 and was born in 1999 when he published *Extreme Programming Explained.* eXtreme Programming (XP) originated with Kent Beck while working at Chrysler in early 1996. In 1999 he published *Extreme Programming Explained* and eXtreme Programming was born!

2. One of XP's important assumptions is that **A UNIFIED CLIENT VIEWPOINT** exists. Where that assumption is correct, XP is productive. Otherwise, it is risky at best. That assumption drives the practice of having an on-site Customer that proponents cite as providing needed flexibility while reducing cost. Critics claim it causes rework and scope creep.

3. The **ARCHITECT** manages one of the biggest challenges for an XP team, maintaining stability while developing a complex solution in an uncertain environment. The Architect guides development through small, safe steps to modify the architecture without undermining its integrity so the best solution emerges as the product evolves.

4. The **PROGRAMMER** accepts responsibility for completing the tasks that ultimately deliver a successful result and estimates Stories, defines tests, and writes code, usually working with a partner as a "pair".

5. The **INTERACTION DESIGNER** chooses a simple description of the program vision as a metaphor the Team uses to guide system development choices as they write Stories and evaluate progress towards the completed system.

6. The **TESTER** guides Programmers on implementing testing techniques. Testers also coach the Customer on selecting system-level tests that will define and validate acceptable functioning of the system before development and improve deployment of the system after development.

7. The **PRODUCT MANAGER** writes Stories and also prioritizes them in quarterly and weekly cycles. The Product Manager encourages communication about important customer concerns so the Team can respond to them. Product Managers groom the logical development sequence for business value, not technical efficiency.

8. The **COACH** helps the Team identify and focus on risks and optimization opportunities. The Coach monitors the process and mentors the Team on XP processes and techniques, but is considered optional.

9. The P**ROJECT MANAGER** packages information so it is helpful to all of the stakeholders and facilitates communication by keeping plans synchronized with reality.

10. Unlike other Agile Frameworks, the **CUSTOMER** can vary the release date by adding or removing Stories from the Backlog to be delivered in any given Release. Similar to other frameworks, the Customer sets the development priorities. The Customer creates and prioritizes the Stories to be developed.

11. The **TRACKER** monitors progress and warns when redistributing Tasks might be required to adjust the schedule. The Tracker, another preferred but optional position, monitors team progress and warns when redistributing Tasks might be required to adjust the schedule. Sometimes a Programmer "doubles" as Tracker for the same pair, and sometimes a Programmer serves as Tracker for a different pair.

12. The **BATMAN** is the super hero who must handle organizational emergencies and support requests so that the Programmers and Team aren't diverted from their work. While a mask and cape are optional, nerves of steel are mandatory!

13. At the highest-level, XP starts with a quarterly Release planning cycle that is focused on **ALIGNING THE PROJECT GOAL WITHIN THE ORGANIZATION'S BIGGER OBJECTIVES.** At the highest-level, XP starts with a quarterly Release planning cycle focused on understanding and aligning the project goal within the organization's bigger objectives. The quarterly plan is progressively elaborated into a weekly cycle of plans.

14. At the start of each week, the Team reviews its progress with the Customer and **PICKS STORIES FOR THE WEEKLY ITERATION.** At the start of each week, the Team reviews its progress and the Customer picks another group of Stories to be the current week's work. Next, acceptance tests are defined. Once the Stories and acceptance tests are defined, the work and daily Stand-up Meetings begin.

15. A **WHOLE TEAM** ceremony addresses the issue that software development, at its core, is a complex challenge in an environment of high uncertainty.

16. The **PLANNING GAME** ceremony is a critical point of collaboration between Customer, Product Manager and Team where business value is defined. The Planning Game defines a rough order of magnitude (ROM) plan for a project so the Team can refine it as the project progresses. It is a critical point of collaboration between Customer, Product Manager and Team where business value is defined. The core purpose is to define the scope of the Release and the order of delivery of features, functions and capabilities and discuss the technical impacts of choosing to implement the requirements in that order. The outcome is a shared understanding of the expected release dates and a collection of specific User Stories that will be broken down into Tasks so the Team can allocate its work.

17. The **TEST-DRIVEN DEVELOPMENT** ceremony helps the Team limit scope creep because expectations are clearly and objectively stated. The Test-Driven Development ceremony requires the test to be written before the code is developed and run frequently while the code is being written. Applying a rigid TDD discipline helps the Team limit scope creep because expectations are clearly and objectively stated. The process of test, code, and refactor is repeated over and over again, creating a cadence that assists the twin goals of speed and quality.

18. The **PLANNING GAME** ceremony defines the scope of the Release and the order of delivery of features, functions and capabilities. The Planning Game defines a rough order of magnitude (ROM) plan for a project so the Team can refine it as the project progresses. It is a

critical point of collaboration between Customer, Product Manager and Team where business value is defined. The core purpose is to define the scope of the Release and the order of delivery of features, functions and capabilities and discuss the technical impacts of choosing to implement the requirements in that order. The outcome is a shared understanding of the expected release dates and a collection of specific User Stories that will be broken down into Tasks so the Team can allocate its work.

19. The goal of **INCREMENTAL ARCHITECTURAL DESIGN** is to minimize waste caused by misunderstanding. The goal of Incremental Architectural Design is to minimize waste caused by misunderstanding about the real functionality needed on Customer and Product Owner side and caused by redundant development and rework on the Team side.

    The ceremony means the Team works hard to create and apply a robust architecture where design investments are in proportion to system needs so the cost of changing during development doesn't rise exponentially. It means defining an incremental design strategy where the system grows through gradual, predictable change, minimizing the cost of complexity and maximizing the probability that the simplest design will actually work.

20. The **PAIR PROGRAMMING** ceremony means that Programmers take personal ownership of specific tasks. The Pair Programming ceremony means that Programmers take personal ownership of specific Tasks and that doing so creates internal team accountability.

    The best approach to pair programming is for the partners to sit side-by-side in front of the computer and concentrate on the code being written as the Driver or Navigator and share observations.

21. A ceremony where anyone on the Team can improve any part of the system at any time is called **COLLECTIVE CODE OWNERSHIP.**

    The Collective Code Ownership ceremony means anyone on the Team can improve any part of the system at any time, as long as fixing it is not out of scope. It means every Programmer creates unit tests as code is developed and every piece of code released into the source code repository is subjected to automated testing as it is changed.

22. The **XP SMALL RELEASES** ceremony is applied by delivering operational, tested software at the end of every Iteration.

    XP teams apply the Small Releases ceremony by delivering operational, tested software at the end of every Iteration, creating the business value prioritized by the Customer.

    The Small Releases ceremony is technical and critical. It is technical because the software coding must be finished properly. It is critical because it is the only way to be absolutely sure the software being developed meets the Customer's expectations.

23. The **TEN-MINUTE BUILD** ceremony requires that the system architecture and design be maintained in a way that allows for an automatic build of the whole system.

    The Ten-Minute Build ceremony means that at all times during development the system architecture and design is maintained in a way that allows for an automatic build of the whole system where all of the tests run in ten minutes or less.

    Having an automated and reliable build of the system that runs in ten minutes means it can be run many times a day, thereby reducing risk. If not, it won't be run and risk will rise as timely feedback decreases.

24. When a team of Programmers can use a divide and conquer strategy, avoid integration problems and develop software that is cohesive and reliable, they are using a(n) **CONTINUOUS INTEGRATION** ceremony.

    The Continuous Integration ceremony means integration is part of the daily workflow where Programmers integrate their code frequently and have it validated by an automated build tool that uses defined tests to detect errors so they can be fixed immediately. As a result, a team of Programmers can use a divide and conquer strategy, avoid integration problems and develop software that is cohesive and reliable.

Each integration involves builds at two levels – the local machine and the integration machine – and both builds must finish and be error free before the Programmer can continue to another Task because XP requires that the build never be broken. The combination of double builds and automated testing means errors are detected rapidly so they can be fixed and a working build properly maintained.

25. When a team member picks up pieces of a conversation in a common area and is then able to make a meaningful contribution, it is called **OSMOTIC COMMUNICATION.**

    Osmotic communication can be described as a team member picking up pieces of a conversation in a common area and then being able to make a meaningful contribution even though he or she was not fully engaged in the discussion.

Answers - Terminology Matching

1:G, 2:D, 3:M, 4:B, 5:C, 6:A, 7:F, 8:J, 9:K, 10:H, 11:I, 12:N, 13:L, 14:O, 15:E

Chapter End Notes

[31]Beck, K., & Andres, C. (2004). *Extreme programming explained: Embrace change, Second edition.* Boston: Addison-Wesley Professional.

Lean Software Development (LSD) Deep Dive

Chapter Highlights

In this chapter you will find an overview of Lean Software Development (LSD) as well as a detailed description of its key elements. Those elements are broken out as the Roles, Workflow, Ceremonies and Artifacts. The people are identified by the Roles they fulfill. The Workflow details how those people work together and produce the planned results. Lastly, the Artifacts are the electronic or printed evidence of the results.

Overview of Lean Software Development (LSD)

As with XP, the name of the Lean Software Development (LSD) framework gives away the context of its start up. The goal of the LSD framework is to eliminate any unnecessary burden or overhead from the software development process. Unlike other Agile Frameworks, LSD is concerned with how the organization perceives and articulates the systems they want, and that concern shows up during requirements gathering and documentation efforts.

Today, because of companies like Google, Amazon, Facebook and YouTube, software development is no longer about just automating business activities. Rather, the process of developing products and services has software development at its core. Therefore, Lean Product Development has become a core principle of business success and underpinning that is Lean Software Development. But it wasn't always so.

Lean Software Development was born in 2003 when *Lean Software Development: An Agile Toolkit* was published by Mary and Tom Poppendieck.[32] The book presented how to use an adapted version of Lean Manufacturing principles, or more specifically, Lean Product Development, to develop software and also compared it to other Agile practices. The Poppendiecks' credibility with the Agile software development community accelerated acceptance of their ideas and LSD by the Agile community, as a whole.

LSD followed close on the heels of eXtreme Programming (Beck, 1999) and the Agile Manifesto (2001) and its specific practices were aimed at overcoming the problems common to software development approaches at that time. Of those flaws, the one that was perceived to be the biggest was the Traditional Project Management practice of developing software using the sequential phases of design, development, test, and deployment. This approach was seen as maintaining large "inventories of information" during each phase, violating Lean wisdom. It also left testing and integration until the end of development creating potentially large "inventories of undetected defects", another violation of Lean wisdom. The goal for LSD was to apply the Lean philosophy of "build quality in", which had previously not been considered practical for software development.

To improve the existing sequential process, the new LSD Framework focused on practices like Test-Driven Development (TDD), Continuous Integration, development Iterations, and Cross-Functional teams. With what is known today it is almost impossible to understand how radical these practices seemed at the time. But as it produced a track record of success, LSD moved from being a radical idea to a mainstream best practice.

LSD evangelists and disciples leveraged the widespread acceptance and growth of Scrum, but felt it had mistakenly only stressed development Iterations and Cross-Functional Teams and overlooked the importance of rigorous TDD and Continuous Integration practices. The differences in Lean "purity" were vigorously debated.

Both LSD and Scrum improved the software development process in IT and Product Development departments, but failed to gain traction creating organizational benefits and "changing the world of work" as expected. The cause of failure at the organizational level may have been the intense focus on optimizing software development and not realizing the system constraint for "changing the world of work" was not how to create software. LSD differed from Scrum rather significantly because of the leadership of the Poppendiecks.

Mary and Tom Poppendieck wanted to improve workflow and organizational throughput across the entire value stream, as highlighted in the subtitle of their book, *Implementing Lean Software Development: From Concept to Cash (2006)*. The idea that the organization's interest in creating value "from concept to cash" aligned with the work of Taiichi Ohno, considered the father of the Toyota Production System and Lean Manufacturing, and the Poppendiecks saw that if it was properly implemented, it really could "change the world of work."

As the years since have passed, the ideas in LSD have become mainstream and Agile software development has gradually extended into more and more of the organization's value stream. Today, with the success of Cloud computing, not only is automated provisioning through code-build-test deployment pipelines practical, it has become mandated as a matter of survival for organizations to embed software in their products and deliver it as a service on the web and via mobile apps.

Ever improving TDD has made error-free, rapid deployment a Customer expectation. However, IT departments are struggling to meet that expectation because of monolithic legacy code frustrating deployment of small independent changes. One of the most difficult, and perhaps biggest, problems this presents for IT departments is overcoming the breakdown in communication between Developers and Customers. It is large and difficult because of the longstanding barriers that were erected and still exist between Subject Matter Experts (SMEs) in IT departments and their colleagues and Customers.

As software continues to grow in significance for business success and improvements in how software is developed and deployed take hold, overcoming the communication barriers between Developers and Customers will fall. That change will release powerful, innovative solutions because Lean's principle of learning through feedback will drive the evolution. Then the principles of Lean will be assimilated and the term Lean will disappear as it becomes mainstream.

Roles

In *Lean Software Development: An Agile Toolkit, as part of the Tool 14: Motivation* section, the Poppendiecks say, *"Think of a software development team as a multisided polygon. Each side of the polygon has its goals."* Then they describe a bit about each facet of the Development Team, at the end of which they say, *"Together, this team has a purpose: Deliver business value."* They start the next paragraph by saying, *"The number of sides of the polygon and the specific disciplines needed to achieve a purpose will vary depending on the type of project."*

The core idea is that the Team is multisided (equivalent to cross-functional), delivers business value as its core purpose, and varies its composition to support delivering the desired project outcomes.

From the Poppendieck's insight, five typical roles in LSD are defined. They are Analyst, Customer, Developer, Support and Tester.

Analyst

Analysts help Customers explain and describe system features in enough detail for the Developers to understand what to build. Analysts are similar to Product Managers in XP and Product Owners in Scrum with an important distinction that they not become a barrier to direct Developer-Customer discussions. Analysts facilitate knowledge transfer for both sides without restricting direct contact.

Customer

Customers focus on the goal of ensuring the system will deliver business value. Customers sometimes benefit from the help of Analysts as they go through the process of translating low granularity "boulders" into high granularity "rocks" Developers can understand. But not every Customer needs help creating and prioritizing the Stories to be developed.

Developer

Developers estimate Stories, write code, and define tests in order to deliver working software. Some Developers have enough experience and domain-savvy to fill the Analyst role. The Developer role is simply to accept responsibility for completing the tasks that ultimately deliver a successful result.

Support

Support includes all the roles that are responsible for system deployment, user training, and the help desk to answer user questions. It is a broad category and can include many domain- and industry-specific roles.

Tester

Testers create comprehensive tests for both the Customer's Conditions of Satisfaction and User Acceptance Tests. The goal is to ensure the system meets the needs of the Customer and end users. Sometimes Testers have the experience and cross-training to also serve as Analyst, and vice versa.

If needed, the Tester will coach the Customer on selecting tests that validate acceptable functioning of the system. Testers may also assist Developers with selecting testing techniques that correctly test what is being developed so it can be properly deployed later.

Workflow

In *Lean Software Development: An Agile Toolkit, as part of the Tool 10: Pull Systems* section, the Poppendiecks say, *"People who routinely deal with fluid situations, such as emergency workers and military personnel ... figure out how to respond to events with the other people who are on the scene. ... One of the keys ways to do this is to let Customers' needs pull the work ..."*

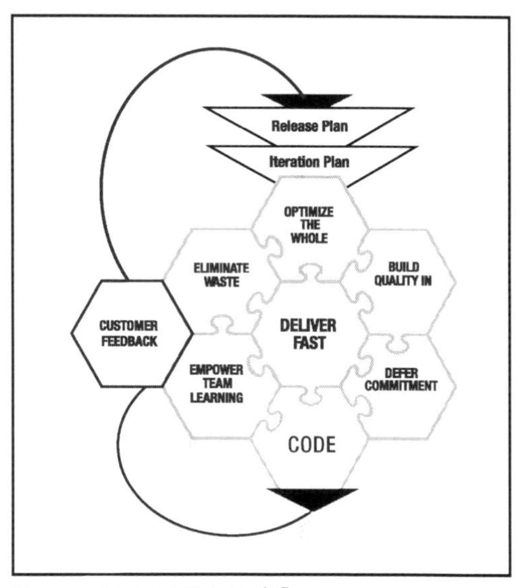

Figure 6.1 | *LSD Workflow*

Because software development by its very nature is fluid, complex and uncertain, the best and only reliable approach is a Pull System based on rules that are both flexible and robust. Diagramming or mapping such a process is challenging at best. (Figure 6.1)

The Poppendiecks adapted Lean principles into seven rules for software development that have evolved into six best practices. The best practices are commonly referred to as: Optimize the Whole, Defer Commitment, Deliver Fast, Eliminate Waste, Build Quality In, and Empower Team Learning.

1. Optimize the Whole

Without the proper perspective there is a continuous risk that development will optimize part of the solution thereby sub-optimizing the overall solution. As Mary and Tom Poppendieck rightly said, the organization's interest in creating value is *"from concept to cash"* and, *"Together, this team has a purpose: Deliver business value."* While the synergy of the sub-systems is critical, the performance of the system as a whole is the key to success.

As the cross-functional team works through development, it must 'begin with the end in mind' as Stephen Covey advised in *Seven Habits of Highly Effective People*, clarifying the entire Value Stream by analyzing back from the future. The solution must solve the current need and avoid technical debt so it is also capable of moving forward to the next generation of technology challenges.

2. Defer Commitment

Deferring commitments allows the best possible design to emerge as part of the development process. Software development always occurs in an atmosphere charged with uncertainty and complexity. Better results come from having the discipline to create as much clarity as possible about the problem then identify the various solution choices and tradeoffs imbedded in each one, and finally making a fact-based decision on which approach or approaches to test and pursue.

This principle drives the success of iterative development approaches by fueling adaptive changes to overcome mistakes that would be potentially costly after the release of the system. It means that planning is concerned with exploring options and adapting to discoveries while the inter-relationships between requirements, which may number in the thousands, are worked out. It requires decisions and commitments be deferred to the Last Responsible Moment.

Last Responsible Moments occur at the point where any advantage of acquiring additional valuable information or insight is offset by the potential risk of delaying the decision any longer.

The Agile and LSD practice of using written Stories as planning placeholders enables the Team to concentrate on developing high-priority items and using resources wisely in time-constrained projects because Customers feel assured that deferred does not mean forgotten.

3. Deliver Fast

The fastest way to deliver the system the Customer expects is to have the Customer pull the pieces – features, functions and capabilities – through an incremental discovery process that creates a deep understanding of how to solve the problem. Therefore the Team develops an initial prototype as quickly as possible and delivers it to the Customer. Then the Customer evaluates if it solves the problem as expected and needed. If not, the new deeper understanding defines the next indicated incremental change to be made as quickly as possible so the Customer can re-evaluate it. The cycle repeats itself until the feature solves a particular piece of the problem and no more.

The process of delivering defect-free, working elements of the solution quickly so they can be evaluated and the feedback used to guide the next step of development also raises quality. First, it raises the quality of requirements gathering by clarifying what is really needed. Second, it raises the quality of features developed by abandoning those deemed unnecessary as soon as it becomes clear they don't help solve the problem.

It sounds like an oxymoron to say that deferred commitments increase speed. It also sounds like an impossibility to say that speed increases quality. But when properly understood, they intersect at the point that optimizes the whole solution.

4. Eliminate Waste

Lean principles insist that anything not adding customer value is waste. When applied to software development, waste includes everything from unnecessary code to development delays to vague requirements.

In Lean, the idea is that waste is a big burden because it consumes precious resources yet fails to deliver value. Knowing that compels LSD not to let the resources spent gathering requirements be left in a binder gathering dust or the developer's time be spent coding more features that are not immediately needed so they keep getting handed off from one Iteration to the next. The goal is to find out exactly what a Customer needs, develop it, deliver it quickly, and get feedback immediately.

The goal of rapidly satisfying a Customer need is driven by the Lean principle to eliminate waste. Therefore, the Team must be vigilant about recognizing any activity that could be bypassed as waste while still satisfying the Customer. Waste-removal must be diligently pursued during every Iteration and every step of the planning process.

Defects lower quality and add waste, but they are also evidence of the process missing an opportunity to produce real value. Value Stream

Mapping identifies waste, but becomes waste itself if not used to eliminate it. Planning minimizes waste as well, but it too becomes waste if it doesn't prevent development of the wrong solution. As famed management consultant and author, Peter Drucker, said, "There is nothing so useless as doing efficiently that which should not be done at all."

5. Build Quality In

Building quality into the solution is more than just the technical notion that individual components and subassemblies work well together as a robust, flexible, and responsive system. It means that the Customer's needs have been understood and integrated into the overall system experience for the Users. It means paying the price to develop a solution that is intuitive to use, solves problems well, and can be maintained, extended and scaled appropriately and efficiently.

It means moving from a Quality Control (QC) mindset of catching bugs to a Quality Assurance (QA) mindset of validating assumptions throughout the process with useful metrics that ensure practices create value or are discarded.

Building quality in is a significant challenge that can only be achieved by developing a comprehensive understanding of the problem domain and solving it with an iterative cycle of discovery and adaptation. It is an application of the quote often attributed to Albert Einstein about "the level of knowledge that got us to this problem is not the level of knowledge needed to solve it." An iterative cycle of discovery reveals the information needed to develop an adaptation that solves it and moves the Team to the next level of knowledge needed to modify the solution until the final solution solves the entire problem.

Only information flowing in a constant feedback loop from Customer to Developer and back again can provide the needed "actionable insight". It is integral to that process that architecture be guided by refactoring so that as more features are added to the solution the coding maintains as much simplicity, clarity and reliability as possible. With the proper use of automated testing and frequent integrations, the best way to reduce risk and build quality in can be determined.

6. Empower Team Learning

In Dan Pink's best-selling book, *Drive: The Surprising Truth About What Motivates Us*, he describes three factors that motivate knowledge workers.

Knowledge workers exactly match the technical professionals working in software development. Those three factors are Autonomy, Mastery and Purpose.

Empowering the Team to learn as much as possible as quickly as possible, gives the Organization the capacity to respond quickly to the future as it unfolds, which is an unassailable competitive advantage. The formula from Dan Pink – Autonomy, Mastery and Purpose (AMP) – is the key to unlocking learning that, dare we say, "AMPs up your Team's voltage!"

Instead of expecting more documentation or additional planning to find the answer, the Team must be given the autonomy to prototype different ideas and refine them by writing code, testing it, and repeatedly improving it. Given that autonomy, they will apply and develop every aspect of their technical mastery until they fulfill the purpose of meeting the Customer's need.

It cannot be denied that planning is worthwhile, but it must be acknowledged that learning is critical. LSD, at its core, is knowledge-based development of solutions. It uses short, iterative cycles to generate and apply knowledge. For such a system to work, it must respect the people on the Team and recognize that only by collaborating with the Customer and the Users can the Team succeed in improving it.

Establishing an environment where the Team is empowered to learn faces challenges because of the decades-old belief taught in famous business schools that decision-making means managers telling workers how to do their job. But, as the Poppendiecks rightly point out, "The Lean approach favors the aphorism 'find good people and let them do their own job'." Furthermore, as William McKnight, the fabled Founder and leader of 3M Corp., was fond of saying, "Hire good people, and leave them alone."

Empowering team learning means Developers must have access to the Customer and the Organization must provide support in difficult situations. It means staying out of the Team's way as they cycle through prototypes so cynicism about LSD just being the latest organizational trick to "extract blood" from the Team does not ruin their motivation.

One final, often overlooked benefit of an organizational commitment to empowered team learning is that it dramatically reduces the risk, and immense cost, of important knowledge workers leaving the project for a better opportunity elsewhere.

Ceremonies

In the chapter on Scrum, four ceremonies – Sprint, Daily Scrum, Sprint Review and Sprint Retrospective – were described. In the chapter on XP, a total of nine ceremonies, composed of three ceremonies at three levels were identified as Whole Team, Planning Game, Test-Driven Development, Incremental Architectural Design, Pair Programming, Collective Code Ownership, Small Releases, Ten-Minute Build, and Continuous Integration.

Describing ceremonies for LSD is quite different because other than the Release and Iteration planning ceremonies held in common with other Agile Frameworks, the only ceremony in LSD is gathering Customer Feedback. It is a ceremony that is not held on a formal periodic basis, like the Daily, Review or Retrospective meetings. Instead, it is an ad hoc, mostly informal ceremony that can be held as often as hourly.

During the Customer Feedback ceremony, the Developer and Customer meet and see, test and use the system changes to decide if they solve the problem or need additional fine-tuning.

Artifacts

In the chapter on Scrum, three artifacts – Product Backlog, Sprint Backlog and Increment – named in the Scrum Guide were described. Potentially Shippable Products, Definitions of Done, and User Stories were other artifacts. In the chapter on XP, the Release, Quarterly, and Weekly Plans were identified as artifacts in addition to User Stories, diagrams, abstractions and wall charts. Also, documentation related to "throw away" code used during development spikes and documentation of experiments and research were called out as artifacts.

Artifacts for LSD include the Product Vision, Roadmap and Release Plans, User Stories, Code, Tests, Configuration Scripts, and Customer Reviews and Approvals. And even though many of the artifacts are intangible and may have a short lifespan, they are still important. They should be captured and maintained in a version control system with a central repository providing a history of changes.

The core concept is that planning leads to units of customer-desired functionality that are approximately defined in Stories. The Stories drive the creation of scripts, tests and code that is reviewed and approved by the Customer. Therefore, the better development becomes at delivering business value, the more focused the artifacts must become in order to support speed and quality.

Since LSD is committed to empowered teams, rather than specifically defining a laundry list of artifacts, it trusts the wisdom of the Team to select relevant then simple metrics, and keep artifacts with appropriate content for later reference. It is essential to realize that relevance is more important than simplicity. Many organizations make the mistake of not collecting important, relevant metrics because they are hard to gather or require judgment when being interpreted or applied. After a relevant metric has been identified the easiest way to collect and measure it should be sought.

Metrics are relevant when they are focused on essential elements and identify corrective actions at the point where threshold values are reached. Metrics are simple when they are easy to collect, easy to understand, and trigger action when something is wrong.

When done correctly, metrics produce artifacts that improve fact-based decision-making at the earliest possible moments in the current Iteration as well as creating an archive of data where trends, such as increasing defects or falling quality, can be observed and corrected in future Iterations and projects. They also fuel process improvement because they unlock insight into the metadata about what works and what does not, often pulling back the veil covering hidden organizational misunderstandings. Finally, artifacts become an invaluable tool when they foster honest, frank discussions in an atmosphere of personal safety and trust.

Recommended Reading

- *Lean Software Development: An Agile Toolkit,* by Mary Poppendieck and Tom Poppendieck (Addison-Wesley Professional; May 2003),
- *Implementing Lean Software Development: From Concept to Cash,* by Mary Poppendieck and Tom Poppendieck (Addison-Wesley Professional; September 2006)

Chapter Close-Out

Practice Test

1. Artifacts for LSD include ________________ and ________________.

   A. Product Vision and Incremental Architectural Design
   B. Code Configuration and Customer Tests
   C. Customer Reviews and Approvals
   D. Roadmap and Product Plans

2. Even though many of the artifacts have a ______________________, they are still important.

   A. Short lifespan
   B. Vague client viewpoint
   C. Limited business value
   D. Software problem

3. Without the proper perspective, there is a continuous risk that development will ______________ part of the solution.

   A. Optimize
   B. Sub-optimize
   C. Increase technical debt in
   D. Reduce technical debt in

4. As the Team works through development, it must solve the current need and ____________________________ so it is capable of moving forward to the next generation of technology challenges.

   A. Optimize
   B. Sub-optimize
   C. Have technical debt
   D. Avoid technical debt

5. Lean Software Development was born in 2003 when Lean Software Development: An Agile Toolkit was published by __________________________.

   A. Kent Beck
   B. Ken Schwaber
   C. Mary and Tom Poppendieck
   D. Mike Cohn

6. One of the ceremonies used by LSD includes _____________________.

   A. Daily Stand-up
   B. Customer Feedback
   C. Sprint Review
   D. Iteration Perspective

7. ______________________ estimate Stories, write code, and define tests.

   A. Analysts
   B. Customers
   C. Developers
   D. Project Managers

8. The _____________________ explains and describes system features in enough detail for the Developers to understand what to build.

   A. Analyst
   B. Customer
   C. Product Manager
   D. Tester

9. The goal of the ______________________ is to ensure the system meets the needs of the Customer and end users.

A. Analyst
B. Customer
C. Developer
D. Tester

10. The ______________________ role is responsible for system deployment, user training, and the help desk.

A. Support
B. Customer
C. Developer
D. Tester

11. The ____________________ exercises the process of translating low granularity "boulders" into high granularity "rocks" that Developers can understand.

A. Analyst
B. Coach
C. Customer
D. Tester

12. ________________ occur when any advantage of acquiring additional information is offset by the risk of delaying the decision.

A. Empowered Team Decisions
B. Last Responsible Moments
C. Customer Prioritizations
D. Architectural Refactoring Assessments

13. ________________________________ means that the Customer's needs have been understood and integrated into the overall system experience for the users.

A. Build Quality In
B. Defer Commitment
C. Eliminate Waste
D. Optimize the Whole

14. Moving from a Quality Control (QC) mindset of catching bugs to a Quality Assurance (QA) mindset of validating assumptions can be described as ________________________________.

A. Building quality in
B. Deferring commitment
C. Eliminating waste
D. Optimizing the whole

15. It is integral to the __________________ process that architecture be guided by refactoring.

A. Building quality in
B. Deferring commitment
C. Eliminating waste
D. Optimizing the whole

16. ________________________ allow the best possible design to emerge as part of the development process.

A. Empowered Teams
B. Deferred Commitments
C. Eliminating Wastes
D. Optimizing the Holes

17. The goal of rapidly satisfying a Customer need is driven by the Lean principle to ____________________.

    A. Empower the Team
    B. Defer Commitment
    C. Eliminate Waste
    D. Optimize the Whole

18. The principle of ____________________ drives the success of iterative development approaches because it fuels adaptive changes to overcome mistakes.

    A. Empower the Team
    B. Defer Commitments
    C. Eliminate Wastes
    D. Optimize the Holes

19. Failure to ____________________ shows up in evidence that the process missed an opportunity to produce real value.

    A. Empower the Team
    B. Defer Commitment
    C. Eliminate Waste
    D. Optimize the Whole

20. The fastest way to deliver the system the Customer expects is to have the Customer ____________________ through an incremental discovery process.

    A. Pull the pieces
    B. Push the pieces
    C. Refine the Stories
    D. Optimize the priorities

Fill-in-the-Blank Challenge

1. Artifacts for LSD include ____________________ and ____________________.

2. Even though many of the artifacts have a ________________ they are still important.

3. Without the proper perspective, there is a continuous risk that development will _____________ part of the solution.

4. As the Team works through development, it must solve the current need and ____ so it is capable of moving forward to the next generation of technology challenges.

5. Lean Software Development was born in 2003 when Lean Software Development: An Agile Toolkit was published by ________________________________.

6. The ceremonies used by LSD include ________________________________.

7. _________________________ estimate Stories, write code, and define tests.

8. The ____________________ explains and describes system features in enough detail for the Developers to understand what to build.

9. The goal of the _____________________ is to ensure the system meets the needs of the Customer and end users.

10. The __________________________ role is responsible for system deployment, user training, and the help desk.

11. The _________________________ exercises the process of translating low granularity "boulders" into high granularity "rocks" that Developers can understand.

12. ________________________________ occur when any advantage of acquiring additional information is offset by the risk of delaying the decision.

13. ______________________________ means that the Customer's needs have been understood and integrated into the overall system experience for the users.

14. Moving from a Quality Control (QC) mindset of catching bugs to a Quality Assurance (QA) mindset of validating assumptions can be described as ____.

15. It is integral to the ___________________________________ process that architecture be guided by refactoring.

16. ______________________________ allow the best possible design to emerge as part of the development process.

17. The goal of rapidly satisfying a Customer need is driven by the Lean principle to ____________________________________.

18. The principle of ____________________________ drives the success of iterative development approaches because it fuels adaptive changes to overcome mistakes.

19. Failure to ______________________________ shows up in evidence that the process missed an opportunity to produce real value.

20. The fastest way to deliver the system the Customer expects is to have the Customer _________________________________ through an incremental discovery process.

Terminology Matching Exercise

In the blank column to the left of the Term, fill in the letter that identifies the correct Definition or Description.

	TERM		DEFINITION / DESCRIPTION
	1. Customer Feedback	A	Focus on the goal of ensuring the system will deliver business value
	2. Developers	B	Write descriptions of the Customer's Conditions of Satisfaction and User Acceptance Tests
	3. Analysts	C	Includes roles responsible for system deployment, user training, and the help desk to answer user questions
	4. Testers	D	Estimate Stories, write code, and define tests in order to deliver working software
	5. Support	E	Help Customers explain and describe system features in enough detail for the Developers to build them
	6. Customers	F	When any advantage of additional insight is offset by the potential risk of delaying the decision
	7. Last Responsible Moment	G	Must be avoided as the Team works through development so the solution is capable of moving forward to the next generation of technology challenges
	8. Build Quality In	H	The Lean principle that drives the goal of rapidly satisfying a Customer need
	9. Deferred Commitment	I	The fastest way to deliver the system the Customer expects
	10. Eliminate Waste	J	Means the Customer's needs have been understood and integrated into the overall system experience for the users
	11. Customer Pull	K	Allow the best possible design to emerge as part of the development process

	TERM		DEFINITION / DESCRIPTION
	12. LSD Artifact	L	The only ceremony in LSD
	13. Technical Debt	M	The principle that says there is a continuous risk that development will optimize only part of the solution
	14. Empower the Team	N	Customer Reviews
	15. Optimize the Whole	O	Gives the organization the capacity to respond quickly to the future as it unfolds

Answers - Chapter Practice Test

1. **C.** Artifacts for **LSD** include **CUSTOMER REVIEWS** and **APPROVALS.**

   Artifacts for LSD include the Product Vision, Roadmap and Release Plans, User Stories, Code, Tests, Configuration Scripts, and Customer Reviews and Approvals. And even though many of the artifacts are intangible and may have a short lifespan, they are still important. They should be captured and maintained in a version control system with a central repository providing a history of changes.

2. **A.** Even though many of the artifacts have a **SHORT LIFESPAN** they are still important.

   Artifacts for LSD include the Product Vision, Roadmap and Release Plans, User Stories, Code, Tests, Configuration Scripts, and Customer Reviews and Approvals. And even though many of the artifacts are intangible and may have a short lifespan they are still important. They should be captured and maintained in a version control system with a central repository providing a history of changes.

3. **A.** Without the proper perspective, there is a continuous risk that development will **OPTIMIZE** part of the solution.

   Without the proper perspective, there is a continuous risk that development will optimize part of the solution thereby sub-optimizing the overall solution. While the synergy of the sub-systems is critical, the performance of the system as a whole is the key to success.

4. **D.** As the Team works through development, it must solve the current need and **AVOID TECHNICAL DEBT** so it is capable of moving forward to the next generation of technology challenges.

   As the cross-functional Team works through development, it must 'begin with the end in mind' as Stephen Covey advises, clarifying the entire Value Stream by analyzing back from the future. The solution must solve the current need and avoid technical debt so it is also capable of moving forward to the next generation of technology challenges.

5. **C.** Lean Software Development was born in 2003 when Lean Software Development: An Agile Toolkit was published by **MARY AND TOM POPPENDIECK.**

   Lean Software Development was born in 2003 when Lean Software Development: An Agile Toolkit was published by Mary and Tom Poppendieck. The book presented how to use an adapted version of Lean Manufacturing principles, or more specifically, Lean Product Development, to develop software and also compared it to other Agile practices.

6. **B.** The ceremonies used by LSD include **CUSTOMER FEEDBACK.**

   Describing ceremonies for LSD is quite different because other than the Release and Iteration planning ceremonies, held in common with other Agile Frameworks, the only ceremony in LSD is gathering Customer Feedback. It is a ceremony that is not held on a formal periodic basis, like the Daily, Review or Retrospective meetings. Instead it is an ad hoc, mostly informal, ceremony that can be held as often as hourly.

   During the Customer Feedback ceremony the Developer and Customer meet and see, test and use the system changes to decide if they solve the problem or need additional fine-tuning.

7. **C. DEVELOPERS** estimate Stories, write code, and define tests.

   Developers estimate Stories, write code, and define tests in order to deliver working software. Some Developers have enough experience and domain-savvy to fill the Analyst role. The Developer role is simply to accept responsibility for completing the Tasks that ultimately deliver a successful result.

8. **A.** The **ANALYST** explains and describes system features in enough detail for the Developers to understand what to build.

   Analysts help Customers explain and describe system features in enough detail for the Developers to understand what to build. Analysts are similar to Product Managers in XP and Product Owners in Scrum with an important distinction that they not become a barrier to direct Developer-Customer discussions. Analysts facilitate knowledge transfer for both sides without restricting direct contact.

9. **D.** The goal of the **TESTER** is to ensure the system meets the needs of the Customer and end users.

   Testers create comprehensive tests for both the Customer's Conditions of Satisfaction and User Acceptance Tests. The goal is to ensure the system meets the needs of the Customer and end users. Sometimes Testers have the experience and cross-training to also serve as Analyst, and vice versa.

10. **A.** The **SUPPORT** role is responsible for system deployment, user training, and the help desk.

    Support includes all the roles that are responsible for system deployment, user training, and the help desk to answer user questions. It is a broad category and can include many domain- and industry-specific roles.

11. **C.** The **CUSTOMER** exercises the process of translating low granularity "boulders" into high granularity "rocks" that Developers can understand.

    Customers focus on the goal of ensuring the system will deliver business value.

    Customers sometimes benefit from the help of Analysts as they go through the process of translating low granularity "boulders" into high granularity "rocks" that developers can understand. But not every Customer needs help creating and prioritizing the Stories to be developed.

12. **B. LAST RESPONSIBLE MOMENTS** occur when any advantage of acquiring additional information is offset by the risk of delaying the decision.

    Last Responsible Moments occur at the point where any advantage of acquiring additional valuable information or insight is offset by the potential risk of delaying the decision any longer.

13. **A. BUILD QUALITY IN** means that the Customer's needs have been understood and integrated into the overall system experience for the users.

    Building quality into the solution is more than just the technical notion that the individual components and subassemblies work well together as a robust, flexible, and responsive system. It means that the Customer's needs have been understood and integrated into the overall system experience for the Users. It means paying the price to develop a solution that is intuitive to use, solves problems well, and can be maintained, extended and scaled appropriately and efficiently.

14. **A.** Moving from a Quality Control (QC) mindset of catching bugs to a Quality Assurance (QA) mindset of validating assumptions can be described as **BUILD QUALITY IN.**

    Build quality in means moving from a Quality Control (QC) mindset of catching bugs to a Quality Assurance (QA) mindset of validating assumptions with useful metrics throughout the process that ensure practices create value or are discarded.

15. **A.** It is integral to the **BUILD QUALITY IN** process that architecture be guided by refactoring.

    Only information flowing in a constant feedback loop from Customer to Developer and back again can provide the needed "actionable insight". It is integral to the build quality in process that architecture be guided by refactoring so that as more features are added to the solution the coding maintains as much simplicity, clarity and reliability as possible.

16. **B. DEFERRED COMMITMENTS** allow the best possible design to emerge as part of the development process.

    Deferred commitments allow the best possible design to emerge as part of the development process. Software development always occurs in an atmosphere charged with uncertainty and complexity. Better results come from having the discipline to create as much clarity as possible about the problem, identify the various solution choices and the tradeoffs imbedded in each one, and making a fact-based decision on which approach or approaches to test and pursue.

17. **C.** The goal of rapidly satisfying a Customer need is driven by the Lean principle to **ELIMINATE WASTE.**

    The goal of rapidly satisfying a Customer need is driven by the Lean principle to eliminate waste. Therefore, the Team must be vigilant about recognizing any activity that could be bypassed as waste while still satisfying the Customer. Waste-removal must be diligently pursued during every Iteration and every step of the planning process.

18. **B.** The principle of **DEFER COMMITMENTS** drives the success of iterative development approaches because it fuels adaptive changes to overcome mistakes.

    The principle of Defer Commitments drives the success of iterative development approaches because it fuels adaptive changes to overcome mistakes that would be potentially costly after the release of the system. It means that planning is concerned with exploring options and adapting to discoveries while the inter-relationships between requirements, which may number in the thousands, are worked out. It requires that decisions and commitments be deferred to the Last Responsible Moment.

19. **C.** Failure to **ELIMINATE WASTE** shows up in evidence that the process missed an opportunity to produce real value.

    Defects lower quality and are waste, but they are also evidence that the process missed an opportunity to produce real value. Value Stream Mapping identifies waste, but it becomes waste if it is not used eliminate it. Planning minimizes waste, but it becomes waste if it doesn't prevent development of the wrong solution.

20. **A.** The fastest way to deliver the system the Customer expects is to have the Customer **PULL THE PIECES** through an incremental discovery process.

    The fastest way to deliver the system the Customer expects is to have the Customer pull the pieces – features, functions and capabilities – through an incremental discovery process that creates a deep understanding of how to solve the problem.

Answers - Fill-in-the-Blank Challenge

1. Artifacts for **LSD** include **CUSTOMER REVIEWS** and **APPROVALS.**

   Artifacts for LSD include the Product Vision, Roadmap and Release Plans, User Stories, Code, Tests, Configuration Scripts, and Customer Reviews and Approvals. And even though many of the artifacts are intangible and may have a short lifespan, they are still important. They should be captured and maintained in a version control system with a central repository that provides a history of changes.

2. Even though many of the artifacts have a **SHORT LIFESPAN** they are still important.

   Artifacts for LSD include the Product Vision, Roadmap and Release Plans, User Stories, Code, Tests, Configuration Scripts, and Customer Reviews and Approvals. And even though many of the artifacts are intangible and may have a short lifespan they are still important. They should be captured and maintained in a version control system with a central repository that provides a history of changes.

3. Without the proper perspective there is a continuous risk that development will **OPTIMIZE** part of the solution.

   Without the proper perspective there is a continuous risk that development will optimize part of the solution thereby sub-optimizing the overall solution. While the synergy of the sub-systems in critical the performance of the system as a whole is the key to success.

4. As the Team works through development, it must solve the current need and **AVOID TECHNICAL DEBT** so it is also capable of moving forward to the next generation of technology challenges.

   As the cross-functional Team works through development, it must 'begin with the end in mind' as Stephen Covey advises, clarifying the entire Value Stream by analyzing back from the future. The solution must solve the current need and avoid technical debt so it is also capable of moving forward to the next generation of technology challenges.

5. Lean Software Development was born in 2003 when Lean Software Development: An Agile Toolkit was published by **MARY AND TOM POPPENDIECK.**

   Lean Software Development was born in 2003 when Lean Software Development: An Agile Toolkit was published by Mary and Tom Poppendieck. The book presented how to use an adapted version of Lean Manufacturing principles, or more specifically, Lean Product Development, to develop software and also compared it to other Agile practices.

6. The ceremonies used by **LSD** include **CUSTOMER FEEDBACK.**

   Describing ceremonies for LSD is quite different because other than the Release and Iteration planning ceremonies, held in common with other Agile Frameworks, the only ceremony in LSD is gathering Customer Feedback. It is a ceremony that is not held on a formal periodic basis, like the Daily, Review or Retrospective meetings. Instead it is an ad hoc, mostly informal, ceremony that can be held as often as hourly.

   During the Customer Feedback ceremony the Developer and Customer meet and see, test, and use the system changes to decide if they solve the problem or need additional fine-tuning.

7. **DEVELOPERS** estimate Stories, write code, and define tests.

   Developers estimate Stories, write code, and define tests in order to deliver working software. Some Developers have enough experience and domain-savvy to fill the Analyst role. The Developer role is simply to accept responsibility for completing the Tasks that ultimately deliver a successful result.

8. The **ANALYST** explains and describes system features in enough detail for the Developers to understand what to build.

   Analysts help Customers explain and describe system features in enough detail for the Developers to understand what to build. Analysts are similar to Product Managers in XP and Product Owners in Scrum with an important distinction that they not become a barrier to direct Developer-Customer discussions. Analysts facilitate knowledge transfer for both sides without restricting direct contact.

9. The goal of the **TESTER** is to ensure the system meets the needs of the Customer and end users.

   Testers create comprehensive tests for both the Customer's Conditions of Satisfaction and User Acceptance Tests. The goal is to ensure the system meets the needs of the Customer and end users. Sometimes Testers have the experience and cross-training to also serve as Analyst, and vice versa.

10. The **SUPPORT** role is responsible for system deployment, user training, and the help desk.

    Support includes all the roles that are responsible for system deployment, user training, and the help desk to answer user questions. It is a broad category and can include many domain- and industry-specific roles.

11. The **CUSTOMER** exercises the process of translating low granularity "boulders" into high granularity "rocks" that Developers can understand.

    Customers focus on the goal of ensuring the system will deliver business value.

    Customers sometimes benefit from the help of Analysts as they go through the process of translating low granularity "boulders" into high granularity "rocks" Developers can understand. But not every Customer needs help creating and prioritizing the Stories to be developed.

12. **LAST RESPONSIBLE MOMENTS** occur when any advantage of acquiring additional information is offset by the risk of delaying the decision.

    Last Responsible Moments occur at the point where any advantage of acquiring additional valuable information or insight is offset by the potential risk of delaying the decision any longer.

13. **BUILD QUALITY IN** means that the Customer's needs have been understood and integrated into the overall system experience for the users.

    Building quality into the solution is more than just the technical notion that the individual components and subassemblies work well together as a system that is robust, flexible, and responsive. It means that the Customer's needs have been understood and integrated into the overall system experience for the users. It means paying the price to develop a solution that is intuitive to use, solves problems well, and can be maintained, extended and scaled appropriately and efficiently.

14. Moving from a Quality Control (QC) mindset of catching bugs to a Quality Assurance (QA) mindset of validating assumptions can be described as **BUILD QUALITY IN.**

    Build quality in means moving from a Quality Control (QC) mindset of catching bugs to a Quality Assurance (QA) mindset of validating assumptions with useful metrics throughout the process that ensure practices create value, or are discarded.

15. It is integral to the **BUILD QUALITY IN** process that architecture be guided by refactoring.

    Only information flowing in a constant feedback loop from Customer to Developer and back again can provide the needed "actionable insight". It is integral to the build quality in process that architecture be guided by refactoring so that as more features are added to the solution the coding maintains as much simplicity, clarity and reliability as possible.

16. **DEFERRED COMMITMENTS** allow the best possible design to emerge as part of the development process.

    Software development always occurs in an atmosphere charged with uncertainty and complexity. Better results come from having the discipline to create as much clarity as possible about the problem, identify the various solution choices and the tradeoffs imbedded in each one, and finally making a fact-based decision on which approach or approaches to test and pursue.

17. The goal of rapidly satisfying a Customer need is driven by the Lean principle to **ELIMINATE WASTE.**

    The goal of rapidly satisfying a Customer need is driven by the Lean principle to eliminate waste. Therefore, the Team must be vigilant about recognizing any activity that could be bypassed as waste while still satisfying the Customer. Waste-removal must be diligently pursued during every Iteration and every step of the planning process.

18. The principle of **DEFER COMMITMENTS** drives the success of iterative development approaches because it fuels adaptive changes to overcome mistakes.

    The principle of Defer Commitments drives the success of iterative development approaches because it fuels adaptive changes to overcome mistakes that would be potentially costly after the release of the system. It means that planning is concerned with exploring options and adapting to discoveries while the inter-relationships between requirements, which may number in the thousands, are worked out. It requires that decisions and commitments be deferred to the Last Responsible Moment.

19. Failure to **ELIMINATE WASTE** shows up in evidence that the process missed an opportunity to produce real value.

    Defects lower quality and are waste, but they are also evidence that the process missed an opportunity to produce real value. Value Stream Mapping identifies waste, but it becomes waste if it is not used eliminate it. Planning minimizes waste, but it becomes waste if it doesn't prevent development of the wrong solution.

20. The fastest way to deliver the system the Customer expects is to have the Customer **PULL THE PIECES** through an incremental discovery process.

    The fastest way to deliver the system the Customer expects is to have the Customer pull the pieces – features, functions and capabilities – through an incremental discovery process that creates a deep understanding of how to solve the problem.

Answers - Terminology Matching

1:L, 2:D, 3:E, 4:B, 5:C, 6:A, 7:F, 8:J, 9:K, 10:H, 11:I, 12:N, 13:G, 14:O, 15:M

Chapter End Notes

[32]Mary Poppendieck and Tom Poppendieck (2003), Lean Software Development: An Agile Toolkit, Addison-Wesley Professional

Kanban Basic Practices Deep Dives

Chapter Highlights

In this chapter you will find an overview of Kanban's basic practices as well as a detailed description of its key elements. Those elements are broken out as the Roles, Workflow, Ceremonies and Artifacts. The people are identified by the Roles they fulfill. The Workflow details how those people work together and produce the planned results. Lastly, the Artifacts are the electronic or printed evidence of the results.

Overview of Kanban

It is well known in project management circles that the core of Goldratt's Theory of Constraints is an approach that identifies a bottleneck and eliminates it until no more performance constraints exist. Of course, when one bottleneck is eliminated a new bottleneck emerges and the cycle repeats and no system ever reaches the point of having zero constraints. Goldratt applied the theory to flow problems and called it, "Drum-Buffer-Rope." It is an iterative approach to improving systemic performance.

Outside of project management circles, Kanban's storied history with the Toyota Production System and Lean Principles has given it much broader recognition and credibility than the Theory of Constraints even though they have an amazing number of similarities. Drum-Buffer-Rope and Kanban are both examples of Pull systems. Pull systems produce deliverables by changing them incrementally at a sustainable pace. With the advance of Lean principles into the project management profession, commonly referred to as Agile Project Management, the science developed in Goldratt's Theory of Constraints may finally get a full wind in its sails. However, those sails will billow under the flag of Kanban.

Kan-ban *(pronounced con-bon)* is a Japanese word that literally means "signal card" in English. The card is used to signal an upstream process to produce more. Kanban does not allow work to occur upstream until a downstream lever pulls it. It has proven to be a very useful technique for handling development in environments with high complexity and uncertainty where the means of production is knowledge workers. Kan-ban, or as used in The United States, Kanban, also has a strong link to Kaizen, a Japanese word for "continuous improvement." In Japanese manufacturing it is believed that Kaizen is the engine that makes Kanban work.

Combining Kanban ideas with techniques from workflow modeling and visualization has created performance breakthroughs in industries where work emerges and changes as it "flows" through a production system. It has generated amazing results because it creates visibility allowing bottlenecks to be seen and removed.

That physiological connection – being able to literally "see" bottlenecks – is one of the big reasons why Kanban works. In your brain, a picture is worth a thousand words or, literally perhaps 10,000 to 50,000 words, because according to brain researchers the human brain processes visual information tens of thousands of times faster than text. In fact, the largest group of nerve fibers connected to the human brain is linked to the eyes. That kind of evolutionary development highly suggests that neurological pathways in the human brain are better adapted to visual displays than text.

Kanban harnesses the power of visual information by using sticky notes on a whiteboard, or an electronic equivalent, to create "pictures" of work. Seeing how work flows within the Team's process makes both the status and the context of the work visible. Kanban takes vital information and turns it into brain candy. So one might ask, "How did all this get started?"

In the late 1940s, Toyota engineered a better automotive production process by extrapolating ideas for a most unlikely source, the American supermarket. They recognized that stores restocked grocery items in order to replace missing inventory and not just because a supplier had the item in stock.

Only when an item's inventory was depleted to a defined minimum level did the store replenish its stock. That observation set in motion Toyota's decision to rethink their production approach and develop a new approach – a Kanban system – where replacement inventory arrived only after being summoned, and only "just-in-time", to replace inventory already consumed.

Kanban surfaced as an idea for developing systems in high-complexity, knowledge-driven environments around 2005 because of the leadership of David Anderson, Rick Garber, Jim Benson, Corey Ladas and others. The Toyota Production System, W. Edwards Deming, Eliyahu Goldratt, and Donald Reinertsen were all influential in sculpting the developing body of knowledge.

In May 2007, at the Lean New Product Development conference in Chicago, Rick Garber and David Anderson presented results from an approach they were developing. Anderson also led an open-space discussion about Kanban systems at the Agile 2007 gathering later that summer. Along with Garber and Anderson, other early adopters like Arlo Belshee with his Naked Planning approach, Karl Scotland, Aaron Sanders, and Joe Arnold from Yahoo!, and Kenji Hiranabe who was published in InfoQ, became well recognized thought leaders in the nascent Kanban community.

There was so much excitement and interest in Kanban that in 2008, the Agile Alliance presented the Gordon Pask Award to Arlo Belshee and Kenji Hiranabe for their contributions to the emergence of Kanban to the Agile community. Clearly a fire had been lit, but there was still a lot of learning to be done.

It was counter-intuitive to software experts, who happen to be manufacturing neophytes, to imagine that engineer-to-order (ETO) manufacturing and software development could share a great deal in common because of the intense amount of knowledge work both contain. As it turned out, ETO and software development share production domains characterized by high variability where creative, leading edge design drives value as well as project success and organizational profitability. Often ETO precedes mass-production manufacturing where the goal is to leverage the intellectual capital acquired in the ETO process in order to replicate deliverables as cheaply as possible. That situation is amazingly similar to the software development cycle that leverages the intellectual capital imbedded in the original code and replicates it at a cost that rapidly approaches zero.

Beyond just being manufacturing neophytes, because Kanban as a methodology used in software is relatively young in the maturity process, it is also supported, and being extended, by a robust community actively discovering new insights and putting them into practice. And those new practices are very good because they are founded on, and tested against, core Lean principles.

Within the Kanban community there are six practices (currently) referred to as "core practices." They are:

1. Visualize
2. Limit Work in Progress
3. Manage Flow
4. Make Process Policies Explicit
5. Implement Feedback Loops
6. Improve Collaboratively, Evolve Experimentally

These core practices aren't carved in stone. As Marcus Hammarberg and Joakim Sunden share in their book, *Kanban in Action*[33], "During our time as kanban practitioners, the principles we talk about have become practices, the practices have gone from three to five to six, the term principles has been redefined, and a new principle has been added. We expect and hope that the discussion around these practices isn't over."

The whole exercise of developing the Kanban Framework is a great example of continuous improvement, as Lean advocates.

Roles

Kanban is fundamentally different from other Agile Frameworks like Scrum, XP, and LSD. Those other Frameworks prescribe roles and responsibilities along with workflows, ceremonies and artifacts. Kanban, on the other hand, maps the workflow in order to understand the current system and make the roles and responsibilities explicit and visible so they can be improved.

Kanban does not prescribe roles. Instead, it seeks to be minimally invasive while improving job roles and responsibilities. That makes it possible to create a Hybrid Project Management system, tailored to the needs of the Team and the Organization, by combining Kanban with any of the other Agile Frameworks.

Because the goal of Kanban is to optimize existing processes using visualization tools to catalyze incremental changes the existing roles and responsibilities do not change, unless and until the Team decides it is necessary.

Workflow

Two Quick, Familiar Analogies

Example 1 - Commercial Laundry Business

Step One – Find the Constraint. How? Observe the environment and identify where laundry is piled up. In this case, the piles are lined up waiting for the dryers. Therefore, the dryer process is the constraint.

Step Two – Optimize the Constraint. How? Observe that each dryer has a loud buzzer that sounds when a load is done. Define an operating control that only allows a washer load to be started when a dryer buzzes and the load is moved to the folding area. The control means work is pulled into the system based on dryer demand, not pushed into the system based on washer demand. (Figure 7.1)

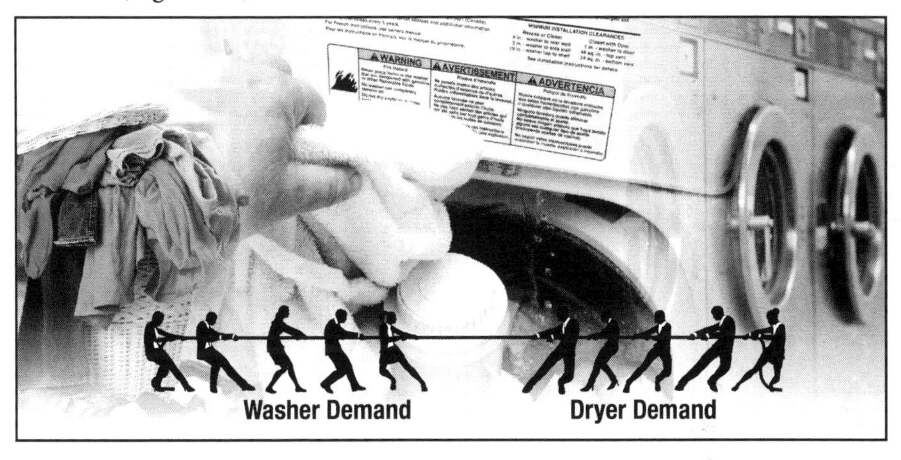

Figure 7.1 | *Kanban Laundry Example*

Step Three, Option 1 – Increase the Capacity. How? Options include buying washers that spin more moisture out of the clothes so they process faster in the dryers, buying dryers with larger capacity or faster drying capability. Bigger dryer, speed drying, offload, drying work by buying a new washing machine that spins clothes faster.

Step Three, Option 2 – Offload Some Work. How? Options include sending batches to an off-site processer or dry-cleaning them on-site.

Step Three, Option 3 – Redesign the Process. How? Options include pre-sorting batches to be air dried on racks after washing or implementing price-controlled levels of service to move more work into off-peak hours.

Example 2 - Rush-Hour Freeway Traffic

Step One – Find the Constraint. How? Observe the environment and identify where traffic is backed up. In this case, traffic is "stop and go" on the in-bound morning and out-bound evening commute. Therefore, freeway capacity is the constraint.

Step Two – Optimize the Constraint. How? Install stoplights on on-ramps that are programmed to control the number of cars entering the freeway during rush hour. Manage the control means work is pulled into the system based on freeway demand, not pushed into the system based on commuter demand.

Step Three, Option 1 – Increase the Capacity. How? Observe that the morning and evening commutes move in opposite directions and the opposing direction has excess capacity. Options include defining a control such as carpool lanes to influence commuter behavior, adding additional freeway lanes, or installing a moveable median so the number of lanes in-bound or out-bound varies depending on the time of day. (Figure 7.2)

Figure 7.2| *Moveable Median*

Step Three, Option 2 – Offload Some Work. How? One option is to define an operating control that prevents a certain class of vehicles, such as semi-trucks, from using the freeway during rush hour thereby offloading that work to the surface streets.

Step Three, Option 3 – Redesign the Process. How? Collaborate with local municipal authorities to extend the boundaries of the programmable stoplights to surface streets within 1.5 miles of freeway off-ramps to raise the number of cars able to exit highly congested off-ramps during rush hour.

Seeing two examples as completely different as commercial laundry and freeway traffic demonstrates that Kanban is powerful and flexible. Let's examine how it's done.

Visualize the Workflow

Visualizing the workflow requires creating transparency by leveraging implicit knowledge to expose and resolve inconsistencies and conflicts between policies and real process behaviors. Using a Kanban board to make the information visible, instead of just being in people's minds, means it can be subjected to continuous improvement.

It is helpful to remember that it is not important that work "fit" in predefined categories however, it is very important that it flows! Likewise, arbitrarily fracturing work so it fits into a predefined time sequence often has a negative impact on work completion, whereas having it properly flow through the process can reduce defects, increase team motivation, and raise total throughput.

So the goal is to visualize the workflow as it actually takes place now then incrementally improve it over time so that the fastest, sustainable pace of quality work can be achieved.

For many years, without calling it Kanban, two famously successful companies have used visualization. Intel® Corp. has a process called "MAPP Day" (Make A Project Plan) and Siemens Corp. has a process called "PACT Day" (Project Acceleration Control Technique). Both use visualization best practices to optimize the workflow of large teams developing major initiatives.

Both processes use an important best practice referred to as "low-tech, high-touch." Over the years, experience has repeatedly demonstrated that collocating the key decision makers and SMEs in a room and having them use sticky notes to do planning at key times, such as project initiation, after a significant change, or beginning a major new release, saves many more dollars and days than the cost of bringing them together to do that planning. Something powerful in human physiology and relationships unlocks a creative genius for solving complex problems in environments of high uncertainty when simple, physical, low-tech sticky notes are used to create a high-touch interactive discussion about how to represent the most logical workflow for development.

There are many electronic tools, from mind mapping to Kanban software, that mimic the whiteboards and walls used in low-tech, high-touch approaches. They can be, and are, invaluable to teams for managing their work and workflow, but the recommended best practice for initially visualizing the workflow remains low-tech, high-touch.

When the Team assembles to visualize the process for the first time it should take into account that it has the freedom to change the visualization as many times and as much as needed to express what is actually happening. Therefore, the process needs to facilitate changing the presentation quickly and easily.

Remember the goal is to visualize the workflow as it actually takes place, which means uncovering the mental and physical closets and cubbyholes where constraints, guidelines, rules and regulations are hiding and drawing them out into the open. That means the members of the Team have to have the experience and expertise to know where to look, the authority and courage to pull it out of hiding, and power and insight to address it.

Step-by-Step

Step 1 - Define the Boundaries

The first step is to put a boundary around which workflow is being visualized. Is it the entire enterprise from end to end? If so, the steps will have to be relatively high-level or else the workflow will be huge and possibly unmanageable making it worthless. Is it at a business unit or product class level? If so, some of the enterprise-level concerns just mentioned must be considered and it must also clearly identify the beginning and end points of the workflow. Those endpoints must include all descriptions of the constraint assumptions being made about the condition of the inputs to the process and the condition of the outputs from the process. One way to root out the constraints and assumptions is to define the acceptance criteria or conditions of satisfaction that must be met before the input enters or the output exits the process. Before finalizing the visualization, those constraints and assumptions must be validated. Regardless of the level of workflow being defined, it is vital that the inputs and outputs be clearly defined along with the constraints and assumptions being made about them.

One caveat worth noting is to avoid information overload. The level of experience a team has with doing visualizations limits the amount of detail they can process. As a rule of thumb, new teams should limit their visualizations to no more than 100 sticky notes. However, one experienced team at Intel® Corp. produced a MAPP Day visualization that was 9 feet tall and 38 feet long, but they had deep, extensive experience with the process. If a team tries to fit too much information or too many branches into the visualization, they will end up with a process that is difficult to understand and therefore impossible to improve.

Step 2 - Name the Phases

Once the frame has been defined, the next step is to name the Phases. The Phases will be the column titles on the Kanban board and the work will flow through them.

Phases can be anything from Preliminary Design Review (PDR), Critical Design Review (CDR), Mock-up, Prototype, Test Set, and Flight Set, commonly used in aerospace hardware manufacturing, to Write Stories, Estimate, Design, Code and Test, User Acceptance Testing (UAT), and Commit, used in software development. The names should be descriptive in a way that is intuitive to the general audience likely to interact with it. One IT team working at a large construction firm decided to name the Phases of their system development workflow according to the construction lexicon their coworkers would recognize. The phases were named Idea, Block Diagram, Blueprint, Construct, and Punch List because those names were familiar to their users, from senior management to crew superintendents. (Figure 7.3)

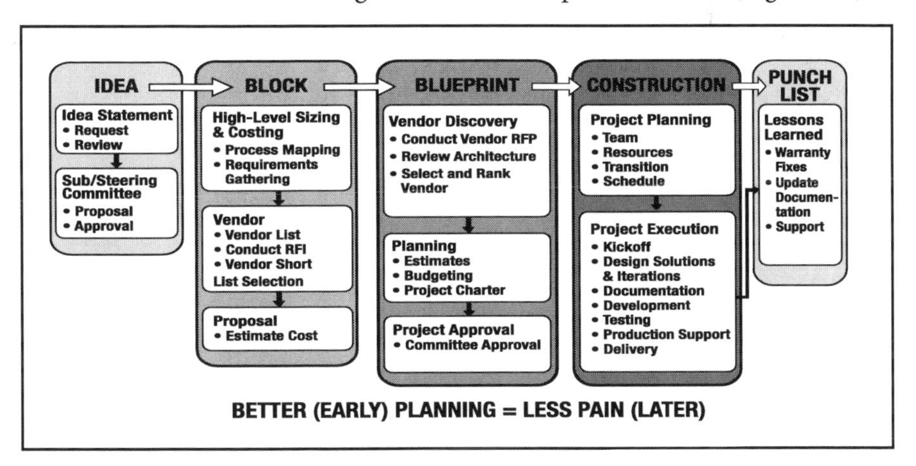

Figure 7.3| *Visualization Example*

Using a familiar lexicon is a great idea, but it does have a couple of inherent risks. The first is that familiar names provide lots of hiding places for assumptions. So it is important to ferret out those assumptions to prevent misunderstandings and achieve a reliable consensus about what the Phases include or exclude. Consider Figure 7.3 as an example. Because activities for defining requirements and selecting a vendor are spread over several Phases, assumptions about who is documenting what can easily hide from view. One way to expose those assumptions is to describe the boundaries of the Phases (and columns) by defining the criteria that must be met before the work item can move to the next column. The columns represent work processes and queues so it is vital that the entry and exit criteria be explicit and concise. If they can be listed as bullet points on a checklist they help crystallize what is visualized as part of the phase and what is being left out.

Having the criteria refined to the correct degree means that each item can be tested against them before being moved across the board. It also means that if a criterion is not being applied, or if a new criterion is needed or requires modification, it will become apparent and continuous process improvement activities, such as root-cause analysis, can be initiated. In this way, policies are made visible by the criteria representing them and can be continuously discussed and incrementally improved over time.

A best practice for naming and validating the phases comes from Honda Motor Co. and is called, "The 3 Actuals." The three Actuals are:

- Go to the actual place.
- Speak to the actual people.
- See them do the actual work.

The 3 Actuals encapsulate the truth that there is nothing better than making your own observations and collecting your own data. Honda insists it is the only way to develop a comprehensive understanding!

The first two steps can be accomplished by bringing together a group of people with appropriate experience in a low-tech, high-touch meeting to visualize the boundaries and phases. The third step is applied to validate the visualization.

Step 3 - Validate the Activities

Focus on capturing the actual workflow. Capturing the company's formal published version of the process because that's the one teams are supposed to use might be easier, but it's a mirage and won't be helpful. It is best to start with one or two of the most common work items that cross the boundary and enter the system then mentally walk down the stream of how the work actually flows in that particular context.

It is important to accept that getting the workflow correctly visualized can be hard and the exercise will consume quite a lot of time. However, the time spent discussing it until it is accurately documented is time well spent. Implicit assumptions are forced to rise to the surface by a clear visualization so they can be fully examined until true transparency about how the work is accomplished is achieved. Until that point, many opinions about how the work flows will exist, and those variances create waste and problems. After the point of clear visualization, assumptions and policies are explicit and can be evaluated and improved. Resist the urge to improve the process until after an accurate map of the current process is completed. The goal is to identify and document the workflow phases as they exist now, including queues (i.e., laundry piles waiting for the next machine), and improve the workflow, second.

Until the visualization produces a complete and validated map of the workflow, the real opportunities for improvement are not likely to be where they first appear in large part because of undiscovered queues. Even though not every type of work follows the exact same workflow, creating the map gives the Team the power to decide how to document those variations. One best practice is to revise a column name if the initial name is too specific to suit all work item types. A more abstract name, such as Verify or Validate, might overcome the limitations of a column name such as Test.

It is important to not be too rigid at first because experience shows that the Team will likely revise the column names several times as they discover work doesn't flow as initially thought. Because of that, it is usually best to delay defining the Kanban Board with an electronic tool or fancy tape on a whiteboard. Let the design be tested and validated and when it is stabilized, move it to a more permanent environment.

Step 4 - Define the Buffers, Queues and WIP

At times, the throughput of a process is sub-optimized by the variability of an input in general, or at specific or peak times. When smoothing that input might improve total throughput, a Buffer or Queue can be inserted into the workflow. Recall the example of cars randomly entering the freeway during rush hour and how the resulting gridlock reduced total freeway throughput. When the stoplights on the on-ramps were activated as a Buffer, a Queue formed and only as many cars as the freeway could process were pulled into that process. Buffers and Queues are a common bottleneck optimization method.

Buffers and Queues are holding places for small inventories of work items used to insure instant availability of input when a downstream process pulls it. They are often used as synonyms and are very nearly so. However, Buffers are external to a process group or step and occur between steps. Queues are different because they are internal to a process group and occur at the end of the process remaining internal to it.

	A	B	C	D	E	F	G	H	I	J
1	WORKFLOW →		BACKLOG			SPECIFICATION		DEV. BUFFER		DEVELOPMEN
2	WIP LIMIT →		7			5		3		3
3	BUSINESS DEFINED FFC ↓	USER STORY	ESTIMATE	QUEUE	DETAILED DESIGN	ACCEPT TESTS	QUEUE	BUFFER	TASKS PLAN	CODE
4	LOGIN									
5	USER ACCT									
6	PASSWORD RESET									
7	CC/BILLING									

Figure 7.4| *Buffers and Queues*

Both Buffers and Queues are illustrated in the Kanban spreadsheet shown in Figure 7.4. There is a Backlog Queue (column D) and a Specification Queue (column G) and both are internal to their respective process group. There is also a Development Buffer (column H) that is external to Specification and Development steps, following the first and preceding the second. It could have been inserted there for a variety of reasons, such as to allow the Product Owner to prioritize Stories with completed specifications that have been queued up. When both the Buffer and Queue are full, the productivity of the downstream development process regulates the production of the upstream process.

The Specification Queue, as shown, has a limit of 5 Stories while the Development Buffer has a limit of 3 Stories. Those limits mean the Product Owner can choose from 5 available Stories to keep the top 3 priorities presented for Development to pull. In that way the Queues and Buffers absorb variation and help maintain a smooth flow so that the Development Team isn't idle or constantly subjected to stop-and-go work conditions due to the differing lengths of time it takes to complete work items. Smoothing the flow improves predictability and increases throughput so more work is finished and delivered.

Although Queues and Buffers are necessary they should be kept as small as possible because they raise the level of Work-in-Progress (WIP) and lengthen lead-time, both of which are undesirable. When the work item count in the Buffer or Queue is below the defined WIP Limit, it is a visual signal that upstream production should engage.

The key to choosing a WIP Limit for a Buffer or Queue is that it must be large enough to ensure smooth flow in the system and avoid idle time for the resource that is the workflow bottleneck. It is also worth noting that if the upstream process has been defined to allow each person or programming pair to have two items-in-progress then production is Buffered for variability so the WIP Limit can be zero or one and the process is still optimized.

When capacity-constrained and non-instant-availability situations have to be managed, sizing Buffers and Queues is more challenging so the techniques applied must be more sophisticated. How to do that is covered in Book Two of the Agile Almanac.

As noted earlier, it was counter-intuitive for manufacturing neophytes to imagine that engineer-to-order (ETO) manufacturing and software development could share a great deal in common. Yet both domains must deal with high variability using creative, leading edge designs to drive value and achieve project success.

Interestingly, a positive, unintended consequence of applying the Pull System logic from manufacturing to the software development domain emerged. Using a Pull System with WIP Limits minimized the resource over allocation that commonly occurred in software development and increased throughput while maintaining agreed-upon quantity standards. It was an unexpected solution to a decades old conundrum.

In order to understand how Kanban helps improve workflow in production systems it is necessary to understand WIP.

Defining WIP

Work in progress, work in process, goods in process, and in-process inventory are all synonyms to a greater or lesser degree, with the terms work in progress and work in process being the most widely used. They all refer to partially finished tangible or intangible goods that an organization develops and delivers to customers or constituents. They are items that started as raw materials, such as fenders or designs, and are being altered, such as attached to a car chassis or written into code, but are unfinished and require further processing. (Figure 7.5) Often they are in a Queue, Buffer, or other storage location.

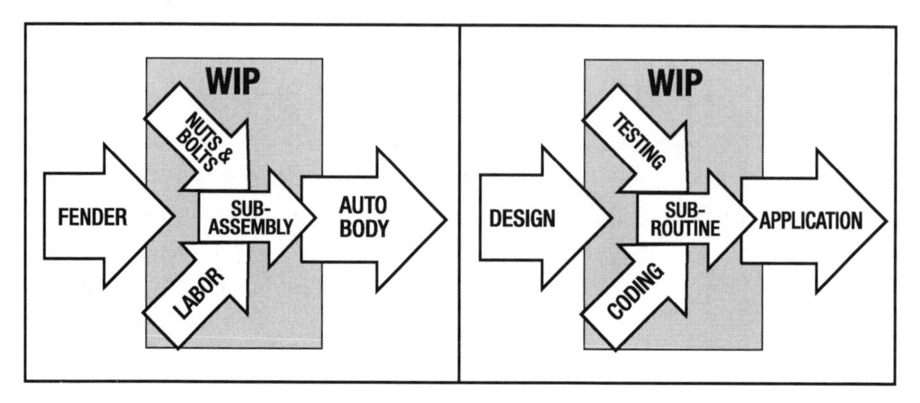

Figure 7.5| *Work in Progress (WIP)*

In manufacturing, the most commonly used term is work in progress, while in accounting it is most common to refer to the item classification as work in process.

Therefore, since Agile Project Management and Kanban both spring from a legacy in manufacturing, when the acronym **WIP** is used it is understood to mean Work In Progress.

WIP is important because it can be used to measure the progress of development work and validate the probable accuracy of project schedules before the actual deliverable is completed. WIP is also important to management because it can be recognized as an asset on the Balance Sheet and impact external stakeholders' evaluation of the performance of the CEO and other senior managers.

Little's Law[34] proves the relationship between WIP and throughput for a production system in a steady state. It is important because it correlates three significant performance measures – inventory, flow time, and throughput – in units per time period. This is very useful because risk can be identified with the amount of time represented by the User Stories in inventory. For instance, if we see 200 Stories of WIP for a team that produces 10 per day, a disaster probably awaits. Conversely, if we see 200 Stories of WIP for a team that produces 100 per day then it is extremely lean.

To leverage Little's Law and improve the process, the values for inventory, flow time, and throughput should be long-term averages measured in consistent units. Once we have those values, we can use them to estimate waiting times, plan WIP levels to reduce variability, and track flow time to ensure high delivery reliability.

Because Little's Law shows that Flow Time = WIP/Throughput, it is clear that reducing WIP while holding throughput constant will reduce flow time. That is very desirable, but leaders must resist the temptation to conclude that WIP reduction will always reduce cycle time. Reducing WIP without making required external process changes would also reduce throughput. An essential part of a Kanban implementation is to reduce variability and enable the Team to achieve greater throughput with less WIP. And that is why WIP Limits are used.

WIP Limits are a tool for managing development bottlenecks by aligning the amount of WIP to the system's capacity, thereby creating planning options, accelerating throughput, and clarifying focus with transparency throughout the production cycle

The scope of this book only includes basic Kanban because that is all that is required for single-team projects. The more complex aspects of scaling Kanban to enable large projects and programs and enterprise-wide agility, are covered in the second and third books of the Agile Almanac, respectively.

Basic Kanban starts with understanding how to manage and improve a Pull System. Generically, it means finding the constraint, optimizing it, then increasing its capacity, offloading some of its work, or redesigning the process to eliminate the constraint so that total system throughput is optimized and can be increased. The four steps for managing workflow just described – Define the Boundaries, Name the Phases, Validate the Activities and Define the Buffers, Queues and WIP – align with and implement the first three of the six core process mentioned earlier – Visualize, Limit Work in Progress, and Manage Flow.

Next, the Ceremonies content will explain how to implement the second three of the six core process mentioned earlier – Make Process Policies Explicit, Implement Feedback Loops, and Improve Collaboratively, Evolve Experimentally.

Ceremonies

Making process policies explicit is possible because combining visualization with information radiators makes the policy obvious. It can then be measured to see if it is helping the Team "do the right things the right way" and continuously improved. Normally, the combination of visualized policies and workflow is presented as an information radiator called the Kanban Board.

The Kanban Board focuses discussions on the process using objective, observable data instead of assumptions and anecdotal evidence to create transparency. Experience has shown that, quite often, an important step occurs, but is not shown on the board. Experience has also shown that transparency can be threatening to people who have chosen to "do things their own way," ignore policies or create a political power base by doing "favors" that fly under the organization's radar. The ceremony, "Create and Manage the Kanban Board" below explains more.

Feedback loops are essential to the Manage Flow core process and must be designed into the environment. Implementing feedback loops applies continuous improvement to the workflow using the Daily Standup, Queue and Buffer Replenishment, and Release Planning ceremonies. Each is explained below.

Lastly, employing the Improve Collaboratively, Evolve Experimentally core process means the Team must have a basic understanding of Lean, the Theory of Constraints and Kanban so they can explore and apply models and inquiries using the scientific method to improve the project environment and organizational ecosystem. The "After" Meeting and Triage ceremonies provide two structures for doing so and are explained below.

Create and Manage the Kanban Board

When a Kanban Board reaches full maturity it can look like the spreadsheet image shown in Figure 7.6 (which can be downloaded from the Members section of the GR8PM website). You can see the signs of maturity in the nesting of lower level processes, such as User Story, Estimate, and Queue, within the higher level Backlog process group, as well as in the use of Buffers and Queues, and, significantly, in the Policies bulleted across the bottom. The granular decomposition of the process groups and the explicit linkage to policies should not be expected in the initial Kanban mapping exercise, but it should be the long-term goal.

WORKFLOW →	BACKLOG			SPECIFICATION			DEV BUFFER	DEVELOPMENT			CODE REVIEW		CODE BUFFER	PRE-RELEASE REVIEW		DEPLOYMENT	
WIP LIMIT →	7			5			3	3			2		6	2			
BUSINESS DEFINED FFC ↓	USER STORY	ESTIMATE	QUEUE	DETAILED DESIGN	ACCEPT TESTS	QUEUE	BUFFER	TASKS PLAN	CODE	DONE/ QUEUE	TEST	COMMIT	BUFFER	UAT	APPROVED/ QUEUE	READY	DONE
LOGIN																	
USER ACCT																	
PASSWORD RESET																	
CC/BILLING																	
USER TEST SCORES ARCHIVE																	
POLICIES ➡	• Product Owner wrote or approved User Stories • Dev Team estimated using Planning Poker • Priority/Class assigned by PO and noted in User Story • Schedule requirements noted in User Story			• Design per Architectural rules • Define Acceptance criteria • Write tests			• PO pulls top 3 priorities from SPEC QUEUE into DEV BUFFER	TASKS PLAN • Programming pairs defined • Tasks listed • Cycle start time noted for alternating roles • Timer set for alternating pairs CODE • TDD practices applied • Refactored as required DONE • Cycle end time noted			TEST • Antipatterns checked • Unit tests conducted • Integration tests completed • Code Coverage checked • Deployment issues fixed Commit • Committed to non-production repository		• PO pulls from CODE COMMIT into CODE BUFFER for UAT process	UAT • Product Owner and Tester present during UAT as required • Appropriately qualified Users may also be involved • Only code functionality checked APPROVED • Approval or exceptions that are basis of rejection documented		READY • Ticket removed • End date recorded • Deployment reviewed and exceptions documented DONE • Statistics on cycle times and KPIs updated • Burn-down chart updated • Cumm. Flow Diagram updated • User Stories re-estimated then re-prioritized in Backlog	

Figure 7.6| *XLSX Kanban Board*

Before the board reaches maturity, the ceremony is focused on understanding and exposing the actual process being used and the real policies being followed. As the board matures, the ceremony is focused on measuring and improving it. When the board has reached a high level of maturity the ceremony focuses on using it to guide and improve how the Team applies it. However, introducing a visual, transparent way of directing work can seem threatening for some participants as mentioned above. Introducing visualization in small steps using a low-tech, high-touch approach will allow the Team to develop a consensus that supports decisions and undergirds accountability.

Daily Stand-Up Meetings

Stand-up meetings are common to Agile Frameworks, but they have evolved differently in Kanban. Because the board contains all the information about who is working on what, the focus is on the workflow process, not the individual's work progress. Each day the Team is looking to see whether a work item is blocked or has become invisible. Typically the group leader will begin at the end of the process and "walk backward" across the board from right to left, following the system's pull. The Stories on the board are discussed to discover if the information on the board presents the situation in a real and transparent way.

When a work item is blocked or being delayed, due to such things as defects or because someone needs help, questions are raised about the assumptions, resources and constraints that are contributing to the problem. One method for improving the visual power of the information is to attach small, round sticky-dots with green, yellow and red colors to tickets, escalating the color the longer the work item stays in a single location and is not actively flowing.

When a problem has been identified, the appropriate team members will accept responsibility to work the issue until it is resolved. As the workflow process, Kanban board, and team matures, the focus of the Daily Standup will narrow to just the stories that have a problem. This allows the Daily Standup to be scaled to larger teams and projects than in other Agile Frameworks.

Queue and Buffer Replenishment Meetings

Replenishment drives prioritization in Kanban, but because, as defined above, Queues are internal to a process group and Buffers are external to them, the mechanism used to replenish them is different.

The most common use of a Queue Replenishment Meeting is to manage the "input Queue" at the front end of a project management process. To be clear, because the "input Queue" is actually external to the development process, it would be better to call it an "input Buffer", but that is not the standard jargon at this time.

During a replenishment meeting for an "input Queue", typically a group of key stakeholders review the work items in the project Backlog and make prioritization decisions to ensure deliverables align with wider organizational objectives. This approach improves decision-making by aligning it to optimize organizational throughput.

Buffers are external to a process group so a specific replenishment process is used. In some cases, such as Kanban being used to improve the throughput of a system based on the Scrum Framework, the Product Owner in the system depicted in Figure 7.6 might act on her own to make decisions about replenishing the Development Buffer or might employ a Queue Replenishment Meeting, held at regular intervals, to make those decisions with a group of business and user representatives. Having a regular cadence for the replenishment meetings makes schedule coordination much easier for the participants while the meeting itself builds the relationship between the business and development team.

Queues are internal to a process group so they replenish, as we like to say, "auto-magically." Because the team responsible for the process group has a daily meeting, if the work item count in the Queue is below the WIP Limit, they decide who will produce what to replenish it.

The frequency of Queue Replenishment Meeting will affect decisions about Queue sizes and must be considered as the Kanban system is visualized and designed. Sometimes a decision will be made to increase the frequency of the Queue Replenishment Meeting in order to optimize total system throughput. Other times, throughput is acceptable so the frequency will be reduced to optimize the time-cost to participants.

Release Planning Meetings

In some organization-level Kanban systems, Release Planning Meetings are used to provide guidance about downstream delivery objectives to Queue Replenishment Meetings and other lower-level Kanban and project management systems. Because release planning is a high-level, long-range activity, it takes place on a regularly scheduled basis. Doing so reduces coordination costs and raises the probability that all key stakeholders will be present.

The "After" Meeting

When we previously described the Daily Scrum, we also explained the "Seven-Second Rule" for keeping synchronization meetings focused and time-boxed. The "After" Meeting in Kanban is comparable to the working group meetings that are often spawned during the Daily Scrum. The "After" Meeting is also ad hoc and typically involves 3 or 4 team members discussing anything from how to get a work item unblocked to options for removing a delay to kicking around a technical issue. Often times it is to discuss a process- or policy-related issue making the After Meeting a vital tool for transforming the current culture into one where Kanban can be leveraged to create more value. Sometimes it is simply an informal sub-team deciding how they'll build a particular feature, function or capability during the next few days.

Triage

Triage is a process for assessing and categorizing urgent work items based on their level of urgency and priority. It is a term borrowed from the medical profession where it is used to manage patients in an emergency room based on the severity of their condition rather than the time of their arrival. Priority is given to the most severe and life threatening situations and scaled down to conditions that are simply scary or uncomfortable. It is helpful in environments where many work items are pulling for limited resources.

For Kanban systems, the most common use of a Triage ceremony is Backlog Grooming. Release Planning ceremonies are regularly scheduled and focus high-level, long-range activity. Backlog Triage is also regularly scheduled, but focuses on mid-level or low-level activities addressed by Product Owners with or without the involvement of business or user representatives depending on the system policies. Typically the Triage ceremony focuses on whether the work item should remain in the Backlog or be removed versus the Backlog grooming done in other Agile Frameworks where work items are prioritized, ranked, or stacked. The goal is simply to reduce the size of the Backlog so that Task dependencies can be more clearly understood and complexity reduced. It enables clearer, quicker replenishment ceremonies.

Artifacts

In the Scrum Guide, three artifacts are named and described, while in general practice, a few others also exist. In XP, several formal artifacts were identified and a few others also described. And the LSD Framework includes at least nine artifacts and even though many are intangible or have a short lifespan, they are still important.

Assuming the Team is using a manual whiteboard to visualize the system, the sticky notes used to name process groups, processes, Buffers, Queues and the work items passing through the system could be kept as artifacts. As they identify and document the policies that govern the workflow – again, often done on sticky notes – the sticky notes could become artifacts.

If and when the Team moves the Kanban system to an electronic environment, such as Microsoft Excel, a PDF printout of each day's board could be kept as an artifact. When that is done, they are often useful for doing variance and trend analysis at a later time.

However with Kanban, the core concept of artifacts is significantly different because it is highly dependent on the underlying system that Kanban is being used to improve. Kanban generates very few independent, Kanban-caused artifacts. However, it does use a reporting tool called a Cumulative Flow Diagram that is uniquely its own.

Cumulative Flow Diagrams (CFDs)

The keys to creating a more sustainable pace are creating accurately sized and testable Stories and focusing on a few Stories at a time in order to finish specific work pieces more quickly. The linkage occurs between the customer-proxy creating better Stories, the Cumulative Flow Diagram (CFD) providing more visibility, and the system reducing WIP levels.

The idea of applying a CFD to Agile development has been articulated by Don Reinertsen[35] and David Anderson[36], two Kanban thought leaders. Their work demonstrates that WIP is a leading metric and can be tracked using a CFD.

That means WIP can predict lead times and delivery dates and be used to adjust for risks before they become serious problems.

Cumulative Flow Diagrams (CFD) are area graphs that create insight about project execution so it can be used to improve performance. They show workload imbalances enabling decisions that can spread the work more evenly, reducing risk and creating a more effective and sustainable pace.

Figure 7.7 shows a basic CFD where the work item status is defined as Backlog, In-Progress or Done. Backlog means the requirements of a feature, function or capability have been decomposed into work items and are available for development. The example shows that three batches of work items were added to the initial Backlog. In-Progress means development work is being executed according to whatever organizational standards have been established. Done means the work has been completed in accordance with the agreed upon Definition of Done, such as the acceptance criteria in the Story or perhaps an organizational standard.

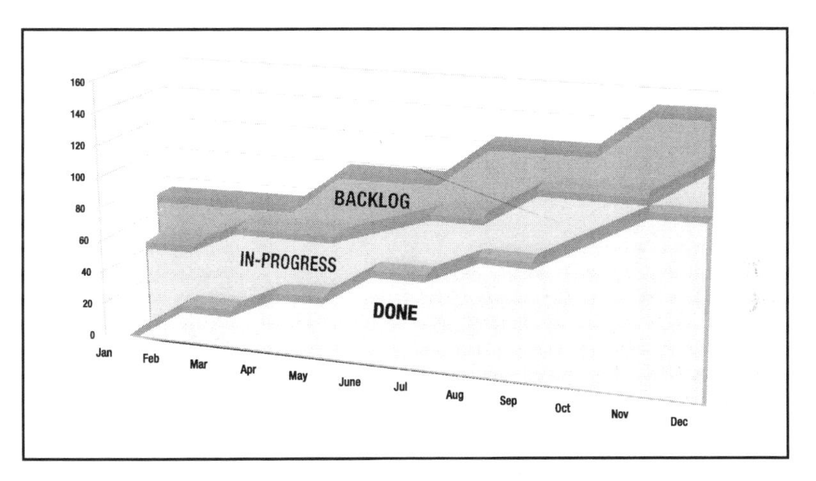

Figure 7.7 | *Basic CFD*

The scale of the vertical, x-axis is a chosen unit-of-measure for WIP, such as Story Points or the count of work items in progress. The scale of the horizontal, y-axis is time shown in the desired units. Lead Time is the distance between the point where a work item is placed in the Backlog and when it is Done. Cycle Time is the distance between the point where a work item is pulled into the In-Progress phase and when it is Done.

Lead Time starts when the work item is made available for development. Cycle Time starts when development work actually begins. Both end when the work item is delivered. Both measures are important because Lead Time impacts customer expectations and satisfaction, whereas Cycle Time is a measure of throughput and provides insight into process improvement choices. Even though both indices measure time, they measure different aspects.

Lead Time is a measure of elapsed time between "ideation and customer receipt." It is expressed as the unit of time between when the work item is made available for development and when it is delivered.

Cycle Time is a measure of process throughput. It is expressed as the average unit of time used per work item produced.

Both Lead Time and Cycle Time are measures of the average time the system requires to accomplish its goal. They are not an expression of time for a specific work item because a large work item started earlier may not be completed before a smaller work item started later. Also, as explained previously, Lead Time and Cycle Time have a relationship with WIP as described by the Little's Law. Therefore, they are useful for analyzing and managing bottlenecks within the system.

Figure 7.8 shows a more advanced CFD where work item status has been defined as Backlog, Design, Code, Review and Complete. Backlog means the requirements of a feature, function or capability have been decomposed into Stories that are queued up and waiting to be designed. Design means creating the specific kind of information at a defined level of granularity, such as a

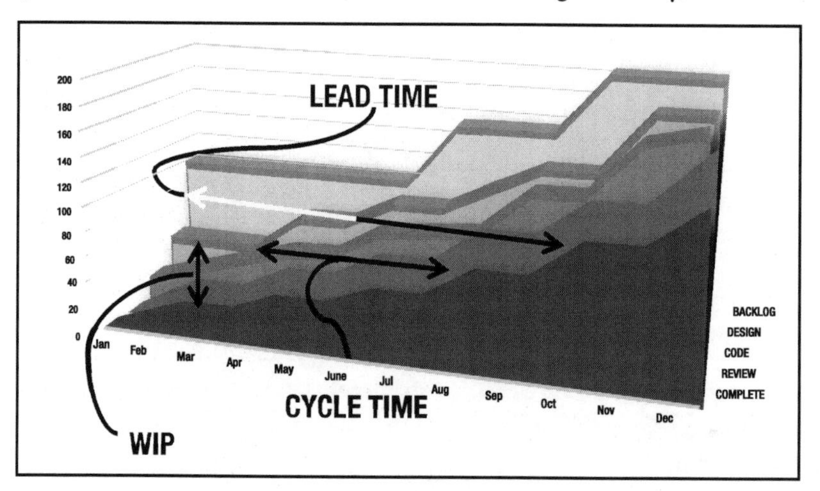

Figure 7.8| *Advanced CFD*

Unified Modeling Language (UML) sequence diagram, as mandated by organizational standards so that the story may be coded. Code means the programming has completed a successful build on both the local and integration machines and is defect-free. Review means the code has been peer reviewed and passed User Acceptance Testing (UAT). Complete means the work has been finished in accordance with the agreed upon Definition of Done, such as the acceptance criteria in the Story.

Unified Modeling Language (UML) is a modeling language used in software engineering that standardizes how to express system design visualizations.

The Backlog shows the project scope with a first Release in June, an increase in the scope for a second Release in October, and an additional increase for a third Release in December. The WIP is subcategorized as Design, Code and Review, each of which shows the various levels of work items processed over time. Finally, the graph for the Complete category shows that the Release scheduled for June was delivered in October.

When a CFD is being reviewed it is useful to remember that a large WIP is undesirable because the complexity of managing the relationships between multiple variables increases in a more than linear way, inducing more opportunities for errors and failure. Also, a large WIP typically contributes to long Lead and Cycle Times, which is undesirable because it increases the probability that the Team's understanding of the Customer's need will deteriorate, again, inducing more opportunities for errors and failure.

CFDs record work completed in a Burn-Up Chart type format. They provide insight into the total scope and the progress of work items using an accessible, visual, proportional image of actual completeness. CFDs radiate a simple analysis of work-in-progress and the trends for Lead and Cycle Time and therefore the probability of delivering a working solution on time. As a leading metric, CFDs enable Agile teams to act appropriately to growing problems in a transparent way.

Recommended Reading

- *Kanban* In Action, by Marcus Hammarberg and Joakim Sunden (Manning Publications; March 2014)
- *Kanban: Successful Evolutionary Change for your Technology Business,* by David J. Anderson (Blue Hole Press; April 2010)

Chapter Close-Out

Practice Test

1. CFDs are area graphs where the scale of the vertical, x-axis is a chosen ________________.

   A. WIP unit-of-measure
   B. Lead Time
   C. Cycle Time
   D. In-progress unit-of-measure

2. ______________ starts when the work item is made available for development.

   A. Work progress unit-of-measure
   B. Lead Time
   C. Cycle Time
   D. In-progress unit-of-measure

3. ______________ is a measure of elapsed time between "ideation and customer receipt."

   A. Work progress unit-of-measure
   B. Lead Time
   C. Cycle Time
   D. In-progress unit-of-measure

4. ______________ is expressed as the average unit of time used per work item produced.

   A. Work progress unit-of-measure
   B. Lead Time
   C. Cycle Time
   D. In-progress unit-of-measure

5. For Kanban systems, the most common use of a ________________ ceremony is Backlog Grooming.

   A. Daily Stand-up Meeting
   B. Release Planning Meeting
   C. The "After" Meeting
   D. Triage

6. During the ______________ ceremony the Team is looking to see whether a work item is blocked or has become invisible.

   A. Daily Standup Meeting
   B. Release Planning Meeting
   C. The "After" Meeting
   D. Triage

7. The ceremony that produces signs of maturity such as the nesting of lower level processes within the higher-level process group is called ________________________

   A. Daily Standup Meeting
   B. Release Planning Meeting
   C. Create and Manage the Kanban Board
   D. Queue and Buffer Replenishment Meeting

8. Before the board reaches maturity the ______________________ ceremony is focused on understanding and exposing the actual process.

   A. Create and Manage the Kanban Board
   B. Queue and Buffer Replenishment Meeting
   C. Daily Standup Meeting
   D. Release Planning Meeting

9. ______________________ are high-level, long-range activities taking place on a regularly scheduled basis.

   A. Create and Manage the Kanban Board Meetings
   B. Queue and Buffer Replenishment Meetings
   C. Daily Standup Meetings
   D. Release Planning Meetings

10. The ______________________ is comparable to the working group meetings often spawned during the Daily Scrum.

    A. "After" Meeting
    B. Triage Meeting
    C. Daily Standup Meeting
    D. Release Planning Meeting

11. When a ____________________ is being reviewed it is useful to remember that a large WIP is undesirable.

    A. Burn-Up Chart
    B. Burn-Down Chart
    C. Cumulative Flow Diagram (CFD)
    D. Lead-Cycle Time Report (LCT)

12. A _______________ radiates a simple analysis of work-in-progress and the trends for Lead and Cycle Time.

    A. Lead-Cycle Time Report (LCT)
    B. Cumulative Flow Diagram (CFD)
    C. Burn-Up Chart
    D. Burn-Down Chart

13. ________________________________ is Goldratt's example of a Pull system.

A. Drum-Pulley-Rope
B. Agile Project Management
C. Theory of Constraints
D. Drum-Buffer-Rope

14. __________________ is a Japanese word that literally means "signal card" in English.

A. Kaizen
B. Yuan-ban
C. Kanban
D. Kai-zen

15. Kanban uses a reporting tool called a ______________________ that is uniquely its own.

A. Burn-Up Chart
B. Burn-Down Chart
C. Continuous Flow Diagram (CFD)
D. Cumulative Flow Diagram

16. ________________________ proves the relationship between WIP and throughput for a production system in a steady state.

A. Kaizen equations
B. Pareto's principle
C. Little's Law
D. Regression testing

17. Because Agile Project Management and Kanban both spring from a legacy in manufacturing, when the acronym WIP is used it is understood to mean ________________________.

    A. Work in progress
    B. Work in process
    C. Work item process
    D. Work inventory processed

18. ____________________ are holding places for small inventories of work items that are external to a process group.

    A. Buffers
    B. Phases
    C. Queues
    D. Steps

19. ____________________ are holding places for small inventories of work items that are internal to a process group.

    A. Buffers
    B. Phases
    C. Queues
    D. Steps

20. Within the Kanban community there are six practices (currently) referred to as "core practices." Three of them are:

    A. Visualize, Triage, and Implement Feedback Loops
    B. Limit WIP, Make Process Policies Explicit, and Manage Flow
    C. Create and Manage the Kanban Board, Limit WIP, and Manage Flow
    D. Improve Collaboratively, Evolve Experimentally and Limit WIP

Fill-in-the-Blank Challenge

1. CFDs are area graphs where the scale of the vertical, x-axis is a chosen ________________.

2. ______________ starts when the work item is made available for development.

3. _____________ is a measure of elapsed time between "ideation and customer receipt."

4. _____________ is expressed as the average unit of time used per work item produced.

5. For Kanban systems, the most common use of a __________ ceremony is Backlog Grooming.

6. During the ________________ ceremony the Team is looking to see whether a work item is blocked or has become invisible.

7. The ceremony that produces signs of maturity such as the nesting of lower level processes within the higher-level process group is called _________________________.

8. Before the board reaches maturity, the ____________________________________ ceremony is focused on understanding and exposing the actual process.

9. ____ is a high-level, long-range activity that takes place on a regularly scheduled basis.

10. The ____________________________ is comparable to the working group meetings often spawned during the Daily Scrum.

11. When a ___________________________________ is being reviewed it is useful to remember that a large WIP is undesirable.

12. A ____________________________________ radiates a simple analysis of work-in-progress and the trends for Lead and Cycle Time.

13. ______________________________ is Goldratt's example of a Pull system.

14. ______________ is a Japanese word that literally means "signal card" in English.

15. Kanban uses a reporting tool called a ______________ ______________ that is uniquely its own.

16. ____________________ proves the relationship between WIP and throughput for a production system in a steady state.

17. Because Agile Project Management and Kanban both spring from a legacy in manufacturing, when the acronym WIP is used it is understood to mean ______________________________.

18. ______________ are holding places for small inventories of work items that are external to a process group.

19. ______________ are holding places for small inventories of work items that are internal to a process group.

20. Within the Kanban community there are six practices (currently) referred to as "core practices." Two of them are ________________ and ________________ .

Terminology Matching Exercise

In the blank column to the left of the Term, fill in the letter that identifies the correct Definition or Description.

	TERM		DEFINITION / DESCRIPTION
	1. CFD	A	A high-level, long-range activity that takes place on a regularly scheduled basis
	2. Lead Time	B	Kanban's most common ceremony for Backlog Grooming
	3. Cycle Time	C	Ceremony used to see whether a work item is blocked or has become invisible
	4. Triage	D	The distance between the point where a work item is placed in the Backlog and when it is Done
	5. Daily Stand-up	E	The distance between the point where a work item is pulled into the In-Progress phase and when it is Done
	6. Release Planning	F	A Japanese word that means "signal card"
	7. Kanban	G	An area graph that creates insight about project execution so it can be used to improve performance
	8. Kaizen	H	Means work-in-progress
	9. Little's Law	I	Holding places for small inventories of work items that are external to a process group
	10. WIP	J	A Japanese word for "continuous improvement"
	11. Buffers	K	Proves the relationship between WIP and throughput
	12. Queues	L	One of the Kanban community's six core practices

	TERM		DEFINITION / DESCRIPTION
	13. Visualize	M	A tool for managing development bottlenecks that creates planning options and accelerates throughput
	14. UML	N	Holding places for small inventories of work items that are internal to a process group
	15. WIP Limits	O	A modeling language used in software engineering

Answers - Chapter Practice Test

1. **A.** CFDs are area graphs where the scale of the vertical, x-axis is a chosen **WIP UNIT-OF-MEASURE.**

   Cumulative Flow Diagrams (CFD) are area graphs that create insight about project execution so it can be used to improve performance. It shows workload imbalances enabling decisions that can spread the work more evenly, reducing risk and creating a more effective and sustainable pace.

   The scale of the vertical, x-axis is a chosen unit-of-measure for WIP, such as Story Points or the count of work items in progress. The scale of the horizontal, y-axis is time shown in the desired units. Lead Time is the distance between the point where a work item is placed in the Backlog and when it is Done. Cycle Time is the distance between the point where a work item is pulled into the In-Progress phase and when it is Done.

2. **B. LEAD TIME** starts when the work item is made available for development.

   Cycle Time starts when development work actually begins. Both end when the work item is delivered. Both measures are important because Lead Time impacts customer expectations and satisfaction, whereas Cycle Time is a measure of throughput and provides insight into process improvement choices. Even though both indices measure time, they measure different aspects.

3. **B. LEAD TIME** is a measure of elapsed time between "ideation and customer receipt."

   Lead Time is a measure of elapsed time between "ideation and customer receipt." It is expressed as the unit of time between when the work item is made available for development and when it is delivered.

   Cycle Time is a measure of process throughput. It is expressed as the average unit of time used per work item produced.

4. **C. CYCLE TIME** is expressed as the average unit of time used per work item produced.

   Cycle Time is a measure of process throughput. It is expressed as the average unit of time used per work item produced.

Both Lead Time and Cycle Time are measures of the average time the system requires to accomplish its goal. They are not an expression of time for a specific work item because a large work item started earlier may not be completed before a smaller work item started later. Also, as explained previously, Lead Time and Cycle Time have a relationship with WIP as described by the Little's Law. Therefore, they are useful for analyzing and managing bottlenecks within the system.

5. **D.** For Kanban systems the most common use of a **TRIAGE** ceremony is Backlog Grooming.

   Release Planning ceremonies are regularly scheduled and focus high-level, long-range activity. Backlog Triage is also regularly scheduled, but focuses on mid-level or low-level activities addressed by Product Owners with or without the involvement of business or user representatives depending on the system policies. Typically the Triage ceremony focuses on whether the work item should remain in the Backlog or be removed versus the Backlog grooming done in other Agile Frameworks where work items are prioritized, ranked, or stacked. The goal is simply to reduce the size of the Backlog so that Task dependencies can be more clearly understood and complexity reduced. It enables clearer, quicker replenishment ceremonies.

6. **A.** During the **DAILY STAND-UP** ceremony, the Team is looking to see whether a work item is blocked or has become invisible.

   Stand-up meetings are common to Agile Frameworks, but have evolved differently in Kanban because the board contains all the information about who is working on what and the focus is on the workflow process not the individual's work progress. Each day the Team is looking to see whether a work item is blocked or has become invisible. Typically the group leader will begin at the end of the process and "walk backward" across the board from right to left following the system's pull. The Stories on the board are discussed to discover if the information on the board presents the situation in a real and transparent way.

7. **C.** The ceremony that produces signs of maturity such as the nesting of lower level processes within the higher-level process group is called **CREATE AND MANAGE THE KANBAN BOARD.**

   When a Kanban Board reaches full maturity it can look like the XLSX image shown in Figure 7.6 (which can be downloaded from the

Members section of the GR8PM website). You can see the signs of maturity in the nesting of lower level processes, such as User Story, Estimate, and Queue, within the higher level Backlog process group, as well as in the use of Buffers and Queues, and, significantly, in the Policies bulleted across the bottom. The granular decomposition of the process groups and the explicit linkage to policies should not be expected in the initial Kanban mapping exercise, but it should be the long-term goal.

8. **A.** Before the board reaches maturity, the **CREATE AND MANAGE THE KANBAN BOARD** ceremony is focused on understanding and exposing the actual process being used and the real policies being followed. As the board matures, the ceremony is focused on measuring and improving it. When the board has reached a high level of maturity, the ceremony focuses on using it to guide and improve how the Team applies it. However, introducing a visual, transparent way of directing work can seem threatening for some participants as mentioned above. Introducing visualization in small steps using a low-tech, high-touch approach will allow the Team to develop a consensus that supports decisions and undergirds accountability.

9. **D. RELEASE PLANNING MEETINGS** are high-level, long-range activities taking place on a regularly scheduled basis.

   In some organization-level Kanban systems, Release Planning Meetings are used to provide guidance about downstream delivery objectives to Queue Replenishment Meetings and other lower-level Kanban and project management systems. Because release planning is a high-level, long-range activity, it takes place on a regularly scheduled basis. Doing so reduces coordination costs and raises the probability that all key stakeholders will be present.

10. **A.** The **AFTER MEETING** is comparable to the working group meetings often spawned during the Daily Scrum.

    The "After" Meeting in Kanban is comparable to the working group meetings often spawned during the Daily Scrum. The "After" Meeting is also ad hoc and typically involves 3 or 4 team members discussing anything from how to get a work item unblocked to options for removing a delay to kicking around a technical issue. Often times it is to discuss a process- or policy-related issue making the After Meeting a vital tool for transforming the current culture into one where Kanban can be leveraged to create more value. Sometimes it is simply an informal sub-team deciding how they'll build a particular feature, function or capability during the next few days.

11. **C.** When a **CFD** is being reviewed it is useful to remember that a large WIP is undesirable.

    When a CFD is being reviewed it is useful to remember that a large WIP is undesirable because the complexity of managing the relationships between multiple variables increases in a more than linear way, inducing more opportunities for errors and failure. Also, a large WIP typically contributes to long Lead and Cycle Times, which is also undesirable because it increases the probability that the Team's understanding of the customer's need will deteriorate, again, inducing more opportunities for errors and failure.

12. **B.** A **CFD** radiates a simple analysis of work-in-progress and the trends for Lead and Cycle Time.

    CFDs record work completed in a Burn-Up Chart type format. They provide insight into the total scope and the progress of work items using an accessible, visual, proportional image of actual completeness. CFDs radiate a simple analysis of work-in-progress and the trends for Lead and Cycle Time and therefore the probability of delivering a working solution on time. As a leading metric, CFDs enable Agile teams to act appropriately to growing problems in a transparent way.

13. **D. DRUM-BUFFER-ROPE** is Goldratt's example of a Pull system.

    Outside of project management circles, Kanban's storied history with the Toyota Production System and Lean Principles has given it much broader recognition and credibility than the Theory of Constraints even though they have an amazing number of similarities. Drum-Buffer-Rope and Kanban are both examples of Pull systems. Pull systems produce deliverables by changing them incrementally at a sustainable pace. With the advance of Lean principles into the project management profession, commonly referred to as Agile Project Management, the science developed in Goldratt's Theory of Constraints may finally get a full wind in its sails. However, those sails will billow under the flag of Kanban.

14. **C.** Kanban is a Japanese word that literally means "signal card" in English.

    The card is used to signal an upstream process to produce more. Kanban does not allow work to occur upstream until a downstream lever pulls it.

    Kanban, also has a strong link to Kaizen, a Japanese word for "continuous improvement." In Japanese manufacturing it is believed that Kaizen is the engine that makes Kanban work.

15. **D.** Kanban uses a reporting tool called a **CUMULATIVE FLOW DIAGRAM** that is uniquely its own.

    However, with Kanban, the core concept of artifacts is significantly different because it is highly dependent on the underlying system that Kanban is being used to improve. Kanban generates very few independent, Kanban-caused artifacts.

16. **C. LITTLE'S LAW** proves the relationship between WIP and throughput for a production system in a steady state.

    It is important because it correlates three significant performance measures – inventory, flow time, and throughput – in units per time period. This is very useful because risk can be identified with the amount of time represented by the User Stories in inventory. For instance, if we see 200 Stories of WIP for a team producing 10 per day, a disaster probably awaits. Conversely, if we see 200 Stories of WIP for a team producing 100 per day, then it is extremely lean.

17. A. Because Agile Project Management and Kanban both spring from a legacy in manufacturing, when the acronym WIP is used, it is understood to mean **WORK-IN-PROGRESS.**

    Work in progress, work in process, goods in process, and in-process inventory are all synonyms to a greater or lesser degree, with work in progress and work in process being the most widely used.

    In manufacturing, the most commonly used term is work in progress, while in accounting it is most common to refer to the item classification as work in process. Therefore, since Agile Project Management and Kanban both spring from a legacy in manufacturing, when the acronym WIP is used, it is understood to mean Work In Progress.

18. **A. BUFFERS** are holding places for small inventories of work items that are external to a process group.

    Buffers and Queues are holding places for small inventories of work items used to insure instant availability of input when a downstream process pulls it. They are often used as synonyms and are very nearly so. However, Buffers are external to a process group or step and occur between steps whereas Queues are internal to a process group and occur at the end of the process, remaining internal to it.

19. **C. QUEUES** are holding places for small inventories of work items that are internal to a process group.

    Buffers and Queues are holding places for small inventories of work items used to insure instant availability of input when a downstream process pulls it. They are often used as synonyms and are very nearly so. However, Buffers are external to a process group or step and occur between steps whereas Queues are internal to a process group and occur at the end of the process, remaining internal to it.

20. Within the Kanban community there are six practices (currently) referred to as "core practices." Three of them are: **LIMIT WIP, MAKE PROCESS POLICIES EXPLICIT, and MANAGE FLOW.** (Any of the 6 below are correct.)

    Within the Kanban community there are six practices (currently) referred to as "core practices." They are:

    1. *Visualize*
    2. *Limit Work in Progress*
    3. *Manage Flow*
    4. *Make Process Policies Explicit*
    5. *Implement Feedback Loops*
    6. *Improve Collaboratively, Evolve Experimentally*

Answers - Fill-in-the-Blank Challenge

1. CFDs are area graphs where the scale of the vertical, x-axis is a chosen **WIP UNIT-OF-MEASURE.**

   Cumulative Flow Diagrams (CFD) are area graphs that create insight about project execution so it can be used to improve performance. It shows workload imbalances enabling decisions that can spread the work more evenly, reducing risk and creating a more effective and sustainable pace.

   The scale of the vertical, x-axis is a chosen unit-of-measure for WIP, such as Story Points or the count of work items in progress. The scale of the horizontal, y-axis is time shown in the desired units. Lead Time is the distance between the point where a work item is placed in the Backlog and when it is Done. Cycle Time is the distance between the point where a work item is pulled into the In-Progress phase and when it is Done.

2. **LEAD TIME** starts when the work item is made available for development.

   Cycle Time starts when development work actually begins. Both end when the work item is delivered. Both measures are important because Lead Time impacts customer expectations and satisfaction, whereas Cycle Time is a measure of throughput and provides insight into process improvement choices. Even though both indices measure time, they measure different aspects.

3. **LEAD TIME** is a measure of elapsed time between "ideation and customer receipt."

   It is expressed as the unit of time between when the work item is made available for development and when it is delivered.

   Cycle Time is a measure of process throughput. It is expressed as the average unit of time used per work item produced.

4. **CYCLE TIME** is expressed as the average unit of time used per work item produced.

   Cycle Time is a measure of process throughput. It is expressed as the average unit of time used per work item produced.

Both Lead Time and Cycle Time are measures of the average time the system requires to accomplish its goal. They are not an expression of time for a specific work item because a large work item started earlier may not be completed before a smaller work item started later. Also, as explained previously, Lead Time and Cycle Time have a relationship with WIP as described by the Little's Law. Therefore, they are useful for analyzing and managing bottlenecks within the system.

5. For Kanban systems the most common use of a **TRIAGE** ceremony is Backlog Grooming.

   Release Planning ceremonies are regularly scheduled and focus high-level, long-range activity. Backlog Triage is also regularly scheduled, but focuses on mid-level or low-level activities addressed by Product Owners with or without the involvement of business or user representatives depending on the system policies. Typically, the Triage ceremony focuses on whether the work item should remain in the Backlog or be removed versus the Backlog grooming done in other Agile Frameworks where work items are prioritized, ranked, or stacked. The goal is simply to reduce the size of the Backlog so that Task dependencies can be more clearly understood and complexity reduced. It enables clearer, quicker replenishment ceremonies.

6. During the **DAILY STAND-UP** ceremony the Team is looking to see whether a work item is blocked or has become invisible.

   Stand-up meetings are common to Agile Frameworks, but have evolved differently in Kanban because the board contains all the information about who is working on what and the focus is on the workflow process not the individual's work progress. Each day the Team is looking to see whether a work item is blocked or has become invisible. Typically the group leader will begin at the end of the process and "walk backward" across the board from right to left following the system's pull. The Stories on the board are discussed to discover if the information on the board presents the situation in a real and transparent way.

7. The ceremony that produces signs of maturity such as the nesting of lower level processes within the higher-level process group is called **CREATE AND MANAGE THE KANBAN BOARD.**

   When a Kanban Board reaches full maturity it can look like the XLSX image shown in Figure 7.6 (which can be downloaded from the

Members section of the GR8PM website). You can see the signs of maturity in the nesting of lower level processes, such as User Story, Estimate, and Queue, within the higher level Backlog process group, as well as in the use of Buffers and Queues, and, significantly, in the Policies bulleted across the bottom. The granular decomposition of the process groups and the explicit linkage to policies should not be expected in the initial Kanban mapping exercise, but should be the long-term goal.

8. Before the board reaches maturity, the **CREATE AND MANAGE THE KANBAN BOARD** ceremony is focused on understanding and exposing the actual process.

   Before the board reaches maturity, the ceremony is focused on understanding and exposing the actual process being used and the real policies being followed. As the board matures, the ceremony is focused on measuring and improving it. When the board has reached a high level of maturity, the ceremony focuses on using it to guide and improve how the Team applies it. However, introducing a visual, transparent way of directing work can seem threatening for some participants as mentioned above. Introducing visualization in small steps using a low-tech, high-touch approach will allow the Team to develop a consensus that supports decisions and undergirds accountability.

9. **RELEASE PLANNING MEETINGS** are high-level, long-range activities taking place on a regularly scheduled basis.

   In some organization-level Kanban systems, Release Planning Meetings are used to provide guidance about downstream delivery objectives to Queue Replenishment Meetings and other lower-level Kanban and project management systems. Because release planning is a high-level, long-range activity, it takes place on a regularly scheduled basis. Doing so reduces coordination costs and raises the probability that all key stakeholders will be present.

10. The **AFTER MEETING** is comparable to the working group meetings often spawned during the Daily Scrum.

    The "After" Meeting in Kanban is comparable to the working group meetings often spawned during the Daily Scrum. The "After" Meeting is also ad hoc and typically involves 3 or 4 team members discussing anything from how to get a work item unblocked to options for removing a delay to kicking around a technical issue. Often times it is to discuss a process- or policy-related issue making the After Meeting a vital tool for transforming the current culture into one where Kanban can be leveraged to create more value. Sometimes it is simply an informal sub-team deciding how they'll build a particular feature, function or capability during the next few days.

11. When a **CFD** is being reviewed it is useful to remember that a large **WIP** is undesirable.

    When a CFD is being reviewed it is useful to remember that a large WIP is undesirable because the complexity of managing the relationships between multiple variables increases in a more than linear way, inducing more opportunities for errors and failure. Also, a large WIP typically contributes to long Lead and Cycle Times, which is also undesirable because it increases the probability that the Team's understanding of the Customer's need will deteriorate, again, inducing more opportunities for errors and failure.

12. A **CFD** radiates a simple analysis of work-in-progress and the trends for Lead and Cycle Time.

    CFDs record work completed in a Burn-Up Chart type format. They provide insight into the total scope and the progress of work items using an accessible, visual, proportional image of actual completeness. CFDs radiate a simple analysis of work-in-progress and the trends for Lead and Cycle Time and therefore the probability of delivering a working solution on time. As a leading metric, CFDs enable Agile teams to act appropriately to growing problems in a transparent way.

13. **DRUM-BUFFER-ROPE** is Goldratt's example of a Pull system.

    Outside of project management circles, Kanban's storied history with the Toyota Production System and Lean Principles has given it much broader recognition and credibility than the Theory of Constraints even though they have an amazing number of similarities. Drum-Buffer-Rope and Kanban are both examples of Pull systems. Pull systems produce deliverables by changing them incrementally at a sustainable pace. With the advance of Lean principles into the project management profession, commonly referred to as Agile Project Management, the science developed in Goldratt's Theory of Constraints may finally get a full wind in its sails. However, those sails will billow under the flag of Kanban.

14. **KANBAN** is a Japanese word that literally means "signal card" in English.

    The card is used to signal an upstream process to produce more. Kanban does not allow work to occur upstream until a downstream lever pulls it.

    Kanban also has a strong link to Kaizen, a Japanese word for "continuous improvement." In Japanese manufacturing it is believed that Kaizen is the engine that makes it Kanban work.

15. Kanban uses a reporting tool called a **CUMULATIVE FLOW DIAGRAM** that is uniquely its own.

    However, with Kanban, the core concept of artifacts is significantly different because it is highly dependent on the underlying system that Kanban is being used to improve. Kanban generates very few independent, Kanban-caused artifacts.

16. **LITTLE'S LAW** proves the relationship between WIP and throughput for a production system in a steady state.

    It is important because it correlates three significant performance measures – inventory, flow time, and throughput – in units per time period. This is very useful because risk can be identified with the amount of time represented by the User Stories in inventory. For instance, if we see 200 Stories of WIP for a team producing 10 per day, a disaster probably awaits. Conversely, if we see 200 Stories of WIP for a team producing 100 per day then it is extremely lean.

17. Because Agile Project Management and Kanban both spring from a legacy in manufacturing, when the acronym WIP is used it is understood to mean **WORK-IN-PROGRESS.**

    Work in progress, work in process, goods in process, and in-process inventory are all synonyms to a greater or lesser degree, with work in progress and work in process being the most widely used.

    In manufacturing, the most commonly used term is work in progress, while in accounting it is most common to refer to the item classification as work in process. Therefore, since Agile Project Management and Kanban both spring from a legacy in manufacturing, when the acronym WIP is used, it is understood to mean Work In Progress.

18. **BUFFERS** are holding places for small inventories of work items that are external to a process group.

    Buffers and Queues are holding places for small inventories of work items used to insure instant availability of input when a downstream process pulls it. They are often used as synonyms and are very nearly so. However, Buffers are external to a process group or step and occur between steps whereas Queues are internal to a process group and occur at the end of the process, remaining internal to it.

19. **QUEUES** are holding places for small inventories of work items that are internal to a process group.

    Buffers and Queues are holding places for small inventories of work items used to insure instant availability of input when a downstream process pulls it. They are often used as synonyms and are very nearly so. However, Buffers are external to a process group or step and occur between steps whereas Queues are internal to a process group and occur at the end of the process, remaining internal to it.

20. Within the Kanban community there are six practices (currently) referred to as "core practices." Two of them are: **CHOOSE FROM THE LIST BELOW**

    Within the Kanban community there are six practices (currently) referred to as "core practices." They are:

    1. *Visualize*
    2. *Limit Work in Progress*
    3. *Manage Flow*
    4. *Make Process Policies Explicit*
    5. *Implement Feedback Loops*
    6. *Improve Collaboratively, Evolve Experimentally*

Answers - Terminology Matching

1:G, 2:D, 3:E, 4:B, 5:C, 6:A, 7:F, 8:J, 9:K, 10:H, 11:I, 12:N, 13:L, 14:O, 15:M

Chapter End Notes

[33]Marcus Hammarberg and Joakim Sunden (2014), Kanban in Action, Manning Publications Co.

[34]Little's law is a restatement of the work of Danish mathematician Agner Krarup Erlang (1878 – 1929) and named for John Little, an Institute Professor at the Massachusetts Institute of Technology, although he was at Case Western Reserve University when he published the first proof was published in 1961.

[35]Reinertsen, D. G. (2009). The principles of product development flow: Second generation lean product development. Celeritas Publishing.

[36]Anderson, D. (2010). Kanban: Successful evolutionary change for your technology business. Sequim, WA: Blue Hole Press.

Hybrid Project Management Deep Dive

Chapter Highlights

In this chapter you will find an explanation of Hybrid Project Management as well as a detailed description of its key elements. Those components are broken out as the Roles, Workflow, Ceremonies and Artifacts. The people are identified by the Roles they fulfill. The Workflow details how those people work together and produce the planned results. Lastly, the Artifacts are the electronic or printed evidence of the results.

Overview of Hybrid Project Management

The project management landscape is one of continuous change where small teams, or groups of small teams, with limited budgets work to fulfill business requirements while being pressed to deliver desirable results faster. Struggling to cope with this environmental backdrop, leaders are integrating, optimizing and adapting new and different strategies. Hybrid has become the name for this way of managing projects, and can be loosely described as flexibly combining Traditional, Agile and other processes and practices to increase the probability of a successful project outcome.

Simply put, according to Jim Highsmith, an Agile Manifesto

signatory and respected Agile expert, "Agility is the ability to both create and respond to change in order to profit in a turbulent business environment." Hybrid Project Management is a clear expression of that maxim.

Everywhere we go to present, teach, coach and mentor, the audiences and teams we work with acknowledge that there is not one right way to do every project. They also agree that for a specific team, on a specific project, given the available resources and constraints, there is one best way – the way with the highest probability of success – to execute that specific project. That means that for any project leader to be a real professional, they must combine as many tools and techniques as the Team may need to effectively empower their performance and growth. Hybrid Project Management is a clear application of that wisdom.

Stated another way, projects allow organizations to operationalize their innovative strategic vision. Executing those projects using the correct project management framework ensures those projects maximize the positive impact of the resources deployed to deliver them. To accomplish this, professional Project Managers are increasingly being tasked by their organizations to synthesize the best practices of Traditional and Agile Frameworks into an approach that is tailored to the environmental demands they face.

Traditional, Agile, and Hybrid Project Management approaches are complementary tools mandatory for professional Project Managers (PMs) to know! Selecting and using the right approach is a significant first step to delivering a successful project.

One factor causing the significant rise in the number of organizations using a Hybrid approach to meet their needs is simply that users of Scrum, XP, and other defined Frameworks invariably tailor their process over time to improve results.

A second factor fueling the drive to Hybrid Project Management is actually the absence in every Agile Framework of two key elements required for scalability. Those components are budgeting and sophisticated scheduling. The organizational need for budgets and schedules drives PMs to adapt and optimize existing Agile Frameworks by integrating needed budgeting and scheduling techniques and tools. In fact, the existence of integrated budgeting and scheduling techniques is a clear marker or identifier of a Hybrid Project Management approach.

Hybrid projects are managed with a combination of Traditional and Agile practices or with a combination of practices from multiple Agile frameworks.

Hybrid Project Management is an Agile Framework where a selected combination of techniques and practices, including those from one or more Agile Frameworks, are used to manage projects in order to best meet the needs of the organization and customer.

One last thought about Hybrid Project Management worth noting is that at its core, it honors the principle that practices should never be carved in stone and should always be subject to continuous improvement, as Lean advocates.

Roles

Hybrid Project Management can apply any useful convention from other defined Agile Frameworks to structure roles and responsibilities along with workflows, ceremonies and artifacts. Because Hybrid does not prescribe roles, it is not possible, or necessary, to describe a new or different set of them here.

Whatever enables a Hybrid system to be tailored to the needs of the Team and the Organization, so that delivery of results is optimized, gets included. Everything else gets excluded. Because the goal of Hybrid approaches is to optimize project results, the roles and responsibilities are defined in the way the Team decides is necessary.

Workflow

As with defining Roles, in Hybrid Project Management the Workflow includes whatever enables the delivery of desirable results while everything else gets excluded. Tailoring the workflow practices can be at the team-level, which is within the focus of this book, or at a higher business level, the focus of Book Two of the Agile Almanac.

To get a better understanding, consider this quick example.

Combining Agile Practices at the Team Level

A small Development Team within a big healthcare company is responsible for the newly mandated Electronic Health Records (EHR) mobile application (app). Luckily the Team is pretty small and mostly self-directed. The Team creates new EHR features and supports and maintains the released production version of the app.

A lot of stakeholders no longer trust the quality of work, estimates or delivery date promises made by the Team. Frank, the IT Manager and project leader, and is having difficulties justifying the erratic pace of deliveries. Meanwhile, the Team feels totally swamped by requests coming from every direction, has no sense of what to do first, and is working as hard as they can. They have been using Scrum and want to apply Kanban, starting right where they are, to improve results.

Currently, Bob, the Business Analyst who does requirements analysis, manages the Product and Iteration Backlogs in a web-based project-tracking system. Anna, the tester, Darry and Evon the developers, and Carol, the Product Owner, all have access to the system to input information and updates. However, in addition to the Scrum work recorded in the project-tracking system, Anna, Darry and Evon also have to deal with support issues, change requests, system maintenance and ad hoc senior management demands often dropped on them in the hallway or break room.

Handling these two different workflows – Scrum and Other Work – might be manageable in the project-tracking system as long as everything got entered and nothing got overlooked or misidentified. However, Kanban's visual pull system has a much higher probably of reliably delivering the best results for both workflows.

The new Kanban system will include standard Scrum elements like Carol doing the typical Product Backlog management activities, and Carol and the Team doing Sprint Planning. Once the Sprint Backlog has been determined, the Stories will be placed in the initial step (i.e., first column) of the new Kanban Board, which includes Buffers, and Queues not found on the old Story Board. Items from the second workflow, the Other Work, will also be added to the initial step as it arrives. The Kanban Board may be configured as a single, combined workflow or it may be divided horizontally into two "swim lanes" where one lane has the Scrum items and the other lane has the Other Work items. The Team will also hold a Daily Scrum covering all of the work items and a standard Review ceremony at the end of the Sprint. The Retrospective will become a monthly ceremony to continuously improve the combined Kanban workflow.

Ceremonies

As with defining Roles and Workflows in Hybrid Project Management, the Ceremonies include whatever enables the system to delivery optimized results while excluding everything else. The only area that tends to be unique to Hybrid Project Management is ceremonies focused on budgeting and sophisticated scheduling.

While budgeting practices vary widely from industry to industry and organization to organization, one highly recommended best practice is to use Earned Value Management (EVM). Regardless of the timing or process used, validating and verifying cost baseline performance against organizational budget and funding standards is very important. EVM is a good choice because its single most important core assumption aligns exactly with Agile Project Management. In EVM, only when work is completed is the corresponding budget value "earned", hence the term Earned Value (EV). This core principle exactly mirrors the Agile principle of measuring work progress by only counting work that is Done-Done in the Velocity.

So even though a detailed in-depth explanation of applying EVM is part of Book Two of the Agile Almanac, introducing it in the context of the team-level environment as a bridge to the other more in-depth coverage is appropriate. Also, this coverage aligns with the purpose of this book by providing the information and structure, which helps ensure adequate PMI-ACP® exam preparation.

Earned Value Management (EVM)

An initial important question that deserves to be addressed is, "Why is EVM even necessary in an Agile environment?" The answer is that none of the Agile Frameworks articulate how to identify, track and manage costs. Yet doing so is the only way to fulfill the fundamental business need to manage the resources that will respond to customer needs. As a program management tool that integrates the technical, cost, and schedule parameters of a contract, EVM may even prove to be the missing link that enables Agile Frameworks to fully function at the enterprise level.

When EVM is configured for use with projects where discrete effort delivers discrete results – in other words, increments or potentially shippable products – it is easily aligned and tailored to any Agile Framework.

During the Release planning process, EVM can be used to create an integrated baseline with time-phased budgets for resources and deliverables. In EVM, as work is completed, the corresponding budget value becomes earned value (EV), and since most Agile Frameworks recognize completed work at the end of the Iteration, defining the EV at that level is quite effective.

However, if circumstances warranted it, EV could be associated with specific features or stories.

Defining EV as part of Release Planning provides a reasonable, integrated way to give the insight the business and customer need. Interestingly, it does so with enough clarity and reliability to assist the Product Owner and Customer with making Backlog adjustments in a timely, effective fashion.

Earned Value Management (EVM) is a program management technique that integrates scope, schedule, and resource consumption information in order to measure project performance against planned cost metrics. It provides quantitative, objective data to supplement qualitative, subjective judgments.

EVM's fundamental premise is that as work is completed, the corresponding budget value is earned, hence the term Earned Value (EV). In EVM, that paradigm of value only being earned for completed work aligns at the most basic level with the core Agile principle of measuring work progress by only counting work that is Done-Done in the Velocity.

The EVM process is defined with the following six steps:

1. Define project scope
2. Assemble team
3. Decompose work
4. Outline project schedule
5. Estimate work package budgets
6. Specify time-phased budget

The EVM process definition can be adapted to Agile as:

EVM:	**Agile-EVM:**
1. Define project scope	1. Create Roadmap and Release plans
2. Assemble team	2. Assemble team
3. Decompose work	3. Document Stories
4. Outline project schedule	4. Define Releases and Iterations
5. Estimate work package budgets	5. Estimate story/feature budgets
6. Specify time-phased budget	6. Specify Iteration budgets

To maximize value and minimize cost when EVM is being implemented, the organization must define standards for data collection, analysis and reporting that align with, and support, decision-making. The organization must choose to limit reporting detail because the more detailed or granular the reporting requirements, the greater the increases in time and effort required to produce it.

There are two basic ways to increase the granularity of reporting – shorten the Iteration or estimate the PV at a lower level.

Shortening the Iteration requires additional work for the Customer-Proxy and Team during Release planning, but that increase is likely to be less-than-linear. However, the effort used defining PV that can be measured with specific User Stories or features will likely be more-than-linear. So there will be a direct correlation between the level of detail required for reporting and the cost of collecting that data.

Mathematically, EVM is also quite easily adapted to Agile Frameworks. Comparing the standard definitions of the three core EVM variables shows that tailoring them for Agile Frameworks is not difficult. (See Figure 8.1)

TERM	EVM DEFINITION	A-EVM DEFINITION
Planned Value (PV)	The budgeted cost of work planned for a ***specific time period.***	The budgeted cost of work planned for an ***iteration.***
Earned Value (EV)	The budgeted cost of work completed during a ***specific time period.***	The budgeted cost of work completed during an ***iteration.***
Actual Cost (AC)	The actual cost of work completed during a ***specific time period.***	The actual cost of work completed during an ***iteration.***

Figure 8.1 | *Comparison of EVM & A-EVM Terminology*

For PMI-ACP® exam preparation, even though there are 13 EVM formulas, 80% of questions only involve 4 of them. We will cover those four formulas and their equations (see Figure 8.2). However, we will not cover the other 9 formulas in this book of the Agile Almanac because it is distracting and counter-productive for exam preparation.

As seen, once the PV has been established, the calculations become quite routine. If the work has been completed, PV becomes EV. Also, as the work is completed, the AC comes from the cost accounting system.

In addition to the calculations being routine, interpreting their meaning is very straightforward. For both the SV and CV, a negative variance is undesirable and indicates the project is *behind* schedule, *over* budget or both. For both the SPI and the CPI, an index value less than 1 is undesirable and indicates the project is *behind* schedule, *over* budget or both.

FORMULA	EQUATION
Schedule Variance (SV)	SV = EV – PV
Schedule Performance Index (SPI)	SPI = EV / PV
Cost Variance (CV)	CV = EV – AC
Cost Performance Index (CPI)	CPI = EV / AC

Figure 8.2 | *Four Core EVM Equations.*

Since the calculations and their interpretations are both quite simple, it is easy to wonder why EVM has received so little positive attention from project managers. Our experience teaching EVM over many years suggests three key insights. The first and most obvious is that it takes a lot of extra work in Traditional approaches to create the PV estimates. Luckily, that is not the case with Agile Frameworks. Second, once the PV estimates are created, the metrics generated are very concrete. Those concrete metrics make it very difficult to avoid drawing conclusions about project manager performance they want to escape.

Finally, a far less obvious reason that explains why project managers avoided EVM is confusion about a single core concept. When we teach EVM, we ask the students whether *completed* work has Actual Cost or Planned Value? Invariably they state that *completed* work has Actual Cost. That is the subtle point where confusion about EVM exists, but often isn't recognized. The question we ask is, in a way, a trick question. We ask it as an either/or question, but the answer is both/and. Completed work has both a PV and an AC. Just because the AC is known when the work is completed does not mean that the PV is lost. PV and AC are simply two pieces of meta-data related to the work. Before it is completed, the work has only one piece of meta-data, PV. Once it is completed it has two pieces of meta-data AC and the original PV that has become EV. Completed work obviously has an AC associated with it, so it is counter-intuitive to think of it as still having a PV expressed as an EV, but completed work has both!

Since it is counter-intuitive to think of a PV for completed work, this is probably the most misunderstood part of EVM.

In preparation for the PMI-ACP® exam, we recommend students master a memorization trick regarding the four core formulas.

The memorization trick is to write the formulas in a grid of 6 columns and 4 rows rather than as sentences or lines. For example, in the first column write Schedule, Schedule, Cost, Cost, then in the second column write Variance, Index, Variance, Index, and so forth. When it is completed the grid looks like:

Schedule	Variance	=	EV	–	PV
Schedule	Index	=	EV	/	PV
Cost	Variance	=	EV	–	AC
Cost	Index	=	EV	/	AC

To make it easy, think of each column as a line of musical "lyrics." Have fun pretending the lyrics are part of a rap song. What's really great is that all you need to commit to memory are the first two lines, "Schedule, Schedule, Cost, Cost" and "Variance, Index, Variance, Index."

Once the first two columns of the rap-song-grid are memorized, the balance of the grid fills itself out "auto-magically." Since the grid expresses equations the equal sign is mandatory in the third column. Because EVM is the name of the technique it stands to reason that the first variable is EV. Luckily the fifth column mirrors the second column so Variance requires a minus symbol and Index requires a division symbol. Equally convenient is the fact that the sixth column mirrors the first column because Schedules require PVs and Cost reporting produces AC.

With minimal effort memorizing then applying the EVM Grid during the PMI-ACP® exam, students can be confident in handling the vast majority of EVM questions.

Artifacts

As with defining Roles and Ceremonies in Hybrid Project Management, the Artifacts include whatever enables the system to deliver optimized results while excluding everything else. Those artifacts usually include information radiators focused on budgeting and scheduling status.

When organizations or teams pursue the benefits of Agile, and especially as they customize their approach and create a Hybrid Framework, the importance of the Agile Mindset becomes apparent.

Agile Mindset

The mindset of a professional Agile practitioner is focused on creating an organizational culture where executive managers endorse Agile principles and champion Agile teams, middle managers commit to coaching and mentoring teams, and Agile teams hold themselves accountable to learn Agile principles and continuously improve Agile practices that serve the customers of the organization.

Creating an Agile culture, first and foremost, means committing to learning and mastering the basics so that continuous improvement techniques can be employed to incrementally and successfully evolve the organization into the most Agile expression of itself.

It is popular in Agile circles to refer to a cycle of training used in martial arts that is expressed with three kanji, Japanese characters, and pronounced, "Shu Ha Ri." It is popular because ***Shu Ha Ri*** is a simple, powerful model of learning not restricted to martial arts.

Shu is the first step in the learning cycle and requires developing and mastering the technical foundation of the designated subject, such as martial arts or Lean manufacturing. In Shu, the student learns by mimicking proven techniques. Shu is absolutely required to build a lasting technical foundation that will later enable a deeper, developed understanding.

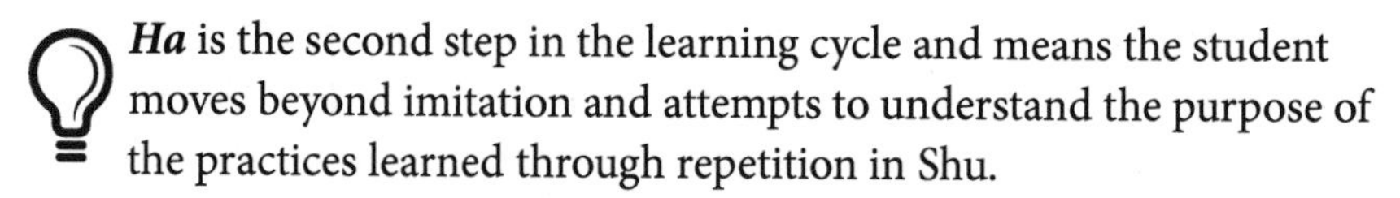

Ha is the second step in the learning cycle and means the student moves beyond imitation and attempts to understand the purpose of the practices learned through repetition in Shu.

Ri is the third step in the learning cycle and transcends Ha because the student is expected to become a practitioner. Because of the hours invested in Shu and Ha, the student has the background knowledge and skills to become a thought-leading practitioner producing original insights about overcoming the inertia of the existing reality.

One of the big challenges of being an Agile thought leader is that it is much more fun to be the guru demonstrating personal mastery in an Agile "dojo" (i.e., martial arts school) than it is to be the diligent master decomposing Ri and Ha into tiny steps that can be mimicked and practiced in Shu, ultimately creating the technical foundation every student needs.

Being the diligent master decomposing Ri and Ha into tiny Shu steps requires hours of painstaking analysis and experimentation to discover and create a viable instructional design, followed by achingly long hours of near-boredom guiding students through the sequence of micro-steps that eventually produce technical mastery. So it is not surprising that many self-proclaimed Agile experts and Certified Scrum Trainers spend so much time in the dojo of their classrooms showing they are an Agile guru instead of being the selfless, diligent master their students really need.

While it is not surprising, it is unfortunate because every Agile Framework could produce far more significant and immediate benefits for the students if they were learning from diligent masters. The overall result would be far more progress towards the Agile goal of transforming the world of work.

Before an organization can be expected to embrace an Agile culture it must have the chance to learn proven techniques for creating high customer involvement, applying test-driven development, and implementing collaborative decision-making. As Shu insists, imitating the micro-steps of techniques that produce the expected outcome must first be learned and mastered. With a good foundation in place, everything gets easier. Without a good foundation, organizational inertia will make every necessary change excruciatingly slow and hard-fought before it is won, if, in fact, it is ever won!

Therefore, the mindset of a professional Agile practitioner starts with focusing on finding or becoming the Agile coach their organization needs. A diligent master is intent on creating an environment of self-reliant, self-directed teams. The coach helps everyone understand and master the micro-techniques and the Agile principles and practices that are the foundation of becoming more Agile.

An initial challenge is determining what training approach provides the best payoff. Is it best to start with generic training for everyone or more specific, robust training for a pilot project team? In order to reduce fear and resistance, the coach must provide enough general information to everyone. But experience has shown that one of the best ways to implement Agile is to carefully choose pilot projects and the teams that will execute them.

The pilot project team must be trained with enough depth to allow them to understand and apply core Agile principles successfully. It is important to remember that they are in the Shu stage so they benefit from starting with a specific, proven methodology. Then when they reach the Ha stage they can use their knowledge and experience to lightly-tailor an approach that is effective for their team and project. The coach's goal is to create an environment where a robust process can be mimicked to produce a successful project outcome. Then, as the team experiences success and grows in knowledge and confidence, the coach's goal evolves to guiding the team's transformation into self-directed action aligned to core Agile principles.

One of those core Agile principles is continuous improvement, which implies the need to map existing organizational processes. As the Team moves from the Ha stage, with mastery of their micro-process, they enter a new Shu stage regarding organizational macro-processes and the need for foundational training in scalable Agile practices begins.

Scaling Agile to an organization is a difficult process because it is a huge change initiative and a major-change initiative. It involves reducing management and increasing leadership. It means moving decision-making power down to where the work is happening while raising goal articulation and vision clarification up so it facilitates group interactions, improves team dynamics, and encourages experimentation and innovation.

The Agile mindset is epitomized in the "Disagree and Commit" philosophy at Intel® Corporation. It honors a culture of opinion-diversity by making it the duty of each team member to disagree with the Team when they see a risk or problem from their area of expertise, yet commit to optimizing the implementation of the Team's perspective once a decision has been made. The magic of Disagree and Commit is that it leverages the power of a diverse team to avoid groupthink and maximize vigorous execution.

The Agile mindset accepts the challenge of expressing leadership through vigorous delegation of decision-making power instead of the threat of sanctions or reprisals. The Agile mindset embraces the dare to earn the respect of the Team and exercises the perseverance to establish a history of successfully delivering projects. The Agile mindset strives to establish a courageous, transparent, collaborative culture where teams excel in a way that energizes the organization that feeds them.

Recommended Reading

Agile Project Management: Creating Innovative Products, by Jim Highsmith (Addison-Wesley Professional; July 2009)

Chapter Close-Out

Practice Test

1. Shu Ha Ri is a simple, powerful model of learning where _______ means attempting to understand the purpose of the techniques.

   A. Dojo
   B. Shu
   C. Ha
   D. Ri

2. A professional Agile practitioner is focused on creating an Agile culture, committed to _________________________________.

   A. Learning and mastering the basics
   B. Deploying Shu Ha Ri
   C. Implementing continuous integration
   D. Extending techniques incrementally and successfully

3. _______________ usually include information radiators focused on budgeting and scheduling status.

   A. User Stories
   B. Workflows
   C. Ceremonies
   D. Artifacts

4. Tailoring the ______________________ practices can be done at the team-level.

   A. Workflow
   B. Ceremony
   C. Artifact
   D. User Story

5. ____________________ uses selected combinations of techniques and practices to best meet the needs of the customer.

A. Agile Project Management
B. Hybrid Project Management
C. Kanban
D. Scrum

6. EVM is a program management technique that integrates ____________________.

A. Scope, schedule, and cost information
B. Quantitative, objective and supplemental data
C. Scope, schedule, and resource consumption information
D. Qualitative, subjective and supplement data

7. EVM's fundamental premise is that as work is ______________, the corresponding budget value is ____________________.

A. Planned; Calculated
B. Released; Approved
C. Designed; Assessed
D. Completed; Earned

8. Schedule Performance Index (SPI) = ____________________ .

A. EV – PV
B. EV / PV
C. EV – AC
D. EV / AC

9. Cost Variance (CV) = ________________________ .

A. EV – PV
B. EV / PV
C. EV – AC
D. EV / AC

10. When the SV registers as a negative integer it is ________________________ .

A. Desirable
B. Undesirable
C. Neutral
D. Incorrect

Fill-in-the-Blank Challenge

1. Shu Ha Ri is a simple, powerful model of learning where ______________ means attempting to understand the purpose of the techniques.

2. A professional Agile practitioner is focused on creating an Agile culture, committed to

   ____.

3. ________________________________ usually include information radiators focused on budgeting and scheduling status.

4. Tailoring the ____________________________ practices can be done at the team-level.

5. ______________________________________ uses selected combinations of techniques and practices to best meet the needs of the customer.

6. EVM is a program management technique that integrates ________________________, ________________________, and ____.

7. EVM's fundamental premise is that as work is ________________, the corresponding budget value is ________________________.

8. Schedule Performance Index (SPI) = ________________________

9. Cost Variance (CV) = ________________________

10. When the SV registers as a negative integer it is ______________________________.

Terminology Matching Exercise

In the blank column to the left of the Term, fill in the letter that identifies the correct Definition or Description.

	TERM		DEFINITION / DESCRIPTION
	1. Shu	A	Integrates scope, schedule, and resource consumption information
	2. Ha	B	Usually include information radiators focused on budgeting and scheduling status
	3. Ri	C	Practices can be tailored at the team-level.
	4. Artifacts	D	Move beyond imitation and attempt to understand the purpose of the practice
	5. Workflow	E	Student becomes a thought-leading practitioner producing original insights
	6. EVM	F	EV – PV
	7. Schedule Variance	G	Requires developing and mastering the technical foundation of the designated subject.
	8. Schedule Index	H	EV / AC
	9. Cost Variance	I	Behind schedule
	10. Cost Index	J	EV / PV
	11. Negative SV	K	EV – AC
	12. CPI >1	L	Under budget
	13. Positive CV	M	Budgeted cost of work completed during an iteration
	14. SPI < 1	N	Ahead of schedule
	15. EV	O	Over budget

Answers - Chapter Practice Test

1. **C.** Shu Ha Ri is a simple, powerful model of learning where **HA** means attempting to understand the purpose of the techniques.

   Ha is the second step in the learning cycle and means the student moves beyond imitation and attempts to understand the purpose of the practices learned through repetition in Shu.

2. **A.** A professional Agile practitioner is focused on creating an Agile culture, committed to **LEARNING AND MASTERING THE BASICS.**

   The mindset of a professional Agile practitioner is focused on creating an Agile culture, committed to learning and mastering the basics so that continuous improvement techniques can be employed to incrementally and successfully evolve the organization into the most Agile expression of itself.

3. **D. ARTIFACTS** usually include information radiators focused on budgeting and scheduling status.

   As with defining Roles and Ceremonies in Hybrid Project Management, the Artifacts include whatever enables the system to delivery optimized results while excluding everything else gets. Those artifacts usually include information radiators focused on budgeting and scheduling status.

4. **A.** Tailoring the **WORKFLOW** practices can be done at the team-level.

   As with defining Roles in Hybrid Project Management, the Workflow includes whatever enables the delivery of desirable results while everything else gets excluded. Tailoring the workflow practices can be done at the team-level, which is within the focus of this book, or at a higher business level, the focus of Book Two of the Agile Almanac.

5. **B. HYBRID PROJECT MANAGEMENT** uses selected combinations of techniques and practices to best meet the needs of the customer

   Hybrid Project Management is an Agile Framework where a selected combination of techniques and practices, including those from one or

more Agile Frameworks, are used to manage projects in order to best meet the needs of the organization and customer.

6. **C. EVM** is a program management technique that integrates **SCOPE, SCHEDULE, AND RESOURCE CONSUMPTION INFORMATION.**

   Earned Value Management (EVM) is a program management technique that integrates scope, schedule, and resource consumption information in order to measure project performance against planned cost metrics. It provides quantitative, objective data to supplement qualitative, subjective judgments.

7. **D.** EVM's fundamental premise is that as work is **COMPLETED** the corresponding budget value is **EARNED.**

   EVM's fundamental premise is that as work is completed, the corresponding budget value is earned, hence the term Earned Value (EV). In EVM, that paradigm of value only being earned for completed work aligns at the most basic level with the core Agile principle of measuring work progress by only counting work that is Done-Done in the Velocity.

8. **B.** Schedule Performance Index (SPI) = EV / PV

9. **C.** Cost Variance (CV) = EV – AC

10. When the SV registers as a negative integer it is **UNDESIRABLE.**

    In addition to the calculations being routine, interpreting their meaning is very straightforward. For both the SV and CV, a negative variance is undesirable and indicates the project is behind schedule, over budget or both. For both the SPI and the CPI, an index value less than 1 is undesirable and indicates the project is behind schedule, over budget or both.

Answers - Fill-in-the-Blank Challenge

1. Shu Ha Ri is a simple, powerful model of learning where **HA** means attempting to understand the purpose of the techniques.

   Ha is the second step in the learning cycle and means the student moves beyond imitation and attempts to understand the purpose of the practices learned through repetition in Shu.

2. A professional Agile practitioner is focused on creating an Agile culture, committed to **LEARNING AND MASTERING THE BASICS.**

   The mindset of a professional Agile practitioner is focused on creating an Agile culture, committed to learning and mastering the basics so that continuous improvement techniques can be employed to incrementally and successfully evolve the organization into the most Agile expression of itself.

3. **ARTIFACTS** usually include information radiators focused on budgeting and scheduling status.

   As with defining Roles and Ceremonies in Hybrid Project Management, the Artifacts include whatever enables the system to delivery optimized results while excluding everything else. Those artifacts usually include information radiators focused on budgeting and scheduling status.

4. Tailoring the **WORKFLOW** practices can be done at the team-level.

   As with defining Roles in Hybrid Project Management, the Workflow includes whatever enables the delivery of desirable results while everything else gets excluded. Tailoring the workflow practices can be done at the team-level, which is within the focus of this book, or at a higher business level, the focus of Book Two of the Agile Almanac.

5. **HYBRID PROJECT MANAGEMENT** uses selected combinations of techniques and practices to best meet the needs of the customer

   Hybrid Project Management is an Agile Framework where a selected combination of techniques and practices, including those from one or more Agile Frameworks, are used to manage projects in order to best meet the needs of the organization and customer.

6. **EVM** is a program management technique that integrates **SCOPE, SCHEDULE AND RESOURCE CONSUMPTION INFORMATION.**

   Earned Value Management (EVM) is a program management technique that integrates scope, schedule and resource consumption information in order to measure project performance against planned cost metrics. It provides quantitative, objective data to supplement qualitative, subjective judgments.

7. **EVM's** fundamental premise is that as work is **COMPLETED** the corresponding budget value is **EARNED.**

   EVM's fundamental premise is that as work is completed, the corresponding budget value is earned, hence the term Earned Value (EV). In EVM, that paradigm of value only being earned for completed work aligns at the most basic level with the core Agile principle of measuring work progress by only counting work that is Done-Done in the Velocity.

8. Schedule Performance Index (SPI) = EV / PV

9. Cost Variance (CV) = EV – AC

10. When the SV registers as a negative integer it is **UNDESIRABLE.**

    In addition to the calculations being routine, interpreting their meaning is very straightforward. For both the SV and CV, a negative variance is undesirable and indicates the project is behind schedule, over budget or both. For both the SPI and the CPI, an index value less than 1 is undesirable and indicates the project is behind schedule, over budget or both.

Answers – Terminology Matching

1:G, 2:D, 3:E, 4:B, 5:C, 6:A, 7:F, 8:J, 9:K, 10:H, 11:I, 12:N, 13:L, 14:O, 15:M

Chapter End Notes

None.

PART THREE
AGILE TOOLS

Estimating and Derived Schedules

Agile estimation tools are, perhaps, the most cogent approach available to project managers to forecast future project outcomes. And when they are combined with Logic Networks, one of the most powerful tools in Traditional Project Management, it is possible to create a Derived Schedule that does more to optimize development progress and manage stakeholder and team expectations than any other technique in existence. This chapter will focus on explaining key principles that will enable the most robust and reliable planning possible. It is a very significant, information-dense chapter.

Understanding Estimating and Derived Schedules

In order to properly frame estimating and scheduling it is important to first define the core purpose of planning in project management. Planning's core purpose is to aid and support decision-making.

Many times stakeholders are described derisively as being irrational. The sad truth is that such an accusation is self-incriminating. Often a lack of well-communicated, reliable planning forces irrational behavior on the part of stakeholders. When project leaders fail to continually teach, reinforce, and re-impress upon stakeholders that estimating, scheduling and planning activities are done in order to support their decision-making they fail to be decision makers. When project leaders give them inadequate, unreliable, and poorly timed information they cannot make rational decisions. The job of the project leader and the Team is to be the expert on every piece of vital project information, frame it in an understandable context, and establish the timeframes for when decisions need to be made. The information needs to be framed as "just an update" or "this information requires a decision by Friday." Information must be structured within a context in order to produce rational stakeholder behavior.

John Maynard Keynes, the well-known economist, said, "It is better to be roughly right than precisely wrong." One commonly ingested assumption that is precisely wrong is that things are going great right now. Far too many projects are nightmares, causing good people to quit. Too many projects exist in an environment where everyone is on blood pressure medicine and dealing with very unhappy customers. The Chaos Studies from the Standish Group have established a longitudinal, statistically validated baseline that only one-third of projects succeed, while one-third are troubled and one-third are outright failures.

Robust estimating integrated to Derived Schedules in a Rolling Wave planning system can correct that situation. Henry Ford, founder of Ford Motors, rightly said, "Thinking is the hardest work there is...that's why so few people do it!" We would add that implementing a Rolling Wave planning system should not be taken lightly because planning is the hardest thinking there is. So this solution is simple, but not easy. It is rigorous, but straightforward.

The idea of using a Rolling Wave plan has been part of the *PMBOK® Guide* for many years. However, the important linkage between estimating at three levels – Rough Order of Magnitude (ROM), Budgetary and Definitive – and aligning them to long-term, mid-term and current time horizons has not been made clear.

Rolling Wave Planning means project-planning goes through multiple passes (i.e., waves) to decompose work elements with increasing levels of detail. Work in the near term has been subjected to more iterations of refinement so they include greater detail, whereas work in the future has lower granularity because it has gone through less decomposition.

The Rolling Wave plan really begins at the organizational level. Those organizational aspects will be covered briefly here in order to facilitate understanding the team-level and exam prep content that is within the scope of this book. It will be covered in more complete detail in Books 2 and 3 of this Agile Almanac.

Rolling Wave Cycle 1 - Affinity Sizes and Derived ROM-Granularity Schedules

The purpose of the first cycle of Rolling Wave planning is to identify the logical order of development from a customer-value perspective. This is a simple-sounding but extremely important principle because it addresses one of the biggest problems in project management – being forced to make major, indiscriminate reductions in scope because of an impending delivery date. The reason that major, indiscriminate reductions in scope occur so often is because the Customer, Project Manager, and Team have ingested and accepted an assumption that is fatally flawed.

They assume, wrongly, that all of the work identified in the original scope will be completed. Therefore, planning is sequenced for development team efficiency and convenience. Countless data exists to prove that the vast majority of projects are correlated, in statistically significant ways, to the delivery deadline and overall cost than those driven by completion of the entire scope. And since development team efficiency rarely aligns with the customer's value-hierarchy, when time is running out the remaining scope invariably contains features, functions and capabilities of greater value than some of those that have already been completed. When development is predicated on the assumption that everything will get done, planning induces a major problem when the delivery date drives mandatory scope adjustments. Ultimately, the customer is forced to sacrifice items of greater value than those previously delivered in order to meet the deadline, leaving them very unhappy!

A properly executed first cycle of Rolling Wave planning overcomes the problem induced by the fatally flawed assumption. It begins by identifying the logical order of development from a customer-value perspective, then staging the development work for efficiency. Creating the first-cycle plan requires that all of the features, functions and capabilities included in the project scope be documented, then sized, and finally integrated into a Logic Network governed by rough-cut capacity analysis so the schedule can be derived.

Document the Features, Functions and Capabilities (FFCs)

As previously noted, FFCs are documented on cards containing information about their attributes and traits with low-level granularity appropriate for planning on long-term time horizons. The information elements include descriptions of desired outcomes, conditions of satisfaction or acceptance criteria, and any other critical content used when determining the best approach for solution development. Because the granularity of the details increases as FFCs are decomposed into User Stories, and ultimately into Tasks, summarized information at the highest level that will still effectively focus the dialogue needed to logically synchronize development work is the goal.

Each card contains one, and only one, FFC in order to size them.

Affinity Estimate the Size of the FFCs

Sizing is applied using two different techniques based on planning granularity. For ROM-level planning, the Affinity approach is used. Later those sizes are refined using Planning Poker to produce Budgetary-level planning. Before learning how Sizing is done, it is valuable to understand why it works.

Sizing works because it is based on solid mathematical and biological science. The first factor that contributes to it working is multiple, independent sources of Expert Judgment determining the size. The cross-functional Team, whose members are the experts, uses independent analysis to estimate the relative complexity, effort and uncertainty impacting the development of each work item. Those multiple, independent sources improve the reliability of the outcome by including the outliers, without being overly influenced by them during comprehensive peer-level discussions, which compensate for missing information and focus on improving estimating accuracy.

The second factor is that each Iteration's selection of User Stories being assessed is a sample size that will be normally distributed, according to the Central Limit Theorem. That means their composite level of accuracy will gather around the mean of the Bell Curve and reduce the risk of a gross error, even though each estimate is likely skewed toward under or over estimation.

The third factor leverages the observable human ability for determining the relative size things and avoids the human limitation for assessing time required to complete Tasks, especially in the abstract. Both Affinity Estimating and Planning Poker are structured to compare work items to each other and assess their relative size.

The fourth factor, which may be the most potent, is also the least intuitive. Modern brain science shows that laughter and fun release biochemicals that enhance the power of the prefrontal cortex to creatively collaborate. That power unlocks the integrative thinking, discussed in the previous chapter, needed by the Team to explore and investigate options in order to synthesize the most realistic assessment of the effort and risk associated with each work item being sized. Both Affinity Estimating and Planning Poker are structured to create an engaging atmosphere (that is sometimes misinterpreted as chaos!).

Together the impact of those factors means that the individual estimates created during Sizing activities are imperfect, but as a group produce reliable input for planning. When they are integrated into a Logic Network the results predicts the most probable outcome of an Iteration or Release. Imperfect sizes and reliable results!

Affinity estimating is a technique used to quickly size a large number of Stories, typically to plan a Roadmap, Release or first Iteration.

The Affinity Estimating process takes the FFC cards and organizes them according to their relative size. The process begins with the process leader creating a workspace, commonly on a whiteboard or wall, where columns are labeled at the top with a scale, typically the Agile "T-Shirt" scale of extra small (XS) to extra large (XL), plus a Parking Lot. Next the leader populates the columns with FFC cards by taking the first guess at their relative sizes.

Then the process leader gives the following simple instructions to the participants:

- All of the participants will approach the workspace together.
- They will work in complete silence and simultaneously assess the first draft currently posted.
- Each participant will evaluate the proposed size of each card relative to the other cards, based on the complexity, effort and uncertainty involved with delivering it.
- If the proposed size seems correct to the participant, they will leave it alone.
- If the proposed size seems incorrect to the participant, they will move it to the correct column, and place a small diagonal line in the bottom right corner of the card. If a diagonal line already exists in the corner, they will add a second line perpendicular to the first such that an "X" will be created. If an X already exists, it must be placed in the Parking Lot column.
- When everyone is satisfied, as indicated by the cessation of cards being moved, the entire team will step back from the workspace. (Figure 9.1)

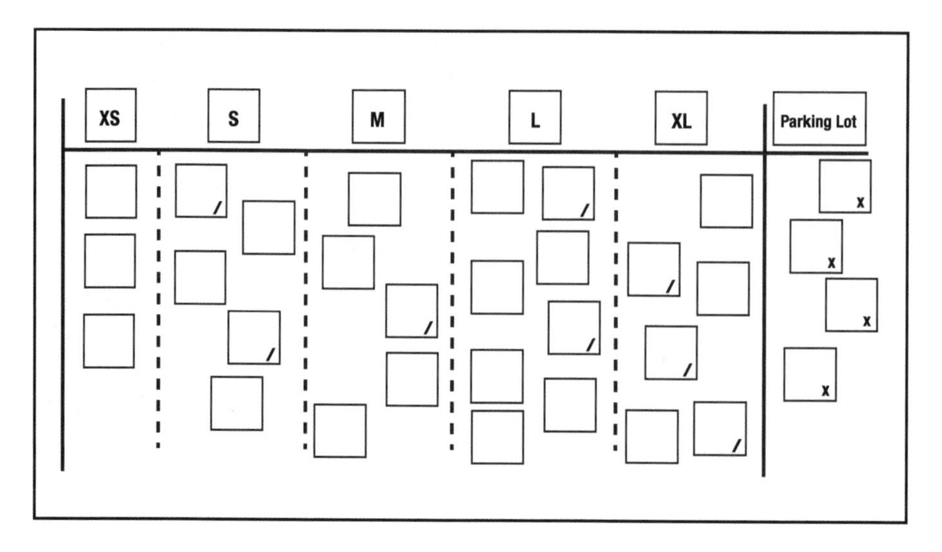

Figure 9.1 | *Affinity Sizing Board*

When the silent phase of the process is completed, the leader will engage the Team to discuss the cards in the Parking Lot. The discussion will focus on clarifying the nature and content of the work represented by the card so that its size may be assessed. Once its size has been assessed, it will be moved into the appropriate column.

After all of the cards have been placed in a column, the process leader initiates a final discussion about the group's impression of how long each size will take to complete. It is important that this step be done last so it does not

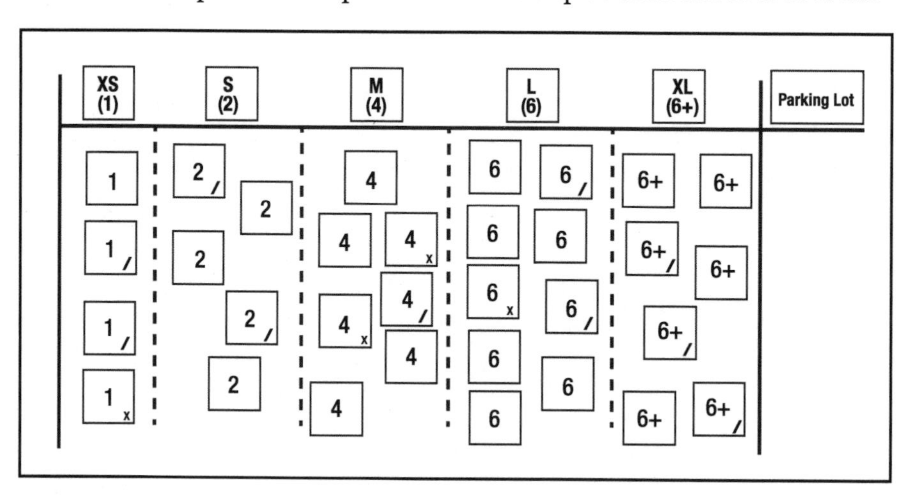

Figure 9.2 | *Affinity Sizing with ROM Estimates*

skew the work done in the prior steps. Only after the relative sizes have been established should a discussion of the abstract measure of the time occur. The result will be something like Extra Small are work items that will likely take less than 1 week, Small less than 2 weeks, Medium less than 4 weeks, Large less than 6 weeks, and Extra Large more than 6 weeks. (Figure 9.2)

The participants should be reminded that the goal is to develop information for use in ROM-level planning decisions so it is counter-productive to try to assign too much precision to the brackets. After all, the five columns suggest that the refinement is only slightly higher than dividing the work in quartile groups. This final step is important because it is needed to integrate the cards into the Logic Network, but it is waste if it becomes an exercise in false precision.

The resulting workspace contains three things. First, it shows all of the FFCs that are currently understood to be part of the project. Second, it defines the relative size of each card. Third, it contains a documented correlation between the T-shirt size and a ROM-level time assessment. All of that information is critical to understanding the best way to approach solution development and delivery.

Rough-cut Capacity Analysis

The Rough-cut Capacity Analysis is created in order to define the ROM-level Forecast Velocity used to build the Roadmap and Release plans. In order to create it, the appropriate decision makers have to define the expected team size and document some basic assumptions. The result must end up looking something like:

- The Team will have 6 SMEs or Developers, each committed at 50%
- Each SME will work on the project for 5 days x 4 weeks (the standard Iteration).
- Therefore, they will have 20 Actual days at 50%, yielding 10 Production days.
- Production days operate at 60% efficiency, yielding 6 days of Throughput.
- 6 SME's x 6 days of Throughput = 36 Planning (aka Ideal) days per Iteration
- Forecast Velocity per Team per Iteration is 36 days.
- 3 teams will be assigned to the project. Therefore the Forecast Velocity for each Iteration of the Release is 108 Planning days.

In Books 2 and 3 of the Almanac, a more in-depth discussion about managing the added complexity of using multiple teams in development will be discussed. For this book we will ignore the overhead burden placed on development throughput due to integration and alignment factors.

Logic Networks

Product Roadmaps and project Release Plans are Agile tools for managing organizational resources and scheduling Programs. Both become more robust and reliable when they apply Logic Networks' best practices. However, because Roadmaps and Releases are program-, portfolio- and organizational-level tools, they will receive more in-depth scrutiny in Books 2 and 3 of the Almanac. However, they must also be covered here in order to fulfill the objective of this book.

Logic Networks are where the dependencies between activities are identified and accurately mapped so they can be optimized. Done properly, the Logic Network overcomes the problem induced by the fatally flawed assumption that was discussed above. It identifies the logical order of development from a customer-value perspective, during this first cycle. Then during the second and third cycles, it stages development work for efficiency.

To begin, the process maps the customer-value perspective of the FFC cards by showing the dependencies impacting the start of an activity, and also what subsequent tasks are affected by the completion of an activity. Responding to a flat tire provides a simple example. (Figure 9.3)

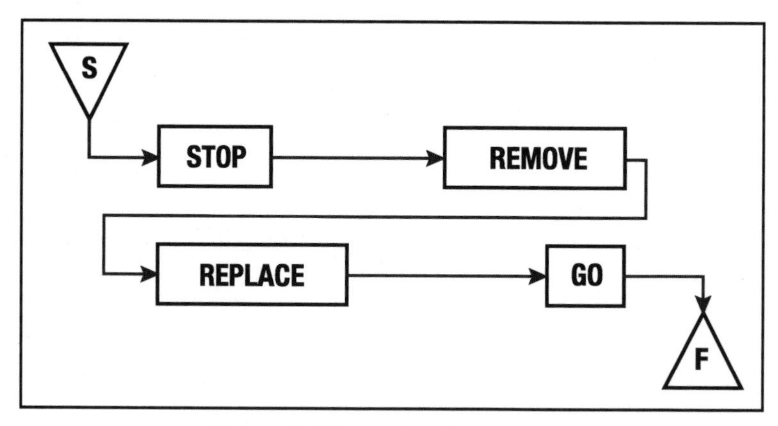

Figure 9.3 | *Flat Tire Logic Network*

As the diagram indicates, there is a start point – like the sound of a tire popping – diagrammed using a triangle with an "S", followed by the activities:

(1) stop the vehicle, (2) remove the flat tire, (3) replace it with a spare tire, and (4) go back to driving as originally intended. The diagram indicates the process is finished using a triangle identified with the letter "F".

The goal of a Logic Network is to ensure that the correct inputs of any given activity are identified, and that the output is correctly linked to subsequent activities. Creating a Logic Network can be accomplished by methodologies as simple as placing each activity on a separate sticky note, arranging them according to predecessor-successor relationships on a whiteboard, and drawing the arrows that show the type of dependency.

Experience has shown that using low-tech, high-touch methods, such as sticky notes, allows the project team to collaborate until a unified vision of project execution emerges. Because it is a simple graphical method, it draws out the optimum level of contribution from each team member. Quite often it also reveals aspects of the interdependence of team members' responsibilities that weren't apparent to every team member initially. As the Team negotiates how tasks are related – adding, removing and rearranging sticky notes – their understanding of project success being related to their interdependency becomes clear.

Typically, the project leader creates a first draft diagram of the workflow (sometimes called a "straw man") before the meeting. The leader takes the FFC cards and User Stories and writes the name of each one on a sticky note. Then the leader arranges them in sequential and parallel paths across the whiteboard. When the participants arrive for the meeting, they revise the straw man by adding or removing sticky notes until their vision emerges. Along the way, or when visioning is complete, they draw in the arrows to complete the Logic Network diagram.

Drawing the arrows correctly is important because they define the type of dependency. Four types of dependencies exist – One-to-One, One-to-Many, Many-to-One, and Many-to-Many – and they are each diagrammed differently. (Figure 9.4)

One-to-One means that one, and only one, activity must be completed before the next activity can begin. For example, drywall must be installed before it can be painted but once it is installed painting may begin without the completion of any other activity.

One-to-Many means that one, and only one, activity must be completed before multiple follow-on activities can begin. For instance, plans must be

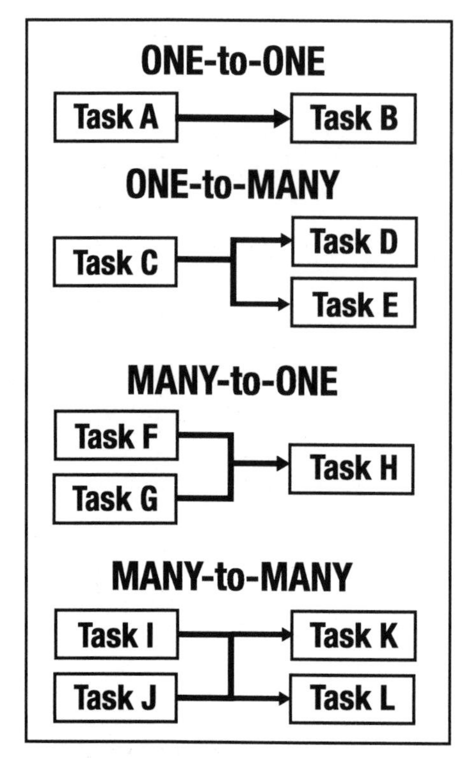

Figure 9.4 | *Relationship Dependencies*

approved before either permits can be obtained or site preparation can be started (in residential construction).

Many-to-One means that two or more Tasks must be completed before the start of a subsequent Task can occur. As an example, the completion of both the engineering design and the manufacturing design are required before production is started in many industries.

Many-to-Many means that two or more Tasks must be completed before multiple subsequent tasks can begin. As an example, many times software code and copyright registration must receive final approval before either marketing or production is started.

When diagramming the relationships in a Logic Network, for one-to-one relationships a single line passes between the activities. In one-to-many relationships, a single line divides after it leaves the predecessor and moves towards the successor activities, indicating mutual dependence on the prior activity. In many-to-one relationships, multiple lines merge after leaving the predecessors, and then it moves towards the successor activity, indicating its dependence on the completion of all prior activities. Finally, in many-to-many relationships, multiple lines merge after leaving the predecessors then re-divide as they move towards the successor activities, indicating mutual dependence on the completion of all prior activities.

Once the FFCs and their relationships have been mapped on sticky notes with their size annotated, the final step of deriving the ROM-level schedule can be done. (Figure 9.5)

Creating the first-cycle plan requires that all of the FFCs included in the project scope be documented, then be sized, and finally integrated into a Logic Network governed by rough-cut capacity analysis so the schedule be derived.

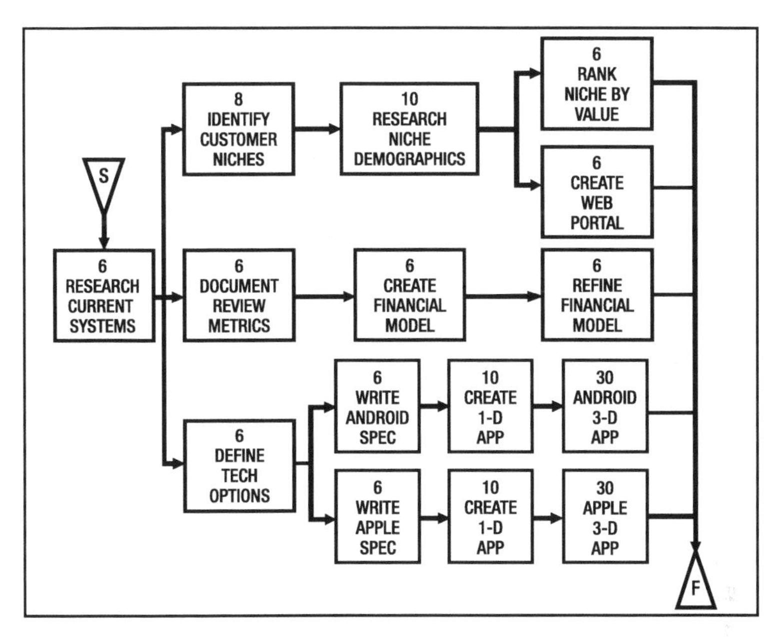

Figure 9.5 | *Logic Network*

Derive the Schedule

Derived Schedules are calculated by identifying and estimating the size of the work items in a group, diagramming their logical relationships in a network, and using a Forecast Velocity to determine the project schedule. The schedule can be recalculated using the Velocity of actual work progress, as it becomes available, without requiring a reassessment of the original work item estimates.

For example, Figure 9.6 shows a ROM-level plan with a Forecast Velocity of 30 weeks of development work. Two of the five Releases have a Forecast Velocity of exactly 30 weeks, one is slightly lower at 24 weeks and two slightly exceed that standard at 32 weeks. Because this is a ROM-level plan, it is acceptable for the plan to have some variance. The purpose is to identify where the Team should spend resources refining the ROM-level information into Budgetary-level data before finalizing it as Definitive-level detail during the next two cycles. Doing this eliminates more waste than the resources it consumes because it aligns development to customer-value expectations.

Rolling Wave Cycle 2 – Planning Poker and Derived Schedules with Budgetary Granularity

Having created the ROM-level plan, the Team now knows the correct place to focus its planning resources is on the four FFCs at the beginning (shown in white at the beginning of Figure 9.6) in order to create an efficient

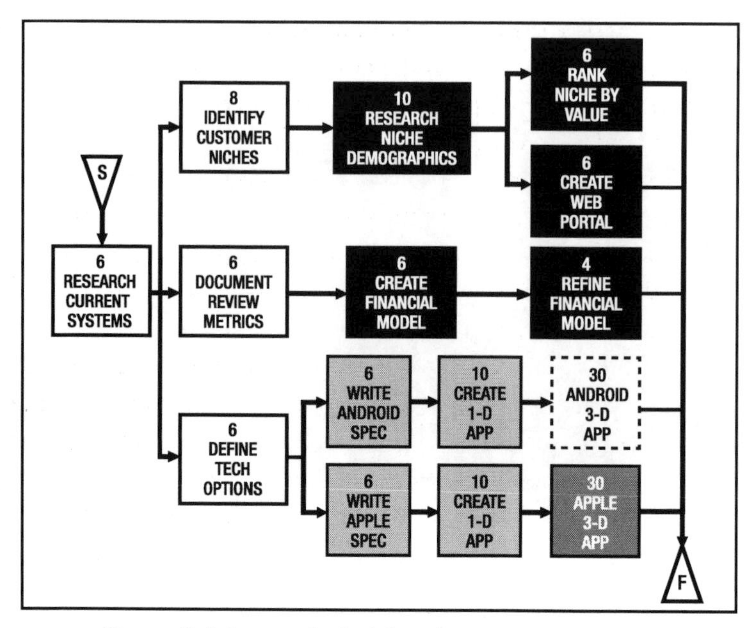

Figure 9.6 | *Derived Schedule with Forecast Velocity of 30*

development workflow. Figure 9.7 shows an example where the Team has decomposed the four FFCs identified as most significant from the customer-value perspective in the ROM-level plan. Each FFC was refined into three lower level work items and assigned a Budgetary size using Planning Poker. Planning Poker will be explained in the next chapter.

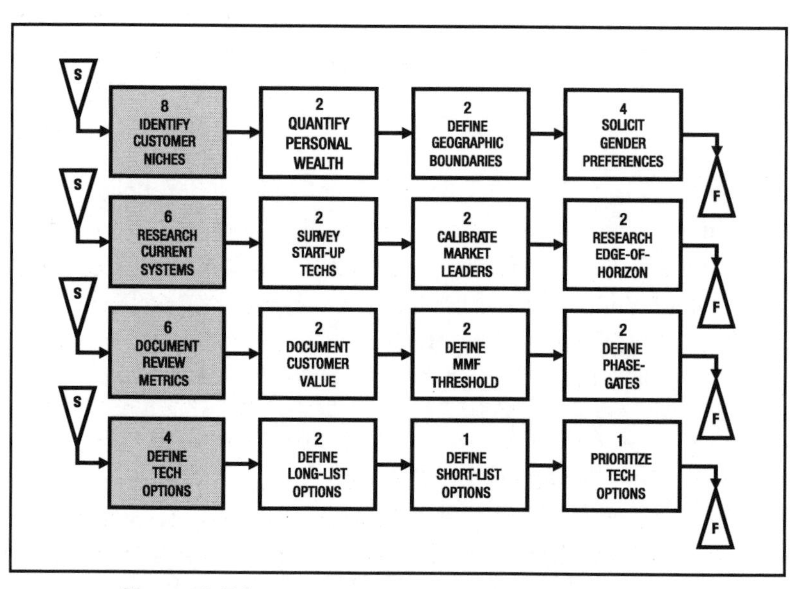

Figure 9.7 | *Derived Schedule with Forecast Velocity of 30*

In real world situations, the amount of Budgetary-level detail is typically far more than the 3 elements shown in the example. It is common to see four FFCs decomposed into 30, 40 or even 50 constituent elements. Also, the example shows Logic Networks that are considerably simpler than in the real world. The point of the illustration is to show that conducting the second cycle of this process produces Budgetary-level planning options used to optimize developmental efficiency, market responsiveness, or whatever variable is most important. This level of detail provides visibility into choices while keeping them framed by customer-value priorities. For example, maximizing quality might mean making the choice to have one Team do all four Iterations. Whereas, accelerating the time-to-market might be better served by having four Teams working in parallel doing one Iteration each. Regardless, choices about how to structure the development approach get moved into plain sight where they can be weighed, measured and assessed against articulated standards of customer-value before being refined one final time in order to produce a definitive plan for work execution.

Rolling Wave Cycle 3 - Engineered Schedules with Definitive Granularity

Now that both the ROM- and Budgetary-level plans have been created, the Team can zero in on the "one best way for this particular team" to execute this project and Iteration. Recall that we previously described how audiences and teams everywhere we work acknowledge that there is not one right way to do every project. However, they also agree that for a specific team, on a specific project, given the available resources and constraints, there is one best way to create the highest probability of success for that project. Using Rolling Wave planning and Derived Schedules improves the Team's performance because it creates a rational, focused understanding of the goal.

In this third cycle, the Budgetary User Stories are decomposed into smaller User Stories and Tasks so that an efficient development workflow can be chosen. Each one is also given a Definitive Estimate including hours, resources, materials, or any other elements defined as the organizational standard.

In real world situations, the level of detail for Definitive Estimates is defined by the organization in order to support its financial management needs. The point of the third cycle is to bucket work items into Iterations that optimize developmental efficiency by aligning with how the project and teams have been structured. Regardless of which choices are made, the important thing is that the choices were made in a transparent environment aligning with customer-value priorities.

Creating a Derived Schedule means ongoing calculations and analysis can be used to continuously improve the probability of a successful outcome. Properly implementing Rolling Wave planning overcomes problems induced by failing to identify the logical order of development from a customer-value perspective first, then staging the development work for efficiency second.

A key principle in Scrum (one shared by other Agile frameworks also) is that complex problems cannot be fully defined in advance. Therefore, using scientifically validated empirical process control– transparency, inspection, and adaptation – is the only thing that can consistently deliver desirable results.

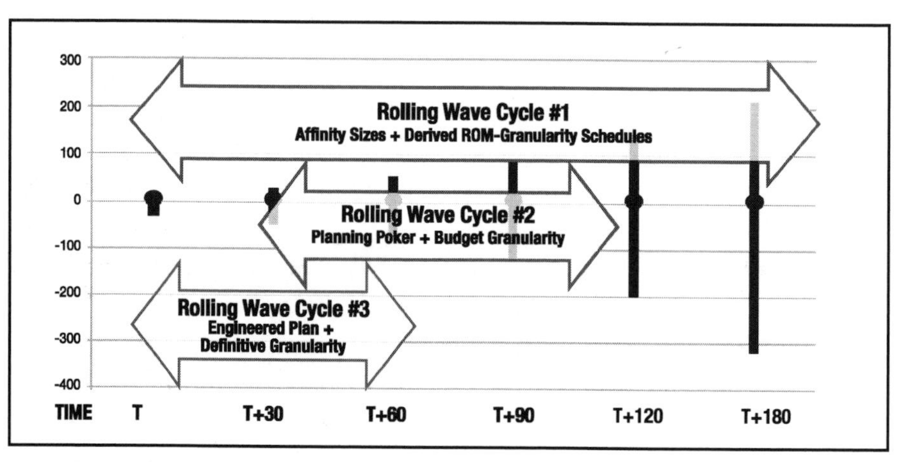

Figure 9.8 | *Rolling Wave Planning*

Figure 9.8 shows how Rolling Wave planning operationalizes empirical process control. The first cycle creates a transparent view of the customer-value priorities. The second cycle adapts development to the Customer's priorities and frames inspection points. The third cycle defines development so that it moves the project towards a viable solution in the midst of emerging requirements.

Recommended Reading

- *Agile Estimating and Planning,* by Mike Cohn (Prentice Hall; November 2005)

Chapter End Notes

None.

Planning Poker

Planning Poker optimizes the development of vital information with appropriate planning-level accuracy. It minimizes resources spent on estimating and planning while increasing clarity and granularity to aid decision-making. After the ROM-level FFCs from the first cycle of Rolling Wave planning have been decomposed into User Stories in the second cycle, Planning Poker efficiently assesses the development work they will require. It reduces the range of variability in the Affinity Estimates produced in the first cycle making the uncertainty of the development schedule also decline. The process supports the production of a more reliable schedule while avoiding undue estimating costs.

Planning Poker stands out among Agile tools because of an interesting dichotomy. It is very popular with teams yet poorly understood. The lack of clarity about the principles underlying Planning Poker means sometimes it is implemented incorrectly and is frequently poorly explained to stakeholders. This chapter will focus on clarifying key principles in order to ensure the tool is used properly. It will also support clearly explaining it to stakeholders so that common misunderstandings can be avoided. It is an information-rich chapter.

Understanding Planning Poker

In the previous chapter, the core science that makes Sizing approaches work was described. The contributing factors included using multiple, independent sources of Expert Judgment, independent analysis of relative complexity, effort and uncertainty, inclusion of outlier data, adequate sample size, observable human capabilities, and laughter to induce brain chemistry that releases the power of the prefrontal cortex.

Both Affinity Estimating and Planning Poker are Sizing approaches structured to compare the relative size of work items. The Sizing assessments they deliver are imperfect, but as a group, produce reliable input for planning.

Planning Poker is a consensus-based estimating technique commonly used by Agile teams employing a simplified Delphi technique to estimate the relative size of User Stories. A Fibonacci sequence is commonly used to establish the range of numbers applied.

Planning Poker typically follows this process:

- The Team quickly sorts through the Iteration Backlog and chooses a medium-*ish* User Story to use as the comparison standard. It is important to note that the selected Story is medium-*ish* and **not** the mean, median, mode or average of the Iteration Backlog. It does not have to be the exact midpoint. It only needs to be in the relative range of a midpoint. If selecting it takes very long, it usually means team members are attempting more precision than is worthwhile. They have forgotten that speed is a driving factor (pun intended). The medium-ish User Story is assigned a size value, typically 8 Story Points.

Each additional User Story is then individually processed as follows:

- The Team briefly discusses what the User Story contains so they can assess whether its size is larger, a lot larger, smaller or a lot smaller than the comparison standard.
- Independently, each member selects a number from their own deck of cards to express his or her estimate of the size of the Story.
- The process leader confirms everyone has selected a size then initiates a voting process for everyone to simultaneously display a size number by holding the card to their forehead so everyone can see it. For example, the leader might say, "Does everyone have a number? Yes. OK, on 3 show your card…1, 2, 3!" It is important that the votes be displayed simultaneously in order to avoid groupthink or anchoring. Also, holding the card to the forehead usually provokes laughter that relaxes the prefrontal cortex.
- The team members presenting the outliers – highest and lowest estimate – then briefly explain their perspective, offering evidence others may have overlooked.

- The process leader then initiates re-voting after which any discussion needed to quickly reach a consensus occurs and the size of the Story is finalized.

There are three common units of estimation used in project management. The first two, Ideal Days and Actual Days, have been used for many years in Traditional project management. The third unit, Story Points, is newer and preferred in Agile project management.

Ideal Days, Actual Days, and Story Points

Ideal Days express the development time required assuming there are no interruptions, obstacles or delays. Ideal Days present a problem because the assumption that work can be completed with 100% efficiency must be factored to compensate for environmental conditions that are not uniformly present.

For example, a task estimated to need 5 Ideal Days to complete could not be done in a typical 40-hour, 5-day workweek. Also, the type of work being done and the role of the person doing it are not homogenous, so factoring for the frequency and type of interruptions, obstacles or delays that will reduce productive work time cannot be done reliably.

Actual days express the development time required factored with assumptions about efficiency based on a particular type of work being done and the role of the person doing it. Actual Days present a problem because the assumptions can be invalid if the production approach or the person doing the work changes.

For example, what assumption should be made if the number of other projects the person is working on changes? Or how much efficiency should be assumed if a new production process is chosen? Or what assumption should be made if the person doing the work has more experience than the one assumed during planning?

Story Points express the development time required relative to other Stories in the Iteration, typically expressed using a non-linear number series such as the Fibonacci sequence.

The key to understanding Story Points as an estimation unit, and being able to explain it to stakeholders, centers on the correlation between human physiology and estimating granularity across time scales. Abstract mathematics and human physiology do not always align in the discipline of estimating and planning.

In mathematics the sequences 1, 2, 3, and 88, 89, 90 share a lot in common. They are both a series of three digits separated by one integer. However, in human physiology they are quite different. For example, consider a situation where you ask a SME for an estimate, they pause to ponder, and then respond, "It will probably take 1 or 2, maybe 3 days" versus "It will probably take 88 or 89, maybe 90 days."

The experience of sharing this example with thousands of students has shown that no one believes the second scenario would ever happen. The most common student response is, "Our SME would never say 88, 89, 90. It would be more like 80, 90, maybe 100 days." That assessment is correct and is driven by the correlation between human physiology and estimating granularity across time scales. (Figure 10.1)

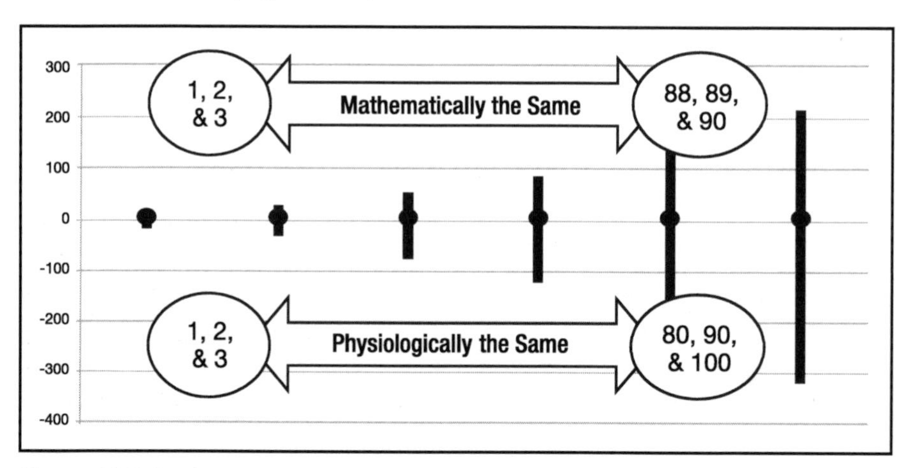

Figure 10.1 | *Mathematics and Human Physiology*

Human physiology includes the capacity to estimate with high-resolution granularity on a near-horizon time scale, but it is limited to low-resolution granularity on longer-term time scales. On the near-horizon time scale, mathematics and physiology align. On longer-term horizons, they do not. That is why Sizing approaches use non-linear number series to define the relative size of work items being compared. The Fibonacci sequence and modified-Fibonacci sequences are the most widely employed number series.

The ***Fibonacci sequence*** is a non-linear number series derived from the sum of two previous numbers and expressed in the equation $F_n = F_{n-1} + F_{n-2}$. The first part of the sequence is 0, 1, 1, 2, 3, 5, 8, 13, 21 and 34.

The Fibonacci sequence is credited to Leonardo of Pisa, also known as

Fibonacci, because he published it in1202 in *Liber Abaci.* His book introduced the sequence to the Western world although it had been documented much earlier in India.

Modified Fibonacci sequences leverage the value of being non-linear, but make it easier to remember by using a pattern such as 1, 2, 3, 5, 8, 13, 20, 40, 60, 80 and 100.

The Fibonacci sequence has seen widespread application in computer algorithms used for searches, data structuring, and cube graphs linking parallel and distributed systems. It is widely recognized in biological and life sciences where it describes phenomena such as tree branching, the arrangement of scales around the axis of a pinecone, and the proportions of successive spirals of many seashells.

Non-linear sequences have received extensive acceptance in Sizing approaches because they provide a mathematical scale that is correlated to the limits of human physiology in expressing estimating granularity across a variety of time scales. (Figure 10.2)

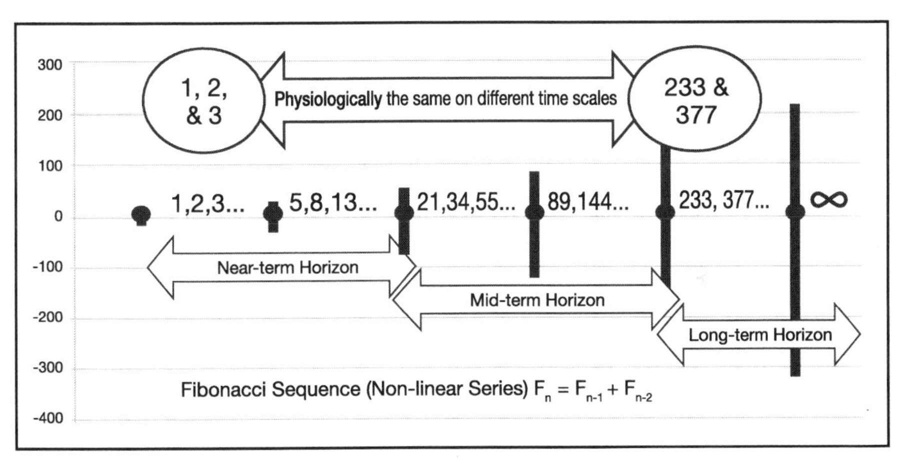

Figure 10.2 | *Sizing and the Fibonacci Sequence*

One best practice that helps integrate non-linear sizes with project planning to create reliable schedules is to set thresholds for maximum acceptable sizes at the outer limit of a time horizon. For example, an organization could state that its near-term time horizon for planning is 90 days and that all work items must be decomposed into elements not larger than 13 Story Points. It could continue that its mid-term horizon is 91 to 180 days and those work item elements must not exceed 144 Story Points whereas its long-term horizon is everything over

181-days and work item elements can be any appropriate Size.

Major frustration occurs for many stakeholders, especially those with an engineering background, when they ask an Agile Project Leader or team member, "How many hours are in a Story Point?" The frustration occurs because many professed Agile experts offer unclear, convoluted answers that are not technically grounded and sound evasive. Explaining that using non-linear sequences in Sizing approaches correlates a mathematical scale to the limits of human physiology to produce reliable estimating across a variety of time scales supports the indisputable recognition that it also creates an association between sizes and hours that varies across the time scales. It can be easily observed that there is a higher correlation between sizes and hours on the near-term horizon and a lower correlation on the long-term horizon. However, the varying association between sizes and hours does not undermine the core purpose of planning and estimating – to aid and support effective decision making!

Recommended Reading

- *Agile Software Development: The Cooperative Game,* Alistair Cockburn (Addison-Wesley Professional; October 2006)

Chapter End Notes

None.

User Stories

User Stories are, perhaps, the most widely discussed Agile tool in existence. Because so many other respected thought leaders have published detailed information about the step-by-step process of writing, formatting, and manipulating them, this chapter will focus on clarifying key principles that will ensure the proper use of the tool. Those principles will also aid in the avoidance of common mistakes and misunderstandings. It is a brief, but very significant, information-dense chapter.

Understanding User Stories

It is interesting that many Agile aficionados are surprised to hear that creating and manipulating User Stories is a technique aligned with the concepts of decomposition and progressive elaboration in the *PMBOK® Guide.* It is equally funny that many Traditional project managers are astonished to hear that Agile has tools that deploy these accepted concepts in powerful and useful ways.

Despite that surprise and astonishment, there is wide agreement that the project management landscape is one of continuous change where small teams, or groups of small teams, with limited budgets work to fulfill business requirements while being pressed to deliver desirable results faster. In that environment, all of Agile's stakeholders – Team, Customer and Organization – often struggle to cope with a nearly overwhelming, chaotic mix of complexity and uncertainty.

One key Agile principle that enables its power to succeed in such a challenging environment, but also induces some aspects of the complexity and uncertainty, is that Customers are free to change their minds about the relative importance of features, functions and capabilities within the logical order of development work. In order to enable that freedom while creating a manageable environment, XP introduced a tool called User Stories. The tool proved useful and became a standard among Agile Frameworks.

User Stories provide the needed flexibility while making progress measurable and manageable even within the chaotic environment of modern project management. For example, the Planning Game in XP defines a ROM-level plan for the project that is a shared understanding of the expected Release using User Stories that the Team can break down into Tasks to allocate its work.

User Stories often have a one-to-many relationship with Tasks, so it is common to have Stories in the Backlog, but more detailed Tasks in the other columns of the Story Board. The structure of a Story Board with User Stories holding elements that need to be developed creates visibility into the work and radiates the level of progress towards the Iteration Goal so it can be tracked and monitored using Velocity. This is very useful because risk can be correlated to the amount of work remaining, as represented by the User Stories in inventory, and the rate of progress, as represented by the Velocity.

In *Extreme Programming Explored*[37], Bill Wake presented the mnemonic **INVEST** to describe the six characteristics of good User Stories.

INVEST was a mnemonic for **I**ndependent, **N**egotiable, **V**aluable, **E**stimatable, **S**mall and **T**estable. The elements can be defined as follows.

Independent means the Story avoids interlocking dependencies in order to simplify decomposition and Task estimation.

Negotiable means the Story encourages frequent Customer conversations (i.e., negotiations) to explore and expand the brief descriptions of functionality on the card. It is the inverse of a contract clause or detailed specification.

Valuable means the Story reflects the priorities that create value for End User and Organizational Customers.

Estimatable means the Development Team can make a good assessment of the relative size of the Story as a piece of the solution, which implies it is not too large or too small.

Small means the Story leans towards minimalism, avoiding being a compound Story with multiple shorter Stories or a complex Story with avoidable complications, so that it fits within the Iteration.

Testable means the Story can be tested, even if the test hasn't been defined yet, which implies acceptance criteria are definable.

A comparable mnemonic that may be a bit easier to remember, $SI^2MP^2LE^2$ suggests a rank-ordered list of nine considerations.

$SI^2MP^2LE^2$ is defined as **S**izable, **I**mportant and **I**nsightful, **M**easurable, **P**review and **P**laceholder, and **L**inked, **E**xtractable and **E**xecutable. The elements can be defined as follows.

Sizable means the principles of good estimating can be applied to define a reasonable and reliable approximation of the development effort. It avoids being too large, which induces complexity, or too small, which causes inefficiency.

Important and Insightful (I^2) means the Story creates and enhances Customer value by encapsulating elements of the solution in a way that improves discernment of progress towards the best solution.

Measurable means the Story can be subjected to the best practices of Test-Driven Development (TDD) within a continuously improved development system, ultimately enhancing stakeholder relationships.

Preview and Placeholder (P^2) means the Story describes an element of a feature, function or capability at a summary level and acts a marker guaranteeing well-timed, appropriate, in-depth discussions.

Linked means the Story can be mapped in a Logical Network or Precedence Diagram of the Iteration or Release that makes dependencies visible, manageable, and productive.

Extractable and Executable (E^2) means the development of the Story is independent of dependencies that hinder its linkage to the Iteration Goal.

Considering the two mnemonics – ***INVEST*** and ***$SI^2MP^2LE^2$*** – exposes the fact that User Stories are much more sophisticated than their simple appearance suggests.

User Stories are an invaluable tool because project deliverables are composed of thousands of inter-related requirements driving an inherent need for flexibility during planning. A best practice for managing that unavoidable complexity is the Lean principle to defer decisions and commitments to the Last Responsible Moment, as previously discussed. Because stakeholders know the User Story is a written placeholder, it alleviates their concern that something important will get overlooked or forgotten. That, in turn, encourages them to be efficient with the precious time of expensive Team resources by deferring discussions until the Last Responsible Moment. Doing so enables the Team to concentrate on developing high-priority Stories and use planning resources wisely, especially in time-constrained projects.

It also increases efficiency by helping avoid the mistake of using resources to do premature planning that creates the illusion of precision where none is possible. Experience has shown that a User Story that appeared necessary or valuable when first conceived, is abandoned when it is supplanted by a better, or simply different, alternative as the project progresses and additional discovery and learning occurs.

In addition to efficiently managing unavoidable complexity in time-constrained projects, User Stories increase the Team's effectiveness with problem solving in the midst of high uncertainty. Highly technical problem solving inherently means engaging uncertainty with a process of experimentation and discovery where a key constraint is the Idea Transfer Rate.

Idea Transfer Rate is the measure of the processing bandwidth needed by a team simultaneously exploring and investigating multiple, often opposing possibilities in search of a synthesized solution containing elements that improve each other in previously unconsidered ways.

Idea Transfer Rates are implied in Roger Martin's article, *The Opposable Mind: How Successful Leaders Win Through Integrative Thinking*, previously mentioned, that explains how great leaders tolerate and embrace ambiguity as long as necessary in order to overcome "either/or" limitations with "both/and" choices.

Martin refers to this leadership capacity as "integrative thinking" and thinking with an "opposable mind." To solve highly technical problems surrounded by uncertainty, a team must overwhelm the known limits by constructing, demolishing, reconstructing, and altering its mental model over and over again until it can envision options that may produce a solution. This process is, perhaps, the only known reliable model for producing solutions in this environment. It works, at least in part, because it applies the Law of Large Numbers used in commonly accepted statistical models.

The cross-functional Team of subject matter experts represents one variable in the equation. The expansive number of potential solutions, including the variants of each solution, which the Team considers, is another variable. And when those variables are multiplied, the result is a large sample of random events where the most desirable solution can be predicted to occur within normal deviations of the mean.

Law of Large Numbers (LLN) is a statistical rule stating that as the quantity of samples increases, the average or mean of the whole population emerges and can be used to predict behavior within normal deviations of outcomes. This allows the transformation of unpredictable outcomes into predictable ones.

With these insights from the science of statistics, it is known that when a team has a high enough Idea Transfer Rate, it will create and synthesize sufficient choices for the LLN to "guarantee" consistent long-term delivery of solutions even though the process will look chaotic and undisciplined.

Agile Frameworks access a minimal Idea Transfer Rate to achieve synchronization during the Daily Meeting. They employ moderate to high Idea Transfer Rates during Working Group meetings to plan work activities. But, they must have very high Idea Transfer Rates to drive problem-solving outcomes.

An interesting and entertaining example of this idea is the individual jet pack invented by Yves Rossy, a Swiss pilot and aviation enthusiast, which uses semi-rigid airplane-type carbon-fiber wings built into a wing-suit system powered by four jet engines. He solved a problem that billions of government dollars failed to overcome, and earned himself the monikers of Jetman and Rocketman.

User Stories are the tangible component of a development system that leverage Idea Transfer Rates and the LLN in order to solve challenging problems. User Stories facilitate exploration, foster discussion and focus planning resources. By making the thousands of inter-relationships between requirements more visible, User Stories expose opportunities to re-prioritize them when needed for planning flexibility. They allow planning to focus on exploring options and adapting to discoveries while the inter-relationships between requirements are still fluid and able to be influenced.

Each Story elicits challenges and clarifications during the vigorous debate occurring while creating and refining them. They also act as a repository for the acceptance criteria and tests that come into view. This participatory decision-making approach has many advantages for the project because the discussion and debate clarifies what is valuable and how it will be created and delivered.

User Stories are a deceptively simple way of integrating the powerful human genius imbedded in purpose-driven customer conversations with drawings, samples, prototypes, and small segments of code. Those kinds of conversations allow customers to evaluate progress in small steps and provide "actionable insight" revealing the optimal way for the project to be successful.

The power of this approach becomes a "blinding flash of the obvious" when you remember that written words, especially in those ever-popular emails, are very tenuous expressions of the unavoidably complex content of most projects. Because, as the saying goes, "The greatest myth about communication is…that it has happened", vigilance is required to prevent misinterpretation. Frequent conversations between the Customer, End Users, and the Team create a tremendously powerful antidote to this common problem.

User Stories are a multifaceted device with tangible and intangible aspects referred to as the "Three Cs" – the Card, Commitment and Criteria. They are composed of a *tangible* Card representing customer requirements used in the planning process; an *intangible* Commitment to have meaningful conversations at appropriate times, and a *collection* of Criteria that will demonstrate when a Story is complete.

Recommended Reading

- *User Stories Applied: For Agile Software Development*, by Mike Cohn (Addison-Wesley Professional; March 2004)

Chapter End Notes

[37]Bill Wake, Extreme Programming Explored (Addison-Wesley Professional, 2001)

PART FOUR
APPENDICES, COMPREHENSIVE EXAM AND GLOSSARY

Exam Prep Appendices

The Exam Prep Appendices are included in an electronic PDF format. Doing so allows them to be updated as changes occur so the reader has the latest information available. Also because the core Agile content presented in the printed book is mature and stable, the Desk Reference has a long-term shelf life and won't need to be replaced frequently, saving the reader a future expense.

Comprehensive Exam

Exam Prep Best Practices

Learning research has proven that the best way to master a subject is to study using multiple modalities. Interacting with the material on many channels reinforces concepts and strengthens recall. That is why the Agile Almanac includes Tests as well as Fill-in-the Blank and Word Matching exercises with each chapter. Those resources unavoidably suffer from being limited to only the content covered on that chapter. To overcome that limitation this Comprehensive Exam is provided. It includes questions that have been randomly selected from throughout the book.

Even though this comprehensive exam is a good first step, it is important to note that it is clearly not adequate preparation by itself. Because the actual exam is computer-based the best practice for preparation is to use an online exam simulator. GR8PM's exam simulator is the most robust one available and it is constantly updated and upgraded as changes to the exam occur. We recommend that you practice on it before sitting for the actual exam. The time and money spent doing so is an inexpensive insurance policy when compared with the cost and aggravation of having to sit for the exam a second time.

Now it is time for you to go forth and conquer the PMI-ACP® exam! Good luck!!

Comprehensive Exam *(120 Questions; 3 Hours)*

001. When the Team clarifies the project objective and the desired final result, in Traditional Project Management it is called creating the ________________ while the same activities in Agile are called defining the ____________________.

A. Project Requirements and Product Specifications
B. Project Specifications and Product Requirements
C. Project Charter and Product Vision
D. Project Vision and Product Charter

002. The foundation for organizing Agile Frameworks can be described as ____________.

A. Processes
B. Approaches
C. Methodologies
D. Philosophies

003. The Scrum Alliance is the largest professional user group in the Agile world and its best known certifications is:

A. Certified ScrumMaster® (CSM)
B. Certified Product Owner® (CSPO)
C. Certified Scrum Professional® (CSP)
D. Certified Scrum Trainer® (CST)

004. Because of work done by ________________, eXtreme Programming (XP) originated in early 1996 and was born in 1999 when he published Extreme Programming Explained.

A. Matt Stephens
B. Ron Jeffries
C. Kent Beck
D. Doug Rosenberg

005. Artifacts for LSD include ________________ and ________________.

A. Product Vision and Incremental Architectural Design
B. Code Configuration and Customer Tests
C. Customer Reviews and Approvals
D. Roadmap and Product Plans

006. CFDs are area graphs where the scale of the vertical, x-axis is a chosen ________________.

A. WIP unit-of-measure
B. Lead Time
C. Cycle Time
D. In-progress unit-of-measure

007. Shu Ha Ri is a simple, powerful model of learning where _______ means attempting to understand the purpose of the techniques.

A. Dojo
B. Shu
C. Ha
D. Ri

008. When the Team initiates a repetitive cyclical process to make choices and define the final objective of the project in Agile Project Management, the timeboxes in the cycle are called a(n) ______________________.

A. Iteration or Sprint
B. Milestone
C. Phase or Stage
D. Release

009. ______________________ are context-specific foundations that have a set of Processes that are used to execute work in a defined way.

A. Frameworks
B. Processes
C. Methodologies
D. Philosophies

010. The seeds of Scrum were planted in 1986 when Hirotaka Takeuchi and Ikujiro Nonaka wrote ______________________.

A. PMBOK Guide®
B. The New New Product Development Game
C. Wicked Problems, Righteous Solutions
D. The Scrum Guide

011. One of XP's important assumptions is that ______________________ exists. Where that assumption is correct, XP is productive. Otherwise it is risky at best.

A. Important PMBOK Guide® guidance
B. A unified client viewpoint
C. Wicked problems with a righteous solution
D. XP solutions for software problems

012. Even though many of the artifacts have a ________________________, they are still important.

A. Short lifespan
B. Vague client viewpoint
C. Limited business value
D. Software problem

013. ______________ starts when the work item is made available for development.

A. Work progress unit-of-measure
B. Lead Time
C. Cycle Time
D. In-process unit-of-measure

014. A professional Agile practitioner is focused on creating an Agile culture, committed to ________________________________.

A. Learning and mastering the basics
B. Deploying Shu Ha Ri
C. Implementing continuous integration
D. Extending techniques incrementally and successfully

015. When the Team completes the work of a specific timebox, the result is called a(n) ____________________________.

A. Minimal Marketable Feature
B. Blueprint or Design
C. Customer Shippable Product
D. Potentially Shippable Product

016. Practical "how to" protocols used to direct things like sponsoring, organizing, funding, and controlling solution development can be described as _____________.

A. Frameworks

B. Processes

C. Methodologies

D. Philosophies

017. Peter DeGrace and Leslie Stahl first referenced the "Scrum approach" in their book ____________________________.

A. PMBOK Guide®

B. The New New Product Development Game

C. Wicked Problems, Righteous Solutions

D. The Scrum Guide

018. The ______________ guides development through small, safe steps to modify the architecture without undermining its integrity so the best solution emerges as the product evolves.

A. Architect

B. Interaction Designer

C. Programmer

D. Tester

019. Without the proper perspective, there is a continuous risk that development will ______________ part of the solution.

A. Optimize

B. Sub-optimize

C. Increase technical debt in

D. Reduce technical debt in

020. _______________ is a measure of elapsed time between "ideation and customer receipt."

A. Work progress unit-of-measure
B. Lead Time
C. Cycle Time
D. In-progress unit-of-measure

021. _______________ usually include information radiators focused on budgeting and scheduling status.

A. User Stories
B. Workflows
C. Ceremonies
D. Artifacts

022. There are two key characteristics that make planning Agile. One of those factors is:

A. Spending time carefully planning in order to manage inevitable changes.
B. Balancing resource consumption against the certainty that the plan is going to change.
C. Using Lean practices to reduce unavoidable waste.
D. Applying Rolling Wave Progressive Elaboration in a robust and meaningful way.

023. The person who prioritizes the Backlog by sorting the most important ones to the top of the stack, and pushing the less important ones to the bottom of the stack is the

_______________________.

A. Project Manager
B. Scrum Master
C. Sponsor
D. Customer-Proxy

024. Jeff Sutherland and Ken Schwaber created ________________ and made it available as a free download.

A. PMBOK Guide®
B. The New New Product Development Game
C. Wicked Problems, Righteous Solutions
D. The Scrum Guide

025. The ________________ estimates Stories, defines tests, and writes code, usually working with a partner as a "pair".

A. Architect
B. Interaction Designer
C. Programmer
D. Tester

026. As the Team works through development, it must solve the current need and ________________________ so it is capable of moving forward to the next generation of technology challenges.

A. Optimize
B. Sub-optimize
C. Have technical debt
D. Avoid technical debt

027. ____________ is expressed as the average unit of time used per work item produced.

A. Work progress unit-of-measure
B. Lead Time
C. Cycle Time
D. In-process unit-of-measure

028. Tailoring the ____________________ practices can be done at the team-level.

A. Workflow
B. Ceremony
C. Artifact
D. User Story

029. An often-overlooked reality of today's competitive marketplace is:

A. An almost unimaginable uncertainty in project management due to budget cuts.
B. The unavoidable truth that organizations competing for tax dollars or consumer dollars must face each other.
C. That some constituents and customers have had their expectations conditioned by the Internet, Amazon, Facebook and Google.
D. The constantly increasing rate of technological capabilities is driving almost unimaginable levels of complexity into every project.

030. During Iteration planning, the ____________________ creates the Reciprocal Commitment.

A. Soft Commitment
B. Hard Commitment
C. Signed contracts
D. Iteration Backlog

031. During Sprint Planning, the ____________________ creates the Reciprocal Commitment.

A. Soft Commit
B. Hard Commit
C. Signed contracts
D. Sprint Backlog

032. The ____________________ chooses a simple description of the program vision as a metaphor that the Team uses to guide system development choices.

A. Architect

B. Interaction Designer

C. Programmer

D. Tester

033. Lean Software Development was born in 2003 when Lean Software Development: An Agile Toolkit was published by ___________________________.

A. Kent Beck

B. Ken Schwaber

C. Mary and Tom Poppendieck

D. Mike Cohn

034. For Kanban systems, the most common use of a ________________ ceremony is Backlog Grooming.

A. Daily Stand-up Meeting

B. Release Planning Meeting

C. The "After" Meeting

D. Triage

035. _____________________ uses selected combinations of techniques and practices to best meet the needs of the customer.

A. Agile Project Management

B. Hybrid Project Management

C. Kanban

D. Scrum

036. Iterative development techniques were being employed ______________________ Lean principles were developed.

A. While Agile and
B. Before
C. After
D. While best practices from the PMBOK® Guide and

037. A ________________ is a product-centric meeting where any interested or impacted Stakeholder can come and see what was just finished.

A. Stakeholder Workshop
B. Daily Stand-Up
C. Review Meeting
D. Retrospective Meeting

038. The Product Owner sets the logical order of ____________________________ for Increments.

A. Stakeholder Expectations
B. Daily Tasks
C. Development Priorities
D. Testing Procedures

039. The ___________________ coaches the Customer on selecting system-level tests that will define and validate acceptable functioning of the system.

A. Architect
B. Interaction Designer
C. Programmer
D. Tester

040. One of the ceremonies used by LSD includes ______________________.

A. Daily Stand-up
B. Customer Feedback
C. Sprint Review
D. Iteration Perspective

041. During the ______________ ceremony the Team is looking to see whether a work item is blocked or has become invisible.

A. Daily Standup Meeting
B. Release Planning Meeting
C. The "After" Meeting
D. Triage

042. EVM is a program management technique that integrates ______________________________________.

A. Scope, schedule, and cost information
B. Quantitative, objective and supplemental data
C. Scope, schedule, and resource consumption information
D. Qualitative, subjective and supplement data

043. The highest-level structure or philosophical foundation of a project management lexicon is called a ______________________________.

A. Methodology
B. Frameworks
C. Best Practice
D. Process or Protocol

044. A process-centric meeting where the Team, with nobody else present, talks about the development process is called the ______________.

A. Stakeholder Workshop
B. Daily Stand-Up
C. Review Meeting
D. Retrospective Meeting

045. The Product Owner's primary responsibility is to ______________________ of the product by optimizing the work of the Development Team.

A. Maximize the Deliverables
B. Maximize the Value
C. Maximize the Quality
D. Maximize the Scope

046. The ____________________ encourages communication about important customer concerns so the Team can respond to them.

A. Coach
B. Customer
C. Product Manager
D. Project Manager

047. ____________________ estimate Stories, write code, and define tests.

A. Analysts
B. Customers
C. Developers
D. Project Managers

048. The ceremony that produces signs of maturity such as the nesting of lower level processes within the higher-level process group is called

____

A. Daily Standup Meeting
B. Release Planning Meeting
C. Create and Manage the Kanban Board
D. Queue and Buffer Replenishment Meeting

049. EVM's fundamental premise is that as work is _______________, the corresponding budget value is _________________________.

A. Planned; Calculated
B. Released; Approved
C. Designed; Assessed
D. Completed; Earned

050. The core purpose of project management is to _______________________________.

A. Provide accurate estimates.
B. Develop accurate plans and reports.
C. Aid and support stakeholder decision-making.
D. Create a competitive advantage by efficient delivery of customer solutions.

051. ____________________ refers to the concept of how unknown facets of a problem decrease over time.

A. Iterative Development
B. Cone of Uncertainty
C. Progressive Elaboration
D. Rolling Wave Planning

052. A process-centric meeting where the Development Team applies continuous improvement to its process of creating Increments is called the ________________.

A. Stakeholder Workshop
B. Daily Stand-Up
C. Sprint Review
D. Sprint Retrospective

053. The ______________________ monitors the process and mentors the team on XP processes and techniques, but is considered optional.

A. Coach
B. Customer
C. Product Manager
D. Project Manager

054. The ______________________ explains and describes system features in enough detail for the Developers to understand what to build.

A. Analyst
B. Customer
C. Product Manager
D. Tester

055. Before the board reaches maturity the ______________________ ceremony is focused on understanding and exposing the actual process.

A. Create and Manage the Kanban Board
B. Queue and Buffer Replenishment Meeting
C. Daily Standup Meeting
D. Release Planning Meeting

056. Schedule Performance Index (SPI) = ________________________ .

A. EV – PV
B. EV / PV
C. EV – AC
D. EV / AC

057. Technology-driven process change means that exploration and experimentation has been altered so that ____.

A. Discovering solutions is both more effective and less costly.
B. Discovering solutions is more effective and somewhat more costly.
C. Discovering solutions is both more efficient and less costly.
D. Discovering solutions is more efficient and somewhat more costly.

058. ________________________ are defined as the smallest set of features that provide enough functionality to fulfills the customer's expectations.

A. Minimal Marketable Features
B. Contract Requirements
C. Minimal Marketable Specifications
D. Minimal Elicited Features

059. A __________________ is a product-centric meeting where any interested or impacted stakeholder can come and see what was just finished.

A. Stakeholder Workshop
B. Daily Stand-Up
C. Sprint Review
D. Sprint Retrospective

060. The ______________________ facilitates communication by keeping plans synchronized with reality.

A. Coach
B. Customer
C. Product Manager
D. Project Manager

061. The goal of the ______________________ is to ensure the system meets the needs of the Customer and end users.

A. Analyst
B. Customer
C. Developer
D. Tester

062. ______________________ are high-level, long-range activities taking place on a regularly scheduled basis.

A. Create and Manage the Kanban Board Meetings
B. Queue and Buffer Replenishment Meetings
C. Daily Standup Meetings
D. Release Planning Meetings

063. Cost Variance (CV) = ______________________ .

A. EV – PV
B. EV / PV
C. EV – AC
D. EV / AC

064. The Agile value proposition says that sustainable advantage comes from ____.

A. Disruptive innovation.

B. Discovering effective solutions quickly.

C. Systematic innovation.

D. Developing solutions that are cost effective.

065. A process that analyzes, and potentially redesigns, the flow of materials and information used to deliver a product or service is called ________________________.

A. Roadmap Planning

B. Logic Network Diagramming

C. Value Stream Mapping

D. Participatory Decision Making

066. The Scrum Master ensures the process is understood, shields the Development Team from outside interference and ___________________________ for the Development Team.

A. Supports Roadmap Planning

B. Removes Obstacles

C. Leads Release Planning

D. Participates in Customer Decision Making

067. The ________________________ creates and prioritizes the Stories to be developed.

A. Coach

B. Customer

C. Product Manager

D. Project Manager

068. The _______________________ role is responsible for system deployment, user training, and the help desk.

A. Support
B. Customer
C. Developer
D. Tester

069. The _______________________ is comparable to the working group meetings often spawned during the Daily Scrum.

A. "After" Meeting
B. Triage Meeting
C. Daily Standup Meeting
D. Release Planning Meeting

070. When the SV registers as a negative integer it is _______________________ .

A. Desirable
B. Undesirable
C. Neutral
D. Incorrect

071. The Team creates a graphical expression of the solution that includes whatever images and narrative content is necessary to convey what the customer expects. This is called the __________.

A. Project Data Sheet
B. Product Vision Box
C. Project Vision Box
D. Product Data Sheet

072. The ______________________________'s primary responsibility is to structure and manage the development work that fulfills the Definition of Done.

A. Scrum Team
B. Product Owner
C. Scrum Master
D. Development Team

073. The ______________________________ monitors progress and warns when redistributing Tasks might be required to adjust the schedule.

A. Batman
B. Coach
C. Customer
D. Tracker

074. The ____________________ exercises the process of translating low granularity "boulders" into high granularity "rocks" that Developers can understand.

A. Analyst
B. Coach
C. Customer
D. Tester

075. When a ____________________ is being reviewed it is useful to remember that a large WIP is undesirable.

A. Burn-Up Chart
B. Burn-Down Chart
C. Cumulative Flow Diagram (CFD)
D. Lead-Cycle Time Report (LCT)

076. A ____________________ presents a project's objectives in a one-page summary of the key objectives and capabilities.

A. Project Data Sheet
B. Product Vision Box
C. Project Vision Box
D. Product Data Sheet

077. Scrum use empirical process control – transparency, inspection, and adaptation. ______________________ means making important aspects of the process visible.

A. Adaptation
B. Inspection
C. Transparency
D. Adoption

078. The ______________ is the super hero who must handle organizational emergencies and support requests so that the Programmers and Team aren't diverted from their work.

A. Batman
B. Coach
C. Customer
D. Tracker

079. ______________ occur when any advantage of acquiring additional information is offset by the risk of delaying the decision.

A. Empowered Team Decisions
B. Last Responsible Moments
C. Customer Prioritizations
D. Architectural Refactoring Assessments

080. A ______________ radiates a simple analysis of work-in-progress and the trends for Lead and Cycle Time.

A. Lead-Cycle Time Report (LCT)
B. Cumulative Flow Diagram (CFD)
C. Burn-Up Chart
D. Burn-Down Chart

081. A simple tool used to communicate how to handle the unavoidable tradeoffs that will arise during solution development is called a ______________________.

A. Project Data Matrix
B. Product Flexibility Grid
C. Project Flexibility Matrix
D. Flexibility Matrix

082. Scrum use empirical process control – transparency, inspection, and adaptation. ________________________________ means frequently examining work products to detect undesirable variances.

A. Adaptation
B. Inspection
C. Transparency
D. Adoption

083. At the highest-level, XP starts with a quarterly Release planning cycle that is focused on ________________________________.

A. Picking Stories for each weekly Iteration
B. Aligning the project goal within the Organization's bigger objectives
C. Progressively elaborating it into a monthly cycle of plans
D. Defining the Stories and acceptance tests for the work

084. ________________________________ means that the Customer's needs have been understood and integrated into the overall system experience for the users.

A. Build Quality In
B. Defer Commitment
C. Eliminate Waste
D. Optimize the Whole

085. ________________________________ is Goldratt's example of a Pull system.

A. Drum-Pulley-Rope
B. Agile Project Management
C. Theory of Constraints
D. Drum-Buffer-Rope

086. A four-step process that begins with creating a well-defined test, then invoking an operation to take the test is referred to as a

____________________.

A. QA/QC Planning
B. Regression Testing
C. TDD
D. Product Refactoring

087. Scrum use empirical process control – transparency, inspection, and adaptation. ____________________________ means adjusting a process input to correct unacceptable deviations.

A. Adaptation
B. Inspection
C. Transparency
D. Adoption

088. At the start of each week, the Team reviews its progress with the Customer and ______________________________.

A. Picks Stories for the weekly Iteration

B. Aligns the project goal with the Organization's bigger objectives

C. Elaborates the monthly cycle

D. Defines the Stories to review at the Stand-up Meeting

089. Moving from a Quality Control (QC) mindset of catching bugs to a Quality Assurance (QA) mindset of validating assumptions can be described as ______________________________.

A. Building quality in

B. Deferring commitment

C. Eliminating waste

D. Optimizing the whole

090. ____________________ is a Japanese word that literally means "signal card" in English.

A. Kaizen

B. Yuan-ban

C. Kanban

D. Kaizen

091. A(n) ________________is an uncomplicated way to prioritized a collection of short descriptions of features, functions and capabilities.

A. Product Backlog

B. Feature List

C. Elevator statement

D. Iteration Backlog

092. A(n) _______________ is an uncomplicated way to prioritize a collection of short descriptions of features, functions and capabilities.

A. Product Backlog

B. Feature List

C. Elevator Statement

D. Sprint Backlog

093. A(n) _______________ ceremony addresses the issue that software development, at its core, is a complex challenge in an environment of high uncertainty.

A. Caves and Commons

B. Planning Game

C. Test-Driven Development

D. Whole Team

094. It is integral to the _________________ process that architecture be guided by refactoring.

A. Building quality in

B. Deferring commitment

C. Eliminating waste

D. Optimizing the whole

095. Kanban uses a reporting tool called a _____________________ that is uniquely its own.

A. Burn-Up Chart

B. Burn-Down Chart

C. Continuous Flow Diagram (CFD)

D. Cumulative Flow Diagram

096. The specific subset of Product Backlog items the Team has committed to develop is referred to as a(n) ______________________.

A. Product Backlog
B. Feature List
C. Elevator statement
D. Iteration Backlog

097. The specific subset of Product Backlog items the Development Team has committed to develop is referred to as a(n) ______________________.

A. Product Backlog
B. Feature List
C. Elevator Statement
D. Sprint Backlog

098. The ______________________ ceremony is a critical point of collaboration between Customer, Product Manager and Team where business value is defined.

A. Caves and Commons
B. Planning Game
C. Test-Driven Development
D. Whole Team

099. ______________________ allow the best possible design to emerge as part of the development process.

A. Empowered Teams
B. Deferred Commitments
C. Eliminating Wastes
D. Optimizing the Holes

100. ______________________ proves the relationship between WIP and throughput for a production system in a steady state.

A. Kaizen equations
B. Pareto's principle
C. Little's Law
D. Regression testing

101. ____________________ is the process that prioritizes and clarifies Backlog items as they move from the long-term to a more near-term time horizon.

A. Roadmap Planning
B. Release Planning
C. Backlog Grooming
D. Iteration Grooming

102. ____________________ is the process that prioritizes and clarifies Backlog items as they move from the long-term to a more near-term time horizon.

A. Roadmap Planning
B. Release Planning
C. Grooming or Refinement
D. Sprint Grooming

103. The ____________________ ceremony helps the Team limit scope creep because expectations are clearly and objectively stated.

A. Caves and Commons
B. Planning Game
C. Test-Driven Development
D. Whole Team

104. The goal of rapidly satisfying a Customer need is driven by the Lean principle to ______________________.

A. Empower the Team
B. Defer Commitment
C. Eliminate Waste
D. Optimize the Whole

105. Because Agile Project Management and Kanban both spring from a legacy in manufacturing, when the acronym WIP is used it is understood to mean ______________________.

A. Work in progress
B. Work in process
C. Work item process
D. Work inventory processed

106. A meeting held primarily to synchronize the team members' activities is called a ____________________.

A. Demonstration Meeting
B. Daily Meeting
C. Review Meeting
D. Retrospective Meeting

107. A meeting held primarily to synchronize the Scrum Master and Development Team members' activities is called a

____________________.

A. Daily Demo
B. Daily Scrum
C. Daily Review
D. Stand-up Meeting

108. The _______________________ ceremony defines the scope of the Release and the order of delivery of features, functions and capabilities.

A. Caves and Commons
B. Planning Game
C. Test-Driven Development
D. Whole Team

109. The principle of _______________________ drives the success of iterative development approaches because it fuels adaptive changes to overcome mistakes.

A. Empower the Team
B. Defer Commitments
C. Eliminate Wastes
D. Optimize the Holes

110. _____________________ are holding places for small inventories of work items that are external to a process group.

A. Buffers
B. Phases
C. Queues
D. Steps

111. A meeting where any interested stakeholder can offer insights and concerns is called a ____________________.

A. Demonstration Meeting
B. Daily Meeting
C. Review Meeting
D. Retrospective Meeting

112. The core process of Scrum is called ___________________.

A. The Daily Scrum
B. The Sprint Review
C. The Product Demo
D. The Sprint

113. The goal of ___________________ is to minimize waste caused by misunderstanding.

A. Small Releases
B. Incremental Architectural Design
C. Pair Programming
D. Collective Code Ownership

114. Failure to ___________________ shows up in evidence that the process missed an opportunity to produce real value.

A. Empower the Team
B. Defer Commitment
C. Eliminate Waste
D. Optimize the Whole

115. ___________________ are holding places for small inventories of work items that are internal to a process group.

A. Buffers
B. Phases
C. Queues
D. Steps

116. ___________________ is the definition of all the activities to finish and tests to fulfill before the work is complete.

A. Refactoring
B. Definition of Done
C. Acceptance Criteria
D. Conditions of Satisfaction

117. ________________ is the definition of all the activities to finish and tests to fulfill before the work is complete.

A. Refactoring
B. Definition of Done
C. Acceptance Criteria
D. Conditions of Satisfaction

118. The ________________ ceremony means that Programmers take personal ownership of specific tasks.

A. Small Releases
B. Incremental Architectural Design
C. Pair Programming
D. Collective Code Ownership

119. The fastest way to deliver the system the Customer expects is to have the Customer ________________ through an incremental discovery process.

A. Pull the pieces
B. Push the pieces
C. Refine the Stories
D. Optimize the priorities

120. Within the Kanban community there are six practices (currently) referred to as "core practices." Three of them are:

A. Visualize, Triage, and Implement Feedback Loops
B. Limit WIP, Make Process Policies Explicit, and Manage Flow
C. Create and Manage the Kanban Board, Limit WIP, and Manage Flow
D. Improve Collaboratively, Evolve Experimentally and Limit WIP

Comprehensive Exam Answers

001. **C.** When the Team clarifies the project objective and the desired final result, in Traditional Project Management it is called creating the Project Charter while the same activities in Agile are called defining the Product Vision. 2-01

002. **C.** The foundation for organizing Agile Frameworks can be described as **METHODOLOGIES.**

Methodologies provide the philosophical foundation for organizing Frameworks. In project management the two dominant choices are Traditional, as embodied in the PMBOK® Guide, and Agile. Methodologies contain and define various Frameworks as context-specific logical foundations. 3-01

003. **A.** The Scrum Alliance is the largest professional user group in the Agile world and its best known certifications is the **CERTIFIED SCRUMMASTER® (CSM)**

The Scrum Alliance is the largest professional user group in the Agile world. Its flagship certification, the Certified ScrumMaster® (CSM), has the highest name recognition and largest market share of any Agile certification at the time of this writing (July 2015). 4-01

004. **C.** Because of work done by **KENT BECK,** eXtreme Programming (XP) originated in early 1996 and was born in 1999 when he published Extreme Programming Explained.

eXtreme Programming (XP) originated with Kent Beck while working at Chrysler in early 1996. In 1999 he published Extreme Programming Explained and eXtreme Programming was born! 5-01

005. **C.** Artifacts for **LSD** include **CUSTOMER REVIEWS** and **APPROVALS.**

Artifacts for LSD include the Product Vision, Roadmap and Release Plans, User Stories, Code, Tests, Configuration Scripts, and Customer Reviews and Approvals. And even though many of the artifacts are intangible and may have a short lifespan, they are still important. They should be captured and maintained in a version control system with a central repository providing a history of changes. 6-01

006. **A. CFDs** are area graphs where the scale of the vertical, x-axis is a chosen **WIP UNIT-OF-MEASURE.**

Cumulative Flow Diagrams (CFD) are area graphs that create insight about project execution so it can be used to improve performance. It shows workload imbalances enabling decisions that can spread the work more evenly, reducing risk and creating a more effective and sustainable pace.

The scale of the vertical, x-axis is a chosen unit-of-measure for WIP, such as Story Points or the count of work items in progress. The scale of the horizontal, y-axis is time shown in the desired units. Lead Time is the distance between the point where a work item is placed in the Backlog and when it is Done. Cycle Time is the distance between the point where a work item is pulled into the In-Progress phase and when it is Done. 7-01

007. **C.** Shu Ha Ri is a simple, powerful model of learning where HA means attempting to understand the purpose of the techniques.

Ha is the second step in the learning cycle and means the student moves beyond imitation and attempts to understand the purpose of the practices learned through repetition in Shu. 8-01

008. **A.** When the Team initiates a repetitive cyclical process to make choices and define the final objective of the project in Agile Project Management the timeboxes in the cycle are called an Iteration or Sprint. 2-02

009. **A. FRAMEWORKS** are context-specific foundations that have a set of Processes that are used to execute work in a defined way.

Frameworks are context-specific foundations created to support particular industry settings, such as aerospace or automotive, or particular categories of activities, such as software or product development. Frameworks have a set of Processes used to execute work in a defined way. 3-02

010. **B.** The seeds of Scrum were planted in 1986 when Hirotaka Takeuchi and Ikujiro Nonaka wrote **THE NEW NEW PRODUCT DEVELOPMENT GAME.**

The seeds of Scrum were planted in 1986 when Hirotaka Takeuchi and Ikujiro Nonaka wrote The New New Product Development Game. (Harvard Business Review). 4-02

011. **B.** One of XP's important assumptions is that **A UNIFIED CLIENT VIEWPOINT** exists. Where that assumption is correct, XP is productive. Otherwise it is risky at best.

That assumption drives the practice of having an on-site Customer that proponents cite as providing needed flexibility while reducing cost. Critics claim it causes rework and scope creep. 5-02

012. **A.** Even though many of the artifacts have a **SHORT LIFESPAN** they are still important.

Artifacts for LSD include the Product Vision, Roadmap and Release Plans, User Stories, Code, Tests, Configuration Scripts, and Customer Reviews and Approvals. And even though many of the artifacts are intangible and may have a short lifespan they are still important. They should be captured and maintained in a version control system with a central repository providing a history of changes. 6-02

013. **B. LEAD TIME** starts when the work item is made available for development.

Cycle Time starts when development work actually begins. Both end when the work item is delivered. Both measures are important because Lead Time impacts customer expectations and satisfaction, whereas Cycle Time is a measure of throughput and provides insight into process improvement choices. Even though both indices measure time, they measure different aspects. 7-02

014. **A.** A professional Agile practitioner is focused on creating an Agile culture, committed to **LEARNING AND MASTERING THE BASICS.**

The mindset of a professional Agile practitioner is focused on creating an Agile culture, committed to learning and mastering the basics so that continuous improvement techniques can be employed to incrementally and successfully evolve the organization into the most Agile expression of itself. 8-02

015. **D.** When the Team completes the work of a specific timebox the result is called a Potentially Shippable Product. 2-03

016. **B.** Practical "how to" protocols used to direct things like sponsoring, organizing, funding, and controlling solution development can be described as **PROCESSES.**

 Processes are practical "how to" protocols used to direct things like sponsoring, organizing, funding, and controlling solution development projects. The Processes guide work to follow or align with context-specific best practices. 3-03

017. **C.** Peter DeGrace and Leslie Stahl first referenced the "Scrum approach" in their book **WICKED PROBLEMS, RIGHTEOUS SOLUTIONS.** 4-03

018. **A.** The **ARCHITECT** guides development through small, safe steps to modify the architecture without undermining its integrity so the best solution emerges as the product evolves. The Architect manages one of the biggest challenges for an XP team, maintaining stability while developing a complex solution in an uncertain environment. 5-03

019. **A.** Without the proper perspective, there is a continuous risk that development will **OPTIMIZE** part of the solution.

 Without the proper perspective, there is a continuous risk that development will optimize part of the solution thereby sub-optimizing the overall solution. While the synergy of the sub-systems is critical, the performance of the system as a whole is the key to success. 6-03

020. **B. LEAD TIME** is a measure of elapsed time between "ideation and customer receipt."

Lead Time is a measure of elapsed time between "ideation and customer receipt." It is expressed as the unit of time between when the work item is made available for development and when it is delivered.

Cycle Time is a measure of process throughput. It is expressed as the average unit of time used per work item produced. 7-03

021. **D. ARTIFACTS** usually include information radiators focused on budgeting and scheduling status.

As with defining Roles and Ceremonies in Hybrid Project Management, the Artifacts include whatever enables the system to delivery optimized results while excluding everything else gets. Those artifacts usually include information radiators focused on budgeting and scheduling status. 8-03

022. **B.** There are two key characteristics that make planning Agile. One of those factors is balancing resource consumption against the certainty that the plan is going to change. 2-04

023. **D.** The person who prioritizes the Backlog by sorting the most important ones to the top of the stack, and pushing the less important ones to the bottom of the stack, is the **CUSTOMER-PROXY.**

The Customer-Proxy prioritizes the Backlog by sorting the most important ones to the top of the stack, and pushing the less important ones to the bottom of the stack. The idea is that the Customer-Proxy will continuously groom the Backlog. This sorting process is an important step that precedes the planning session and occurs at the beginning of each Iteration or Sprint. 3-04

024. **D.** Jeff Sutherland and Ken Schwaber created the **SCRUM GUIDE** and made it available as a free download.

The Scrum Guide was created by Jeff Sutherland and Ken Schwaber and the most recent version of the Scrum Guide (2013) is available as a free download. 4-04

025. **C. The PROGRAMMER** estimates Stories, defines tests, and writes code, usually working with a partner as a "pair", and accepts responsibility for completing the Tasks that ultimately deliver a successful result. 5-04

026. **D.** As the Team works through development, it must solve the current need and **AVOID TECHNICAL DEBT** so it is capable of moving forward to the next generation of technology challenges.

As the cross-functional Team works through development, it must 'begin with the end in mind' as Stephen Covey advises, clarifying the entire Value Stream by analyzing back from the future. The solution must solve the current need and avoid technical debt so it is also capable of moving forward to the next generation of technology challenges. 6-04

027. **C. CYCLE TIME** is expressed as the average unit of time used per work item produced.

Cycle Time is a measure of process throughput. It is expressed as the average unit of time used per work item produced.

Both Lead Time and Cycle Time are measures of the average time the system requires to accomplish its goal. They are not an expression of time for a specific work item because a large work item started earlier may not be completed before a smaller work item started later. Also, as explained previously, Lead Time and Cycle Time have a relationship with WIP as described by the Little's Law. Therefore, they are useful for analyzing and managing bottlenecks within the system. 7-04

028. **A.** Tailoring the **WORKFLOW** practices can be done at the team-level.

As with defining Roles in Hybrid Project Management, the Workflow includes whatever enables the delivery of desirable results while everything else gets excluded. Tailoring the workflow practices can be done at the team-level, which is within the focus of this book, or at a higher business level, the focus of Book Two of the Agile Almanac. 8-04

029. **D.** An often-overlooked reality of today's competitive marketplace is the constantly increasing rate of technological capabilities is driving almost unimaginable levels of complexity into every project. 2-05

030. **B.** During Iteration planning, the **HARD COMMIT** creates the Reciprocal Commitment.

The Hard Commit creates the Reciprocal Commitment. During Step One of Iteration planning the Team makes the "Soft Commit" meaning they think they can fulfill the proposed Iteration Backlog." In Step Two, after some analysis, if they are confident they can do it, they make the "Hard Commit." 3-05

031. **B.** During Sprint Planning the **HARD COMMIT** creates the Reciprocal Commitment.

The Hard Commit creates the Reciprocal Commitment. During step one of Sprint Planning, the Development Team makes the "Soft Commit" meaning they think they can fulfill the proposed Sprint Backlog. In step two, after some analysis, when they are confident they can do it, they make the "Hard Commit." 4-05

032. **B.** The **INTERACTION DESIGNER** chooses a simple description of the program vision as a metaphor that the Team uses to guide system development choices as they write Stories and evaluate progress towards the completed system. 5-05

033. **C.** Lean Software Development was born in 2003 when Lean Software Development: An Agile Toolkit was published by **MARY AND TOM POPPENDIECK.**

Lean Software Development was born in 2003 when Lean Software Development: An Agile Toolkit was published by Mary and Tom Poppendieck. The book presented how to use an adapted version of Lean Manufacturing principles, or more specifically, Lean Product Development, to develop software and also compared it to other Agile practices. 6-05

034. **D.** For Kanban systems the most common use of a **TRIAGE** ceremony is Backlog Grooming.

Release Planning ceremonies are regularly scheduled and focus high-level, long-range activity. Backlog Triage is also regularly scheduled, but focuses on mid-level or low-level activities addressed by Product Owners with or without the involvement of business or user representatives depending on the system policies. Typically the Triage ceremony focuses on whether the work item should remain in the Backlog or be removed versus the Backlog grooming done in other Agile Frameworks where work items are prioritized, ranked, or stacked. The goal is simply to reduce the size of the Backlog so that Task dependencies can be more clearly understood and complexity reduced. It enables clearer, quicker replenishment ceremonies. 7-05

035. **B. HYBRID PROJECT MANAGEMENT** uses selected combinations of techniques and practices to best meet the needs of the customer

Hybrid Project Management is an Agile Framework where a selected combination of techniques and practices, including those from one or more Agile Frameworks, are used to manage projects in order to best meet the needs of the organization and customer. 8-05

036. **B.** Iterative development techniques were being employed before Lean principles were developed. 2-06

037. **C. A REVIEW MEETING** is a product-centric meeting where any interested or impacted stakeholder can come and see what was just finished.

The Review Meeting is a product-centric meeting where any interested or impacted stakeholder can come and see what was just finished as the next piece of the project puzzle. They give feedback and ask questions that produce actionable insight for the Customer-Proxy to use to groom the Product Backlog. 3-06

038. **C.** The Product Owner sets the logical order of **DEVELOPMENT PRIORITIES** for Increments.

The Product Owner is the "voice of the customer" representing the stakeholders and the business, and setting the logical order of development priorities for Increments. 4-06

039. **D.** The **TESTER** coaches the Customer on selecting system-level tests that will define and validate acceptable functioning of the system before development and improve deployment of the system after development. Testers also guide Programmers on implementing testing techniques. 5-06

040. **B.** The ceremonies used by **LSD** include **CUSTOMER FEEDBACK.**

Describing ceremonies for LSD is quite different because other than the Release and Iteration planning ceremonies, held in common with other Agile Frameworks, the only ceremony in LSD is gathering Customer Feedback. It is a ceremony that is not held on a formal periodic basis, like the Daily, Review or Retrospective meetings. Instead it is an ad hoc, mostly informal, ceremony that can be held as often as hourly.

During the Customer Feedback ceremony the Developer and Customer meet and see, test and use the system changes to decide if they solve the problem or need additional fine-tuning. 6-06

041. **A.** During the **DAILY STAND-UP** ceremony, the Team is looking to see whether a work item is blocked or has become invisible.

Stand-up meetings are common to Agile Frameworks, but have evolved differently in Kanban because the board contains all the information about who is working on what and the focus is on the workflow process not the individual's work progress. Each day the Team is looking to see whether a work item is blocked or has become invisible. Typically the group leader will begin at the end of the process and "walk backward" across the board from right to left following the system's pull. The Stories on the board are discussed to discover if the information on the board presents the situation in a real and transparent way. 7-06

042. **C. EVM** is a program management technique that integrates **SCOPE, SCHEDULE, AND RESOURCE CONSUMPTION INFORMATION.**

Earned Value Management (EVM) is a program management technique that integrates scope, schedule, and resource consumption information in order to measure project performance against planned cost metrics. It provides quantitative, objective data to supplement qualitative, subjective judgments. 8-06

043. **A.** The highest-level structure or philosophical foundation of a project management lexicon is called a Methodology. 2-07

044. **D.** A process-centric meeting where the Team, with nobody else present, talks about the development process is called the **RETROSPECTIVE MEETING.**

The Retrospective Meeting is a process-centric meeting where the Team, with nobody else present, talks about the development process. It is the application of the Lean principle of continuous improvement. 3-07

045. **B.** The Product Owner's primary responsibility is to **MAXIMIZE THE VALUE** of the product by optimizing the work of the Development Team.

The Product Owner's primary responsibility is to maximize the value of the product, for both the customer and organization, by optimizing the work of the Development Team. The Product Owner's biggest tool for achieving their goal is managing the Product Backlog by defining the logical order of development with clearly expressed stories. 4-07

046. **C.** The **PRODUCT MANAGER** encourages communication about important customer concerns so the Team can respond to them. The Product Manager writes Stories and also prioritizes them in quarterly and weekly cycles. Product Managers groom the logical development sequence for business value, not technical efficiency. 5-07

047. **C. DEVELOPERS** estimate Stories, write code, and define tests.

Developers estimate Stories, write code, and define tests in order to deliver working software. Some Developers have enough experience and domain-savvy to fill the Analyst role. The Developer role is simply to accept responsibility for completing the Tasks that ultimately deliver a successful result. 6-07

048. **C.** The ceremony that produces signs of maturity such as the nesting of lower level processes within the higher-level process group is called **CREATE AND MANAGE THE KANBAN BOARD.**

When a Kanban Board reaches full maturity it can look like the XLSX image shown in Figure 7.6 (which can be downloaded from the Members section of the GR8PM website). You can see the signs of maturity in the nesting of lower level processes, such as User Story, Estimate, and Queue, within the higher level Backlog process group, as well as in the use of Buffers and Queues, and, significantly, in the Policies bulleted across the bottom. The granular decomposition of the process groups and the explicit linkage to policies should not be expected in the initial Kanban mapping exercise, but it should be the long-term goal. 7-07

049. **D.** EVM's fundamental premise is that as work is **COMPLETED** the corresponding budget value is **EARNED.**

EVM's fundamental premise is that as work is completed, the corresponding budget value is earned, hence the term Earned Value (EV). In EVM, that paradigm of value only being earned for completed work aligns at the most basic level with the core Agile principle of measuring work progress by only counting work that is Done-Done in the Velocity. 8-07

050. **C.** The core purpose of project management is to aid and support stakeholder decision-making. 2-08

051. **B. CONE OF UNCERTAINTY** refers to the concept of how unknown facets of a problem decrease over time.

Cone of uncertainty refers to the concept of how unknown facets of a problem decrease over time as customers traverse through an unavoidable, ambiguous process where discovery and learning occur. 3-08

052. **D.** A process-centric meeting where the Scrum Team applies continuous improvement to its process of creating Increments is called the **SPRINT RETROSPECTIVE.**

 Sprint Retrospectives are process-centric meetings where the Scrum Team applies continuous improvement to its process of creating Increments. 4-08

053. **A.** The **COACH** monitors the process and mentors the Team on XP processes and techniques, but is considered optional. The Coach helps the Team identify and focus on risks and optimization opportunities. 5-08

054. **A.** The **ANALYST** explains and describes system features in enough detail for the Developers to understand what to build.

 Analysts help Customers explain and describe system features in enough detail for the Developers to understand what to build. Analysts are similar to Product Managers in XP and Product Owners in Scrum with an important distinction that they not become a barrier to direct Developer-Customer discussions. Analysts facilitate knowledge transfer for both sides without restricting direct contact. 6-08

055. **A.** Before the board reaches maturity, the **CREATE AND MANAGE THE KANBAN BOARD** ceremony is focused on understanding and exposing the actual process being used and the real policies being followed. As the board matures, the ceremony is focused on measuring and improving it. When the board has reached a high level of maturity, the ceremony focuses on using it to guide and improve how the Team applies it. However, introducing a visual, transparent way of directing work can seem threatening for some participants as mentioned above. Introducing visualization in small steps using a low-tech, high-touch approach will allow the Team to develop a consensus that supports decisions and undergirds accountability. 7-08

056. **B.** Schedule Performance Index (SPI) = EV / PV 8-08

057. **A.** Technology-driven process change means that exploration and experimentation has been altered so that discovering solutions is both more effective and less costly. 2-09

058. **A. MINIMAL MARKETABLE FEATURES** are defined as the smallest set of features that provide enough functionality to fulfill the customer's expectations.

Minimum Marketable Features are defined as the smallest set of features that provide enough functionality to fulfill the customer's expectations and create a desired level of engagement (i.e., consumer purchases or constituent votes). 3-09

059. **C. A SPRINT REVIEW** is a product-centric meeting where any interested or impacted stakeholder can come and see what was just finished.

The Sprint Review is a product-centric meeting where any interested or impacted stakeholder can come and see what was just finished as the next piece of the project puzzle. They give feedback and ask questions that produce actionable insight the Product Owner uses to groom the Product Backlog. 4-09

060. **D. The PROJECT MANAGER** facilitates communication by keeping plans synchronized with reality and packaging that information so it is helpful to all of the stakeholders. 5-09

061. **D.** The goal of the **TESTER** is to ensure the system meets the needs of the Customer and end users.

Testers create comprehensive tests for both the Customer's Conditions of Satisfaction and User Acceptance Tests. The goal is to ensure the system meets the needs of the Customer and end users. Sometimes Testers have the experience and cross-training to also serve as Analyst, and vice versa. 6-09

062. **D. RELEASE PLANNING MEETINGS** are high-level, long-range activities taking place on a regularly scheduled basis.

In some organization-level Kanban systems, Release Planning Meetings are used to provide guidance about downstream delivery objectives to Queue Replenishment Meetings and other lower-level Kanban and project management systems. Because release planning is a high-level, long-range activity, it takes place on a regularly scheduled basis. Doing so reduces coordination costs and raises the probability that all key stakeholders will be present. 7-09

063. **C.** Cost Variance (CV) = EV – AC 8-09

064. **C.** The Agile value proposition says that sustainable advantage comes from systematic innovation. 2-10

065. **C.** A process that analyzes, and potentially redesigns, the flow of materials and information used to deliver a product or service is called **VALUE STREAM MAPPING.**

Value Stream Mapping is defined as a process that analyzes, and potentially redesigns, the flow of materials and information used to deliver a product or service to the customer in order to reduce the total time required from the beginning to end of the production stream without taking shortcuts at the expense of future opportunities. 3-10

066. **B.** The Scrum Master ensures the process is understood, shields the Development Team from outside interference and **REMOVES OBSTACLES** for the Development Team.

The Scrum Master (SM) ensures the process is understood and followed, shielding the Development Team from outside interference and removing impediments for the Development Team. The Scrum Master's primary responsibility is to ensure the Scrum Team understands and applies the principles of Scrum properly. 4-10

067. **B.** The **CUSTOMER** creates and prioritizes the Stories to be developed. Unlike other Agile Frameworks, the Customer can vary the release date by adding or removing Stories from the Backlog to be delivered in any given Release. Similar to other frameworks, the Customer sets the development priorities. 5-10

068. **A.** The **SUPPORT** role is responsible for system deployment, user training, and the help desk.

Support includes all the roles that are responsible for system deployment, user training, and the help desk to answer user questions. It is a broad category and can include many domain- and industry-specific roles. 6-10

069. **A.** The **AFTER MEETING** is comparable to the working group meetings often spawned during the Daily Scrum.

The "After" Meeting in Kanban is comparable to the working group meetings often spawned during the Daily Scrum. The "After" Meeting is also ad hoc and typically involves 3 or 4 team members discussing anything from how to get a work item unblocked to options for removing a delay to kicking around a technical issue. Often times it is to discuss a process- or policy-related issue making the After Meeting a vital tool for transforming the current culture into one where Kanban can be leveraged to create more value. Sometimes it is simply an informal sub-team deciding how they'll build a particular feature, function or capability during the next few days. 7-10

070. When the SV registers as a negative integer it is **UNDESIRABLE.**

In addition to the calculations being routine, interpreting their meaning is very straightforward. For both the SV and CV, a negative variance is undesirable and indicates the project is behind schedule, over budget or both. For both the SPI and the CPI, an index value less than 1 is undesirable and indicates the project is behind schedule, over budget or both. 8-10

071. **B.** When the Team creates a graphical expression of the solution that includes whatever images and narrative content is necessary to convey what the customer expects. This is called the **PRODUCT VISION BOX.**

Product vision boxes are a graphical expression of the solution that includes whatever images and narrative content is necessary to convey what the customer expects from the product. The content is expressed in end user language and not techno-jargon. 3-11

072. **D.** The **DEVELOPMENT TEAM'S** primary responsibility is to structure and manage the development work that fulfills the Definition of Done.

The Development Team is a cross-functional group, which creates solutions by analyzing, designing, developing, testing, and implementing deliverables. The Development Team's primary responsibility is to structure and manage the development work that fulfills the Definition of Done committed to during Sprint Planning. 4-11

073. **D.** The **TRACKER** monitors progress and warns when redistributing Tasks might be required to adjust the schedule.

The Tracker, another preferred but optional position, monitors team progress and warns when redistributing Tasks might be required to adjust the schedule. Sometimes a Programmer "doubles" as Tracker for the same pair, and sometimes a Programmer serves as Tracker for a different pair. 5-11

074. **C.** The **CUSTOMER** exercises the process of translating low granularity "boulders" into high granularity "rocks" that Developers can understand.

Customers focus on the goal of ensuring the system will deliver business value.

Customers sometimes benefit from the help of Analysts as they go through the process of translating low granularity "boulders" into high granularity "rocks" that developers can understand. But not every Customer needs help creating and prioritizing the Stories to be developed. 6-11

075. **C.** When a **CFD** is being reviewed it is useful to remember that a large **WIP** is undesirable.

When a **CFD** is being reviewed it is useful to remember that a large WIP is undesirable because the complexity of managing the relationships between multiple variables increases in a more than linear way, inducing more opportunities for errors and failure. Also, a large WIP typically contributes to long Lead and Cycle Times, which is also undesirable because it increases the probability that the Team's understanding of the customer's need will deteriorate, again, inducing more opportunities for errors and failure. 7-11

076. **A. A PROJECT DATA SHEET** presents a project's objectives in a one-page summary of the key objectives and capabilities.

Project data sheets (PDS) capture a project's objectives in a one-page summary of the key objectives, capabilities, and information needed to understand the purpose and progress of the project. The PDS is a minimalist document. 3-12

077. **C.** Scrum uses empirical process control – transparency, inspection, and adaptation. **TRANSPARENCY** means making important aspects of the process visible.

Scrum uses empirical process control – transparency, inspection, and adaptation. Transparency is defined as making important aspects of the process visible for those making decisions about the outcome to enable a shared understanding of what has occurred. 4-12

078. **A.** The **BATMAN** is the super hero who must handle organizational emergencies and support requests so that the Programmers and Team aren't diverted from their work.

While a mask and cape are optional, nerves of steel are mandatory! 5-12

079. **B. LAST RESPONSIBLE MOMENTS** occur when any advantage of acquiring additional information is offset by the risk of delaying the decision.

Last Responsible Moments occur at the point where any advantage of acquiring additional valuable information or insight is offset by the potential risk of delaying the decision any longer. 6-12

080. **B.** A **CFD** radiates a simple analysis of work-in-progress and the trends for Lead and Cycle Time.

CFDs record work completed in a Burn-Up Chart type format. They provide insight into the total scope and the progress of work items using an accessible, visual, proportional image of actual completeness. CFDs radiate a simple analysis of work-in-progress and the trends for Lead and Cycle Time and therefore the probability of delivering a working solution on time. As a leading metric, CFDs enable Agile teams to act appropriately to growing problems in a transparent way. 7-12

081. **D.** A simple tool used to communicate how to handle the unavoidable tradeoffs that will arise during solution development is called a **FLEXIBILITY MATRIX.**

Flexibility Matrices are a simple tool that help the Customer-proxy communicate to the Team how to handle the unavoidable tradeoffs that will arise during solution development. The matrix clarifies which constraints are flexible and which are not, hence the name. It is a top-level decision-making tool for guiding tradeoff decisions when resource, time, or cost conflicts arise during execution. 3-13

082. **B.** Scrum uses empirical process control – transparency, inspection, and adaptation. **INSPECTION** means frequently examining work products to detect undesirable variances.

Scrum uses empirical process control – transparency, inspection, and adaptation. Inspection is defined as frequently examining work products to detect undesirable variances that could negatively impact progress toward a desired outcome. 4-13

083. **B.** At the highest-level, XP starts with a quarterly Release planning cycle that is focused on **ALIGNING THE PROJECT**

GOAL WITHIN THE ORGANIZATION'S BIGGER OBJECTIVES.

The quarterly plan is progressively elaborated into a weekly cycle of plans. 5-13

084. **A. BUILD QUALITY IN** means that the Customer's needs have been understood and integrated into the overall system experience for the users.

Building quality into the solution is more than just the technical notion that the individual components and subassemblies work well together as a robust, flexible, and responsive system. It means that the Customer's needs have been understood and integrated into the overall system experience for the Users. It means paying the price to develop a solution that is intuitive to use, solves problems well, and can be maintained, extended and scaled appropriately and efficiently. 6-13

085. **D. DRUM-BUFFER-ROPE** is Goldratt's example of a Pull system.

Outside of project management circles, Kanban's storied history with the Toyota Production System and Lean Principles has given it much broader recognition and credibility than the Theory of Constraints even though they have an amazing number of similarities. Drum-Buffer-Rope and Kanban are both examples of Pull systems. Pull systems produce deliverables by changing them incrementally at a sustainable pace. With the advance of Lean principles into the project management profession, commonly referred to as Agile Project Management, the science developed in Goldratt's Theory of Constraints may finally get a full wind in its sails. However, those sails will billow under the flag of Kanban. 7-13

086. **C.** A four-step process that begins with creating a well-defined test then invoking an operation to take the test is referred to as a **TDD (TEST-DRIVEN DEVELOPMENT)**

Test-driven development (TDD) is a four-step process that begins with creating a well-defined test, invoking an operation to take the test and having a "fail" outcome, followed by doing something to change the operation, and finally invoking the modified operation to take the test and having a "pass" outcome. 3-14

087. **A.** Scrum uses empirical process control – transparency, inspection, and adaptation. **ADAPTATION** means adjusting a process input to correct unacceptable deviations.

Scrum uses empirical process control – transparency, inspection, and adaptation. Adaptation is defined as adjusting a process input or the development process to correct unacceptable deviations from the defined standard that were detected during inspection. 4-14

088. **A.** At the start of each week, the Team reviews its progress with the Customer and **PICKS STORIES FOR THE WEEKLY ITERATION.**

At the start of each week, the Team reviews its progress and the Customer picks another group of Stories to be the current week's work. Next, acceptance tests are defined. Once the Stories and acceptance tests are defined, the work and daily Stand-up Meetings begin. 5-14

089. **A.** Moving from a Quality Control (QC) mindset of catching bugs to a Quality Assurance (QA) mindset of validating assumptions can be described as **BUILD QUALITY IN.**

Build quality in means moving from a Quality Control (QC) mindset of catching bugs to a Quality Assurance (QA) mindset of validating assumptions with useful metrics throughout the process that ensure practices create value or are discarded. 6-14

090. **C.** Kanban is a Japanese word that literally means "signal card" in English.

The card is used to signal an upstream process to produce more. Kanban does not allow work to occur upstream until a downstream lever pulls it.

Kanban, also has a strong link to Kaizen, a Japanese word for "continuous improvement." In Japanese manufacturing it is believed that Kaizen is the engine that makes Kanban work. 7-14

091. **A. A PRODUCT BACKLOG** is an uncomplicated way to prioritize a collection of short descriptions of features, functions and capabilities.

Product Backlogs are a prioritized collection of short descriptions of features, functions and capabilities included in the solution being developed. 3-15

092. **A. A PRODUCT BACKLOG** is an uncomplicated way to prioritize a collection of short descriptions of features, functions and capabilities.

The Product Backlog is a prioritized collection of cards or a list of all the features that are envisioned in the final product. The Product Owner holds it in a specific place, physical or electronic, and each item has a description, prioritization, approximation of development cost, and assessment of customer value. 4-15

093. **D. A WHOLE TEAM** ceremony addresses the issue that software development, at its core, is a complex challenge in an environment of high uncertainty.

The XP ceremony of Whole Team directly addresses the issue that software development at its core is a complex challenge in an environment of high uncertainty. 5-15

094. **A.** It is integral to the **BUILD QUALITY IN** process that architecture be guided by refactoring.

Only information flowing in a constant feedback loop from Customer to Developer and back again can provide the needed "actionable insight". It is integral to the build quality in process that architecture be guided by refactoring so that as more features are added to the solution the coding maintains as much simplicity, clarity and reliability as possible. 6-15

095. **D.** Kanban uses a reporting tool called a **CUMULATIVE FLOW DIAGRAM** that is uniquely its own.

However, with Kanban, the core concept of artifacts is significantly different because it is highly dependent on the underlying system that Kanban is being used to improve. Kanban generates very few independent, Kanban-caused artifacts. 7-15

096. **D.** The specific subset of Product Backlog items the Team has committed to develop is referred to as an **ITERATION BACKLOG.**

Iteration Backlogs are the specific subset of Product Backlog items the Team has committed to develop in a particular timebox period. Once the specific subset of items for the Iteration Backlog are agreed upon and fully committed to, they are not changed. 3-16

097. **D.** The specific subset of Product Backlog items the Development Team has committed to develop is referred to as a **SPRINT BACKLOG.**

The Sprint Backlog contains descriptions of the items to be developed and the Development Team's plan for development that fulfills the Sprint Goal. It creates transparency and also provides enough detail to enable the Development Team to make adjustments during the Daily Scrum as progress is better understood. 4-16

098. **B. The PLANNING GAME** ceremony is a critical point of collaboration between Customer, Product Manager and Team where business value is defined.

The Planning Game defines a rough order of magnitude (ROM) plan for a project so the Team can refine it as the project progresses. It is a critical point of collaboration between Customer, Product Manager and Team where business value is defined. The core purpose is to define the scope of the Release and the order of delivery of features, functions and capabilities and discuss the technical impacts of choosing to implement the requirements in that order. The outcome is a shared understanding of the expected release dates and a collection of specific User Stories that will be broken down into Tasks so the Team can allocate its work. 5-16

099. **B. DEFERRED COMMITMENTS** allow the best possible design to emerge as part of the development process.

Deferred commitments allow the best possible design to emerge as part of the development process. Software development always occurs in an atmosphere charged with uncertainty and complexity. Better results come from having the discipline to create as much clarity as possible about the problem, identify the various solution choices and the tradeoffs imbedded in each one, and making a fact-based decision on which approach or approaches to test and pursue. 6-16

100. **C. LITTLE'S LAW** proves the relationship between WIP and throughput for a production system in a steady state.

It is important because it correlates three significant performance measures – inventory, flow time, and throughput – in units per time period. This is very useful because risk can be identified with the amount of time represented by the User Stories in inventory. For instance, if we see 200 Stories of WIP for a team producing 10 per day, a disaster probably awaits. Conversely, if we see 200 Stories of WIP for a team producing 100 per day, then it is extremely lean. 7-16

101. **C. BACKLOG GROOMING** is the process that prioritizes and clarifies Backlog items as they move from the long-term to a more near-term time horizon.

Backlog Grooming, sometimes referred to as Backlog Management, is a process that prioritizes and clarifies Backlog items as they move from the long-term edge of the time horizon into a time horizon that is more near-term. 3-17

102. **C. GROOMING** or **REFINEMENT** is the process that prioritizes and clarifies Backlog items as they move from the long-term to a more near-term time horizon.

Grooming, or as the Scrum Guide calls it, Product Backlog refinement, is an ongoing activity that increases the granularity of the details about Product Backlog items as they move from a more distant time horizon to a more current time horizon and the likelihood of understanding what will actually be developed increases. 4-17

103. **C. The TEST-DRIVEN DEVELOPMENT** ceremony helps the Team limit scope creep because expectations are clearly and objectively stated.

The Test-Driven Development ceremony requires the test to be written before the code is developed and run frequently while the code is being written. Applying a rigid TDD discipline helps the Team limit scope creep because expectations are clearly and objectively stated. The process of test, code, and refactor is repeated over and over again, creating a cadence that assists the twin goals of speed and quality. 5-17

104. **C.** The goal of rapidly satisfying a Customer need is driven by the Lean principle to **ELIMINATE WASTE.**

The goal of rapidly satisfying a Customer need is driven by the Lean principle to eliminate waste. Therefore, the Team must be vigilant about recognizing any activity that could be bypassed as waste while still satisfying the Customer. Waste-removal must be diligently pursued during every Iteration and every step of the planning process. 6-17

105. **A.** Because Agile Project Management and Kanban both spring from a legacy in manufacturing, when the acronym WIP is used, it is understood to mean **WORK-IN-PROGRESS.**

Work in progress, work in process, goods in process, and in-process inventory are all synonyms to a greater or lesser degree, with work in progress and work in process being the most widely used.

In manufacturing, the most commonly used term is work in progress, while in accounting it is most common to refer to the item classification as work in process. Therefore, since Agile

Project Management and Kanban both spring from a legacy in manufacturing, when the acronym WIP is used, it is understood to mean Work In Progress. 7-17

106. **B.** A meeting held primarily to synchronize the team members' activities is called a **DAILY MEETING.**

     Daily Meetings are held primarily to synchronize the team members' activities and secondarily, to provide information for reporting work progress towards the Iteration Goal. The Daily Meeting is sometimes referred to as a Daily Stand-up or Scrum meeting. 3-18

107. **B.** A meeting held primarily to synchronize the Development Team members' activities is called a **DAILY SCRUM.**

     The Daily Scrum is time-boxed to 15-minutes. The Scrum Master and Development Team use it to synchronize activities. The meetings are held at the same time and place each day. Every Development Team member answers three questions. 4-18

108. **B. The PLANNING GAME** ceremony defines the scope of the Release and the order of delivery of features, functions and capabilities.

     The Planning Game defines a rough order of magnitude (ROM) plan for a project so the Team can refine it as the project progresses. It is a critical point of collaboration between Customer, Product Manager and Team where business value is defined. The core purpose is to define the scope of the Release and the order of delivery of features, functions and capabilities and discuss the technical impacts of choosing to implement the requirements in that order. The outcome is a shared understanding of the expected release dates and a collection of specific User Stories that will be broken down into Tasks so the Team can allocate its work. 5-18

109. **B.** The principle of **DEFER COMMITMENTS** drives the success of iterative development approaches because it fuels adaptive changes to overcome mistakes.

The principle of Defer Commitments drives the success of iterative development approaches because it fuels adaptive changes to overcome mistakes that would be potentially costly after the release of the system. It means that planning is concerned with exploring options and adapting to discoveries while the inter-relationships between requirements, which may number in the thousands, are worked out. It requires that decisions and commitments be deferred to the Last Responsible Moment. 6-18

110. **A. BUFFERS** are holding places for small inventories of work items that are external to a process group.

    Buffers and Queues are holding places for small inventories of work items used to insure instant availability of input when a downstream process pulls it. They are often used as synonyms and are very nearly so. However, Buffers are external to a process group or step and occur between steps whereas Queues are internal to a process group and occur at the end of the process, remaining internal to it. 7-18

111. **C.** A meeting where any interested stakeholder can offer insights and concerns is called a **REVIEW MEETING.**

    Review Meetings are product-centric meetings where any interested stakeholder can offer insights and concerns about the deliverables, as well as considerations for future enhancements. 3-19

112. **D.** The core process of Scrum is called **THE SPRINT.**

    The Sprint is the core process of Scrum. It uses a time-box with a consistent duration throughout development. Each Sprint starts immediately following the previous Sprint with a Sprint Planning ceremony. 4-19

113. **B.** The goal of **INCREMENTAL ARCHITECTURAL DESIGN** is to minimize waste caused by misunderstanding.

    The goal of Incremental Architectural Design is to minimize waste caused by misunderstanding about the real functionality needed on the Customer and Product Owner side and caused by redundant development and rework on the Team side.

The ceremony means the Team works hard to create and apply a robust architecture where design investments are in proportion to system needs so the cost of changing during development doesn't rise exponentially. It means defining an incremental design strategy where the system grows through gradual, predictable change, minimizing the cost of complexity and maximizing the probability that the simplest design will actually work. 5-19

114. **C.** Failure to **ELIMINATE WASTE** shows up in evidence that the process missed an opportunity to produce real value.

    Defects lower quality and are waste, but they are also evidence that the process missed an opportunity to produce real value. Value Stream Mapping identifies waste, but it becomes waste if it is not used eliminate it. Planning minimizes waste, but it becomes waste if it doesn't prevent development of the wrong solution. 6-19

115. **C. QUEUES** are holding places for small inventories of work items that are internal to a process group.

    Buffers and Queues are holding places for small inventories of work items used to insure instant availability of input when a downstream process pulls it. They are often used as synonyms and are very nearly so. However, Buffers are external to a process group or step and occur between steps whereas Queues are internal to a process group and occur at the end of the process, remaining internal to it. 7-19

116. **B. DEFINITION OF DONE** is the definition of all the activities to finish and tests to fulfill before the work is complete.

    Definition of Done is the definition of all the activities to finish and tests to fulfill before a Story or Task is considered complete. It is an agreement between the Team and Customer-Proxy appropriate to the context of a project. 3-20

117. **B. DEFINITION OF DONE** is the definition of all the activities to finish and tests to fulfill before the work is complete.

Definition of Done is defined as the description of all the activities to finish and tests to fulfill before a Story or Task is considered complete. It is an agreement between the Development Team and Product Owner appropriate to the context of a project. 4-20

118. **C. The PAIR PROGRAMMING** ceremony means that Programmers take personal ownership of specific tasks.

The Pair Programming ceremony means that Programmers take personal ownership of specific Tasks and that doing so creates internal team accountability.

The best approach to pair programming is for the partners to sit side-by-side in front of the computer and concentrate on the code being written as the Driver or Navigator and share observations. 5-20

119. **A.** The fastest way to deliver the system the Customer expects is to have the Customer **PULL THE PIECES** through an incremental discovery process.

The fastest way to deliver the system the Customer expects is to have the Customer pull the pieces – features, functions and capabilities – through an incremental discovery process that creates a deep understanding of how to solve the problem. 6-20

120. Within the Kanban community there are six practices (currently) referred to as "core practices." Three of them are: **LIMIT WIP, MAKE PROCESS POLICIES EXPLICIT,** and **MANAGE FLOW.** (Any of the 6 below are correct.)

Within the Kanban community there are six practices (currently) referred to as "core practices." They are:

1. Visualize
2. Limit Work in Progress
3. Manage Flow
4. Make Process Policies Explicit
5. Implement Feedback Loops
6. Improve Collaboratively, Evolve Experimentally 7-20

Glossary

Note: *This glossary provides definitions that describe the main purpose or usage of terms in Agile project management. The definition is intended to be a guide to understanding the concept with enough differentiation to avoid confusing it with similar or related terms.*

The glossary includes terms that are project management centric or are used differently or with a narrower meaning in project management than in general usage.

This glossary does not include general terms whose usage does not differ in a material way when used in project management, most application-specific terms, compound terms whose meaning is clear from the component parts, or variants when the meaning is clear from the base term. When synonyms are included, no definition is given and the reader is directed to the preferred term (i.e., See alternate term).

A-EVM: A version of EVM. *See Agile earned value management.*

Abnormal sprint termination: *See abnormal termination.*

Abnormal termination: Prematurely ending an iteration due to some extraordinary situation because of a significant change of priorities, or because the Team declares it cannot reach the iteration goal. This should be very rare.

AC: *See actual cost.*

Acceptance criteria: Defined metrics for determining how a User Story satisfies a customer need.

ACP: An incorrect abbreviation for a PMI Agile Certified Practitioner (PMI-ACP®).

Active listening: Is the practice of intentionally focusing on the speaker in order to understand what is meant and not just what has been said.

Actual Cost (AC): An earned value management (EVM) variable expressing the cost of work completed during the iteration. Also known as the actual cost of work performed or ACWP in Traditional EVM.

Actual cost of work performed (ACWP): An earned value management (EVM) variable expressing the cost of work completed during a specific time period.

Actual day: *See actual time.*

Actual Percent Complete (APC): A value derived by dividing the total number of Story Points completed by the total number of Story Points planned.

Actual time: Work time required to complete an activity that has been factored for typical interruptions. See ideal time.

ACWP: *See actual cost of work performed.*

Adaptation: The process of using frequent inspections in order to discover requirements and design issues that arise while building the product.

Adaptive planning: A tool for applying iterative cycles to create incremental deliverables.

Adaptive software development: An Agile software development approach using a continuous adaptation process defined as having speculate, collaborate, and learn phases.

Affinity estimating: A technique used to quickly size a large number of Stories, typically to plan a Roadmap, Release or first Iteration.

Agile: (1) Organizational cultures aligned with the values and principles of the Agile Manifesto for Software Development. (2) Iterative, incremental approaches to developing software that apply the Agile Manifesto principles.

Agile Ethos: The notion that having human beings act like biological machines cannot solve the significant, complex problems faced by most organizations, and therefore organizations need the creative, non-linear, and imaginative insights that only come from fully engaged people.

Agile Manifesto: Short for the Agile Manifesto for Software Development where the values and principles for developing a culture and work environment focused customer satisfaction through fast delivery of value and self-organizing teams are documented.

Agile Modeling (AM): A tool for incremental modeling used in conjunction with Agile frameworks.

Anchoring: A condition that exists when a single, strong-willed team member with an outlier opinion exerts undue influence and prevents the Team from progressing.

APM: The abbreviation for Agile Project Management.

Applied simplicity: The practice of creating the simplest possible model to address a problem and avoiding large, complex models.

Artifacts: The tangible or intangible output of development and production processes such as printed vision statements, elevator statements and team agreements or completed code files archived in a system repository.

Automated Test: Test cases that run without human intervention and makes sure system code produces the expected output.

Backlog: A prioritized list of capabilities, features, and Stories to be completed during the Release or Iteration. *See Product Backlog, Release Backlog, and Iteration Backlog.*

Backlog grooming: The process that prioritizes and clarifies Backlog items as they move from the long-term edge of the time horizon into a time horizon that is more near-term. Sometimes referred to as Backlog management.

Backlog management: *See Backlog grooming.*

Barely sufficient: The practice of only doing the minimum necessary to delivery everything required and nothing that is not required. It is the balance point between insufficient and gold plating.

BART: Acronym for the four dimensions of team dynamics, Boundary, Authority, Role, and Task.

BART analysis: Analysis of team dynamics in four categories, Boundary, Authority, Role, and Task.

Batman: An eXtreme Programming (XP) term referring to the person dealing with organizational emergencies and supporting requests so that the other developers can focus on programming work.

BCWP: *See budgeted cost of work performed*

BCWS: *See budgeted cost of work scheduled.*

BDUF: *See Big design up front.*

Behavior: A measurement used in team self-assessments to express how well the Team applied best practices from the chosen framework as well as its own working agreements. It is a measure of team cooperation, cohesion, and commitment aligned to the value of personal safety and transparent, productive tension.

Big design up front (BDUF): The Traditional project planning process that tries to define all the requirements of a product at the beginning of the project.

Big upfront design (BUFD): *See big design up front.*

Blitz planning: A Crystal practice where the sponsor, business representative, expert user, and developers use an index card-based planning session to quickly build the project map and timeline.

Brainstorming: A collection of processes used to produce insight by first generating a large number of ideas then filtering through a set of criteria. To maximize effectiveness it is important to maintain the two-step discipline.

Branch: An action that splits the repository into distinct "alternate histories" or "branches." Typically all files exist in both branches such that changes can be made in one branch independently of all other branches.

Budgeted cost of work performed (BCWP): The planned value of work completed during the Iteration. Also known as the earned value (EV)

Budgeted cost of work scheduled (BCWS): The planned value of work scheduled during the iteration. See planned value (PV).

BUFD: *See Big design up front.*

Buffer: Buffers are holding places for small inventories of work items used to insure instant availability of input when a downstream process pulls it. Buffer is often used as a synonym for Queue and it is very nearly so. However, Buffers are external to a process group or step and occur between steps whereas Queues are internal to a process group and occur at the end of the process, remaining internal to it.

Buffer iteration: The practice of adding an iteration to accommodate changes or deal with risks without jeopardizing the project end date.

Burn chart: A graph of features to be developed shown over time. Typically includes a baseline of the plan as well as the progress-to-date shown as work remaining or work completed.

Burn-Down chart: A chart with time indicated on the x-axis and showing the work remaining, based on the results of the team's daily meeting, compared to the baseline plan on the y-axis.

Burn-Up chart: A chart with time indicated on the x-axis and showing the work completed compared to the baseline plan for the project or release on the y-axis.

Business case: A written document that explains how the project is aligned with a business goal.

Buying points: The total cumulative Story Points of the Stories developed during the iteration, as used in eXtreme Programming (XP).

Cancel-for-convenience clause: Commonly used in government contracts, the clause stipulates that the customer may cancel the agreement for any reason. Such clauses usually define the limit of the buyer's liability and the scope of the seller's right to recover monetary compensation.

CAPM: Abbreviation for a PMI Certified Associate in Project Management (CAPM®).

Card: A written representation of customer requirements.

Caves and commons: The workspace design approach that creates "commons" space that fosters osmotic communication by having team members collocated, but also includes private areas, called "caves", that team members use when they need quiet to focus or to handle personal issues.

CCB: *See change control board.*

Central feature list: A rough sketch of features and functions for planning the project prior to initiating the project.

Certified ScrumMaster (CSM): One of the Agile certifications issued by the Scrum Alliance. The ScrumMaster is the person responsible for ensuring the process is understood and followed, coaching and facilitating the Team, shielding the Team from outside interference, and removing impediments for the Team.

Certified Scrum Product Owner (CSPO): One of the Agile certifications issued by the Scrum Alliance. The Product Owner is the person who acts as the voice of the customer and is responsible for grooming the Backlog, negotiating the sprint goals, and setting the Definition of Done.

Certified Scrum Professional (CSP): One of the certifications issued by the Scrum Alliance. The CSP has more documented expertise and has passed a more rigorous exam than a CSM or CSPO. Being a CSM or CSPO is one of the required perquisites for becoming a CSP.

Change control board (CCB): A committee that decides whether or not proposed changes to a project should be implemented. Commonly used in Traditional project management environments to control change. All changes that are outside the baseline scope must be approved by the CCB before resources are spent. The authority of the CCB will vary from organization to organization.

Check In: Returned completed code files to the repository.

Check Out: Remove a copy of the source code from the repository.

Chicken: A comical reference used in Agile to refer to a person who has an interest in the project, but who is not directly responsible for product delivery. See Pig.

Coach: An eXtreme Programming (XP) role that helps the Team use discipline to apply XP practices. Someone who watches the whole process and calls attention to impending problems or opportunities for improvement.

Code freeze: A term used in software development to identify a period of time during the iteration when no changes are permitted to source code while the Team ensures that it works correctly, usually in preparation for a release or deployment.

Code of Ethics: Short for PMI's Code of Ethics and Professional Conduct. Codes of ethics define the expectations of practitioners in specific community and articulate the ideals and behavioral norms of that community.

Collocation: The practice of arranging the project team in the same or adjacent rooms to facilitate optimum communication.

Collective code ownership: An eXtreme Programming (XP) practice empowering any member of the Team to make necessary changes to fix or improve the code because the Team shares joint responsibility for the quality of the code.

Commit: *See Check In.*

Commitment Schedule: Release dates refined one iteration at a time and adjusted with revised estimates.

Compliance documentation: Any artifact or document used to meet regulatory requirements. Such documentation often has little value to the Team in understanding or communicating customer value.

Cone of uncertainty: The concept of how unknown facets of a problem decrease over time as customers traverse through an unavoidable, ambiguous process where discovery and learning occur.

Constraint: Anything that restricts or controls the actions of the project team in developing a solution, such as cost or time limits.

Continuous improvement: Incremental or disruptive changes to the design of the delivery process that increase efficiency, effectiveness and flexibility.

Cooperative Game: From the book by Alistair Cockburn, Agile Software Development: The Cooperative Game, where he describes development as a process of delivering the software iteration and creating an advantageous position for the next game.

COQ: *See cost of quality.*

Cost of quality (COQ): The cost of NOT creating a quality product is the correct (and counter-intuitive) definition of this often-misunderstood term.

Another way to express it is as the inverse of the cost of things like re-work, re-testing, re-processing a deliverable due to a lack of quality in the original.

Cost performance index (CPI): A measure used to determine the efficiency of expenditures for a given time period on a given project, used in Earned Value Management.

Cost plus award fee (CPAF): A type of contract where the seller is paid for all allowable expenses plus an additional award payment that is typically determined on a subjective basis by an awards fee board.

Cost plus contract: A type of contract where the seller is paid for all allowable expenses plus a profit based on predefined parameters.

Cost plus fixed fee (CPFF): A type of contract where the seller is paid for all allowable expenses plus an additional fee based on predefined parameters.

Cost plus incentive fee (CPIF): A type of contract where the seller is paid for all allowable expenses plus an additional fee when predefined parameters are reached or exceeded. Typically related to cost saving performance metrics.

Cost variance (CV): A measure used to show cost performance for a given time period on a given project, used in Earned Value Management. A positive value is favorable and a negative value is unfavorable.

Cowboy coding: Is a development process where programmers exercise complete autonomy with minimal formality or discipline, and typically has a negative derogatory connotation.

CPAF: *See cost plus award fee.*

CPF: *See cost plus fee.*

CPFF: *See cost plus fixed fee.*

CPI: *See cost performance index.*

CPIF: *See cost plus incentive fee.*

CPM: *See critical path methodology.*

Critical path methodology (CPM): A tool, developed in the 1950's, for analyzing project schedules using an algorithm applied to interdependent activities.

Criticality: The potential damage system failure can cause, as used in Crystal.

Cross-functional team: A team of people, each with different functional expertise, working on a project and typically operating as a self-directing unit for decision-making.

Crystal: A family of Agile frameworks created by Alistair Cockburn that focuses on people and applies two variable Size and Criticality.

CSM: Abbreviation for Certified Scrum Master.

CSP: Abbreviation for Certified Scrum Professional.

CSPO: Abbreviation for Certified Scrum Product Owner.

Cumulative flow diagram (CFD): A graphical tool that shows work in progress, for a given time period and a given project, and can be used to reduce risk by identifying and correcting a workload imbalance creating a more effective and sustainable pace.

Customer: (1) The user of the product who is trying to solve a problem. (2) The purchaser of the product who understands the business problem, constraints, has the authority to make decisions about the product, and may be different than the user. Referred to as the Product Owner in Scrum, and as the voice of the customer or customer-proxy in other Agile frameworks.

Customer-proxy: The Agile role answers the question, "What does the project have to do to deliver value to the customer and to the organization?" Comparable to the Product Owner role in Scrum. Has various responsibilities, the most important of which is grooming the Product Backlog. See also customer.

CV: *See cost variance.*

Cycle Time: A measure of process throughput. It is expressed as the average unit of time used per work item produced. See also Agile Cycle Time.

Daily meeting: A daily meeting during the iteration that is typically timeboxed to no more than 15 minutes during which the team members synchronize by reporting their progress by answering three specific questions. Traditionally, the meeting is done while standing, hence the common convention of adding stand-up to the meeting.

Daily scrum: *See daily meeting.*

Daily stand-up meeting: *See daily meeting.*

Dashboard: A printed or electronic display of project data that answers critical questions and help the Team and stakeholders assess performance of key activities quickly. Dashboards are one type of information radiator.

Decomposition: The process of breaking larger items, such as features, into smaller items or components, such as Stories and Tasks, which can be repeated until the point of irreducibility is reached. See project chunking and progressive elaboration.

Defined process control: Commonly used in manufacturing environments where well-defined inputs plus repeatable processes produce predictable outputs so that quality variances and tolerances can be readily measured and managed. Waterfall-based development processes use defined process control. Compare to empirical process control.

Definition of done: All the activities to finish and tests to fulfill before a Story is considered complete.

Delivery performance: A measurement used in team self-assessments to express how efficiently and effectively the Team delivered the features and Stories that were defined as the iteration goal, and at project closing the release goal. See behavior.

Demonstration (or Demo) Meeting: *See Product demonstration.*

Development Team: A cross-functional group, in Scrum, that creates solutions by analyzing, designing, developing, testing, and implementing deliverables. It is assumed that it has all the needed skills, is highly trusted and self-managing. See also Scrum Team and Team.

Discounting: The process of adjusting future values to reflect their present value.

Disruptive innovations: Changes that displace an existing technology or business process in an unexpected way, creating new market value.

Done: The degree of completeness when a feature conforms to mutually agreed upon metrics, standards, conventions and guidelines. *See done-done.*

Done-done: A degree of completeness generally defined in software development as coded, tested, defect-free, and accepted by the Product Owner.

DSDM: *See Dynamic Systems Development Method.*

Dynamic Systems Development Method (DSDM): An Agile software development framework using rapid application development plus iterative and incremental delivery of code. It was developed in the 1990s in the UK.

EAC: *See estimate at completion.*

Early finish date (EF): The earliest date when all work can be completed for the designated Story.

Early start date (ES): The earliest date on which all preceding Stories will be complete thereby allowing work to begin on the designated Story.

Earned Value (EV): An earned value management (EVM) variable that expresses the planned value of work completed during the iteration. Also known as the budgeted cost of work performed (BCWP).

Earned Value Management (EVM): A program management technique integrating scope, schedule, and resource consumption information in order to measure project performance against planned cost metrics.

EF: *See early finish date.*

Elevator statement: An uncomplicated way to define the product vision in a short statement using language everyone can understand such that the project could be concisely explained to someone "in an elevator."

Emotional intelligence: The ability to identify, assess, and manage one's own emotions plus the ability to identify, assess, and influence the emotions of others.

Empirical Process Control: Commonly used in new product development and R&D environments where high uncertainty exists, but processes produce reliable results using frequent inspections and adaptation, especially early in the development cycle. Agile development processes apply empirical process control. Compare to defined process control.

Engineering Task: A single thing the system must do that is derived directly from a Story. Typically requires one to three days of programming.

Epic: A high-level Story expressing a feature or function to be developed, that is typically decomposed into smaller Stories as planning progresses. It fits into the commonly used Agile taxonomy of Theme, Epic, Story, and Task.

ES: *See early start date.*

Escaped defects: Any product deficiency that was not detected by testing and quality assurance processes and therefore escaped remediation before the product was delivered to the customer.

Estimatable: A User Story characteristic that means the Development Team can make a good assessment the relative size of the Story as a piece of the solution, which implies it is not too large or too small.

Estimate at completion (EAC): An earned value management (EVM) variable that expresses the forecast total cost of an activity, component, sub-project or project when the work is completed.

Estimate to complete (ETC): An earned value management (EVM) variable that expresses the forecast cost required to complete an activity, component, sub-project or project.

ESVP: Abbreviation for a common check-in activity used in retrospective meetings where team members identify their attitude about the retrospective using the terms Explorer, Shopper, Vacationer, or Prisoner.

ETC: *See estimate to complete.*

EV: *See earned value.*

EVM: Abbreviation for Earned Value Management.

Evo: An Agile project management approach focused on delivering high-value-first through evolutionary progress toward goals created by Thomas Gilb.

Exciters and delighters: Product features that can create a price premium, but will not decrease customer satisfaction below neutral if they are not included.

Exploration: The development phase when the customer communicates what the system must do.

Exploratory spike: *See spike.*

Extractable and Executable (E2): A User Story characteristic meaning the development of the Story is independent of the dependencies that link it to the Iteration Goal.

Extreme Programming (XP): A software engineering programmer-centric framework appling engineering techniques and practices with extreme rigor to create higher quality of software and support more responsiveness to customer needs. Also referred to as eXtreme Programming.

Fairness: One of the four hallmark values defined in the PMI Code of Ethics and Professional Responsibility that requires careful avoidance of conflicts of interest and discrimination. See honesty, respect and responsibility.

Feature: A function, requirement or component of the system being developed that provides value to the customer, and typically described in a Story.

Feature breakdown structure (FBS): A hierarchical, graphical or numerical, expression of product features or Stories showing larger items progressively decomposed into smaller items. It is analogous to the Traditional work breakdown structure (WBS).

Feature Driven Development (FDD): An Agile framework beginning with a defined domain model used to drive development activities into building features during iterations that are typically no more than two weeks long.

Feature Stories: Document a business goal as specific pieces or components of business functionality with perceived value for the customer or user. See Story and User Story.

FBS: Abbreviation for Feature Breakdown Structure.

FDD: *See feature driven development.*

FF: *See finish-to-finish.*

FFP: *See firm fixed price.*

Fibonacci sequence: A non-linear number series derived from the sum of two previous numbers and expressed in the equation Fn = Fn-1 + Fn-2. See planning poker.

Finish-to-finish (FF): One of four types of dependencies used to create logic networks for project schedules. FF describes a relationship where one activity, A, cannot be completed unless another activity, B, is also finished. For example, printing this book, A, cannot be completed unless the last chapter is written, B.

Finish to start (FS): One of four types of dependencies used to create logic networks for project schedules. FS describes a relationship where one activity, B, cannot be started until another activity, A, is finished. For example, digging the foundations, A, must be completed before, B, pouring the concrete foundation occurs.

Firm fixed price (FFP): A type of contract where the seller is paid a mutually agreed upon price regardless of the costs incurred to fulfill the contract.

Fishbone diagram: *See Ishikawa diagram.*

Fist of five: A validation process used by the team to demonstrate individual support for a particular decision by holding up a hand and displaying fingers representing agreement; five fingers means I strongly agree, three means I can support it, and one means I am very concerned and opposed.

Fixed price incentive fee (FPIF): A type of contract where the seller is paid a mutually agreed upon price and the seller can earn an additional fee based on meeting or exceeding predefined parameters.

Flexibility matrix: A tool that communicates how to handle unavoidable tradeoffs via a grid showing the relative importance of constraints such as scope, schedule, cost, and quality by defining them as fixed, firm, or flexible; only one constraint may be fixed.

Float: The time difference between when a Story is scheduled for completion and the latest allowable time it can be completed without negatively impacting the finish of development.

Flow: The concept that the development and delivery of continuous value to customers is a process, similar to throughput in Lean manufacturing.

Force Field Analysis: A tool used to examine organizational factors supporting or inhibiting a desired change. First, the issue is defined, then the desired state is defined, and finally factors are listed in two columns – Driving and Restraining. Afterwards, the Team evaluates how to increase the strength of supporting factors, called drivers, and mitigate the impact of inhibiting factors, called restrainers.

Forecast velocity: An estimate of team velocity used when actual velocity is not available because the Team has not run an iteration and therefore do not have historical data to use.

FPIF: *See fixed price incentive fee.*

Fractional assignment: An organizational human resource practice of assigning a single person to multiple projects simultaneously. This practice is not recommended by Agile frameworks.

Frameworks: Context-specific foundations created to support particular industries or activities.

Free-for-all: A creative process for solving problems, stimulating thinking, developing new ideas characterized by unrestrained responses from participants being recorded by a facilitator without any evaluation of merit (which will follow in a separate step). It is one of three brainstorming approaches. See round robin and silent idea generation.

FS: *See finish to start.*

Functional Test: A test written from the Customer's perspective.

Ground rules: See rules of engagement and team working agreements.

Handoff iteration: An iteration used to make documentation meet regulatory requirements, or to get other deliverables ready for production, or to finish other support Tasks, possibly including attending final approval meetings, while avoiding work on any new features.

Hard commit: The second level of commitment made by the Team during the iteration planning meeting as part of the negotiation with the customer-proxy. It follows the soft commit and occurs after the Team has analyzed the stories in the iteration Backlog, agreed they can deliver them successfully, then commits to doing so by the end of the iteration. See soft commit.

Hard logic: Mandatory relationship-logic for a Sstory that must precede subsequent Stories.

Hardening iteration: A final iteration before the release or deployment of a deliverable, or set of deliverables, where activities like user training, creating marketing materials, or final testing are done, but not as a testing cycle substituting for the Agile norm of delivering potentially shippable products. Iterations 0 (Zero) and Hardening Iterations precede and follow standard development Iterations, respectively, but typically do not include new development work. See Iteration 0 (Zero).

Head: *See Tip.*

Honesty: One of the four hallmark values defined in the PMI Code of Ethics and Professional Responsibility that requires never deceiving others. See fairness, respect and responsibility.

Hybrid project: Projects using a combination of Traditional and Agile practices or a combination of practices from multiple Agile frameworks.

Hybrid Project Management: An Agile Framework where a selected combination of techniques and practices, including those from one or more Agile Frameworks, are used to manage projects in order to best meet the needs of the organization and customer.

Idea Transfer Rate: A measure of the processing bandwidth needed by a team simultaneously exploring and investigating multiple, often opposing possibilities in search of a synthesized solution that contains elements that improve each other in previously unconsidered ways.

Ideal day: *See ideal time.*

Ideal time: Work time required to complete an activity assuming there are no interruptions so that work can be completed with 100% efficiency. See actual time.

IID: *See iterative and incremental development.*

Impediment: Any obstacle that interferes with the Team efficiently completing work.

Impediment backlog: A prioritized list of obstacles that interfere with efficiently completing work. See risk backlog.

Important and Insightful (I2): A User Story characteristic that means the Story creates and enhances Customer value by encapsulating elements of the solution in a way that improves discernment of progress towards the best solution.

Increment: As used in Scrum, the portion of product functionality completed during the Sprint, whether or not it can be deployed independently of other functionality.

Incremental innovations: Changes that evolve an existing technology or business process to create more market value.

Incremental revenue: The additional revenue generated by delivery of a specific increment of the product.

Independent: A User Story characteristic that means the Story avoids interlocking dependencies in order to simplify decomposition and Task estimation.

Information radiator: A visible display of the current work status, typically in the project workspace, that consolidates key information so interested persons can evaluate it. See visual control.

Inspection: Frequently examining work products to detect undesirable variances that could negatively impact progress toward a desired outcome, such as the Sprint Goal.

INVEST: A mnemonic for the six qualities of a well-developed User Story – Independent, Negotiable, Valuable, Estimatable, Small and Testable. See Independent, Negotiable, Valuable, Estimatable, Small and Testable.

Ishikawa diagram: Cause-and-effect diagrams created by Kaoru Ishikawa in 1968 commonly used to identify potential factors causing errors and imperfect output. The causes are typically grouped by categories, such as people, methods, machines, materials, measurements, and environment.

Iteration: A single cycle of development with a fixed-length that is not varied during the Release. Commonly the length is fixed at one to four weeks. It is the basic operational process used in Agile to deliver desired results in small increments. The standard Iteration typically delivers new development work that has been subjected to full quality assurance and user acceptance testing. It is begins with the Iteration Planning meeting and concludes with a Review meeting for interested stakeholders and a Retrospective meeting for the team. In Scrum it is called a Sprint.

Iteration 0 (Zero): An optional initial Iteration preceding the first standard development Iteration, where activities like acquiring needed technology, procuring team work space, or defining the product vision are done. Iterations 0 (Zero) and Hardening Iterations precede and follow standard development Iterations, respectively, but typically do not include new development work. See Hardening Iteration.

Iteration backlog: Specific prioritized subsets of Product Backlog items the Team has committed to develop in a particular timebox period. Called a Sprint Backlog in Scrum. See Backlog.

Iterative and incremental development: The Plan-Do-Check-Act product development approach that delivers a portion or increment of the product each cycle or iteration.

Iteration plan: A combination of the detailed work effort descriptions that the Team has committed to completing in the iteration timebox.

Iteration planning meeting: The meeting where the Team determines what Stories will be developed during the iteration and then decomposes them into Tasks with estimates.

Kanban: A Lean manufacturing control or signaling system where needed inputs are produced based on actual usage being pulled by work centers. It can be contrasted with inputs being produced into inventories based forecasted usage and demand scheduling assumptions. It has been adapted to Agile project management as a framework for continuous-flow product development without strict iteration lengths.

Kanban board: A physical board or virtual table showing a collection of Stories or Tasks represented by cards that are pulled through the development system within the boundaries of the scheduling process. They are often used to manage limits on work-in-progress (WIP) and thereby increase development throughput.

Knowledge worker: A phrase coined by Peter Drucker, famed management guru, to describe persons who combine structured and unstructured data with creative thinking to solve mostly non-routine problems.

Label: *See Tag.*

Last responsible moment: The point where any advantage of acquiring additional valuable information or insight is balanced or offset by the potential downside of delaying the decision any longer.

Late finish date (LF): The latest date upon which work on the designated Story can be completed without delaying the completion of development.

Late start date (LS): The latest date upon which work can begin on the designated Story without delaying the completion of development.

Law of large numbers (LLN): A statistical model or rule that states that as the quantity of samples increases, the average or mean of the whole population emerges and can be used to predict behavior within normal deviations of outcomes. This allows the transformation of unpredictable outcomes into predictable ones. Also known as Bernoulli's Law.

Lead Time: A measure of elapsed time between "ideation and customer receipt." It is expressed as the unit of time between when the work item is made available for development and when it is delivered. See also Cycle Time.

Lean Manufacturing: The production methods focused on eliminating waste in order to create better, faster outcomes for customers, and made famous as the Toyota Production System.

Lean Software Development (LSD): An Agile framework that applies the principles of Lean Manufacturing to software development.

Learning Matrix: A tool commonly used during the retrospective meeting to generate and record learning and insight by discovering what was significant in the Team's experience of the just completed iteration.

LF: *See late finish date.*

Linear feature: Product features creating customer satisfaction that has a linear correlation with the quantity of the features. Contrast with exciters and delighters and threshold features.

Linked: A User Story characteristic that means the Story can be mapped in a Logical Network or Precedence Diagram of the Iteration or Release that makes dependencies visible, manageable, and productive.

Lock: An action that secures a file and prevents anyone else from editing it.

Logic Network: A graphical representation of the relationships within portfolio, program, and project schedules.

LS: *See late start date.*

LSD: *See lean software development.*

Macro-dynamic: Refers to organizational frameworks.

Manifesto: Short for the Manifesto for Agile Software Development.

Many-to-Many: Each and every one of two or more Stories must be completed before multiple subsequent Stories can begin.

Many-to-One: Each and every one of two or more Stories must be completed before a subsequent Story can begin.

Measurable: A User Story characteristic that means the Story can be subjected to the best practices of Test-Driven Development (TDD) within a continuously improved development system, ultimately enhancing stakeholder relationships.

Merge: An action that combines multiple programming changes and resolves any conflicts. For example, when two programmers change a file separately and both check it in, the second programmer must merge the first programmer's changes into the code they are checking in.

Metaphor: A simple description of the program's vision that it is easy to understand and communicate. It is used by the XP team to guide and focus development work.

Methodology: A philosophical foundation for organizing frameworks.

Micro-dynamic: Refers to team management frameworks.

Minimum marketable feature (MMF): The smallest set of features that provide the level of functionality required to fulfill customer expectations.

MMF: Abbreviation for minimal marketable features.

MoSCoW: An acronym for a feature prioritization approach that identifies them as M for "must have", S for "should have", C for "could have" and W for "won't have".

Mute mapping: An Extreme Programming (XP) practice where the team gathers at a whiteboard and silently develops ideas that will make future iterations more successful. An application of silent idea generation.

Natural Fracture Lines: The line where a potentially shippable product becomes an actually shippable, testable, or implementable product, component or subsystem.

Negotiable: A User Story characteristic that means the Story encourages frequent Customer conversations (i.e., negotiations) to explore and expand the brief descriptions of functionality on the card. It is the inverse of a contract clause or detailed specification.

Noise: Any impediment that interferes with or prevents the Team from being productive. *See Impediment.*

OBS: *See organizational breakdown structure.*

Obstacle: *See impediment.*

One-to-One: One, and only one, Story must be completed before the next Story can begin.

One-to-Many: One, and only one, Story must be completed before multiple follow-on Stories can begin.

Open space meeting: A product-centric, typically ad hoc, team meeting during the iteration where attendees discuss ideas for dealing with technical challenges impeding delivery of iteration goal. See reflective workshop.

Open workspace: *See team space.*

Organic risk management: Practices that are inherent to agile frameworks, such as release and iteration planning and daily stand-up meetings that address project risks. *See overt risk management.*

Osmotic communication: Team members unintentionally pick up information from conversations occurring near them then can contribute insight to the discussion.

Overt risk management: Practices that are external to Agile frameworks, such as identifying and tracking risks on a risk board, that address project risks. See organic risk management.

Pair programming: A practice used in eXtreme Programming (XP) where two programmers work together, typically on one computer. The first programmer types in code while the second programmer reviews each line of code as it is written. The first programmer is called the driver. The second programmer is called the observer or navigator. They switch roles frequently.

Participatory decision-making: A creative process for finding effective options where ownership of decisions belongs to the team.

PDCA: Acronym for the Plan-Do-Check-Act cycle taught by W. Edwards Deming.

PDM: *See precedence diagramming method.*

PDS: Abbreviation for project data sheet.

Performance Measure Baseline (PMB): The total number of Story Points planned for a release.

Personal safety: Occurs when team members feel support during the unavoidable productive tension and respectful disagreements that accompany developing solutions.

PgMP®: Abbreviation for a PMI Program Management Professional, a certification offered by the Project Management Institute.

Pig: A comical reference used in Agile to refer to a person who is directly responsible for delivery of the product. *See Chicken.*

Planned Percent Complete (PPC): The number of the current sprints divided by the total number of planned sprints.

Planned Value (PV): An earned value management (EVM) variable that expresses the budgeted value of work scheduled during the iteration. See budgeted cost of work scheduled (BCWS).

Planning by date: Occurs when the release date is defined first then the final list of features is adapted to the reality of development.

Planning by scope: Occurs when the MMF is defined first then a release date is calculated.

Planning Game: An eXtreme Programming (XP) technique used to elicit new requirements from the business and Customers with the Team then giving an estimate of the effort required to develop and implement it.

Planning onion: A phrase coined by Mike Cohn, famed Agile expert, that refers to the layers of planning used in Agile where details are appropriately aligned to a given time horizon.

Planning poker: A consensus-based estimating technique commonly used by Agile teams that employs a simplified Delphi technique approach to estimate the relative size of Stories. A Fibonacci sequence is commonly used to establish the range of numbers applied.

PMBOK®: Abbreviation for the Project Management Institute's Project Management Body Of Knowledge

PMI®: Abbreviation for the Project Management Institute.

PMP®: Abbreviation for a PMI Project Management Professional.

Portfolio management: Practices and techniques for making decisions about investment choices to align them with organizational objectives so that resource allocations balance risk and desired performance. *See Project Portfolio Management (PPM).*

Potentially shippable product: The deliverable(s) at the end of the iteration that add value to the customer's understanding project progress.

Pre-assignment: A process where someone in the organization has allocated, appointed or designated some or all of the specific persons who will make up the Team without the project manager's involvement.

Precedence Diagramming Method (PDM): A technique for constructing a logic network to represent a project schedule using symbols, typically boxes, referred to as nodes connected by arrows to show the logical relationships so calculations and analysis can be done.

Predictive release planning: The Traditional project planning approach where the entire plan is created in advance. Agile adaptive planning approaches are a contrast to this approach.

Preview and Placeholder (P2): A User Story characteristic that means the Story describes an element of a feature, function or capability at a summary level and acts a marker guaranteeing well-timed, appropriate in-depth discussions.

Prioritize with Dots: A tool used by the Team to prioritize lists so they can focus on the top ideas, issues, or opportunities. Voting with dots is not intended to be scientific. It is used after activities to generate insights as a tool to narrow a list of choices.

Process analysis: A step-by-step description of a process that includes the inputs, operations, and outputs used and created as part of the process. A process analysis is typically used to increase the understanding of how a process works so that process improvement opportunities can be isolated.

Processes: Practical "how to" protocols used to direct solution development.

Product backlog: A prioritized collection of short descriptions of features, functions and capabilities included in the solution being developed. It is similar to the specification list used in Traditional project management.

Product backlog grooming: *See backlog grooming.*

Product demonstration: Commonly, yet inaccurately, used as a synonym for the Review Meeting. The demonstration, or "demo", is a product-centric meeting where the Agile team demonstrates working features, prior to a Release (not the end of an Iteration as with the Review Meeting), to the customer-proxy, key stakeholders, and selected end users.

Product Owner: *See customer.*

Product Roadmap: An artifact that shows the strategic development path a product is intended to follow, including what specific features it will contain, in broad strokes, at given future release points.

Product Vision Box: A tangible expression of the solution that includes whatever content is necessary to convey what the product will be.

Programmer: A role on an XP team for the person who analyzes, designs, tests, programs, and integrates code.

Progressive elaboration: The Agile process of refining the product vision so that the high priority features are developed and the waste of developing unneeded or low priority features is avoided.

Project chunking: The Agile process of breaking larger items, such as features, into smaller pieces, such as Stories and Tasks, to plan development so it reduces risk and adds customer value. See decomposition and progressive elaboration.

Project constraint: *See constraint.*

Project data sheet (PDS): One-page summary of key project objectives, capabilities, and information.

Project Portfolio Management (PPM): Practices and techniques used by project management offices (PMOs) for making decisions about current or proposed projects to determine resource mixes and schedule activities to achieve organizational goals within constraints. PPM best practices are described as five knowledge areas in the PMI Standard for Portfolio Management®. *See Portfolio Management.*

Promise: Intangible commitment to have conversations with the customer.

Promising innovations: Products or services that occur at the intersection of novel concepts and probability-managed development methods.

PV: *See planned value.*

QA: *See quality assurance.*

QC: *See quality control.*

Quality assurance: Planned and systematic procedures implemented to ensure confidence that a product or service will consistently adhere to a defined set of quality criteria and meets the requirements of the customer.

Quality control: Observation techniques and measurement activities intended to ensure that a product or service adheres to a defined set of quality criteria, and where a failed evaluation against those standards will trigger needed corrective actions.

Queue: Queues are holding places for small inventories of work items used to insure instant availability of input when a downstream process pulls it. Queue is often used as a synonym for Buffer and it is very nearly so. However, Queues are internal to a process group and occur at the end of the process remaining internal to it whereas Buffers are external to a process group or step and occur between steps.

RACI: An acronym for responsible, accountable, consult, and inform as used in a responsibility assignment matrix (RAM).

RAM: *See responsibility assignment matrix.*

Reciprocal commitment: During the Iteration planning meeting the Team and the customer-proxy exchange commitments, hence the name reciprocal. The Team commits to completing the User Stories specified in the Iteration Backlog and in return, on behalf of the organization, the customer-proxy commits to not changing those priorities or adding new Stories. To be clear, requirements outside the Iteration are allowed to change.

Recovery: An XP planning action where the Customer preserves the Release date by reducing scope due to increased estimates or decreased team speed.

Refactoring: The process where a programming tool makes changes to the code that do not modify its functionality, but improve attributes like readability, simplicity, and extensibility, and also improve compliance with architecture or object model standards.

Reflective workshop: Process-centric, self-organized meetings that occur during the iteration where attendees discuss how to correct flawed processes, to introduce new ones, or to augment working agreements. See open space meetings.

Release: A logical, deployable set of product functionality developed over the course of multiple iterations. Releases may be defined as internal, incremental or final. A final release indicates it is ready for deployment to customers and end users.

Release backlog: A version of the backlog that includes all items for a particular release. *See backlog.*

Release plan: A planning tool used to guide development of logical, deployable sets of product functionality over the course of multiple iterations. Releases are typically delivered on quarterly or longer basis. They are equivalent to a Traditional program plan.

Repository: A repository is a storage location. For software development it refers to a location where software packages can be retrieved and installed on a computer. As an eXtreme Programming (XP) practice, it is the storage area used for the Team's files where those at the top of the repository are the latest version that have been checked in.

Request for information (RFI): A business process used to collect and compare information about the capabilities of potential suppliers. An RFI is primarily used to gather information to help guide the process for developing a request for proposal (RFP) or a request for quotation (RFQ).

Request for proposal (RFP): A business process used to collect and compare information about the various approaches and costs of producing a desired outcome from potential suppliers. An RFP is primarily used to rank options and make buying decisions. It usually follows a request for information (RFI) and is a synonym for a request for quotation (RFQ).

Requirement: A term not commonly used in Agile because of a belief that it requires detail too granular for the time horizon and places the emphasis on the technology instead of functionality and user value.

Respect: One of the four hallmark values defined in the PMI Code of Ethics and Professional Responsibility that requires showing esteem for others. See fairness, honesty, and responsibility.

Responsibility: One of the four hallmark values defined in the PMI Code of Ethics and Professional Responsibility that requires taking ownership of one's decisions, actions, and related outcomes. *See fairness, honesty, and respect.*

Responsibility assignment matrix (RAM): A tool for defining the level of accountability and rights belonging to various roles on project or business teams. Those levels are generally defined as responsible, accountable, consult, and inform, or RACI.

Retrospective Meeting: A process-centric meeting where the Team identifies how it can improve its development process.

Revert: An action that discards programming changes to the point of the last update. Used by programmers when the local build has been broken and the cause can't be identified or fixed get the build working again.

Review Meeting: A product-centric meeting to present completed work products and collect stakeholder feedback at the end of the Iteration. Commonly, yet inaccurately, confused as a synonym for the "demo" or product demonstration review meeting that occurs prior to a Release.

RFI: *See request for information.*

RFP: *See request for proposal.*

RFQ: Synonym for request for quote.

Risk-adjusted backlog: An overt risk management practice where the customer-proxy and key stakeholders define feature priorities with requirements that include risk factors such as regulatory or industry best practice compliance like Six Sigma. The objective is to adjust the Backlog by balancing value generating Stories and risk reduction Stories to maximize value creation.

Risk-based spike: A type of spike to address a specific risk or category of risks. See spike.

Roadmap: A planning tool used to align Agile's short development cycles with a desired future business result. They are equivalent to a Traditional portfolio plan.

Roll Back: An action used by programmers to checked-in code from the tip of the repository.

Rolling Wave Planning: The process of planning projects where multiple passes (i.e., waves) decompose the work required with increasing levels of detail. Work in the near term has been subjected to more iterations of refinement so they include greater detail, whereas work in the future has lower granularity because it has gone through less decomposition. *(aka Progressive Elaboration)*

ROM: Abbreviation for rough order of magnitude.

Round-robin: A creative process for solving problems, stimulating thinking, developing new ideas characterized by participants offering responses in a sequential, repeated order, and having those responses recorded by a facilitator without any evaluation of merit (which will follow in a separate step). It is one of three brainstorming approaches. See free-for-all and silent idea generation.

Rules of engagement: Norms and expectation for team member interactions set by the Team. *See team working agreements.*

Sandbox: A common name for a location – physical or electronic – where work can be discarded if it fails testing. For software development it refers to a location where software can be thrown away or reverted to a prior version. It is useful when the current build fails, the cause of the failure cannot be easily determined, and it is more productive to start over than to try to debug the new code.

Scanning: The Agile practice of proactively gathering of information with the goal of reducing future uncertainty and risk.

Schedule Baseline (SB): The total number of planned iterations multiplied by iteration length.

Schedule performance index (SPI): An earned value management (EVM) variable that expresses schedule efficiency as a ratio of earned value versus planned value. The SPI equals Earned Value divided by Planned Value.

Schedule variance (SV): An earned value management (EVM) variable that expresses the difference between the scheduled completion and the actual completion of an activity. The SV equals Earned Value minus Planned Value.

Scopeboxed plan: A type of plan where the required features, commonly referred to as the minimal marketable features (MMF), are defined first and then the release date is calculated.

Scrum: A project management framework developed by Jeff Sutherland and Ken Schwaber that uses an iterative and incremental process to produce a potentially shippable set of functionality during the iteration.

Scrum Alliance: The largest Agile organization and issuer of certifications for Scrum Masters, Scrum professionals and several other designations.

Scrum Master: *See Certified ScrumMaster.*

Scrum Team: A group in Scrum that has three members – Product Owner, Scrum Master and Development Team. *See also Team and Development Team.*

Servant leader: A project leader who practices servant leadership.

Servant leadership: A philosophy that emphasizes awareness, listening, and persuasion as the path to creating value.

SF: *See start-to-finish.*

Showcase: An eXtreme Programming (XP) term that is synonymous with the generic Agile term Review Meeting and the Scrum term Sprint Review.

Shu Ha Ri: A martial arts concept that describes the stages of learning as "shu", repeating forms and disciplines with no deviation, then "ha", making innovations, and finally "ri", developing creative techniques that are unrestricted without breaking laws. It is sometimes used as a model for mastering Agile.

Shuffle time: The time is takes to shift between activities or topics during meetings.

SI²MP²LE²: A mnemonic for the nine qualities of a well-developed User Story – Sizable, Important and Insightful, Measurable, Preview and Placeholder, Linked, and Extractable and Executable. See Sizable, Important and Insightful, Measurable, Preview and Placeholder, Linked, and Extractable and Executable.

Silent idea generation: A creative process for solving problems, stimulating thinking, developing new ideas characterized by participants writing ideas on index cards and handing them to a facilitator without speaking, usually for a defined time period, which will be followed by an evaluation of merit process. It is one of three brainstorming approaches. See free-for-all and round-robin.

Sizable: A User Story characteristic that means the principles of good estimating can be applied to define a reasonable and reliable approximation of the development effort. It avoids being too large, which induces complexity, or too small, which causes inefficiency.

Size: A term used in the Crystal frameworks referring to the number of people on the Team.

Sizing: An Agile estimating technique used to define the relative development effort required to complete stories so that reliable planning can be done. The objective, at a high level, is to assess how much complexity, uncertainty, and risk will be encountered while developing a Story as compared to other Stories in the same iteration or project.

Small: A User Story characteristic that means the Story leans towards minimalism, avoiding being a compound Story with multiple shorter Stories or a complex Story with avoidable complications, so that it fits within the Iteration.

Soft logic: Flexible relationship-logic for a Story that may precede or follow subsequent Stories.

Soft commit: The first level of commitment made by the Team during the Iteration planning meeting as part of the negotiation with the customer-proxy. It precedes the hard commit and occurs after the Team has clarified the Stories proposed for the Iteration Backlog, decide it is appears the Stories can be delivered successfully, and agrees to analyze them enough to decide if they can commit to completing them by the end of the iteration. See hard commit.

SOW: *See statement of work.*

Speed-to-market: Bringing a product to market as quickly as possible to create or defend a competitive advantage.

SPI: *See schedule performance index.*

Spike: A short experiment or Task carried out to gain knowledge so that estimating and planning can be based on data instead of purely hypothetical assumptions, and where the result is typically intended to be discarded. The goal of a spike is to solve a difficult technical problem or to learn enough to posit how to solve it.

Sprint: Scrum uses the term Sprint whereas Agile uses Iteration. See Iteration.

Sprint 0 (zero): *See Iteration 0.*

Sprint backlog: *See backlog.*

Sprint planning meeting: *See iteration planning meeting.*

Sprint retrospective meeting: *See retrospective meeting.*

Sprint review meeting: *See review meeting.*

SS: *See start-to-start.*

Standard iteration: *See iteration.*

Stand-up meeting: *See daily meeting.*

Start to start (SS): One of four types of dependencies used to create logic networks for project schedules. SS describes a relationship where one activity, B, cannot start unless another activity, A, also starts. For example, charging costs to the project, B, cannot start unless, A, the charge numbers are set up.

Start to Finish (SF): One of four types of dependencies used to create logic networks for project schedules. SF describes a relationship where one activity,

B, cannot finish unless another activity, A, starts. For example, the officers on the graveyard shift cannot clock out and leave the prison, B, until the morning shift the following day, A, starts.

Statement of work (SOW): A physical document or electronic file that defines the deliverables a seller must provide for a buyer. Typically a SOW includes detailed requirements, a timeline, pricing, and any regulatory or governance terms and conditions. Usually a SOW precedes and is attached to a contract.

Story: A tool, device or technique used to capture a description of important functionality considered valuable to the customer or user of the solution being developed. Can be a feature Story or User Story depending on the level of detail it includes.

Story board: A physical board or virtual table showing a collection of Stories or Tasks represented by cards that can be updated, estimated, and moved as development progresses in the Iteration. Called a Task Board when the level of detail is decomposed down to Tasks.

Story map: A device used to plan a Roadmap by arranging Stories in a way that aligns with the goals of a market and product development plan. A Story Map can also be used to plan Releases by decomposing Stories into greater granularity.

Story Point: A measure used to quantify the work effort and complexity required to develop a Story relative to other Stories and provide a high-level indicator of how difficult development will be typically expressed using the Fibonacci sequence of numbers.

Sustainable pace: Working, individually or as a team, at a pace that can be maintained indefinitely without a loss of effectiveness caused by exhaustion that leads to increased mistakes and a decrease in quality.

SV: *See schedule variance.*

Swarming: The practice of bringing together all of the people, and their insights, needed to define a roadmap that decreases the overall time required to complete the product.

SWOT: Acronym for strengths, weaknesses, opportunities, and threats as used in strategic planning.

Synchronous integration: The practice that confirms a build and tests succeeded before moving on to the next task.

System Metaphor: *See metaphor.*

T&M: *See time and material.*

Tacit knowledge: Information, insight, and inferences held in a person's mind about a business, project, or activity that may be of a procedural, technical, or relational type. Tacit knowledge can represent a risk when it is held by one person and is not shared within the organization.

Tag: An action used by programmers to mark a particular time in the history of the repository, typically so it can be easily accessed in the future.

Task board: *See Story board.*

TDD: Abbreviation for Test-driven development.

Team reflective workshop: *See reflective workshops.*

Team: In Scrum, one of three roles in the Scrum Team, specifically called Development Team. *See also Scrum Team and Development Team.*

Team Space: A physical work area with defined boundaries over which the Team exercises control. It has two major characteristics. First, the common area that is shared by the whole team where they work on tasks and have ad hoc collaboration. Second, it also includes private space, such as meeting rooms that can be used when privacy is needed. Ideally, team space provides visual lines of site, open meeting areas, and whiteboards in an environment that is comfortable and easily reconfigurable. *See open workspace.*

Team Speed: In XP it is the number of ideal programming weeks the Team can produce in a given amount of time. (Similar to velocity.)

Team working agreements: Work standards and norms, set by the Team, that define the expectations for how the Agile team will work and communicate with one another. They are important because the high level of daily interaction can cause friction without clear, explicit guidelines. They are often displayed as an information radiator.

Technical debt: The total amount of imperfect design and implementation decisions that have created problems that will have to be fixed in order to deliver a quality product.

Test Case: An automated set of stimuli and responses for the system. Each test case should leave the system the way it found it, so tests can run independently of each other.

Test-driven development (TDD): A four-step development process used with an Agile project management framework that begins with creating a well-defined test, then invoking an operation to take the test and having a "fail" outcome, followed by doing something to change the operation, and finally invoking the modified operation to take the test and having a "pass" outcome.

Testable: A User Story characteristic that means the Story can be tested, even if the test hasn't been defined yet, which implies acceptance criteria are definable.

Theory of Constraints (TOC): A management model that uses a focusing process to identify the states small number of constraints that are limiting the system from achieving more of its goals and then realigning the organization mitigate those processes that adversely affect results. TOC was published by Dr. Eliyahu M. Goldratt in 1984 in his book The Goal.

Threshold features: Product features that must be present to create customer satisfaction before a product can be successful. Contrast with exciters and delighters and linear features.

Time-to-value: The time between the initial delivery of a product or service and when a defined business goal is achieved.

Time-to-volume: The time it takes to deliver product volumes sufficient to be profitable.

Time and Material (T&M): A type of contract where the seller is paid for all time (i.e., labor) and material costs incurred to fulfill the contract.

Timebox: Work periods used to manage product development cycles in Agile project management. Examples include Iterations that are fixed-length timeboxes and Releases and Roadmaps that are variable-length timeboxes.

Timeboxed plan: A type of plan where the release date is defined first and then the specific features to be included in the release are determined or negotiated.

Tip: The part of the repository that contains the latest checked in code changes.

Total Quality Management (TQM): A management system defined by a customer-focused organizational paradigm that involves all employees in process-centric continuous improvement to create an integrated system that enables fact-based decision making and communication

Toyota Production System: The widely respected process that organizes manufacturing, logistics, and relationships with suppliers and customers at Toyota and emphasizes improving the value and flow product delivery by eliminating waste.

TQM: S*ee Total Quality Management.*

Trade-off matrix: *See flexibility matrix.*

Tracker: An XP role for the person who measures progress with numbers.

Transparency: Making important aspects of the process visible, using an understood standard, for those making decisions about the outcome to enable a shared understanding of what has occurred.

Trend analysis: The process of collecting time-series data points about one or more variables and then examining that data to detect patterns or relationship between the variables that may predict the future trajectory of the variable or variables.

Unified Modeling Language (UML): A modeling language used in software engineering that standardizes how to express system design visualizations.

Unit Test: A test written from the perspective of the programmer.

Update: An action used by programmers to retrieve the latest code changes from the repository. Updates can also be defined to a particular point in the past.

User Story: The most common of the various types of Stories, they include necessary and important details like acceptance criteria, tests, and a definition of done. They are used for planning Iterations. See feature story and story.

Valuable: A User Story characteristic that means the Story reflects the priorities that create value for End User Customers and Organizational Customers.

Value stream: The flow of materials and information required to deliver a product or service that the customer values.

Value stream mapping: A Lean manufacturing process developed to improve the production flow that delivers value to the customer by analyzing, and potentially redesigning how raw materials are turned into finished goods so the process delivers more value without sacrificing future opportunities.

Variance analysis: The process of calculating the difference between actual and estimated levels of performance followed by identifying the cause or causes of the differences. See trend analysis.

Velocity: The number of Story Points completed by the Team during the iteration.

Velocity-driven iteration planning: A development planning process that uses a team's velocity to estimate how many Story Points should be planned into the Iteration in order to improve the probability of reaching the goal.

Visual control: A Lean manufacturing process that uses a visual signal card as a tool for managing the production process. In Agile development environments, teams display current work status information as a visual control. See information radiator.

Walking Skeleton: A Crystal practice where a minimal framework of the system executes end-to-end functionality that demonstrates the main architectural components without providing all the in-depth features that will come in future development.

Waterfall: A common name for Traditional project planning and management using a sequential phase-gated approach to project delivery.

WBS: *See work breakdown structure.*

Wideband Delphi: A consensus-based estimating method used in many industries on tasks ranging from data collection to sales forecasts that was derived from the Delphi method created by the Rand Corporation.

WIP: Work-in-progress, as used in Agile Project Management and Kanban.

WIP Limits: A tool for managing development bottlenecks by aligning the amount of WIP to the system's capacity, thereby creating planning options, accelerating throughput, and clarifying focus with transparency throughout the production cycle

Wireframes: Visual guides that start with a skeletal structure or framework and layer on additional detail levels of the desired solution. The term originates from the website development lexicon where fast, emergent designs are mandatory for success.

Wiki: An intranet site where content, such as the details of stories, updates, and reports can be edited and stored during development.

Work breakdown structure (WBS): A deliverable-oriented artifact used in Traditional project management to define a project in hierarchical layers that are decomposed into smaller discrete work elements that can be used for cost and schedule estimating and control.

Work-in-progress (WIP): A Lean manufacturing concept developed to manage unfinished items in the production because, by definition, they produce no value until they are finished. In Agile, the WIP concept is used in Kanban-type continuous-flow development environments.

Working agreements: See Team working agreements.

Working software: Software that has met the Definition of Done and, in Lean thinking, is the most reliable indicator of project progress. Can be understood as working increments of the solution in non-software environments.

XP: *See Extreme Programming.*